BEST
FOOD
WRITING
2006

Also edited by Holly Hughes

Best Food Writing 2005
Best Food Writing 2004
Best Food Writing 2003
Best Food Writing 2002
Best Food Writing 2001
Best Food Writing 2000

Also by Holly Hughes

Frommer's New York City with Kids

BEST
FOOD
WRITING
2006

Edited by
HOLLY HUGHES

Marlowe & Company
New York

BEST FOOD WRITING 2006

Copyright © 2006 by Holly Hughes

Published by
Marlowe & Company
An Imprint of Avalon Publishing Group, Incorporated
245 West 17th Street • 11th Floor
New York, NY 10011-5300

AVALON
publishing group incorporated

Library of Congress Cataloging-in-Publication Data is available.

ISBN-10: 1-56924-287-9
ISBN-13: 978-1-56924-287-2

9 8 7 6 5 4 3 2 1

Designed by Michael Walters and Susan Canavan
Printed in the United States of America

Contents

Home Cooking

Dining Around

Someone's in the Kitchen

The Restaurant Biz

Reviewing Life

Introduction

by Holly Hughes

E ach year, the process begins a little earlier. The stack of books in the corner of my office gets taller, the piles of newspapers and magazines threaten to tip over, the cache of unsolicited submissions—my "slush pile"—becomes truly slushy, and the hard drive on my computer registers less and less available disk space. Yet I find myself putting off the moment when I plunge in—because I don't want to gobble up the fun too soon. It's my favorite season of the working year: the food writing–reading season.

There is a certain glorious serendipity to it. Every day I open my mailbox, there could be another manila envelope from some hopeful writer, or at the very least another glossy magazine with a glistening color photo on the cover to whet my appetite. Every time I enter my e-mail program, I wonder what goodies will be embedded in attached files or those tantalizing blue Web links. We talk of food writing as if it were one narrow genre, but in reality it spans so many different things. One day I might come across a dreamy essay on the joys of cooking soup, the next I'm swept up in a dramatic narrative, complete with dialogue, about a night at a restaurant. An intensively researched article about the economics of our food supply system crops up one morning; a colorful travelogue describing exotic cuisine arrives on my desk later that afternoon. Some writers are poets when it comes to communicating sensory details—the tastes, aromas, and textures of the food we eat—while others are supreme storytellers, transporting you vividly into whatever kitchen, dining room, or market, bringing an entire cast of characters to life. The prose may be tender, or savage, or erotic, or drop-dead funny. So long as they awaken our curiosity about food, it's all good.

Partly, I suppose, the avalanche of submissions is due to the fact that this book series has gained visibility over the seven years of its existence. I'm always gratified when writers whose work appeared in previous editions brag about it in their magazine bios. But even with the general public, the Best Food Writing series has made a name for itself. Among my special thrills this year: getting reconnected with a close friend from grade school when she spotted my name on the spine of *Best Food Writing 2005* on her bedside table. (It's so much more fun when your friends buy your book without even knowing you were responsible for it.) Then there was the day a fellow subway passenger, seeing me reading last year's book, remarked that he had just picked up his own copy; when he learned that I was its editor, he actually said, "*The* Holly Hughes?" (I could feel the clock ticking on my fifteen seconds of fame.) As it turned out, he was a chef, and we had a great conversation about the restaurant business the rest of the way downtown. Like I said, serendipity.

Over the past seven years, I've developed a handful of rituals around editing this anthology. My Year in Food Writing cannot truly begin until I've made my annual visit to Manhattan's Kitchen Arts and Letters, the sort of overflowing little specialty bookshop every city should be so lucky to have. Owner Nach Waxman and his knowledgeable staff are unfailingly eager to dart around the store, grabbing new "finds" off the shelves for me, enthusiastically describing their contents. I always manage to leave toting at least two shopping bags full of books. (Can anyone explain to me why food books invariably have to be so *heavy?*)

Reading each year's submissions from certain writers has come to feel like being reunited with old friends: I look forward to finding out where Robb Walsh has been chowing down in Houston (page 332), or Jason Sheehan in Denver (page 192), or John Kessler in Atlanta (page 113), or John T. Edge (page 187) wherever in the deep South he's been hanging out lately. What foods has Jeffrey Steingarten (page 33) been parsing in the pages of *Vogue*? What has pumped up Anthony Bourdain's culinary adrenaline lately (page 269)? I must admit that my first thought when news of Hurricane Katrina hit the media was, *Ohmigod, I hope Brett Anderson and Lolis Eric Elie are okay.* (They are: check out their reports from the disaster's front lines on pages 354 and 326). I don't know any of these people personally, mind you; I only know what they eat and how they feel about it. But in some ways, that means I know them more intimately than most people I encounter every day.

Was there a theme to this year's food writing? I did notice a slight course correction in the realm of food politics: the holy mantra of "cooking organic" has lost some luster, to be replaced by "eating locally." (Purists seem increasingly willing to forgive a small producer for not hewing to the organic orthodoxy, so long as the produce is heirloom and the meats free-range). I detect a backlash, too, among fed up gourmands who refuse to renounce foie gras and caviar just because they are produced by less-than-noble methods.

Maybe it's just coincidence, but I can't recall a year when I read so much about fish, from Molly O'Neill's memoir of a Midwestern girl discovering seafood on Cape Cod (page 253) to Megan Wetherall's portrait of a Cornish fishing village (page 42) to Maria Finn Dominguez's farewell to New York's historic Fulton Street Fish Market (page 51). It was also a year for considering cookbooks: Jane Kramer's tale of a lifelong passion for cookbooks (page 133), Steven Rinella's quest to scavenge ingredients for a blowout feast from Escoffier (page 28), or Julie Powell's account (page 147) of how she worked her way through Julia Child's *Mastering the Art of French Cooking.*

Yes, it makes me hungry, those months of reading about food all day; it's the one occupational hazard of this job. I find myself craving the most inexplicable foods. If it's not Audrey Petty whetting my appetite for chitlins (page 74), it's Henry Alford making me long for silky homemade tofu (page 116), or Bill Buford unlocking the secrets of authentic tortellini (page 243). However, other writers help me keep my standards high. I can't be content with the neighborhood burger joint when I'm reading about Pete Wells's long-awaited meal at Le Bec-Fin (page 160) or Jeff Gordinier's sublime experience at Masa (page 176), not to mention Jane and Michael Stern's manifesto on the cross-country joys of local diners (page 338). And forget about fast food, now that I've read Michael Pollan's *The Omnivore's Dilemma* (page 2). I herewith formally apologize to every person I've bored at cocktail parties this spring by insisting they read Pollan's book—but really, you must, it's the most important book I've read all year . . . oops, there I go again.

So here I am, at the end of another food writing–reading season. Am I a better cook than when I started? No, I'm afraid I'm still only a passable home cook. Am I eating healthier than I did when I started? I wish I could say so, but I'm still all too easily swayed by an ode to the perfect french fry. But even if I haven't fed my body well these past few months, my mind and imagination have dined richly. I feel I've been around the world, even though I've never left my home office.

The only thing left is for you to sample this buffet of fine food writing. Grab a plate and dig right in, while it's still hot.

BEST
FOOD
WRITING
2006

The Food Chain

The Meal: Grass-Fed

by Michael Pollan

from *The Omnivore's Dilemma*

We humans can eat anything we please—so why do we make such bad food choices? In Pollan's stunning new book, science and journalism are woven into a persuasive argument for change.

Before I left [Joel Salatin's Polyface] farm Friday, I gathered together the makings for that evening's dinner, which I'd arranged to cook for some old friends who lived in Charlottesville. I had originally thought about filling a cooler with Polyface meat and bringing it home with me to California to cook there, but decided it would be more in keeping with the whole local food chain concept to eat this particular meal within a leisurely drive of the farm where it had been grown. After all, it was the sin of flying meat across the country that had brought me to Swoope in the first place, and I hated for Joel to think that an entire week of his instruction had left me unimproved.

From the walk-in, I picked out two of the chickens we had slaughtered on Wednesday and a dozen of the eggs I'd helped gather Thursday evening. I also stopped by the hoop house, and harvested a dozen ears of sweet corn. (In consideration of my week's labors, Joel refused to accept payment for the food, but had I paid for it, the chicken would have cost $2.05 a pound, and the eggs $2.20 a dozen—prices that compare very favorably with Whole Foods's. This is not boutique food.)

On the way into Charlottesville, I stopped to pick up a few

other ingredients, trying as best as I could to look for local produce and preserve the bar code virginity of this meal. For my salad, I found some nice-looking locally grown rocket. At the wine shop I found a short, chauvinistic shelf of Virginia wines, but here I hesitated. How far could I take this local conceit before it ruined my meal? I hadn't had a sip of wine all week and was really looking forward to a decent one. I'd read somewhere that wine-making in Virginia was "coming into its own," but isn't that what they always say? Then I spotted a Viognier for twenty-five bucks—the priciest Virginia wine I'd ever seen. I took this as a sign of genuine confidence on somebody's part, and added the bottle to my cart.

I also needed some chocolate for the dessert I had in mind. Fortunately the state of Virginia produces no chocolate to speak of, so I was free to go for the good Belgian stuff, panglessly. In fact, even the most fervent eat-local types say it's okay for a "foodshed" (a term for a regional food chain, meant to liken it to a watershed) to trade for goods it can't produce locally—coffee, tea, sugar, chocolate—a practice that predates the globalization of our food chain by a few thousand years. (Whew . . .)

During the week I'd given some thought to what I should make; the farm's varied offerings certainly gave me plenty of choices. Working backward, I knew I wanted to make a dessert that would prominently feature Polyface eggs, having heard so much from the chefs about their magical properties. A chocolate soufflé, since it calls for a certain degree of magic, seemed the obvious choice. For a side dish, sweet corn was a no-brainer; there'd be kids at the table and no one had tasted corn yet this summer. But what meat to serve? Because it was only June, Polyface had no fresh beef or pork or turkey; Joel wouldn't begin slaughtering beeves and turkeys till later in the summer, hogs not till the fall. There was frozen beef and pork in the walk-in, last season's, but I preferred to make something fresh. Rabbit seemed risky; I had no idea whether Mark and Liz liked it, and the chances that their boys would eat bunny were slim. So that had left chicken, the animal with which I'd been most intimate this week. Which, truth to tell, left me feeling vaguely queasy. Was I going to be able to enjoy eating chicken so soon after my stint in the processing shed and gut-composting pile?

That queasiness perhaps explains the multistep preparation I finally settled on. When I got to Mark and Liz's house, there were still several hours before dinner, which meant there was enough time for me to brine the chicken. So I cut each of the two birds into eight pieces and immersed them in a bath consisting of water, kosher salt, sugar, a bay leaf, a splash of soy sauce, a garlic clove, and a small handful of peppercorns and coriander seeds. My plan was to slow roast the chicken pieces on a wood fire, and brining—which causes meat to absorb moisture and breaks down the proteins that can toughen it on the grill—would keep the chicken from drying out.

But the brining (like the carving of the birds into pieces) promised to do something else, too, something for me as much as the meat: It would put a little distance between the meal and Wednesday's kill, certain aromas of which were still lodged in my nostrils. One of the reasons we cook meat (besides making it tastier and easier to digest) is to civilize, or sublimate, what is at bottom a fairly brutal transaction between animals. The anthropologist Claude Lévi-Strauss described the work of civilization as the process of transforming the raw into the cooked—nature into culture. For these particular chickens, which I had personally helped to kill and eviscerate, the brining would make a start on that transformation even before the cooking fire was lit. Both literally and metaphorically, a saltwater bath cleanses meat, which perhaps explains why the kosher laws—one culture's way of coming to terms with the killing and eating of animals—insist on the salting of meat.

After a few hours, I removed and rinsed the chicken pieces, and then spread them out to dry for an hour or two, so that the skin, now slightly waterlogged, would brown nicely. Since Mark and Liz had a gas barbecue, I'd have to simulate my wood fire. So I snipped a couple of twigs off their apple tree, stripped the leaves, and placed the twigs on top of the grill, where the green wood would smolder rather than burn. I turned the gas down low and, after rubbing a little olive oil on the chicken pieces, arranged them on the grill among the apple branches, leaving some room to add the corn later.

While the chicken roasted slowly outside, I got to work in the kitchen preparing the soufflé with Willie, Mark and Liz's twelve-year-old. While Willie melted the chocolate in a saucepan, I separated the eggs. The yolks were a gorgeous carroty shade of orange and they did seem to possess an unusual integrity; separating them from the whites was a cinch. After adding a pinch of salt, I began beating the egg whites; within minutes they turned from translucent to bright white and formed soft, rounded peaks, which is when Julia Child says to begin adding sugar and to turn the beater on high. Now the egg whites rapidly doubled in volume, then doubled again, as billions of microscopic air pockets formed amid the stiffening egg proteins. When the heat of the oven caused these air pockets to expand, the soufflé would rise, assuming everything went according to plan. Once the egg whites formed a stiff, spiky snowscape, I stopped. Willie had already blended the yolks into his melted chocolate, so we now gently folded that thick syrup into my egg whites, then poured the airy, toast-colored mixture into a soufflé dish and put it aside. I could see why pastry chefs in Charlottesville swore by Polyface eggs: What Joel had called their "muscle tone" made baking with them a breeze.

Willie and I brought the corn out on the deck to shuck. The ears were so fresh that the husks squealed as you peeled them back. I mentioned to Willie that our entire meal would be a celebration of the chicken—not only the eponymous entrée, which we could smell sweetly roasting on the grill, but the soufflé with its half-dozen eggs, and even this corn, which I explained had grown in a deep bed of composted chicken manure. Probably not the sort of detail you'd want to mention on a menu, but Willie agreed there was something pretty neat about the alchemy involved, how a plant could transform chicken crap into something as sweet and tasty and golden as an ear of corn.

Golden Bantam, the corn in question, is an heirloom variety introduced in 1902, long before the hybridizers figured out how to amp up the sweetness in sweet corn. This momentous change in the genetics of our corn is an artifact of an industrial food chain, which demands that vegetables be able to endure a cross-country road trip after picking so that they might be available everywhere the year round. This was a particular problem for corn, the sugars of which begin turning to starch the moment it is picked. So in the early sixties the breeders figured out a way to breed in extra copies of the genes responsible for producing sugars. But something was lost in the translation from local to cosmopolitan corn: The kernels lost much of their creaminess, and the specific taste of corn was overwhelmed by a generic, one-dimensional sweetness. The needs of a long industrial food chain might justify such a trade-off, but when you can eat corn picked a few hours before dinner, there's no reason for it. Unless of course an industrial diet of easy sugars has dulled your taste for the earthy sweetness of corn, now that it has to compete with things like soda.

How different does a pastured chicken actually taste? It certainly smelled wonderful when I raised the lid on the barbecue to put the corn on. The chicken was browning nicely, the skin beginning to crisp and take on the toasty tones of oiled wood. The corn, on which I'd rubbed some olive oil and sprinkled salt and pepper, would take only a few minutes—all it needed was to heat up and for a scattering of kernels to brown. The browning of the chicken skin and the corn looked similar but in fact it owed to completely different chemical reactions, reactions that were contributing to their flavors and smells. The corn was caramelizing, as its sugars broke apart under the heat and formed into hundreds of more complicated aromatic compounds, giving a smoky dimension to the corny sweetness. Meanwhile, the chicken skin was undergoing what chemists called the Maillard reaction, in which carbohydrates in the chicken react in dry heat with certain amino acids to create an even larger and more complicated set of compounds that, because they include atoms of sulfur and nitrogen, give a richer, meatier aroma and taste to the meat than it would otherwise possess. This, at least, is how a chemist would explain what I was seeing and smelling on the grill, as I turned the corn and chicken pieces and felt myself growing hungrier.

While the corn finished roasting, I removed the chicken from the grill and set it aside to rest. A few minutes later I called everyone to the table. Ordinarily I might have felt a little funny serving as both dinner host and guest, but Mark and Liz are such close friends it seemed perfectly natural to be cooking for them in their home. That's not to say I didn't feel the cook's customary preprandial apprehension, compounded in this instance by the fact that Liz herself is such a good cook, and holds very definite opinions about food. I certainly hadn't forgotten the time she'd wrinkled her nose and pushed away a Polyface steak I'd served her. Grass-fed beef is fla- vored by the pastures it grows on, usually but not always for the best. It had tasted fine to me.

I passed the platters of chicken and corn and proposed a toast. I offered thanks first to my hosts-cum-guests, then to Joel Salatin and his family for growing the food before us (and for giving it to us), and then finally to the chickens, who in one way or another had provided just about everything we were about to eat. My secular version of grace, I suppose, acknowledging the various material and karmic debts incurred by this meal, debts which I felt more keenly than usual.

"At the beginning of the meal," Brillat-Savarin writes in his chapter "On the Pleasures of the Table" in *The Physiology of Taste,* "each guest eats steadily, without speaking or paying attention to anything which may be said." And so we did, aside from a few sub-lingual murmurs of satisfaction. I don't mind saying the chicken was out of this world. The skin had turned the color of mahogany and the texture of parchment, almost like a Peking duck, and the meat itself was moist, dense, and almost shockingly flavorful. I could taste the brine and apple wood, of course, but also the chicken itself, which more than held its own against those strong flavors. This may not sound like much of a compliment, but to me the chicken smelled and tasted exactly like chicken. Liz voiced her approval in similar terms, pronouncing it a more chickeny chicken. Which is to say, I suppose, that it chimed with that capitalized idea of Chicken we hold in our heads but seldom taste anymore. So what accounted for it? The grass? The grubs? The exercise? I know what Joel would have said: When chickens get to live like chickens, they'll taste like chickens, too.

The flavors of everything else on the table had a similarly declar- ative quality: the roasted corn and lemony rocket salad, and even the peachy Viognier, all of them tasting almost flamboyantly them- selves, their flavors forming a bright sequence of primary colors. There was nothing terribly subtle about this meal, but everything about it tasted completely in character.

Everyone was curious to hear about the farm, especially after tasting the food that had come off it. Matthew, who's fifteen and cur- rently a vegetarian (he confined himself to the corn), had many more questions about killing chickens than I thought it wise to answer at the dinner table. But I did talk about my week on the farm, about the Salatins and their animals. I explained the whole synergistic ballet of chickens and cows and pigs and grass, without getting into specifics about the manure and grubs and composted guts that made the whole dance work. Thankfully all of that, the killing cones, too, had retreated to the mental background for me, chased by the smoky-sweet aromas of the meal, which I found myself able to thoroughly enjoy.

The unexpectedly fine wine helped too, as did the fact that the dinner table conversation drifted off as it will do, from my Paris Hilton adventures as a farmhand to Willie's songwriting (he is, mark my word, the next Bob Dylan), Matthew's summer football camp, Mark and Liz's books-in-progress, school, politics, war, and on and on, the topics spiraling away from the table like desultory rings of smoke. Being a Friday late in June, this was one of the longest evenings of the year, so no one felt in a rush to finish. Besides, I'd just put the soufflé in to bake when we sat down, so dessert was still a ways off.

In his chapter Brillat-Savarin draws a sharp distinction between the pleasures of eating—"the actual and direct sensation of a need being satisfied," a sensation we share with the animals—and the uniquely human "pleasures of the table." These consist of "considered sensations born of the various circumstances of fact, things, and persons accompanying the meal"—and comprise for him one of the brightest fruits of civilization. Every meal we share at a table recapitulates this evolution from nature to culture, as we pass from satisfying our animal appetites in semisilence to the lofting of conversational balloons. The pleasures of the table begin with eating (and specifically with eating meat, in Brillat-Savarin's view, since it was the need to cook and apportion meat that first brought us together to eat), but they can end up anywhere human talk cares to go. In the same way that the raw becomes cooked, eating becomes dining.

All such transformations were very much on my mind that evening, coming at the end of a week of farmwork that had put me in much closer touch with the biology of eating than the art. The line from composting chicken guts to gastronomy is almost unimaginably long, but there is a line. While we talked and waited for the soufflé to complete its magic rise, the smell of baking chocolate seeped out of the kitchen and filled the house. When at last I told Willie the time had come to open the oven, cross your fingers, I saw his smile blossom first, then the great crown of soufflé puffing out from the cinched white waist of its dish. Triumph!

Here was the most improbable transformation of all. There's something wondrous about any soufflé, how a half dozen eggs flavored by nothing more than sugar and chocolate can turn into something so ethereally Other. Soufflé, "to blow," comes from the Latin word for breath, of course, in recognition of the air that a soufflé mostly is. But soufflé has a spiritual sense, too, as in the breath of life (in English the word "spirit" comes from breath), which seems fitting, for isn't the soufflé as close as cookery ever comes to elevating matter into spirit?

This particular soufflé was good, not great; its texture was slightly grainier than it should be, which makes me think I may have beaten the eggs a little too long. But it tasted wonderful, everyone agreed, and as I rolled the rich yet weightless confection on my tongue, I closed my eyes and suddenly there they were: Joel's hens, marching down the gangplank from out of their Eggmobile, fanning out across the early morning pasture, there in the grass where this sublime bite began.

A Grand Experiment

by Bill McKibben

from *Gourmet*

> How easy is it to carry out a program of eating only locally produced foods? Well, it depends on where and how you live, as McKibben's engaging firsthand account reveals.

From before the first frost until after the salad greens had finally poked their heads above the warming soil, most of my food for seven months came from within a couple dozen miles of my house. For a few things, I traveled to the corners of this watershed, which covers the northwest third of Vermont and a narrower fringe along the New York shore of Lake Champlain. (I did make what might be called the Marco Polo exception—I considered fair game anything your average thirteenth-century explorer might have brought back from distant lands. So pepper and turmeric, and even the odd knob of ginger, stayed in the larder.) Eating like this is precisely how almost every human being ate until very recently, and how most people in the world still do eat today. But in contemporary America, where the average bite of food travels 1,500 miles before it reaches your lips, it was an odd exercise. *Local* and *seasonal* may have become watchwords of much new cooking, but I wanted to see what was really possible, especially in these northern climes. I know that eating close to home represents the history of American farming—but I sense it may have a future, too. The number of farms around Burlington, Vermont's chief city, has grown 19 percent in the past decade. Most of them are small, growing food for local consumers instead of commodities for export; the same trend is starting to show up nationwide. Something's happening, and I wanted to see exactly what.

I'm writing this, so you know I survived. But, in fact, I survived in style—it was the best eating winter of my life. Here's my report:

SEPTEMBER The farmers market in Middlebury, Vermont, is in absolute fever bloom: sweet, sweet corn; big, ripe tomatoes; bunches of basil; melons. This is the bounty of our short but intense summer, when the heat of the long days combines with the moisture of these eastern uplands to produce almost anything you could want. It's the great eating moment of the year.

But I'm wandering the market trying to keep the image of midwinter in mind—the short, bitter days of January, when the snow is drifted high against the house and the woodstove is cranking. I'm used to getting the winter's wood in, but not to putting the winter's food by. In our world, it's always summer somewhere, and so we count on the same produce year-round. But that takes its toll: on the environment, from endless trucking and flying and shipping; on local farmers, who can't compete with the equatorial bounty and hence sell their fields for condos; and most of all, perhaps, on taste. There's nothing that tastes like a June strawberry; whereas a January supermarket strawberry tastes like . . . nothing.

All of which explains why I'm bargaining for canning tomatoes, the Romas with perhaps a few blemishes. Though mostly I want to spend the winter buying what's available, I'll put up a certain amount. My friend Amy Trubek volunteers to help—a food anthropologist, she's the head of the Vermont Fresh Network, which partners farmers with chefs; she and her husband, Brad Koehler, one of the chefs at (and general manager of) Middlebury College's renowned dining halls, also own a small orchard and a big vegetable garden, not to mention a capacious freezer. "A lot of people associate canning with their grandmother, hostage in the kitchen for six weeks," she says. "But, hey, this is the twenty-first century. We can freeze, we can cure, we can Cryovac—we can do all this a hundred different ways." An afternoon's work, with the Red Sox beginning their stretch drive on the radio, and I've got enough tomato sauce frozen in Ziplocs to last me through the winter.

OCTOBER Fall lingers on (and the Red Sox, too). I'm already regarding the leaf lettuce in our local food co-op with a kind of nostalgia, knowing it's about to disappear from my life. And I'm regarding two small bins in the co-op's bulk section as my lifeline. They're filled with local flour, 59 cents a pound. Once upon a time, the Champlain Valley was the nation's granary—but that was back before the Erie Canal opened the way west and vast rivers of grain began rolling back from the deep topsoil of the Plains. Grain farming all but disappeared from the region; the most basic component of the American diet had to be imported from Nebraska.

But there's always an oddball, and, in this case, his name is Ben Gleason, who came to Vermont, as did many others, as a part of the back-to-the-land movement of the 1970s. He found an old farm in the Addison County town of Bridport and began to plant it in a rotation of organic hard red winter wheat. Last year, for instance, he grew 30 tons on 28 acres, perfectly respectable even by Midwest standards, and he ground all of it with the small, noisy machine in the shed next to his house. He only does whole-wheat flour—white would require another machine, and anyway, as he points out, it's not nearly as good for you. In any event, his is delicious—making pancakes flavorful enough to stand up to the Grade B maple syrup that's the only kind we buy. (Grade A, Fancy—it's for tourists. The closer to tar, the better.)

"There's maybe four or five hundred acres altogether that's planted in wheat around the area," says Samuel Sherman, who owns Champlain Valley Milling, in Westport, New York. Mostly he grinds wheat that arrives by train car from the west, but he'd love to see more local product. "We can sell it in a minute," he says. The proof is just down the lakeshore, in the town of Crown Point, where a young baker named Yannig Tanguy makes artisanal bread—*fougasse,* baguette, Swabian rye—entirely with local wheat that he grinds himself, sometimes 300 pounds in a day. Crown Point is a poor town next to an aging paper mill—and yet the door to the little bakery keeps popping open constantly. Here's someone who wants to reserve ten loaves for an elementary school dinner the next week; here's a woman to buy a cookie and say thanks for letting her park in the tiny lot during church that morning. "It's not like I'm trying to invent anything with local food," says Tanguy. "It all obviously worked for a long time. That we're here today is proof that it worked. And it can work again."

NOVEMBER The traditional Thanksgiving dinner is also the traditional local foods dinner in this part of the world. Which makes sense, since the Pilgrims weren't in any position to import much food—they just hunkered down with the beige cuisine that begins to predominate as the summer becomes mere memory. (On Cape Cod, cranberries provide a flash of deep color; here, we have beets, which make a ruby slaw.) The kind of self-sufficient all-around farm with which the colonists covered the continent has essentially disappeared, at least outside of Amish country. Even the tiny growers in this valley specialize in order to stay afloat—I can show you a potato farmer in the hills above Rutland with 50 varieties on his three acres, or a bison wrangler on the lakeshore, or an emu rancher. Some of America's original community-supported agriculture farms (CSAs) are in this area, and none produce vegetables more glorious than those from Golden Russet Farm, in Shoreham, where Will and Judy Stevens are busy threshing dried beans when I stop by one afternoon to pick up some squash. If you pay them a few hundred dollars in the winter, they'll keep you supplied with a weekly bin of vegetables throughout the growing season and deep into the fall. But even Will and Judy go to the store for their milk.

Not so Mark and Kristin Kimball, the young proprietors of Essex Farm, on the New York side of the lake. If you want to join their CSA, you pay more like a few thousand dollars. But when you stop by on Friday afternoons for your pickup, it's not just vegetables: They have a few milking cows, so there's milk and cheese and butter; they have a small herd of grass-fed cattle, so there are steaks and burgers; the snorting tribe of pigs behind the barn provides bacon and lard; there are chickens and turkeys. Except for paper towels and dental floss, you'd never have to set foot in a store again—think Laura Ingalls Wilder, complete with a team of big Belgians. "There's nothing inherent about modern ways that I don't support," Mark insists. "It just so happens that working with horses is—not better than working with tractors, but more fun. It's a more dynamic relationship. You can understand an engine. You'll never understand a horse."

You can't leave the farm without Mark loading your trunk full of food—"Do you have room for another chicken in there?"—and all of it tastes of the place. As you bump down the driveway, a look in the rearview mirror reveals Mark juggling carrots and grinning. "Occasionally I feel like I'm doing some work," he says. "But usually it feels more like entertainment for myself."

Is this realistic? Could you feed Manhattan in this fashion? You could not—every place is different. (And Manhattan is lucky to have New Jersey right next door, with some of the best truck-farming soil and weather anywhere on earth.) But you could feed Essex, New York, this way—Mark figures the 50 acres they're farming can support ten families, a reminder of just how fertile the earth is in the right hands.

DECEMBER Here's what I'm missing: not grapefruit, not chocolate. Oats. And their absence helps illustrate what's happened to American agriculture, and what would be required to change it a little bit.

Once upon a time, oats were everywhere—people grew them for their horses, and for themselves. But oats aren't easy to deal with. They have a hull that needs removing, and they need to be steamed, and dried, and rolled. You can do that more efficiently on an enormous scale in places like Saskatoon, Saskatchewan, where a single mill can turn out more than half a million pounds of oat products a day. For the moment, this centralization works. But that may change if the price of oil (the lifeblood of industrial agriculture) continues to climb, or as the climate continues to shift, or if global politics deteriorates. Even now, stubborn people keep trying to rebuild smaller-scale food networks, but it's hard going against the tide of cheap goods flowing in. A few years ago, for instance, a Vermonter named Andrew Leinoff decided to go into oats—he and his friend Eric Allen found some old equipment and started experimenting. But after a few years of struggling, they gave up, and a little bitterly. The state's Agency of Agriculture talks a good game—a public service ad on the radio urges Vermonters to buy 10 percent of their food from within the state—but in the opinion of many small farmers, it spends most of its time and money propping up the state's slowly withering dairy industry, not supporting the pioneers trying to build what comes next.

They sold their equipment across the border in Quebec, to an organic miller named Michel Gaudreau, who does everything from hulling spelt to pearling barley. And Gaudreau found a farmer in the province's Eastern Townships, Alex Brand, whose family had been growing oats for many years. I tracked him down, delighted to find that Brand's Fellgarth Farm was right on the edge of my Champlain watershed. But shipping a bag of oats across the border was going to be hard work—it might, they warned, require a trip to Customs. Happily, Brand had an American distributor—Joe Angello, in New York's Columbia County. By the time all was said and done, my "local" oats had traveled on a truck from Canada to the lower Hudson Valley, and then back to Vermont in a UPS sack. Not precisely an ecological triumph. On the other hand, they were delicious—plump, if oats can be plump. So now it's pancakes only every other morning.

JANUARY Truth be told, my eleven-year-old daughter has used the words *icky* and *disgusting* on several occasions, always in connection with root vegetables. Not potatoes, not carrots—but turnips, and parsnips, and rutabagas. It is a little hard to imagine how people got through winter on the contents of their root cellars alone.

Which is why I'm glad for the Ziplocs full of raspberries and blueberries my wife froze in the summer. And why I'm glad for the high-tech apple warehouse just down the road in Shoreham. Here's the thing about apples: The best ones rot pretty fast. Sure, those brick-hard Red Delicious and Granny Smiths can be picked in New Zealand or South Africa or China or Washington and flown and trucked halfway around the world and sit on a shelf at the supermarket for a week and still look like an apple. (Taste is another story—they've been bred for immortality, and immortality alone.) But the great apples of the Northeast—your Cortland, your Empire, your Northern Spy, and, above all, your McIntosh—are softer, more ephemeral. For generations, people solved that problem by converting them to cider—hard cider, fermented for freezerless storage. That's what most of those apple trees around New England were planted for. But there's another solution if, like Barney Hodges, you have a storage shed where you can pump in nitrogen. "We push the oxygen level down from its normal twenty percent to just under three percent. The apple's respiration is slowed to the point where the ripening process is nearly halted," he explains. Every few weeks he cracks open another room in the warehouse, and it's as if you're back in September—the apples in his Sunrise Orchard bags head out to nearby supermarkets, where he frets that they won't be kept cool.

Apples help illustrate another point, too: In the years ahead, *local* may be a more important word than *organic* in figuring out how to eat. In fact, a British study published this winter found that buying food from close to home prevented twice as much environmental damage as buying organic food from a distance.

Now, the best solution might be local *and* organic; most of the food I've been eating this winter falls into that category. But apples aren't easy—an orchard is a monoculture, prey to a bewildering variety of insects and blights. And very few consumers, even at the natural foods co-op, will pick up a Macoun or a Paula Red if it's clear that some other creature has taken the first nibble, so almost all the area growers do a little spraying. "How little spray can I get away with, and still produce fruit that people will buy?" asks Bill Suhr, who runs Champlain Orchards, down the road just above the Ticonderoga ferry dock. *His* saving grace is the cider press that's clanking away as we talk: He can take the risk of using fewer chemicals because if the apples aren't perfect, he can always turn them into cider. Absolutely delicious cider, too—I've been drinking well north of two gallons a week, and I'm not sure I'll ever go back to orange juice. And each batch, because it draws on a slightly different mix of varieties, tastes a little different: tartest in early fall, sweetest and most complex at the height of the harvest, but always tangy and deep. It may not be organic, but it's neighborly, which is good enough for me.

FEBRUARY By now an agreeable routine has set in: pancakes or oatmeal or eggs in the morning, soup and a cheese sandwich for lunch. (I could eat a different Vermont cheese every day of the winter, but I usually opt for a hunk off the Orb Weaver farmstead round.) And for dinner, some creature that until quite recently was clucking, mooing, baaing, or otherwise signaling its pleasure at the local grass and hay it was turning into protein. Also potatoes. And something from the freezer—it's a chest-type, and in a dark corner, so you basically just stick a hand in and see what vegetable comes out.

And, oh, did I mention beer? Otter Creek Brewing, a quarter mile down the road from my daughter's school, makes a stellar *wit bier,* a Belgian style that is naturally cloudy with raw organic wheat from Ben Gleason's farm. It's normally sold in the summer, but I hoarded some for my winter drinking. "We'd love to use local barley for the rest of our beers," says Morgan Wolaver, the brewery's owner. But that would mean someone building a malting plant to serve not just Otter Creek but the state's seven other microbreweries. Perhaps right next to the oat mill . . .

MARCH I can see spring in the distance—there are still feet of snow in the woods, but the sun is September strong, and it won't be long before down in the valley someone is planting lettuce.

But there's one last place I must describe, both because it's provided many of my calories and because it embodies the idea of a small-scale farmer making a decent living growing great food. Jack and Anne Lazor bought Butterworks Farm, in the state's Northeast Kingdom, in the mid-'70s, after a stint of working at Old Sturbridge Village, in Massachusetts: Dressed in nineteenth-century costumes, they milked cows by hand and talked to the tourists. As it turns out, they weren't actors—they were real farmers. Slowly they've grown their business into one of the state's premier organic dairies: Their yogurt is nearly a million-dollar business. I've been living off their dried beans, too, and their cornmeal. It's great fun, then, to sit in their kitchen eating bacon and eggs and watch Anne mix up some salve for the teats of her cows, and listen to them describe their life. The talk's a mix of technical detail (they milk Jerseys, not the more common Holsteins, which means less milk but higher protein, so their yogurt needs no pectin to stay firm) and rural philosophy. "We have such a 'take' mentality," Jack is saying. "It's part of our psyche, because we came to this verdant land as Europeans and were able to exploit it for so long."

But here the exploitation feels more like collaboration. We stroll over to his solar barn, where the 100 cows in the herd loiter patiently, mulling over the events of the day. "That's Morel, that's Phooey, that's Vetch, that's Clover, that's Jewel. . . ." It's very calm in here, no sound but cud being chewed, and it's warm out of the late winter wind. Jack, who's a talker, is explaining how Vermont could market itself as the Sustainable State, and how he's hoping to sell masa harina for making tortillas next year, and so forth. I'm sort of listening, but mostly just absorbing the sheer pleasure of the scene—that this place works, that I've been connected to it all winter long, that it will be here, with any luck, for the rest of my life.

Look—eating this way has come at a cost. Not in health or in money (if anything, I've spent less than I usually would, since I haven't bought a speck of processed food), but in time. I've had to think about every meal, instead of cruising through the world on autopilot, ingesting random calories. I've had to pay attention. But the payoff for that cost has been immense, a web of connections I'd never have known about otherwise. Sure, I'm looking forward to the occasional banana, the odd pint of Guinness stout. But I think this winter has permanently altered the way I eat. In more ways than one, it's left a good taste in my mouth.

Proud Heritage

by Patric Kuh

from *Bon Appetit*

Though normally Patric Kuh can be found reviewing hot new restaurants for *Los Angeles* magazine, here he takes a very different journey through the New Mexico countryside, seeking native suppliers quietly devoted to preserving a distinctive regional cuisine.

Española, New Mexico, lies 25 miles northwest of Santa Fe on State Highway 68. If you keep going north, the road narrows into the gorge of the Rio Grande, which, after many curves, opens up into the Taos Plateau. With its car dealerships and fast-food franchises, the small town's main drag seems like an unlikely sliver of Middle America dropped between the turquoise and adobe radiance of Santa Fe and Taos.

In the predawn darkness of an autumn morning, I peeled off that strip into the parking lot of the town's Burger King. I couldn't suppress a smile. I'd come to northern New Mexico to find out about native foods, not about Whoppers. I'd wanted to do it my way; apparently that meant starting where they do it your way.

The previous day I had met Pat Montoya at his apple stall in the Los Alamos Farmers' Market. Although it was only late October, a cold wind was blowing down from the mountains. Montoya was wearing a Windbreaker and looked like a coach, lean and concentrated. I talked; he listened. I was talking about native foods; he was trying to sell apples. I asked if I could go see his farm, and he told me to meet him in the parking lot of the Española Burger King at quarter to seven the next morning.

As someone who reviews restaurants for a living, I've been bombarded with the terms *native* and *heirloom* on menus and from chefs in recent years. The terms beckon one to go deep, yet end up having all the meaning of rare, medium, and well-done. At the table, they become a description of quality, but little more.

A transformation has taken place in the nation's eating habits wherein we feel the need to go back. Back to an approach to food that is preindustrialized and firmly planted in the native soil. New Mexico's Anasazi beans and posole are charter members of a group that also includes heirloom vegetables, heritage breeds such as Berkshire pork and Narragansett turkeys, and traditional foods as diverse as small-batch bourbon and stone-ground grits.

But I still had issues. Tradition seemed to be such a trend, heritage such a sales pitch. Even in my own cooking I stayed away from heirloom vegetables. Whatever was stacked, polished, and on the manager's special was actually my life. And what tradition, exactly, were blue corn chips saving?

And so I went to New Mexico. While all American regions have ingredients that throw a shaft of light into a culture and a people, the role of native foods in the Southwest is unique. Perhaps the best way to explain this is through the names: From the Telephone Tall pea to the Country Gentleman corn, heirlooms that originated elsewhere have the lovely improvised quality of having been thought of while resting with hoe in hand. In New Mexico they seem to share both the austerity and the resonance of the land. Posole—corn kernels cooked in vats of slaked lime—was being prepared this way long before there was a nation. Beans such as pinto and Anasazi were staples of the Pueblo Indians' food. They don't share the narrative thread of so many other heirloom vegetables, which tell of seeds being sewn into pockets, carried down rivers in western expansion, planted in orchards or log cabin gardens, and propagated from there. They weren't what came afterward but what was here before.

Pat Montoya's truck was idling. I parked beside him and he rolled down his window. I think he was surprised I showed up. We pulled out of the lot and started up Highway 84. There isn't much talk in a farmer's truck at that time of the morning, and I found myself looking out the window. New Mexico makes a big deal about its enlightening powers. Desert expanse, native jewelry, Georgia O'Keeffe —who wouldn't feel the scales drop from their eyes? What I hadn't been prepared for was the power of the landscape. Now it was coming to life before me as a looming mesa that ran along the road, a river valley thick with yellow-leaved cottonwoods, and a massive, brightening sky that seemed to mirror the expanse of the land.

The previous day Montoya told me that the only way he'd held on to his orchard—an orchard his father first planted—was thanks to the farmers' markets. At his orchard, Montoya showed me around with farmer's pride, pointing out the new plantings and where he'd cleared brush. But what I remember most is looking down at the acequia with which his trees were irrigated. Built hundreds of years ago by the Pueblo Indians and the Spanish to bring water from the Rio Grande, these channels have since been maintained by generations of farmers. I looked down at the channel and felt the centuries compress before me. In New Mexico you can go from a Burger King to an acequia in minutes flat.

For the following two days as I drove from farm to farm, the past and the present would constantly be winding around each other, playing off each other, creating, I would come to understand, a new prism through which to see native foods.

At Algo Nativo, a farmers' market producer farther up the gorge from Pat Montoya's orchard, Margaret Campos and her mother, Eremita, were putting up the last jellies and tomatoes of the season, which they'd sell at the farmers' market. Mother and daughter, who also run a cooking school called Comida de Campos, seemed like the picture of an eternal farmhouse ritual. Margaret took me outside to show me the wild purslane that her great-grandmother would eat stir-fried with pepper seeds. Eremita, her thin hair held back in a ponytail with a scrunchie, laughed at life's peculiarities. "We used to grow pinto and *bolita* beans, but now we grow French filet beans—haricots verts!"

Still higher, at the end of an unpaved road in the town of Dixon, Fred Martinez walked me around his craggy apple orchard before inviting me into his home. On a terrace lay the dried peppers Martinez threads onto traditional *ristras*. On a table nearby was a charging cell phone—a more modern but equally important part of the business.

In the town of Alcalde I went to see Max Martinez, who makes posole that he dries and sells. The sky was low. The land seemed exhausted. "Every fall I wonder if I should continue," he said, then paused and eventually smiled. "Then spring comes around again and I start right up."

I thought of what I had read about native foods before coming here. Each one drew a bead on a corner of the nation. The dátil chile pepper, for example, introduced by Minorcan immigrants in the late eighteenth century, was until a few decades ago only found in the cooking of natives of St. Augustine, Florida. Louisiana Creole cream cheese was originally made by hanging clabbered milk in cheesecloth from the branches of oaks in the Delta.

The success with which the heirloom ingredients were preserved only seemed to underscore how the survival of others was endangered. Once believed to be lost forever, the Moon and Stars watermelon, with its speckled leaves and high-ridged rind, has been successfully propagated from a single crop found in Missouri. The Marshall strawberry that once thrived in Washington, Oregon, and Northern California today exists only at the USDA's National Clonal Germplasm Repository in Corvallis, Oregon. Its flavor—its uniqueness—will never be tasted again. In Martinez's slow walk back to the car I saw how food traditions survived, not in a statement, not as a principle, but in the very everydayness of a farmer forcing himself out of bed at first light.

On my last day in New Mexico I go to the Santa Fe Farmers' Market. By the entrance Don Bustos is roasting the chiles he grows up in Española in a blazing hand-cranked drum. Not far from him is Antonio Manzanares of Shepherd's Lamb, who raises organic lambs in the high plateaus west of Taos.

I am having a moment of truth. I am holding a one-pound bag of Anasazi beans at Max Martinez's stand. An impulse purchase, perhaps, but what exactly is the impulse? It's the yawning gap between culinary theory and culinary practice. I am going back home, but will I take them with me? I look down at their purple mottled surfaces. I open my wallet and purchase them.

I have one more stop. I find myself driving out of Santa Fe, past the Española Burger King and along Highway 84, and I don't stop till I get to the vista of the Taos Plateau. The expanse of scrub- and juniper-studded hillsides spreads out before me. It is magnificently large; the great plains themselves seem to have rolled up into the mesa before me. I stand there and look north and feel the very pull of the West. I take in the view almost like a breath, like something I want to keep with me after I've left.

And I have. I went to New Mexico a cynic; I came back a believer. It is a place of compacted cultures, of Indian pueblo and adobe chapel and all the different settlers who came after that. Sometimes the space between them broadens into impregnable bands; at other times whatever it is that separates them blows away in an eddy of dust. The snap of morning, the clear early light, the sight of *ristra* wreaths hanging from beams, and the stark beauty of the evening sun on the Sangre de Cristo range—these are moments and sensations that remain with you.

But it has stayed with me in my cooking, too. It has happened gradually. It started when I heard the soft drift of crushed chile *caribe* as I poured it into a jar and placed it in a cupboard at home. It grew when I found myself thinking about how I would cook the Anasazi beans.

I have a chipped sauceboat that I bring out at Thanksgiving. It belonged to my grandparents, and nothing else remains of the set. The reason I don't bring it out at any other time of the year is not because of my wish to preserve it, but because it doesn't seem to fit. It's hard to fit an heirloom into everyday life. At Thanksgiving it is different, however. It is not that we reach some elevated state—I have spent my share of hours waiting for a turkey to finish cooking while entertaining kids with a SpongeBob impersonation. In fact, a little mayhem is itself a part of Thanksgiving. The reason I bring out the sauceboat is that for this one meal, we allow a table and everything that is placed on it to have all the symbolism it can.

Historians tell us that the first Thanksgiving feast was like a big potluck. The pilgrims were thankful that the land they had imagined in Leyden had not proved as dangerous as their darkest fears. They were thankful that the coastline they had first seen less than twelve months before, while far from bountiful, had provided for their needs.

Thinking of it as a potluck places the meal within the domain of my life. It sounds like the kind of neighborhood gatherings we take the kids to, where one person may bring Persian rice, another a great guacamole with the avocado seed in it, and yet another a favorite popover that might still be warm. Native foods had to make a transition from the domain of tradition to that of Tupperware. I knew that each one carried the heritage of centuries; it was the four hours of simmering on my stove that I couldn't get past. No longer.

This Thanksgiving on my family's table, together with my grand-parents' sauceboat and our mismatched silver, there will be Anasazi beans. I have done the practice run. I will sweat some onions and carrots, add Hunt's canned tomatoes and garlic, and simmer that down before adding some chorizo for flavor. Then I'll add the beans, cover with water, and cook slowly with a bay leaf taken from my windowsill. It's not the recipe Max Martinez told me. No, these Anasazi beans are my own.

Posole Stew

This combination of pork, hominy, and vegetables is New Mexico soul food at its best. The recipe is based on one prepared by Evangeline Martinez. Her husband, Max, makes and sells the white hominy with which it is made at the Santa Fe Farmers' Market.

1 ½ pounds boneless country-style pork ribs, cut into 1-inch
    pieces
12 cups low-salt chicken broth
12 cups (about) water, divided
1 pound dried posole (white hominy)*
2 tablespoons (¼ stick) butter
1 large onion, chopped

*Dried posole is available at some specialty foods stores and by mail from the Martinezes at M&S Farms, 505-852-4368.

2 carrots, chopped

4 large plum tomatoes, chopped

4 ounces green beans, cut into 1-inch lengths

1 dried New Mexico chile,** stemmed, halved, seeded, thickly
    sliced

2 large garlic cloves, chopped

1 ½ teaspoons ground cumin

1 cup chopped fresh cilantro

3 Anaheim chiles,** roasted, seeded, chopped, and mixed with
    3 minced garlic cloves

Hot pepper sauce

Warm corn tortillas

Place pork in large pot. Add 12 cups broth and 8 cups
water and bring to boil. Boil 1 minute, skimming surface
with slotted spoon to remove foam. Add posole and bring
to boil. Reduce heat to medium-low. Partially cover and
simmer until posole is tender, skimming surface occasionally, about 4 hours. *(Can be prepared 1 day ahead. Cool
slightly. Refrigerate pork and posole in cooking liquid, uncovered,
until cold; cover and refrigerate.)*

Melt butter in heavy large skillet over medium-high
heat. Add onion, carrots, tomatoes, and green beans; sauté
5 minutes. Mix onion mixture. New Mexico chile, 2 garlic
cloves, and cumin into posole. Boil until posole is very
tender, adding more water by cupfuls as needed to cover
posole, about 1 hour. Mix in cilantro. Season to taste with
salt and pepper.

Ladle posole into bowls. Serve with roasted chile-garlic
mixture and hot sauce. Pass tortillas separately.

SERVES 8

⸺◦⸺

** *Chiles are available at some supermarkets, specialty foods stores, and Latin markets.*

Herbed Goat Cheese with
Roasted Chiles and Olive Oil

3 large fresh Anaheim chiles*
2 large garlic cloves, peeled
1 5-ounce log soft fresh goat cheese, crumbled
1 tablespoon chopped fresh cilantro
2 teaspoons chopped fresh oregano
¼ cup extra-virgin olive oil
1 baguette, sliced, toasted

Char chiles over gas flame or in broiler until blackened on all sides. Wrap in paper bag; let stand 10 minutes to steam. Peel and seed chiles, then cut into strips.

Blanch garlic in small saucepan of simmering water 3 minutes. Drain and cool. Chop 1 garlic clove; thinly slice remaining garlic. Mix cheese, cilantro, oregano, and chopped garlic in small bowl. Season to taste with salt and pepper. Crumble cheese mixture onto plate. Top with roasted chiles and sliced garlic. *(Can be made 1 day ahead. Cover and refrigerate. Let stand 1 hour at room temperature before continuing.)*

Drizzle oil over chiles and goat cheese. Serve with toasted baguette.

SERVES 4

---

* *Also known as California chiles; available at many supermarkets and Latin markets.*

Anasazi Beans with Chorizo

2 tablespoons vegetable oil
2 carrots, peeled, diced
1 large onion, chopped
5 garlic cloves, chopped
1 14 ½-ounce can diced tomatoes in juice
8 ounces link chorizo sausage, casings removed, crumbled
6 large fresh thyme sprigs
2 bay leaves
¼ teaspoon dried crushed red pepper
1 16-ounce bag dried Anasazi beans* or pinto beans

Heat vegetable oil in heavy large pot over medium-high heat. Add carrots and onion; sauté until pale golden, about 7 minutes. Mix in garlic, then tomatoes with juice and cook until liquid is almost evaporated, about 3 minutes. Mix in sausage, thyme, bay leaves, and crushed red pepper. Add beans and enough cold water to cover by 2 inches (about 10 cups). Bring to boil. Reduce heat, cover partially, and simmer until beans are tender, adding more water by cupfuls if dry and stirring occasionally, about 2 hours 15 minutes. Season with salt and pepper. Discard bay leaves and serve.

SERVES 8

*Available at specialty foods stores, natural foods stores, and shopnatural.com.

Fleshy and Full of Life

by Steven Rinella

from *The Scavenger's Guide to Haute Cuisine*

Rinella's hare-brained project—to hunt and scavenge all the ingredients for a blowout feast from Auguste Escoffier's classic cookbook—may sound like a recipe for disaster, but with wry humor and wild escapades he somehow pulls it off.

It's almost time for Thanksgiving dinner and I'm just now beginning to stuff the bird. But no matter how hard I stuff, I can't get it to fit inside the bladder. I'm following a recipe from French master chef Auguste Escoffier's 1903 magnum opus, *Le Guide Culinaire,* a 5,012-recipe compendium on haute cuisine. The book is pinned open on the counter with a one-quart jar of stingray marinade. Technically, the dish I'm making calls for a duck to be poached inside a pig's bladder. But when I killed a wild boar in northern California last summer, I accidentally nicked its bladder with my skinning knife. So I'm trying to forge ahead with an antelope bladder and half a duck. I push and pull and stretch, but it won't go.

The poached bladder is just one of the courses from *Le Guide Culinaire* that I'm attempting to construct tonight. All together, I have the ingredients for fifteen dishes scattered throughout the kitchen here in Miles City, Montana. Or, I should say, I have the ingredients for thirteen dishes scattered around; the makings of the other two courses are still wearing their feathers and fur.

My two squabs, or baby pigeons, are cooing and preening in

the coop that I built last summer. The birds' names are Red and Lil' Red, and I'll be using them in Escoffier's *pigeonneaux cra-paudine.* In an hour they need to be plucked, flattened, dipped in butter, grilled, then served with gherkins and Escoffier's *diable,* or devil sauce.

The remaining dish is a pâté of cottontail rabbit. For all I know, the key ingredient for that is still hopping around south of town. My two brothers, Matt and Danny, left this morning with a group of our friends to hunt pheasants and rabbits along the Powder River, but it's getting dark and they still haven't returned.

I keep busy as I wait for the rabbit. After lifting some strips of black bear fat out of a bowl of brandy, I refill the bowl with a handful of wild boar sausage. Then I begin prepping the fix-ings for a freshwater matelote, a soup made from white wine, stock, and a medley of fish. I've already peeled the crayfish tails, so I trim some fillets of smallmouth bass, walleye, and bluegills and remove the long, serpentine spine from an eel.

If everything goes right, I will prepare forty-five courses from *Le Guide Culinaire* over the next three nights. I have at my fin-gertips a collection of the book's ingredients that I gathered from all corners of the country. As I work along, converting raw material to food, the last year of my life literally passes through my fingers. The stingray marinade takes me back to a Florida beach, where my buddy Kern and I wrestled in a stingray amid a throng of hostile tourists. The black bear fat makes me remember the glaciers of Alaska's Chugach Range, which turn the eerie blue color of gel toothpaste when the sun breaks through the clouds. The eel makes me think of Ray Turner, a self-proclaimed "old hairbag by the river" who operates an eel weir in upstate New York, keeps an emu for company, and once built a fireplace from a rock that he found by the grave site of an Indian princess.

Back when I first discovered *Le Guide Culinaire,* I knew I'd stumbled into a strange, lost world. In his day, Escoffier was known as the King of Chefs and the Chef of Kings; he cooked for the likes of Kaiser Wilhelm II, Frederick VIII, the Duke of Orleans, Queen Victoria, the Prince of Wales, the Khadid of

Egypt, the emperors of Austria and Brazil, the shah of Persia, and the king of Greece. If Escoffier's list of clients just sounds like a bunch of people who figured into World War I, you might approach Escoffier through the more familiar lens of American music:

> Now, if you're blue
> And you don't know where to go to
> Why don't you go where fashion sits
> Puttin' on the Ritz

That ditty from 1929 was written by Irving Berlin, the same dude who wrote "God Bless America." In "Puttin' on the Ritz," Berlin is referring to the Swiss hotelier César Ritz, whose name is synonymous with taste and class and ostentatious display. In large part, Ritz's reputation rested on his long partnership with Auguste Escoffier. Ritz ran the hotels; Escoffier ran the kitchens in the hotels. When Escoffier collected his methods in *Le Guide Culinaire,* he produced a work that single-handedly revolutionized French *haute,* or "high," cuisine.

As old as it is, the book didn't seem to me like a historical document when I found it. Instead, I saw it immediately as a scavenger's guide, an inventory of all that is bizarre and glorious and tantalizing about procuring your own food and living off the wild. I tore into the book, hell-bent on recreating as much of it as I could. I allowed myself a year, and now all that time has come down to these moments, these three nights, and I'm filled with overwhelming giddiness. And an equal dose of anxiety. I've got friends here from all over the country tonight. If I can't pull off this feast, this last year of my life will seem a little less extraordinary.

I go outside to see if my brothers are back yet with some rabbits. They're not. I take a peek into the pigeon coop. It's dark out, and the two squabs are sitting on their perches, oblivious to what lies ahead. The older pigeon, Red, has one of the younger pigeon's feathers stuck in his bill. There's plenty of room for the two to spread out, but they make a sport of pecking at each other in a ritualistic sort of dance. They usually shadowbox, but now and then Red connects. I'm visited by this weird sense of guilt that I get every time I look at them. Catching the squabs required almost a year's time and several near-death experiences. When I first started chasing pigeons with the thought of trying some of Escoffier's thirty-four squab recipes, I thought of the birds as dirty pests. But after catching a few pigeons and raising the squabs by hand, I came to see the birds as a metaphor for the contradictions of a society that has distanced itself from the production of its food. Now that I'm moments away from "prepping" the birds, I lament that it's going to be an awfully abrupt ending for such a long story. In Escoffier's day, people killed squabs by smothering them. The ancient Romans drowned their squabs in red wine. I might use a hatchet.

I go back to the kitchen to finish plucking a box of twenty English sparrows that I got in Iowa. The birds are so small, I can hold four or five of them in my palm at once. Plucking the little things is delicate work. I lift one from the box and pinch a tuft of feathers from its breast just as my girlfriend, Diana, walks into the kitchen. At the sight of her, I reflexively drop the sparrow back into the box and kick the lid closed. At the same time, I toss a scrap of cheesecloth over the plate of wild turkey bones that will go into tomorrow's game stock. Escoffier often recited the maxim, "If you want to keep your appetite, stay out of the kitchen." I'm trying to enforce Escoffier's advice on Diana, because she's a struggling vegetarian. I'm hoping that this feast will serve as a rite of passage for her, and that she'll emerge from the experience as a full-on carnivore. She's agreed to try as much of the food as physically possible tonight. I'm counting on her getting blown away by the beauty of the finished products and I don't want her to get turned off prematurely.

Once I shoo Diana from the kitchen, two of my buddies from childhood, Kern and Drost, come running through the front door in their hunting boots and then go out the back door. As they disappear, I yell, "Hey, did you get the rabbits?" But they don't hear me.

I go outside and see that my brothers and Drost are helping Kern pin down one of his hunting dogs. The dog got hung up on a barbed-wire fence. Kern's wife, Deirdre, is a doctor. She's got a curved needle and a long thread, and she's sewing the dog back up.

When she finishes tightening the last knot, I look at Danny. "Rabbits?"

"Two. I'll skin 'em for you."

When Danny comes in with the rabbit loins, I have what I need to finish the fourteenth dish. I slice the loins in long, thin strips and put them to soak in the brandy. Fourteen down. Now there's just one dish left.

I step outside with the hatchet. Someone's turned on the yard light, so Red thinks the sun has risen. I can hear him cooing.

Stuffed Animals

by Jeffrey Steingarten

from *Men's Vogue*

2006 seemed to be the year of the Great Foie Gras Debate; who better to weigh in than Steingarten, whose in-depth articles in Vogue have established him as a smart, entertaining, and very sane critic of America's foodie scene.

> *our sweet scent is a lyre*
> *On our palates. Your harmony*
> *Plays cymbals on our tongues*
> *And runs through us*
> *With a long shudder of pleasure.*
> — Pablo Neruda on foie gras

Do you think it's all right to eat foie gras? That would be an easy question if foie gras were not one of the most delectable foods on Earth. If they passed a law banning broccoli, nobody would utter a peep, except for farmers whose livelihood depends on broccoli. Plus a few peeps from people whose inexplicable yearning for broccoli cannot be satisfied by brussels sprouts.

Foie means "liver"; *gras* means "fat." It's French. Foie gras is the fattened liver of a force-fed duck or goose. These days 80 percent of the world's foie gras comes from ducks. Their livers expand by eight to ten times during the final month of feeding. Animal-rights advocates, notably PETA and Farm Sanctuary, argue that force-feeding ducks is cruel and causes unacceptable suffering. The practice is illegal in Argentina, two-thirds of Austria, the Czech Republic,

Denmark, Finland, Germany, Ireland, Israel (until recently a large producer of foie gras), Italy, Luxembourg, Norway, Poland, Sweden, Switzerland, the Netherlands, and the United Kingdom, most of which never produced foie gras in the first place. I've heard that Israeli farmers are thinking of moving their operations to the West Bank; most of their current workers now are Palestinians.

Foie gras is the new fur. Except that you can't eat fur. Foie gras is an incomparably delicious food, and there's no substitute, no such thing as faux gras. What does it taste like? Most writers use the word *buttery,* but if that were all, you could save lots of money and grief by eating butter. I'd like to take a stab at it, but I'd first have to eat lots more foie gras, and I can't do that until I decide whether it's ethically right. Maybe now is the time to decide. We can't put it off forever.

I had my first taste long ago, when I was twenty and on a trip to Europe with two old friends. We had saved up for a three-Michelin-star meal in Paris, at the restaurant Laserre. (In those days you could hold the bill to $15 if you were careful ordering wine.) My first course was a generous round foie gras baked into a buttery brioche pastry encircled by a very light and savory version of sauce Périgueux—meat juices reduced with Madeira and flavored with finely minced black truffles. I ate more and more slowly so that it would never disappear. It taught me that there were gastronomic worlds I had never even imagined.

A whole, raw foie gras is naturally pink-beige and shiny and weighs about a pound and a half. It can be eaten hot—in crisp, dark-brown sautéed slices with creamy insides, the most popular form in restaurants these days; or braised until evenly tender throughout, then dramatically served whole at the table; or poached in its own fat or turned into a luxurious sausage, or pureed into a soup with chestnuts, or wrapped into dumplings or turnovers, or confected into an eggy custard, which is among my favorites. Then it is best accompanied by something acidic and fruity. When foie gras is served cold, it is often in a terrine—mildly flavored with cognac or liqueur and pinches of spice and salt, or not flavored at all, then pressed into a loaf pan and baked until the insides are barely hot (unless you follow USDA warnings), and finally cooled and allowed to develop its flavor for a day or two. (You can see a hundred ways of cooking foie gras in an excellent book, *Foie Gras: A Passion,* by Michael Ginor with Mitchell Davis and others.) People who don't know anything much about foie gras promiscuously call it pâté. Pâté de foie gras is something distinct, a mixture of ground foie gras and pork or veal or duck, baked en terrine and cooled. In France, pâté de foie gras must contain at least 50 percent foie gras, but it doesn't compare to pure, unalloyed foie gras, the genuine article.

Traditional force-feeding in the southwest of France, where foie gras is a historic specialty, is still done on some small farms by a member of the farmer's family, who inserts the tube end of a funnel filled with corn some inches down the duck's throat while massaging its neck. This aids the passage of food and checks that there is no corn left over from an earlier feeding. An auger revolving within the tube can also propel the corn. This method of feeding is known as gavage.

Many varieties of duck are migratory, and they instinctively overeat before the long voyage; birds have the remarkable ability to store excess nutrients as fat in their livers, which regularly double in size, but not much more than that without force-feeding. (As you may have noticed in the mirror this morning, mammals store fat all about their bodies and not in their livers, unless they are very sick.) The duck's anatomy also includes a crop, "a pouchlike enlargement of the esophagus . . . in which the food undergoes a partial preparation for digestion before passing on to the true stomach," according to the *Oxford English Dictionary.* Ducks don't chew—they have no teeth, and they have no gag reaction. A duck's crop can hold the excess corn it is fed, unless it is forced to swallow too much, in which case some of the corn gets forced into the bird's stomach or clogs its throat, a rare occurrence when ducks are fed by hand. The ducks are kept in an ample yard and crowd around the feeder when she appears. Near the end, when their fattened livers weigh a pound or more, the ducks may possibly have trouble walking.

This is about as benign as force-feeding gets. It accounts for less than 20 percent of French foie gras and an indeterminate amount of foie gras in America. If what I've described is too harsh for you, then you'll not be consuming much foie gras, until they've found a nicer way to fatten a duck's liver. To me, this is acceptable. Industrially produced foie gras is not.

If Jesus were alive today, would he eat foie gras? The New Testament offers no guidance. I've skimmed all four Gospels, and I have yet to find a scene in which Jesus is actually eating, except maybe the dinner in the house of the Pharisees, which was so totally tense that I doubt anybody ate much of anything. Nor is there even one verse about the humane treatment of animals. I went out and bought a popular book called *What Would Jesus Eat,* by Don Colbert, M.D. It was in the Christian Inspiration section of my local Barnes & Noble. There's not a word in it on the foie gras issue. There's nothing about animal cruelty. Or about what Jesus did, in actual point of fact, eat. But I'll bet he never ate pork or lobster, because Jesus was a Jewish person. Colbert guesses that Jesus mostly ate manna. My corner bodega is plumb out of manna.

Is it possible that Jesus actually did eat foie gras? It certainly is an ancient delicacy. The Egyptians force-fed geese, though their purpose was most likely to obtain nice fat geese for the table, not fat livers. The first people to value the liver in itself were, naturally, the Romans. In his *Natural History,* Pliny the Elder wrote, at about the time of Christ, "Our countrymen are wiser, who know the goose by the excellence of its liver. Stuffing the bird with food makes the liver grow to a great size, and also when it has been removed it is made larger by being soaked in milk sweetened with honey." The Romans employed Jewish slaves to force-feed their geese, and the Jewish aristocracy in Palestine emulated the Roman upper classes as their social models. Foie gras would have been just the thing.

Throughout the Dark and Middle Ages, it was the Jews who kept alive the art and science of fattening geese. By the year 1100, many Jews had migrated to France and northern Germany, and with them went the practice of force-feeding geese. As they were prohibited from eating lard and could no longer obtain the olive oil of the Mediterranean, their only cooking medium was poultry fat, and a force-fed goose was the most abundant source of schmaltz known to man or woman. But the great French-Jewish medieval scholar Rashi worried that the Jews would have to pay in the afterlife for the force-feeding they practiced. In those days, I've read, the geese were blinded and their webbed feet nailed to the floor.

By the time of the Renaissance, Jewish butchers were serving Christian lovers of fatted goose liver in Italy and northern Germany, and Strasbourg in Alsace became the world capital of foie gras. When Germans immigrated to the Midwestern United States in the nineteenth century, they brought with them the talent for force-feeding geese. Watertown, Wisconsin, was the center of the stuffed-goose industry, according to the *Watertown Daily Times,* which characterized it as an old German tradition; the force-feeding was accomplished with noodles. Until the 1970s, Watertown supplied German butcher shops in New York City and the storied restaurant Lüchow's, on Fourteenth Street. People believe that the later influx of relatively inexpensive semi-cooked French foie gras put the Midwest farmers out of business. But for all we know, the German-American housewives of Wisconsin still hasten to their poultry sheds under cover of night to stuff their geese. I guess this means that force-feeding geese is as American as Snack Well's or Kraft Singles.

So far, the animal-rights people have not succeeded in France, which is the largest producer and consumer in the world—17,500 tons a year. The foie gras industry there has created 130,000 jobs, direct and indirect, and in 2005, the national assembly declared foie gras a "cultural and gastronomic patrimony protected in France." In the United States, foie gras is produced on only three farms, two in New York State and one in Sonoma County, California. In late 2004, the California legislature passed a bill (S.B. 1520) banning the production or sale of foie gras, and Governor Schwarzenegger signed it into law. Although this was generally seen as a great victory for the anti–foie gras forces, it was in reality just a tiny triumph because the ban goes into effect in 2012, and until then the one producer in the state is shielded from civil lawsuits. The response of animal-rights groups was divided. Some were outraged, seeing the new law as a betrayal; others, for various reasons, preferred to claim it as a famous victory. California has seen episodes of vandalism and harassment against restaurants, private houses, and Sonoma Foie Gras, a small, largely artisanal farm. The animal-rights people seem to be as strongly convinced of their cause as anti-abortion protesters.

Early in 2005, a bill against the production of foie gras in New York State was posted on the legislative calendar. This could have been cataclysmic for foie gras lovers, as most of the foie gras in the

United States comes from a company called Hudson Valley Foie Gras, in Ferndale, New York. Michael Ginor, its proprietor (and the coauthor of *Foie Gras: A Passion*), helped write the law himself, which included a ten-year grace period. Ginor tells me that he simply wanted the kind of certainty a businessman needs to make decisions, such as whether to put a new roof on a barn. Understanding that Ginor truly did not want the bill to pass, the Republicans in the state Senate killed it. No new bill appears to have been posted this year. Have I found the one reason to vote Republican?

In the abstract, the foie gras question is simple. All Americans fall into one of three categories: Some believe that exploitation of any animal, even milking a cow or taking honey from a hive, is immoral, impermissible. I don't fall into this small group and neither, probably, do you. At the opposite extreme are people who argue that man was created at, or evolved to, the top of the heap and can do whatever he wants with other species, even administer agonizing pain. I've been surprised to discover how many of my fellow humans make this claim. I'm not in that category either. If you are, then you'll happily continue to gorge on foie gras while the rest of us follow a middle way.

Most of us are not vegans or vegetarians. When we buy the flesh of a mammal, bird, or fish in a restaurant or food shop, we are an agent in the slaughter of another living thing. We are taking life. This is a serious act, not a casual one. But our purpose is not survival or even sustenance; most of us can live comfortably without eating meat. No, our goal is pleasure, pure sensory pleasure. We chew on the succulent muscle of a steer, crunch through the crackling skin of a pig or turkey, suck out the marrow from the shin of a calf. If we are willing to kill for our pleasure, shouldn't we also be willing to force-feed ducks for our pleasure? It all depends on how much pain and distress we cause.

Although they neglected to nominate me for sainthood in the last go-around, I do try to follow a few modest practices. I don't eat animals that were raised or slaughtered chemically or inhumanely, preferring animals that grew up in pastures and fields, were cared for individually and by hand, and were not given growth hormones or unnecessary antibiotics. I don't eat veal from anemic calves confined in the darkness of a crate that keeps their meat desirably pale. I haven't eaten supermarket pork for the past ten years, except at important Southern BBQ events. Or eggs laid by battery hens. Or chickens on growth hormones raised by the thousands on the floors of barns covered with several weeks of their own waste—except when they have been fried by an incontestable master. I don't eat meat that doesn't matter—crumbled onto a pizza or scattered over a slimy salad or cooked to cardboard grayness and wedged between two buns. Meat and fowl of the highest quality are extremely expensive, and so I can't afford a great quantity of them. This cuts down on the volume of slaughter for which I'm responsible, as does my attempt not to waste animal flesh. That is how I've made my peace with slaughter.

Animal-rights advocates are much more likely to be vegetarians, vegans even, than the rest of us. That's been my experience. They argue for humane husbandry and slaughter, but underneath it all they won't rest until we stop killing animals for food. Foie gras is an easy target. Luxurious and expensive, it is eaten by only a fraction of the populace, and for much of the rest it carries the stink of decadence and excess. In France, foie gras has long been a required part of Christmas dinner, so being against foie gras in America is deliciously, mouthwateringly anti-French.

In this country, the animal-rights people distribute documented, photographed examples of revolting scenes in the barns and feeding sheds. Foie gras producers argue that the number of injured, ill, or prematurely dead ducks and geese is less than in the average poultry operation. Most of these problems can be ameliorated by getting closer to the artisanal, hands-on methods of the French housewife in southwest France. In the United States, improving the conditions of tube feeding can be achieved through regulation instead of prohibition. After all, there are just three foie gras farms in the entire country—it's not a difficult activity to watch.

And so, at last, the question comes down to this: How much distress does the most careful sort of tube feeding cause to the duck? I know of only two medical or scientific attempts to answer this question. Neither of them has been cited by animal-rights advocates, who instead encourage us to anthropomorphize, to imagine how we would feel getting tube-fed and fattened. But this may be the wrong question. How would we like to be a duck under any circumstances? How would we feel having to paddle all day on cold New England rivers and among the sodden marshes? I wouldn't be able to take it. Think of all the bugs and crawling things. Isn't there a better way of gauging a duck's distress?

Maybe there is. I telephoned Daniel Guémené, Ph.D., a research director at INRA, the prestigious French Institute for Agricultural Research. Guémené is an extremely prolific author of papers published in French and English journals, places such as *World's Poultry Science* and *British Poultry Science*. One of Guémené's keen interests is in discovering and refining ways of knowing whether poultry, ducks in this case, are in pain. He began his work on force-feeding in 1995, and as far as he can tell, his group at INRA is still alone in scientifically assessing the effect of tube feeding.

His first experiments examined the concentration of corticosterone —a hormone closely associated with stress—in ducks' bloodstreams before and after feeding. He expected a sharp rise—but found none at all. Over the following years, Guémené's group also looked at other indications of distress—avoidance of the feeder, withdrawal, pain signals in the medulla—and found possibly some pain in the final days of feeding, probably caused by inflammation of the crop; minor signs of avoidance, but not aversion, among some ducks at feeding time; and an increase in panting. Ducks showed the most stress when they were physically handled in any way or moved to new cages. Mortality on foie gras farms appears to be lower than in standard poultry operations. Guémené's group confirmed that although a grossly fattened liver is not natural, it is not a sign of disease: after feeding is stopped and the liver shrinks, there is no necrosis—no liver cells have been killed.

The American Veterinary Medical Association (the largest and oldest veterinary organization in America) has also considered tube feeding. In 2004, a resolution opposing the practice was introduced in its House of Delegates and referred to a study committee, which over the following year analyzed the limited amount of peer-reviewed literature and visited at least one of the three American foie gras farms. In July 2005, delegates presented their arguments on both the original resolution and a compromise version, apparently approved by an animal-rights representative. One opponent of tube-feeding who had made the farm visit conceded that the birds were not in distress or pain, that, although obese, they could still walk, and that they were better cared for than most chickens raised for food. But he still concluded that this was "not a good use of these animals." When a vote was taken, both ban resolutions were overwhelmingly defeated. Some delegates were influenced by the argument that if the organization disapproved tube-feeding, who knew what might follow? Why, next year they might condemn the confinement of veal calves, or the batteries of small, mechanized cages in which egg-laying hens are kept for their entire adulthood. Not a bad idea.

Well, there it is. The scientific evidence is pretty much unanimous in not condemning foie gras, but the evidence is still limited. So, though it seems unnecessary to stop eating foie gras altogether, the data is not unambiguous enough to encourage unbridled gorging. For now, the most sensible policy is to eat just a little of this sublime and ancient delicacy. Which is what most of us are doing already.

Mackerel Punts and Pilchards

by Megan Wetherall
from *Saveur*

As fishing boats pull into the harbor in Cornwall, *Saveur* contributor Megan Wetherall waits on the dock, watching to see how a traditional fishing community clings to its traditions and yet still smartens up for its role in a global marketplace.

It is barely light outside on a misty Cornish morning in the village of Newlyn, on the southwestern tip of England. Inside a nondescript waterfront warehouse, though, fishermen clad in yellow waterproof overalls and Wellington boots bring a flash of color to the scene as they mill around seafood brokers and merchants standing over red plastic crates full of sea creatures: ink-sprayed squid, gruff-looking ling with bulbous eyes, iridescent mackerel, strapping great monkfish and turbot, and delicate lemon sole are among the more than twenty species represented. Two auctioneers work the room quickly, and I can't follow any of it; then I realize that most of their communicating, with buyers from all over the United Kingdom, is done cryptically, in winks and nods.

The town of Newlyn came into its own when the historically important east-coast fishing ports like Grimsby and Hull began drying up in the 1970s, mainly because they were being shut out (for political reasons) from the cod-rich waters off of Iceland and in the Barents Sea. Unlike the big cod ports, Newlyn had a diverse small fleet, made up of some 170 boats—predominantly day boats, like netters and punts, with a small percentage of beamers, trawlers, and potters—that brought in a varied catch from the surrounding waters stretching westward out toward the continental shelf. Since that time, little Newlyn, with its higgledy-piggledy rows of granite cottages and its history of dashing smugglers and pirates, has become one of the most important fishing ports in the United Kingdom.

I'm standing with Andrew Pascoe, a tall fisherman in his mid-30s with tousled fair hair and the ruddy complexion of a man who has never suffered an office job, watching brightly painted mackerel punts chugging into the harbor and being unloaded in time for the auction. I got to talking with Pascoe on my first visit to Newlyn, last spring, while he was untangling nets. I was struck then, as I am now, by his unquenchable love of fishing and of this town, where he was born. As we walk around, he explains the seasonal cycles of the local catch: "The only time when mackerel aren't around is January through April. From April to June, we have monk and turbot, ray, lobsters, spider crabs and brown crabs, prawns, and brill. In July we start fishing for crayfish, and then later in the year we go for cod, bass, pollack, and some hake. In the new year it's mainly pollack and ling."

We're both hungry after our early start, so Andrew suggests that we adjourn to the fishermen's "caff" across the road for some breakfast. Sadly, as Andrew has warned me, most fishermen don't fancy the taste of fish this early in the day, so there isn't a kipper in sight; instead we make do with tea and hot buttered toast. Sitting next to us is a feisty-looking fellow called Mick Mahon, better known as "Grimmy Mike", because he once lived in Grimsby. I gather that Mahon is something of a local maverick, having moved down to Newlyn when Grimsby, once one of the largest fishing ports in the country, lost all but a handful of boats, and he isn't shy about airing his grievances against European Union quotas and what he views as a callous lack of support for the fishing industry from the British government. He leans in toward me and wags a large, grubby finger. "When we joined the EU, thirty-three years ago, we had huge fleets all over the place," he says. "Today there are only 10,000 fishermen left in the entire country. When I started there were 40,000. It used to be the best job in the world, fishing. If a boy could do a man's job he'd make a man's wage. It isn't the same now; it's swamped with bureaucracy."

My ears still ringing from Mick's impassioned outburst, I walk up the hill to visit Sally, Andrew's wife, to help her make sandwiches of brown crab meat on thickly buttered bread for lunch. She greets me with a wide smile, her tall, slender frame like a willowy tree around which her three-year-old, Archie, is clamped. We clamber up the steep staircase to her attic bedroom and peek out the skylight for a bird's-eye view of the harbor. "When there's a high tide we can see *Lamorna*," she says, that being the larger of Andrew's two boats. "We're always perched up here, me and the boys."

Sally has already boiled and cracked the crab, so we have only to extract and season the meaty flesh and pack it between slices of sandwich bread as the family cat meows plaintively. "You can't cut the sandwiches into triangles, because [fisherman believe] it makes the wind come," Sally cautions with a smile, slicing them into two rectangles. Are fishermen really that superstitious? I ask. "Well, he won't take my green Tupperware to sea, and he won't even dream about taking a pasty [the Cornish meat turnover]," she replies. Other rules: do not say the word *rabbit* at sea, never set out to sea on a Friday—and don't go at all if you happen to pass a nun or a vicar on your way down to the harbor.

We don't see either as we stroll down to the waterfront, Archie waving excitedly from atop his mother's shoulders, to deliver the sandwiches to Andrew, his brother, and his uncle, who wolf them down with enthusiasm and then get back to their nets. I leave them to it and walk on through the village, past stone cottages bearing such lyrical Cornish names as Chy-an-Psycador (House of Fisher), Pol-du (Bridge House), and Huers (Cliff Watchman), up to the other end of Newlyn, where Andrew's parents, Mary and Denys—he is also a fisherman—live with their daughter, Hannah. Over mugs of tea, Mary talks proudly about her family and their connection to the Newlyn area, which goes back to the 1700s. "They were all fishermen—drifters, really—but when the weather was bad they would walk ten miles to the tin mines on the north coast, and the wives would make them enough pasties to last the week." Mary's husband, Denys, on the other hand, and his brother Thomas were the first in a family of masons to get into fishing. "They used to have a little punt and go before and after school, and that's how they got started. They ended up running a bigger boat and fished together until a few years ago, when Denys had a heart attack, so now he's back in his punt again, back to his roots. He goes out about four in the morning, comes home for lunch and a sleep, and then goes out again until around ten. He loves it; he never gets lonely." Of Mary's four sons, three are fishermen. "They didn't ever have a choice," she says. "There was never anything else they wanted to do."

The Pascoes have invited me to a family "tea"—which means supper—the following day, and there is some preparation to be done this afternoon, so Mary and I move into the kitchen. "I'm too short for my work top," she explains, as she sets a bowl down on a green stool and begins rubbing margarine into flour with her fingers and then adding sugar—the beginnings of exotic-sounding saffron buns. She throws in handfuls of a mixture of dried currants, sultanas, raisins, assorted peels, and soaked saffron. (Phoenician traders are credited with introducing saffron to Cornwall, having bartered it for local tin more than two thousand years ago.) Next, she washes and pats dry two dozen pilchards (adult sardines), those modest slips of things on which the Cornish fishing industry was founded, back in the mid-16th century. (Newlyn even has a museum devoted to the fish, the Pilchard Works, temporarily closed.) She lays them head to toe in a baking tin, douses them in malt vinegar, sprinkles pickling spices and fresh bay leaves over them, ties a piece of brown paper around the tin, and slides them into a barely warm oven, where they will gently marinate until morning.

Later that afternoon, I stop off to visit Thomas, Andrew's nine-year-old middle son and the only one of the three who ardently desires to become a fisherman when he grows up. I glimpse his curly head as he bobs about on a rowboat while he pootles around the shallow end of the harbor, stopping to inspect his many prawn pots. When Andrew was a boy, there were at least twenty of them down in their punts after school, but now it's just Thomas and a friend. "I'm happy in m' boat," he says when I ask him what it is that draws him there every afternoon.

The following day, I'm back at the market and meet Robin Turner, the head auctioneer for J. H. Turner & Co. His ancestors used to follow the pilchard shoals around the country and settled in Newlyn in the late nineteenth century, he tells me, his gaze flitting around the warehouse. Remembering the complaints voiced by Mick Mahon, I ask him how he sees the future of Newlyn's fishing industry, and he says that his main concern is in "getting young blood". He continues, "Basically, the media have cast serious aspersions on what we do. We fishermen are perceived as greedy pillagers of the seabed, but here in Newlyn we operate from a small inshore fleet. We have no industrial vessels, and we're not interfering with the food chain." Turner is a board member at the University of Plymouth, where he encourages university applicants to consider careers in the fishing industry while also developing initiatives to get retired fishermen to teach schoolchildren about the sea. "In the eyes of most youngsters, being a fisherman is the equivalent of being a dustman [garbage collector], and we just have to change that. We're bursting with knowledge for our kids."

All this fish talk has given me a craving for the superlative fish pie I discovered last year at the Tolcarne Inn, so at lunchtime I go back there, stooping so as not to bump my head on the low beams when I enter the building, a pair of former farmhouses that have been run as a public drinking house for about 300 years. I order from Maura Thompson, the petite but no-nonsense Irish co-owner (along with her husband), who, as it happens, buys some of her fish from Andrew. "You pay more for his fish because it's hand caught," she says, "but that means that it's good fish and the right size." The pie arrives golden and bubbling, the chunks of fish an inspired combination of fresh and smoked cod, with a creamy mashed-potato covering topped with a crust of cheddar cheese.

Happily replete, I head back to Mary Pascoe's, where I am to assist in making the pasties and other goodies for the early-evening meal. "We usually have pasties once a week," she tells me, rolling up her sleeves. "It's lovely 'cause you've no washing up!" She finishes making a rough puff pastry and then puts it into the fridge to let it rest, while we chop onions, grate swedes (rutabaga), turn spuds, and cut chuck steak into small pieces. Mary divides the dough into balls, rolls them into circles, and neatly arranges the filling in their centers. As she seals each one shut, she crimps the edges at astonishing speed, without even looking, like an accomplished knitter.

Soon the grandchildren come bursting into the house from school, followed by Sally and Andrew, Hannah, and, eventually, Denys, who stumbles down bleary-eyed from his nap. Denys beams when his nose picks up the scent of the golden-brown pasties fresh from the oven, and it's not long before he has a whopping one clasped in his hands. The pasty surpasses my expectations, the pastry beautifully dry and flaky, the beef tender and moist with juice and sweetened by the vegetables. The children dive into the fish cakes their mother has also made, and there are salty-sweet marinated pilchards and mackerel pâté to spread on crackers. I ask Andrew at what age fishermen retire, and he replies that hardly any do; they prefer to go on fishing, even if it's just in a little punt, and those who do retire don't seem to live for long. "A chap died last year in his early 80s, and he was still fishing up to two days before. He wanted to go to sea the day he died, but they wouldn't let him." The boys listen as their father and grandfather reflect on their lives at sea.

How does Denys feel about the future? I ask, as he pushes back his chair to head out. "I feel positive about it," he declares, his eyes twinkling. "You can always paint a dull picture, but there's a big ocean out there, and there'll always be a fish that'll come along."

Fish Pie

Maura Thompson sometimes uses pollack or haddock in this dish.

3 cups milk

1 small leek (white part only), chopped

1 small onion, chopped

½ rib celery, chopped

3 large sprigs parsley, plus 1 tablespoon chopped parsley

3 black peppercorns

1 bay leaf

1 ½ pounds skinless, boneless cod filets, cut into 2-inch pieces

½ pound skinless, boneless hot-smoked cod filets, cut into
     1 ½-inch pieces

2 pounds russet potatoes, peeled and quartered

Salt

12 tablespoons butter

½ cup heavy cream

Freshly ground white pepper

⅓ cup flour

1 teaspoon prepared English mustard, preferably Colman's
¾ cup grated mild white English cheddar

1. Put milk, leeks, onions, celery, parsley sprigs, peppercorns, and bay leaf into medium pot and bring to a boil over medium-high heat. Remove from heat, cover, and let infuse for 20 minutes. Strain milk, discarding solids, and return milk to pot. Add fresh and smoked cod, cover, bring to a simmer over medium heat, and simmer until cooked through, 7–8 minutes. Strain, reserving milk. Transfer cod to a bowl and cover.

2. Meanwhile, cook potatoes in large pot of salted boiling water over medium heat until tender, about 25 minutes. Drain potatoes, return to pot, and set aside to let dry out for about 20 minutes. Add 8 tablespoons of the butter, cream, and salt and pepper to taste and mash coarsely. Cover pot and set aside.

3. Preheat oven to 400°F. Melt remaining butter in medium pot over medium heat. Add flour and stir with a wooden spoon until slightly dried out, but not golden, about 4 minutes. Remove pot from heat and gradually add reserved milk, whisking constantly, until smooth. Return pot to heat, add mustard, 1 teaspoon of the chopped parsley, and salt and pepper to taste. Cook, stirring, until thickened, 5–7 minutes. Transfer sauce to a 3-quart casserole dish and stir in cod.

4. Spread potatoes over top of cod mixture; top with cheese. Bake until hot, about 20 minutes. Preheat broiler; broil until top is golden, 2–3 minutes. Scoop pie onto plates and garnish with remaining parsley.

SERVES 6

Cornish Pasties

Mary Pascoe, who provided this recipe, tells us that in the old days Cornish pasties were sometimes made with a savory filling at one end and a sweet one, such as strawberry jam and cream, at the other, so that they'd make a meal—dessert included—in themselves.

2 ¼ cups flour, plus more as needed
9 tablespoons cold lard, cut into ½-inch pieces
9 tablespoons cold margarine, cut into ½-inch pieces
1 cup peeled grated rutabaga (about ¼ pound)
1 large russet potato, peeled, halved lengthwise, and thinly
    sliced crosswise
1 small yellow onion, chopped
1 pound chuck steak, cut into 1-inch pieces
Salt and freshly ground black pepper
1 egg, lightly beaten

1. Put flour, lard, margarine, and 1 cup water into large bowl and, using your hands, gently form mixture into a dough ball without mixing the fats into the flour. Transfer dough to a lightly floured surface and roll out into an 8-inch × 10-inch rectangle. Fold over short edges of dough into thirds, overlapping them, as if you were folding a letter. Rotate dough clockwise until long edges are parallel to you, then roll again into an 8-inch × 10-inch rectangle. Repeat folding, rotating, and rolling process 8 more times, lightly flouring work surface as necessary. Wrap dough in plastic and refrigerate for 2 hours.

2. Preheat oven to 400°F. Divide dough into 4 equal pieces, shape into balls, and flatten each into a disk. Working with 1 disk at a time (rewrap and refrigerate remaining disks), roll out into a 9-inch round. Lay half of the round over the rolling pin. Place one-quarter of the rutabaga on flat half of dough and layer with one-quarter each of potatoes, onions, and beef; season generously with salt and pepper. Brush edge of dough with egg; fold dough over to form a half-moon shape. Pinch edges together to form a seam; pleat seam by folding and pinching dough over in small increments. Transfer pasty to an 8-inch × 12-inch piece of parchment paper. Repeat process

to make 4 in all, placing them on individual pieces of parchment paper. Arrange the pasties on a baking sheet, pressing them against one another while pulling the edges of the paper up between them. Brush tops and sides of pasties with remaining egg.

3. Bake pasties until light golden, about 15 minutes. Spread the pasties on the baking sheet, reduce heat to 350°F, and continue to bake until deep golden, about 50 minutes more. Set pasties aside and let cool to room temperature. Serve pasties with a cup of hot, sugary tea, if you like.

MAKES 4

Fulton Street Fish Market

by Maria Finn Dominguez

from *Gastronomica*

As the great New York fish market prepared to move to new, less romantic quarters uptown, far from its nineteenth-century seaport roots, Dominguez wandered the aisles for one last fond look.

At four in the morning, Fulton Street fish market is already in full swing. Forklifts honk. Men with gaffs slung over their shoulders and fillet knives tucked into their belts haggle and joke. Fussy buyers from restaurants and retail markets check fish gills for freshness. The shoreline in Brooklyn is nearly dark except for the red and green running lights of ships passing down the East River. Fish arriving at Fulton Street still carry tales of international roguery, intrigue, weather phenomena, and finance. Orders are routinely delayed when pirates rob Malaysian trawlers or when tuna long-liners front for drug cartels in Colombia. A drought in Chesapeake Bay is slowing the oyster harvest, so prices for New Zealand shell-fish rise. Salmon from Alaska compete with Norwegian stock.

I'm down here waiting on a fresh halibut from Alaska. I used to live in Alaska, and I miss the fresh fish terribly. My friend Bill Sullivan, owner of Kachemak Bay Seafoods in Homer, Alaska, bragged that in just twenty hours he could get a fish to me at the Fulton Street Fish Market from the long-line hooks. So we placed a friendly wager on it: if my halibut makes it in twenty hours, I pay for it; anything over, I get a fish for free.

A favor he'll flake on, but a bet he'll keep.

Bill is originally from New York. His father was an Irish fireman, and his mother, a Scandinavian beauty, crowned Miss Norway in Bay Ridge in 1954. That's about as romantic as the story gets. After the divorce Bill's dad moved into an apartment and decorated it in "Early New York Irish Style"—with junk he dragged in off the streets.

The Norwegians and the Irish make up a big part of the seaport's history. In the early 1800s, ships flying the flag of Norway, the maritime heavyweight, were a common sight in the harbor. Meanwhile, the Irish, hordes of them, were arriving by boat, all desperate for work. Ships from every corner of the globe moored at the South Street Seaport. The Dutch imported bricks, calves, and sheep. Rum, sugar, and molasses arrived from the West Indies. Boats from China brought unloaded tea and silk and then carted ginseng back to the Far East. The shipments of fruit had to be unloaded at night so they wouldn't rot in the sun. Fish came in from the rich waters of Jamaica Bay and Long Island Sound, to be sold to New Yorkers or shipped by rail to the inland towns. The neighborhood bustled with bars and brothels. Hustlers scammed newly arrived immigrants, muggers rolled drunken sailors, and fishmongers hawked their wares.

Now we have new vices, and the last industry remaining from those times is the fish market. As historian Richard McKay writes in *South Street: A Maritime History of New York,* the course of American commerce can be traced from this "street of ships." When fish and spices were currency, the seaport was the world trade center. Then trade switched to stocks and bonds, and the center of world commerce was symbolized by two huge towers that used to cast shadows on Fulton Street.

And now the towers are also gone.

This is a place that bespeaks our capacity for destruction, resilience, and innovation. Fishermen used to tow nets full of cod from nearby waters, and people could scoop them out, still live, for supper. But the bays around New York City were quickly fished out and the rivers polluted with industrial waste. Technology, at least until now, has compensated for the destruction. In Alaska, the boats that fish halibut search by radar for deep ravines in the ocean bottom and then lay out their lines and hooks, carefully marking the spots on their LORAN (long-range navigation system). Then they wrap the lines around a hydraulic head that pulls them in while fishermen gaff the huge fish, pull them on board, gut them, and layer them with ice. From the Pacific Ocean, the halibut then travel five thousand miles—from ship, to shore, to truck, to plane, to the Fulton Street Fish Market—in less than a day.

According to scientists, the effects of technology used by fishing boats have been devastating to saltwater fish. Marine biologists Ransom Myers of Dalhousie University in Halifax and Boris Worm of the Institute for Marine Science in Kiel, Germany, created a comprehensive study to assess the fish stocks remaining in the ocean. The results were grim. They reported that over the past fifty years 90 percent of each type of saltwater fish they tracked has disappeared, due mainly to innovations in technology. Furthermore, the fish now being caught are drastically smaller. Evidence of environmental decline is also indicated by the locations where fish are being caught. Fewer and fewer fish are harvested from the western Atlantic and the eastern seaboard, including the once-bountiful Grand Banks, which has been overfished for some time. Sea bass from the southern hemisphere that are fished in Latin America and South Africa are coming in smaller every year.

The smaller fish haven't gone unnoticed at the fish market. Joe, a third-generation worker at Crescent City Seafoods, points out a box of newly arrived fish.

"What, look at the size of these snapper," he groans. "Am I supposed to be selling butterfly wings?"

"The fish are getting smaller, and this place has changed. Let me tell you about this place," he says, icing down a box of flounder. "It used to be its own city, with its own rules. Nowadays, you can make a living here, but it used to be that you made a lot of money."

Joe doesn't like the term mafia and just smiles when ex-mayor Giuliani is mentioned. Giuliani built much of his reputation for toughness by going after the Genovese family, one of the big mobs in New York City, and prosecuting businesses accused of extortion in the Fulton Street Fish Market.

"Now you had your criminals around here," Joe says. "But I wouldn't say mafia."

Several families were accused of laundering and skimming money from the fish dealers, and the bogus unloading and security companies that ran rackets at the fish market were closed down. Beginning in 1995, thirty companies were ejected from Fulton Street.

The fish buyers say that, after the mafia crackdown, everybody got fingerprinted and the Feds ran background checks on them. Only the cleanest of the clean are still there. Many of the workers have been there for twenty years. When asked why they stayed so long, most just shrug and say the money is good—good enough that they get used to working while the rest of the city sleeps. The men who work here now—and there are almost no women around—have fish slime crusted on their coveralls. Accents from Long Island, Jersey, and Brooklyn abound. Many of these men are second-, third-, even fourth-generation fish suppliers. In the early morning, the smell is pervasive, and gurry covers the ground. Scales swing; white Styrofoam boxes labeled "carp," "crab legs," or "Atlantic farmed salmon" are stacked outside the small storefronts. Inside, workers fillet sharks and tunas on stainless-steel tables.

"Annie" (not her real name, but the one she has gone by for the past fifty years at the Fulton Street Fish Market) sells black market cigarettes from a huge garbage bag she wheels around in a shopping cart. She calls every guy who passes by her "boyfriend" and calls out to them "whoo-whoo"—which sounds somewhere between a honk and a catcall—as they drive forklifts by. She knows everybody's brand of cigarette, and some pay her on the spot, but the others she trusts. She won't tell her age, but the fish sellers swear she must be pushing eighty. A beauty in her youth, Annie raised three children by working in the fish market as a prostitute and, as rumor has it, in the meatpacking district as well. She had something of a monopoly and did very well for herself. Those gratifying days are long gone, but Annie is Fulton Street Fish Market's biggest fan. She's one of the guys, and practically the only woman regularly down here. When a customer reaches for a pack of cigarettes, she cackles, "You can put it in, then take it out," in a suggestive way. She can't stop talking about how wonderful the guys at the fish market are.

"Look," she points out. "You got Portuguese, Irish, Ecuadorian, Korean, black, and they all get along just great. It used to be all Italian here, with Jewish fish buyers. Now the buyers are Korean, and the sellers are from all over the world. And there's young men now—it used to be all old men."

Although monogender, it was very multicultural.

"Now him," she says, and points to a man gaffing red snapper from a box. "He's like me."

"What, you Jewish?" he asks.

She only laughs in response.

Details of Annie's life can be gleaned only from what she tells about fish. She points to a carp, large and orange, overlapping the wax box. "See that fish, that's a carp," she says. "Poor Jewish families used to buy the whole fish for fifty cents, and it would last for the entire week."

Inside one fish seller's booth is a picture of Annie running down a dirt road in Alaska. Her hair is flowing behind her, she has sharp cheekbones, and her legs are tan and muscular. In the photo, she's young and beautiful, like a young Raquel Welch. The man who owns the booth said he met Annie when he first started working at the Fulton Fish Market. She flashed him one day, and when he told his mother about it, she became furious. He chuckles at the memory now.

"After the towers were attacked, they moved us temporarily to Hunt's Point," he says. "She still didn't miss a day. She rode the subway all the way up there and sold her cigarettes and newspapers."

The fish sellers grumble about no running water up at Hunt's Point, but they can't argue with the plans for the permanent move. The city has constructed a vast horizontal building with state-of-the-art refrigeration, the latest in European ice technology, lots of sinks, and floor drains to make it all more sanitary. At Fulton Street, open boxes of fish are stacked outside under FDR Drive. The vendors can't wait to go, but the move keeps getting held up by cost concerns as New York City struggles to revive financially after 9/11 and work out the logistics of moving a place that has been operating for so long. A man at a shellfish stand tells me that lawyers are working out which stand will go where. "Lawyers!" Alliances and rifts have deepened over the years, and businesses don't want to move away from allies and next to foes.

As the sun starts to rise, spirits are high in this place out of sync with the rest of the world. Young men with cigarettes tucked behind their ears, with accents from around the world but clothes tagged with New York City insignias—the Mets sweatshirts, the *New York Post* aprons—toss snowballs packed from the fish ice. Older men tease them and one another. Bags of clams are also tossed. Cash trades hands. Here, fish are a currency, and the old laws of supply and demand still rule. With the recession and the war in Iraq, business has been slower. Restaurants have been buying fewer fish, which means the fish sellers can't move them, so fishermen also slow down.

But the fish are still coming in: tilefish from Florida, Jamaican butterfish from Brazil, massive stone bass from the deeps off North Carolina's shores. I see that the boxes of halibut have arrived at Crescent City Seafood. Despite heavy weather, the boats were out fishing in Alaska. These fish were unloaded in Homer, then trucked to Anchorage, then flown to New York City. My halibut arrived in twenty hours. I look over these decapitated fish—the flat white bellies and greenish brown backs. I run a finger along the smooth skin and pick out a forty-pounder to take home, fillet, and freeze for the next few months.

The market winds down as daylight spreads over the river. Traffic hustles over the Brooklyn Bridge. Manhattan is coming to life; shops open and cars roar by. The market will close in an hour, and the only hint of the nocturnal bustle will be the scent of fish that has soaked into this place over the last 130 years. The masts of the *Pioneer* and the *Lettie G. Howard* tower over the docks like schooners of the past. In the distance, foghorns of incoming ships whistle through the early morning.

Personal Tastes

Tales of a Supertaster

by David Leite

from *Ridgefield Magazine*

David Leite has always had a lively palate, well matched to his sprightly sense of humor. In this essay, he discovers it's no accident, but a quirk of genetic fate.

D on't eat anything for the next few hours," my dentist said, snapping off a pair of latex gloves and dropping them into the trash. "You could bite your cheek or tongue. Could be nasty."

I'd been white-knuckling it in the chair for almost an hour because I had to get a filling regrouted. Owing to a pain threshold of a third grader, I insisted he dope me up as much as possible. The result was my mouth was numb from the divot of my upper lip all the way back to my right ear. I rubbed my fingers across the side of my face; it felt as if I were touching the stubble of an unkempt stranger.

"Remember—" he called after me as I walked out of the office.

"No eating, got it," I said and headed to my favorite burger joint. I've downed hundreds of thousands of meals in my life without incident, I reasoned, I'm sure I can manage another.

As I took a bite of my cheeseburger, I experienced that curious post-dental sensation, as if I'd lost muscle control on the side of my face. I couldn't tell if the food was being demurely chewed or was dribbling down the doughy-feeling chin of that stubbled stranger. But an even curiouser thing happened: On the numbed side of my mouth, I couldn't taste anything. It was as if my taste buds had been

Novocained, too. I wasn't about to let a little anesthesia keep me down—there was food at stake here—but after a few more bites, I gave up. The anxiety of wondering if I looked like a slobbering Saint Bernard proved too much, and I headed home.

There were only a few hours left before the medication wore off, and I wanted to test a hypothesis. I opened the refrigerator door and sat on the floor. I ate as many of the foods I find unpleasant to see if they'd register. Endive, which I had always found so bitter, had no effect. Frisée from the bag of mesclun? The same thing. Horseradish: zero. Even some suspicious-looking sour cream the color of slate tasted like nothing. Then I reached for a favorite of mine—a fragrant raspberry. All I got was the grit of tiny seeds. I thought how horrible it must be like to live life without the ability to taste. Then I thought what if something happened, some strange, one-in-a-million medical roll of the dice that caused me to remain this way? A food writer with no capacity for taste. A wave of nausea hit. I had no idea if it was the sour cream or white-hot panic.

After the last bit of Novocain prickled away and I no longer sounded like a bourbon-soaked barfly, I contacted Dr. Linda Bartoshuk, a professor at Yale University who specializes in genetic variations in taste. In fact, she was the person who in the '80s coined the term "supertaster," which refers to the 25 percent of the population who have significantly more sensitive taste receptors. (Medium tasters, aka regular tasters, make up 50 percent, while nontasters make up the remaining 25 percent.) We set up an appointment to meet that Sunday at her lab for me to undergo some tests to learn more about the vagaries of, in my estimation, the most important sense after sight.

Bartoshuk is an energetic, articulate woman with appalling housekeeping skills. Her office was packed with years of professorial detritus. She shifted piles of books, newspapers, and food containers from one stack to another until she was eventually able to displace enough mass to clear off a small chair. We chuckled at our alarming physical proximity.

While I explained my cheeseburger experience, Bartoshuk nodded profusely, barely able to wait until I finished. The reason I couldn't taste my burger, she said, had to do with the intricate interaction of smell and taste. She explained that we have two kinds of smell: orthonasal and retronasal olfaction. Orthonasal olfaction is regular, through-the-nose smelling. Put your nose near a bowl of chicken curry; you smell chicken curry because the odors gather in your nasal cavities and are processed by your brain. In retronasal olfaction, smell occurs in the mouth. The odors from the food you're eating travel up behind the palate, where they gather and are processed just like orthonasal smells.

"You could smell cheeseburger," clarifies Bartoshuk, "because of orthonasal olfaction, but you couldn't taste cheeseburger because your mouth was anesthetized. Your brain didn't know where the odors were coming from, so it didn't bother processing them."

Skeptical? Bartoshuk suggests this experiment to demonstrate retronasal olfaction: Hold your nose and eat a few root beer jelly beans. All you'll taste is sweet, because your taste buds can detect only sweet, sour, bitter, and salty. Then let go. Root beer flavor will explode in your mouth.

Now that she explained my taste dilemma, it was time to test exactly what was going on in my mouth. I didn't mind, really. Being the overachiever that I am, I was convinced I was a supertaster, one of those extraordinary and rare persons with an exquisitely tuned tasting instrument who by dint of divine intervention is the envy of a world of plebeian tasters. Bartoshuk sat me in an uncomfortable chair in her lab and proceeded to swab isolated parts of my tongue and palate with different solutions. My job was to identify the tastes—sweet, sour, bitter, salty—and rate their intensity on a scale developed by Bartoshuk; a scale, she said, that flies in the face of all that came before, by correcting long-standing measurement errors. "There are a lot of people whose whole careers are based on the old scale, and, boy, are they not friendly." Her pride in one-upping the male-dominated establishment of science was palpable.

Testing proceeded without incident until a horribly bitter solution called 6-n-propylthiouracil, PROP for short, was washed on my tongue. It was so bitter, I had to lean over the sink, nauseated.

"Do people normally have this reaction?" I asked, spluttering.

"Supertasters do." There was that word again. Even in my compromised position, I swelled with ego. I could feel it was only a matter of time before I would be officially knighted by the Queen of Taste.

For the last part of the test, Bartoshuk dyed my tongue a deep blue, pressed a piece of plastic against the tip to flatten it, then swung a Zeiss microscope attached to a video camera into place. She turned her head to the lunar landscape glowing on the monitor.

"Oh, is this gorgeous." All I saw was a collection of blue-colored circles with dark rings around them. "You have small ringed fungiform papillae!" Fungiform papillae are the bumps on the tongue that contain taste buds. The more of these a person has, the smaller they get. And according to Bartoshuk, the rings are rare and are practically a confirmation of supertasterdom.

"But your tongue is difficult to classify," she said. What? The Queen giveth and the Queen taketh away? To clarify things, she placed a template over the screen and began counting the dots inside. Within a six-centimeter circle, she found more than fifty fungiform papillae. "And that puts you on the extreme supertaster end," she said. "You're actually one of the highest testing male super tasters I've ever seen."

"Yes!" Genetically irrefutable confirmation of my taste superiority. Surely this now catapults me into the pantheon of food-writing greats that includes Molly O'Neill, Jeffery Steingarten, Ruth Reichl, Calvin Trillin, and Alan Richman. Quite frankly, I wouldn't be surprised if it bumped me even higher. After all, if only 25 percent of the population are supertasters, and I'm pushing against upper limits of the chart, as Bartoshuk says, chances are I'm in a class by myself.

"But that's not necessarily a good thing."

"I beg your pardon?"

According to Bartoshuk, the prefix "super" was intended to signify an unusual sensitivity to tastes, especially bitter, not, as I imagined, a surfeit of gustatory discernment and supremacy. Because supertasters react so strongly to bitter foods, most don't eat enough vegetables. I certainly don't. The result is a higher incidence of colon cancer among supertasters. In addition, most of us tend not to like high-fat foods, reducing the chance of cardiovascular disease. But there's a subset of supertasting men, of which I discovered I'm a card-carrying member, that craves fatty foods. So the list of health risks grows by the addition of an increased risk of heart attack and stroke, not to mention unbridled girth. Oh, and let's not forget diabetes.

I tried to shake the my-tongue-is-better-than-your-tongue mentality and look at my newly crowned status as a supertaster for what it is: a liability. But that word super. Why couldn't she have called my people unfortunate tasters or to-be-pitied tasters? I certainly never would have agreed to be tested in order to be categorized as unfortunate. But Bartoshuk did offer this consolation: "You inhabit a world of neon tastes where everything is more intense, while, as a nontaster, I live in a pastel world."

Nonetheless, I still have to eat my vegetables.

Italian Butcher Shop Blues

by Matthew Gavin Frank

from *Gastronomica*

The challenges of eating authentic food in a foreign culture can sometimes lead a hungry traveler into tense diplomatic situations. Navigating Italy, nonfiction writer Matthew Gavin Frank recalls one such encounter.

I walk the quiet cobblestoned streets of Barolo, Italy. It is early evening. My day has been spent harvesting the Nebbiolo grape crop for Luciano and Luca Sandrone, brothers whose distinctive features—one's red suspenders and the other's bald head—will stay in my mind forever. I've been working in the vineyard for a month as a way to stay in Italy, as a way to be less of a tourist. At the moment, I'm a little stunned by the day's heat and hard physical labor. Stunned, relaxed, and suddenly very hungry.

I step toward the counter, the butcher hidden from view in the back room behind the meat ease. I hear the sound of a handsaw. I look to the walls, mostly blank, save for a poster of a bikini-clad woman holding a porterhouse in the air. The poster is signed in silver ink by "Valentina" and addressed to "Franco." Next to Valentina, encased in a black frame, is a picture of Barolo's castle with a man-shaped shadow clinging to its cast wall. I step closer and see that the man, like a comic book superhero, is adhered to the ancient orange stone at least fifty feet off the ground. The man is facing the camera, sun in his eyes. His head is enormous, too big for his body, as if he's been pieced together by Barolo's resident mad scientist. A thick black moustache, curving over the sides of his mouth, is spread nearly horizontal in the force of his grin. He's dressed in rock climbing gear, leg muscles bursting in effort, his bauds gripping a strange and bulbous rope. I step even closer to the picture, my nose nearly pasted to the wall, my breath fogging the frame's glass, and see that this man is rappelling down the façade of the Castello di Barolo on a fifty-foot string of salami.

Before I can laugh, before I can even exhale, I hear the sound of thick flesh behind me, spreading into a massive smile. I turn. It is, of course, the man in the picture, Franco the Butcher, his moustache crawling over his face like a caterpillar on steroids. He wears brown-framed glasses that stretch from his eyebrows to his upper lip, from his black sideburns to the bridge of his boxer's nose. A billow of black hair shoots geyser-wise from his head, calling to the florescent lights. His hands, strong enough to lift me by the top of my head, are streaked with blood. And yet—I never thought I'd describe someone like this—Franco the Butcher is *jolly*.

"Ciao," I say, "Franco?"

"Si, si, Franco," he replies in a quiet, gentle voice, a voice as hairy as he is. He rubs his hands together as if compressing the air into a pancake.

"Este carne," I say, running my hand over the expanse of display case, "e bellisima."

"Grazie," Franco says, truly touched by the compliment to his meats.

I watch as he rounds the counter, kicking sawdust from his shoes, and joins the scales, knives, and cleavers on the back wall. I examine his wares, salamis of all kinds: white salamis, red ones, pink ones, purple; salamis that nearly stray to black; duck salami, donkey salami, Barolo salami, truffle; salami as long as my legs, salami as short as my thumb; and there, twisted into cylinders as thick as my forearm, *salami di cinghiale*. Wild boar. Wild boar salami. I repeat the word in my head like a cured and fatty mantra, "Salami, salami, salami, salami . . ." until I descend into a cow-pig meditation. I wonder which meat held him to the walls of Barolo's castle. I wonder if he celebrated his climb by eating his equipment. I smile and he sees it, his hands now on his hips, his white apron smeared with blood and hit.

"Americano, no?" Franco slurs.

"Si, americano," I say, "pero adesso, en este macelleria, sono italiano."

Franco laughs at my wish to be Italian, then sighs, turns abruptly left, waves to me, and utters, "Viene, viene qua."

He leads me away from the salami display, and I watch reluctantly over my shoulder as these lovely jeweled life vests float farther and farther away. Franco stops in front of the fresh meats: tenderloin, strip, porterhouse, sausages, pork chop, whole chickens, whole ducks—feet intact and orange, webbed and clinical in the light; pigs' feet, pigs' ears, pigs' blood, veal chops, veal scallops, headcheese, and sweetbreads. And tripe, beautiful white tripe spread wide in its container like a Chinese fan; *trippa,* resting in recline like the aurora borealis on its lunch break. Franco reaches for the tripe with an ungloved finger. It yields like a lover to his touch. The tripe, for lack of a better word, is *kissable.*

I feel my feet slowly spinning across that high school dance floor, slowly building a tango confidence to ask the beckoning girl out for a cup of coffee.

"Te piace trippa?" Franco asks.

I shrug. I've never had it before. But how can I not like tripe?

"Si," I say.

"Ah," Franco smiles, "serio."

"Si," I nod, "serio," and I feel more substantial for saying so. I feel like I could knock down buildings with my bare hands. I feel like I could keep up with Franco the Butcher.

He lifts the tripe from its tray, and like delicate lingerie, it unravels in the air. I want to rub its texture between my fingers; I want to try it on for size. I imagine taking a few pieces home to Il Gioco dell'Oca's kitchen, asking my friend Raffaella for preparation advice, and cooking a tripe dinner together: soup, casserole, napoleon, whichever. I watch as Franco cuts a small piece the size of a finger joint. He holds the white gem to the light like a coin.

"Ah, trippa," he says, and hands me the piece.

Amazing, I think. *Amazing that he sensed my desire to experience its texture.*

The tripe coin is soft and perforated, rich and heady like a chunk of Styrofoam soaked in black tea. I, like Franco, hold it to the light and can almost see through it. I think I'm seeing ghosts. I think I can see my family back in Chicago. They're all sitting in rush hour traffic, car radios blaring classic rock. I allow them all to return home safe, then lower the tripe to the counter to give it back to Franco.

"No, no," he says, holding his bloody-but-innocent palms at me, "Prego."

"Che?" I ask, not quite understanding.

"Si, si, prego," he offers again.

I'm confused. I think he wants me to keep the tripe. I'm not sure what to do with such a small piece. I reach to put it into my pocket; possibly I'll play with it like a rubber stress ball on the way back to Il Gioco.

"No, no," Franco says, and I raise the tripe again from my pocket to the counter, "Prego."

I look at him and shrug. I shake my head. Somewhere behind me, Valentina, in her golden bikini, is comfortably holding her porter-house. Franco opens his mouth. For a second, I think he's going to take a bite out of me. I lean back, and he points to the tripe, then points to his mouth, and again says, "Prego."

I get it now, but that doesn't mean I believe it. He wants me to eat the tripe.

"Crudo?" I say.

"Si," Franco says.

He wants me to eat the tripe raw.

What kind of culinary hazing is this? Why? Why? Don't get me wrong, I have nothing against the pig stomach, but the raw ingesting of such items sends my own organs into disarray; my once hungry stomach now closes in on itself like a fist. My mouth goes dry. I'm having trouble swallowing.

"Prego," Franco says again, and I feel there's no way around this.

My stomach recoils deeper into my ribs, and I want to cry. I hold the tripe to the light again, and it goes from beautiful to revolting in no time flat. Raw tripe, if about to be cooked, is one thing, but raw tripe that wants to stay raw is another.

I look at Franco. His eyes are wide, his cheeks are glowing red. Jolly never looked so evil. I stare at the tripe, wriggling in the toddler laughter of my little sister whenever I got into trouble with my parents. I look to Franco. I look for a way out. The fluorescents burn into me like a spotlight. The audience is waiting; there's no turning back now. After all, I told Franco I was "serious."

I close my eyes and bring my fingers to my mouth.

I smell it before it hits my tongue: dust, metal, morning saliva, bathroom tile, campfire. It squirms in my mouth like a goldfish fighting for its life, a mini skinned bronco bucking my teeth, surely stirring a cowboy-shaped splatter from my stomach.

Hold on, I think, as the taste of pure gut struggles to pass over my taste buds, *Hold on.* I don't dare bite into it, don't dare explode the taste of unmentionable pig over my tongue.

So I swallow it whole, think of oysters, hold my breath, and wait.

"Bravo," Franco claps and laughs in descending octaves.

A sweat breaks from my forehead. I gag audibly but keep it down.

Opening my mouth to exhale, I know I have passed a hideous test and am surprised to find that the taste, if not the memory, has already faded. I rode the bull and returned a little trampled, but ungored.

Franco pulls a necklace of wild boar salami from the wall and hands it to me as my reward, laughing all the way. I can't believe I'm going to thank this man.

"Grazie," I say.

All Franco does is laugh.

As I turn to leave the *macelleria,* paper bag shifting in my arms, Franco the Butcher raises a bloody, tight-fingered hand into the air and, smiling his biggest smile of the day, dangles another slice of tripe into the light.

"Domani," he says, pointing to the horrendous thing.

I shake my head. I wave.

Tomorrow, I think, opening the door to the street, *Tomorrow I'm not coming anywhere* near *this place.*

Taking the (Fruit) Cake

by Jack Turner

from *Bon Appetit*

Most of us cringe at the thought of another obligatory Christmas fruitcake. Not Jack Turner, author of the delightful culinary history *Spice*—in fact, his devotion to his family's recipe is so fierce, you may well long to try the recipe.

In the last ten years I have moved house or country twenty-eight times—an occupational necessity for a writer on Asia and its spices who is married to an itinerant aid worker. This has taken me to some exotic locations for Christmas, which meant some exotic yuletide menus, but everywhere I've gone, so too has Mrs. Mackinnon's Christmas cake.

Throughout my childhood Mrs. Mackinnon's cake was as much a part of our Australian Christmases as the turkey, the summer sun, the cricket games on the beach. Christmas always arrived a little early in our household—every Martinmas, the 11th of November, to be precise, when my mother would assemble the tins, the eggs, the rum, and the fruits, and we would settle down to the annual ritual of making the cake. A similar ritual has been observed, I suppose, in hundreds of other families, for centuries. For Mrs. Mackinnon's is an ancient Scottish recipe, a dense, dark, moist mix of flour, butter, eggs, rum, glacéed fruits, and memories—as rich, ripe, sweet, and soulful as a glass of vintage Port.

The recipe itself is not complicated, but neither is it convenient. After the chopping and stirring, we'd leave the mix to settle overnight, followed by the ceremony of the twine and newspaper.

According to the inherited wisdom, the cake has to be wrapped in several layers of newspaper to keep it from drying out in the oven. My brother and I would hold our fingers on the twine as Mum tied on the newspaper—the pinch it gave our fingers always made me think of the present-wrapping to come.

In the first few years after I left home, my mother used to send me cakes, but eventually, as I moved farther afield, she complained that she could no longer face the annual scene in the post office. I think what really bothered her was the sympathy shown by the others queuing up to dispatch their Christmas mail—their cards already written and neatly arranged, oozing a smug sense of self-satisfaction. Each year Mum would wander in weighed down by her cake, whereupon the manager would smile knowingly and offer a polite "So, the boy's away again. And where's he off to now, then?" The pleasantries out of the way, Mum would hand over a parcel the weight of a bowling ball, followed by a small fortune for the postage.

So there came a Christmas when Mum got fed up, and I had no choice but to make the cake myself. On the whole, I can report, Mrs. Mackinnon has traveled well, but not always easily. When I was a student at Oxford, the main problem was one of equipment. In the misguided belief that students would not want to cook for themselves (though the quality of the food in college practically ensured otherwise), the student accommodation was equipped with nothing but pathetic tin-pot ovens that, when switched on, would immediately turn an angry red, emitting foul-smelling coils of smoke. To make Mrs. Mackinnon's cake I had to talk my way into the kitchen of a sympathetic if somewhat bemused professor. I was disappointed to find that his oven was bigger but not much better than ours—as perhaps befitted his cerebral occupation. I wrapped the cake tin in copies of the *Times Literary Supplement*, and the cake struggled through, more or less—it was edible, once I'd shaved off the blackened bits. But with those crunchy edges and faint aroma of carbon, she was somehow not the same.

After Helena and I were married, I looked back on even those Oxford ovens with nostalgia, given my wife's occupation. In East Timor, where we lived in the ruins of a war zone, amid cockroaches, fighting cockerels, and peacekeeping troops, a friendly diplomat couriered in the glacéed fruits in the diplomatic pouch. Eggs came from the chickens that used to wake us at dawn—the one occasion I did not curse their existence. With all the soldiers there on peace-keeping duty, rum was not a problem.

A more serious hurdle was that no one had an oven. When the Timorese cook, they do so, like everyone else in Southeast Asia, over a gas ring. I made friends with a fellow expat who, like me, seemed to spend most of his time thinking about food, and he was happy to help. Together we rigged up a tin box with a door and a latch, and we then set the contraption above a gas burner. It looked like a large letter box. In lieu of newspaper we wrapped the tin with wet banana leaves and turned the gas on as low as we could get it. I am not a religious person, but I am convinced that there are gods of cooking and spirits that haunt ovens, some malign, some benign, some just temperamental. That day, gods, spirits, and oven were on our side. Or maybe it was the trick of the banana leaves; whatever it was, Mrs. Mackinnon emerged in all her soggy glory.

In the Republic of Georgia, in the former Soviet Union, I found myself pining once more, this time for my improvised oven and the tropical heat of our Timorese Christmas. Outside it was ten below, and not much warmer inside. There were ovens, but no electricity. As for the ingredients, there was no hope. Even the bare necessities were a challenge. The market offered little more than lurid pink sausages of indeterminate origin, pickles and more pickles, vodka, and a seemingly endless supply of frozen battery hens donated by the U.S. government. My heart would sink at the sight of those long lines of cardboard boxes containing a gray mass of reconstituted frozen and refrozen chicken, a long way from Kansas.

Fortunately, Mum came to the rescue. She wouldn't send the cake, but she did send a parcel of the requisite glacéed fruits to the central post office. I waited a month or so, then rode an ancient, clattering streetcar down to a vast, echoing cavern of a building: a typically Soviet-style marble palace, all but abandoned after the country fell apart. The power had long since been turned off, even for civic buildings, and the place was forlorn. The only person around was a shrunken old crone hunched over a gas heater, doing her best to hide beneath the counter.

I showed her my passport, which apparently conveyed no useful information other than the fact that I was a foreigner. She rummaged through a sack of mail before producing a random selection of ancient, long-forgotten letters, selected purely on the basis of their vaguely Western names. I remember the joy when from the bottom of the sack she eventually produced a battered parcel bearing the familiar stamps and postmarks—and the glacéed cherries and apricots.

With no electricity, there was no chance of making the cake at home: The whole country had returned to the days of communal baking. So I hunted out a communal wood-fired oven where the Georgians baked their Christmas meal of suckling pigs. I took my place in a queue of men cradling piglets in their arms like infants, me with my cake tin. While our various meals baked away, we stood around stamping our feet and drinking vodka against the cold, and I tried with a combination of pidgin Georgian and inadequate Russian to explain the concept of an Australian Christmas, by the beach, in the sun. The cake, when it emerged, was altered, but not impaired. It was the only Christmas cake I ever had that tasted of roast pork.

Even New York City posed a challenge, but Dean & Deluca came to the rescue. Standing at the checkout, amid the SoHo crowd—models with their minimalist baskets of truffles and porcini, and computer programmers plugged into their iPods—I clasped my precious tin of treacle and glacéed fruits. Later, I wrapped the cake tin with the Sunday Styles section of *The New York Times* and sat down in our tiny, noisy apartment to eat the cake. It tasted like condensed sun, and home.

Now I live in France, and things are almost too easy. We even have a little British "mini-market" down the road, an otherwise sorry place that nevertheless supplies some crucial ingredients. In one of the oddest business models I have ever encountered, the mini-market is attempting to introduce the French to such British deli-cacies as crumpets and digestive biscuits—and treacle. Everything else I get up the road at the local market, at the weekly stalls of fruits and spices.

Some of the challenge has gone out of our annual ritual. The move to France united for the first time all of our possessions, which had been scattered across the globe in the course of our various relocations. All sorts of objects turned up, most of which we had done without quite happily. One such was an ancient waxed fishing jacket that last saw useful service, so far as I can remember, during a fishing trip to Scotland nearly a decade ago. There in the pocket, covered in plastic wrap, I found a chunk of Mrs. Mackinnon's cake. To my amazement, it looked perfectly preserved—all the rum, I suppose. I left it out on display to show to my wife, but before she arrived my two-year-old son had sniffed it out and, with his usual sense of initiative, devoured it. He tracked me down amid the packing cases to demand more. Though he barely knows it, he too is now looking forward to Martinmas and to the ritual of the rolled-up newspapers.

Mrs. Mackinnon's Christmas Fruitcake

The cake takes its name from the wife of Jack Turner's former headmaster, but the recipe is reportedly an ancient Scottish one. Aluminum foil stands in for the traditional newspaper.

2 ½ cups golden raisins (about 12 ounces)
2 cups dark raisins (about 9 ounces)
1 ¾ cups dried currants (about 8 ounces)
1 ¾ cups chopped glacéed fruits (such as red cherries, pineapple, and apricots)
¾ cup chopped candied orange peel
½ cup water
½ cup plus 6 tablespoons dark rum
2 teaspoons each grated orange and lemon peels
1 teaspoon Lyle's Golden Syrup or light molasses
¾ teaspoon baking soda

1 ¾ cups all purpose flour
⅓ cup self-rising flour
½ teaspoon salt
1 cup plus 2 tablespoons (2 ¼ sticks) unsalted butter, room temperature
1 ½ cups (packed) dark brown sugar
5 large eggs

Mix first 6 ingredients in large saucepan. Add ½ cup rum; bring to simmer over medium heat, stirring often. Remove from heat. Mix in grated orange and lemon peels, syrup, and baking soda. Let stand until fruit mixture absorbs liquid, stirring often, about 1 hour. Preheat oven to 325°F. Butter 10-inch-diameter springform pan, then line bottom and sides of pan with parchment; butter parchment. Sift both flours and salt into medium bowl. Beat butter and sugar in large bowl until well blended. Beat in eggs 1 at a time. Add flour mixture; beat until just blended. Stir in fruit mixture. Transfer batter to pan. Cover pan with foil.

Bake cake 2 hours. Reduce oven temperature to 275°F; continue to bake covered until tester inserted into center comes out clean but slightly moist, about 50 minutes longer. Transfer to rack; remove foil. Pierce top of cake all over with skewer. Drizzle 6 tablespoons rum very gradually over cake. Cool completely in pan. Cut around pan sides to loosen; remove pan sides. *(Can be made 3 weeks ahead. Wrap in foil; chill. Bring to room temperature before serving.)*

SERVES 12

Late-Night Chitlins with Momma

by Audrey Petty

from *Saveur*

Within every family is a complex set of food memories—some good, some bad. Complicate it even further with a subtext of cultural stereotypes, and you get Audrey Petty's conflicted, tender, multifaceted reminiscence.

Ours came frozen solid in a red plastic bucket. Butchered and packaged by Armour. Ten pounds in all. Cleaned, they'd reduce to much less, not even filling my mother's cast-iron pot.

We usually ate them in the wintertime, Momma and I. Negotiations regarding their appearance began weeks in advance, usually around the dinner table. My mother would tell my father she was considering fixing chitlins for the holidays. My father would groan, twist his mouth, and complain in vain.

"Why you got to be cooking them?"

My two sisters backed him up with exaggerated whimpers, calls for gas masks, threats to run away from home.

"I'll cook them next Saturday," Momma would say, suddenly matter-of-fact. Daddy would plan that next Saturday accordingly: out of the house for hours, in protest, then coming back with the Sunday papers, opening the living-room windows wide before heading upstairs to read and watch football in his La-Z-Boy behind a closed door.

My mother would turn to me, smiling and winking. "You'll help me eat them, won't you?"

I was a pleaser, plagued by the classic middle-child complex. With the exception of fierce bickering and the occasional smack-down match with my sisters, dissent tended to make me nervous. Maybe my love of chitlins all began with my feeling sorry for my mother. In terms of labor and attention, cooking proper chitlins is as involved as cooking paella or fufu or risotto milanese. Cleaning them took hours. Hours. So I'd keep Momma company while she rinsed the tangles of pig intestines in the basement sink. And I'd sit with her in the kitchen once they'd simmered down to something that needed watching. By that time, the house was filled with their sharp scent. Despite the addition of a potato to the pot to help absorb some of the odor, the smell was pervasive—vinegary and slightly farmy. When one of my sisters would storm in holding her nose and proclaiming her disgust, I'd puff out my bony chest and call her stupid.

I'd stay up late with Momma, and we'd eat the chitlins off of small saucers as a bedtime snack. For all their potent smell, their flavor was calm and subtle. They had a distinct taste; they didn't remind me of anything. Their texture was pleasing, tender but not soft. My mother's were never greasy, though I marveled at how the leftovers emerged from the fridge congealed in a murky gelatin. Momma would warm up a few in a frying pan, and we'd douse them with hot sauce and put some cornbread on the side. They never failed to build a craving after the first bite. Precious, strange, and furtive food; I longed for them even as I consumed them.

I am a first-generation Northerner. My mother was reared in a middle-class family in El Dorado, a boomtown in southern Arkansas; my father, in a coal-mining camp in Alabama. The two met and fell in love in the late '50s while students at Talladega (a historically black college in Alabama), married, and then moved to Chicago. My sisters and I came of age in Hyde Park, at the time one of the city's few intentionally racially integrated neighborhoods. My dearest friend was Jewish (and white). We shared Sasson jeans, Jolly Ranchers, Judy Blume books, and plenty of secrets. My mother grew to love Karyn, but in the first days of our acquaintance, her anxiety about our closeness showed itself. She had lots of questions about how I was treated by the Levins. Were they kind? Had they *made* me eat the matzo ball soup? Did Karyn have other black friends? Gradually it emerged: Momma was trying to prepare me for the prospect of rejection, once recalling to me how little white girls in El Dorado customarily grew out of their friendships with little black girls. At the time, my only response was confused irritation. Karyn was my best friend.

As my sisters and I reached adolescence, my parents became more visibly concerned about our assimilated ways. While the Jackson 5's *ABC* had been our very first album and we still crowded around the television to watch *Soul Train,* we also knew all the words to "Bohemian Rhapsody." And at seventeen I fell for a boy with blond hair and blue eyes. He also fell for me. On more than one occasion, my sisters and I were summoned to a dialogue that began with my father's question "Do you all know that you're black?" As adults, my sisters and I laugh about it now. My parents do, too. But their uneasiness was real and deadly serious, and I'd sensed it for years. Maybe I ate chitlins to please Momma *and* Daddy.

My grandfathers died before I was born; my grandmothers, when I was quite young. I have missed their embraces, their indulgence, and seeing my face in theirs. I have especially missed their stories. The down-South tales my parents passed on to me and my sisters were rather limited. We'd hear about my uncle Booker T.'s setting the mean goat after my father or how my mother's father was a high-school principal and an avid fisherman and how my mother's mother taught piano and Latin. What we didn't hear were the bloody details, the chronicles of Jim Crow. My parents gave us their South as best they could: in their politesse and their hymns and verses. In their ways with words. They gave us only what they hoped would be nourishing: a sip of pot liquor for our growing bodies and black-eyed peas for good luck at New Year's dinner.

I never saw anyone's chitlins but my family's when I was coming up. At least a few of my classmates must have eaten chitlins at home, but I, for one, never raised the subject. Chicago was a Great Migration city, where a wave of black folks had begun arriving in the early 1900s and been redlined to black belts on the South and West sides. That was my story and the story of so many of my childhood friends. We all had roots and people down South. And we ate like it, too. I remember red beans and rice at Kim Odoms's house, fried gizzards at LaTonya Mott's, and my junior-high business teacher Miss Rice's eating take-out rib tips from Ribs n' Bibs during our fourth-period typing class. I remember hot sauce on everything. But chitlins were their own category of soul food. Chitlins were straight-up country. If you called someone country, you were calling that someone out. Country meant backwoods, backwards, barefoot, 'Bama-fied. K-U-N-T-R-E-E.

I once believed that my father didn't like chitlins because of how they smelled, but as I got older, I began to contemplate my father's childhood and I formulated a more complex theory. My father had seven brothers and sisters; his father was a miner and a preacher and his mother was a domestic worker (a fact I discovered only this year). I assumed that Daddy rejected chitlins as suffering food—a struggling people's inheritance. It wasn't until I began brainstorming for this essay that I finally learned the truth. "He had a bad plate of chitlins as a boy," my mother recently told me. "He never got over it."

When my mother cleaned our chitlins, she never failed to stress how important it was to clean them well. That meant washing them, one section of intestine at a time, with a mild saltwater solution. "You don't just eat any old body's chitlins." I knew that rule by heart. When a cafeteria called Soul by the Pound opened and quickly closed down on State Street, my mother was not at all surprised. "Black people don't live that way. Risk taking for no reason at all. Flying from bungee cords or buying all-you-can-eat chitlins made by God knows who."

My mother has not cooked a pot of chitlins in fifteen years. Perhaps the ritual ended the year I lived in France and sorely missed Christmas with my family. My mother and I shared a good laugh when I told her about chitlins in France, how they called them andouillette de Lyon and topped them with dijon mustard. I smelled them before I saw them, in a Left Bank bistro. Et voilà!—there they were, on a nearby plate. I trusted the chef at Les Fontaines, but I couldn't imagine eating his chitlins. Not without my mother's company. And not without Louisiana-style hot sauce as generous seasoning.

As my mother has gotten used to the idea of my going public with our chitlins habit, she's reminded me that she cooked hers with onion and a green bell pepper or two, and she also splashed in cider vinegar to taste. I've learned how some people add white bread instead of potatoes for the odor. And I've shared Momma's excitement about the new technology in chitlin processing. "They really clean them now. More expensive, but you don't have to do all that work."

She didn't have to ask me twice; we have a date for chitlins this December.

Chitlins

Simmering the chitlins with a potato is said to help reduce their aroma.

9–10 pounds frozen cleaned chitlins (sometimes labeled
    "chitterlings"), thawed and drained
Salt
1 large onion, peeled
1 russet potato, peeled
1 green bell pepper
4 cloves garlic, peeled
½ cup cider vinegar
¾ teaspoon crushed red pepper flakes
2 bay leaves
Freshly ground black pepper
Hot sauce, preferably Frank's brand

1. Put chitlins into a large colander and rinse under tepid running water in the sink. Transfer chitlins to a very large bowl or pot. Cover chitlins by at least 2 inches with tepid mildly salty water (dissolve 1–2 tablespoons salt in every 2 gallons of water needed) and wash, one section at a time. Drain in a colander set in the sink, rinsing them again under tepid running water. Set colander over a bowl and let chitlins drain well.

2. Put chitlins into a large pot and cover with cold water. Add onion, potato, bell pepper, garlic, vinegar, red pepper flakes, bay leaves, and salt and pepper to taste. Partially cover pot and bring to a boil over high heat. Reduce heat to medium-low and cook, partially covered, until chitlins are very tender, about 6 hours.

3. Pour off most of the cooking water from the pot, leaving enough to keep chitlins moist. Discard potato and bay leaves.

Cut chitlins on a cutting board into 1-inch pieces, return them to the pot, and bring to a simmer.

4. Using a slotted spoon, serve chitlins (drained fairly well and apart from the vegetables) in bowls and douse with hot sauce to taste.

SERVES 4–6

My Life with Rice

by Mei Chin

from *Saveur*

For every immigrant child who loves the foods of one's forebears, there is another who secretly loathes it. Novelist Mei Chin traces every step of the guilt trip that ensued when she faced the truth: she just doesn't like white rice.

Rice, and specifically white rice, may be the most ladylike of all grains—with its ivory hue, its luminescent perfume evocative of clean things and cream—but it is also my kitchen demon, the bane of my existence, which has led me to kick the walls and weep. Really, I feel that my world would be a better place without it.

Such an attitude marks me as a traitor to my culture. Every true Chinese regards rice as the ultimate comfort food, whereas I am more partial to mashed potatoes. I *like* mashed potatoes, and, more important, I make heavenly mashed potatoes. I cannot say the same about my rice. To be honest, I've never been crazy about the taste of rice, either, especially when it is cooked the Chinese way, with no salt, butter, or oil. Chinese parents tell their children that every grain of rice they leave in their bowl will linger on as a blemish on their adult face. Luckily, I've survived to the age of twenty-eight acne-free, but I believe that—at the risk of sounding melodramatic—every grain of rice I have left uneaten has left its scar on my soul.

In my opinion, there is no food whose importance quite matches that of rice at the Asian table—not bread for the French, not pasta for the Italians. In the Asian household, rice is more than a staple; it's an assumption. The Chinese term for "eat" is *chi fan,* which, translated, means "eat rice."

Because of its ubiquity, most people don't know that rice is also a problem grain. After all, many things that are desirable are also dangerous. Historically, rice is the Helen of Troy of crops, leaving behind it a wake of devastation and heartbreak. Rice violence, ignited by famine, has been so prevalent in Chinese and Japanese history that historians have taken to describing any incident of a village's or a city's going crazed over a lack of its beloved foodstuff as a "rice riot"; 158 Japanese rice riots were recorded in the first half of the eighteenth century alone.

Let us also consider the pearly good looks of rice, which, in a culture that prizes a snowy complexion, remain revered. Every grain of rice—even the whitest—starts out encased in a coarse brown husk. A process known as milling strips the grain of its plain exterior but also of its vitamins; those who eat white rice as the main part of their diet are vulnerable to malnutrition and the disease beriberi. Worse, certain mills have taken to coating their rice with glucose and cornstarch to enhance the whiteness; eating a grain is like biting into a second-rate beauty hidden underneath a mask of powder and paint.

There is also rice snobbery, usually bred of blind national pride. It polarizes people. In the early 1990s, the Japanese were forced by the World Trade Organization to import rice in the name of fair trade, but instead of eating the grains that were sent from Thailand, Australia, China, and the United States, they stockpiled it in warehouses. There are also rice sects: long-grain versus medium-grain, jasmine versus Japanese sushi. One pal of mine eats only a brand called Nishiki; another, only Tamaki Gold. My mother eats only Kokuho Rose. The one thing on which they all agree is that long-grain rice—your jasmines and basmatis and what have you—is "common-folk crap." I myself cannot tell the difference between their three brands (and neither, I wager, could they), but that doesn't matter; it's the principle that counts.

I primarily associate rice with childhood visits to China in the late 1980s. In retrospect, I imagine that those must have been marvelous experiences, but at the time they meant days of drinking orange pop and preboiled water for fear of bacterial infection and bouts of diarrhea suffered on toilets that were holes dug into concrete. On top of that there was rice, three times a day, seven days a week. There was also rice back home in New England—and the humiliation of getting sneered at by my third-grade classmates when they saw rice in my lunch box—and rice for the holidays. My father's side of the family celebrated Thanksgiving and Christmas in Chinese fashion. Perhaps if they had been a pleasant group I might recall holiday rice with more affection, but my father's family was not pleasant. My grandfather was mealy, my grandmother was loud, and my dad was even louder. Everyone argued at a thunder pitch. My brother and I would creep out of hiding from the walk-in closet for meals, and I distinctly remember my longing, in the tense hours that followed, to be a member of one of those happy families chomping on cranberries and stuffing instead of a soy sauce–basted turkey with rice on the side.

Certainly I have happier rice memories: The crispy-but-not-quite-burnt bottom layer of a rice pot, called *guoba,* which is a real art form when achieved (you know you're the spoiled child when you get the biggest bit), and which I use as a base for a delicious crab and soybean stir-fry. Snacking on deep-fried puffed rice crisps, also referred to as guoba, bought from a street vendor in the city of Zhenjiang. The nicely salty, slightly greasy rice noodles fried quickly with beef that every hole-in-the-wall in Manhattan's Chinatown does so well. Still, there are two particularly awful dishes that balance my happiness with horror. The first is my mother's favorite, congee, or rice porridge, which is otherwise recognizable as the mush that results when you combine a small quantity of rice and a large amount of water and let it sit on the stove to fester. I can attest to the fact that stirring in sugar or salt or Tabasco does nothing to improve the flavor.

The second dish is fried rice. When I was growing up, my father, notoriously penny-wise, was allergic to throwing away any leftovers. This attitude led to some creative culinary inventions. Take his fried rice. That ordinarily simple dish—usually composed of eggs, scallions, and salt—would become a trove of antiques and unknowns. I have eaten, on numerous occasions, meat loaf fried rice, lobster newburg fried rice, and, on one unforgettable evening, bluegill fried rice, the bluegill being a fish that my father had caught in our local pond and kept in our fish tank until it expired.

There is a more prosaic reason for my distaste for rice, and that is that I'm not terribly good at cooking it. If you tasted rice the way I've made it, you wouldn't be too enthusiastic about it either. I may be the only person on the planet who has messed up that Near East stuff that comes in a box.

In many ways, making rice is like having sex; it is a trial-and-error process that goes on throughout your life. The only way you improve is through disaster. For a long time I was a rice virgin, unaware that there was more than one kind of rice or even that there was more than one way of preparing it. Until I was twelve, I believed that all rice was medium-grain, was slightly sticky, and came out of a stainless-steel rice cooker that had baby pink roses on it. When my mother left my father, she left behind the dog, the cat, her savings, her clothes, her books, and the rice cooker. That is when I discovered that rice could also be instant, boil-in-the-bag, or steamed on a stove.

Let me say this: my mother, who is a talented cook, makes decent rice. My stepfather, who rarely cooks, makes superb rice. His is a mysterious ritual, one that involves paper towels, perfectly temperate water, and a two-step dance in honor of Ceres. He succeeds because he is patient; I fail because I am not. Bad rice boils down—quite literally—to carelessness. Over the years, I have learned that rice must be scientifically prepped. My mother uses her finger to judge how much she needs. Now I know to use a measuring cup.

But before you measure rice, you have to wash it. Every idiot knows that, right? I didn't—not until many, many bad rice dishes later, for the simple reason that nobody had told me. You have to rinse it to get rid of the grit, starch, and cosmetic additives. Recently I decided to make the Chinese rice dumplings called zongzi, using a recipe whose secrets have been guarded and maintained by my family for years and that requires at least 14 hours of chopping, marinating, and folding of bamboo leaves into tortuous triangular shapes. After spending three hours on a hot July afternoon boiling the dumplings, I unwrapped one of the delectable little packages and took my first taste. They were terrible. The contents had acquired the texture of Saran Wrap. Even after years of rice washing, the folly of my youth came back to haunt me: I had forgotten to run the rice under the tap before I began.

By neglecting this oh-so-fundamental step, I found myself once again embroiled by rice. Zongzi, by the way, is a suicide dish; it is sometimes made in honor of the Chinese martyr Qu Yuan (who died around 280 B.C.), to be tossed from the riverbank where he leapt to a watery grave. His story certainly tantalized me at the moment I figured out my mistake—the river nearest to me lies just three blocks away—but instead I tearfully bade farewell to my hard work, rinsed some new grains clean, and started over.

The second batch was delicious, good enough to banish my thoughts of death by drowning. I make my dumplings smaller than my grandmother's, marinate the rice longer than my mom does (my current rice of choice is that "common-folk crap" Thai long-grain jasmine), and—though tradition dictates that I should boil—steam them for more savor. My mother disapproves of my methodology, but I don't care. I have come up with something that I can call my own. I can even bring myself to eat congee now. It's not my mother's congee; it is the Cantonese variety she disdains, stewed with dried seafood and pork bones.

When my father died, I made fried rice. I made it out of love, but no sooner had I finished preparing it than I realized I had created anti-father fried rice. It was fresh with vengeance. It was exactly what he would have hated the most because the rice, sausage, and shrimp were the best, and also the most obnoxiously expensive, varieties that I could find. Still, the funeral came and went, night descended, and my fried rice was the first dish to be consumed. No one knew, no one judged, and, best of all, no one remembered the bad things. For me, it was sort of a triumph.

Jambon Dreams

by Floyd Skloot

from *Boulevard*

All happy families are alike; all unhappy families have dysfunctional attitudes toward food. Take essayist Floyd Skloot's family: just trying to figure out whether they kept Kosher or not was enough to screw him up for *years.*

It was a winter night in 1952. My brother Philip was thirteen and famished, though we'd finished dinner only an hour earlier. He tiptoed into the kitchen and approached a pan of leftover stuffed cabbage cooling on the counter. I followed, wearing black Hopalong Cassidy pajamas and an empty holster on my hip, toy six-gun cocked in my hand. I was five and learning how to be a food thief.

It was vital to know the whereabouts of the authorities: my mother sat at her desk in the foyer, talking on the phone, and my father slept, hoping to get eight hours in before waking at four to open his poultry market. *Don't make a sound,* Philip whispered.

The kitchen window was steamed over, but I could still see lights from apartments that faced ours in the east Flatbush neighborhood. I could hear traffic below on Lenox Road. The room smelled of tomato, ground beef, onion, and the rank biology of cabbage wrappings cooked so long that the outer leaves flopped into the sauce. My parents called this concoction *galooptchy,* and loved to eat it for days as leftovers. Those loosed leaves were Philip's target. If he could be delicate enough in his touch so that nothing looked out of place afterwards, and careful not to drip sauce once he'd liberated the goods, he could pilfer a few and eat them without getting caught.

He didn't particularly like cabbage leaves. But he liked foiling our parents' plans, he liked taking forbidden food, and he needed the practice. I was there to appreciate the moves.

The week before, I'd witnessed his failed Velveeta Caper. My mother had brought home the smallest available block of the cheese, Philip's favorite, and placed it on the refrigerator shelf with a warning: *this has to last the whole week*. When she'd gone downstairs to visit her friend Ann, Philip opened the box, unfolded the foil packaging, and cut chunk after chunk, devouring each one plain—without crackers or bread, without offering any to me, and without pause—until just a thin slice was left. Then he crumpled up wax paper and shaped the mass into a rectangle, stuffed it against the remaining slice, refolded the packaging, and slipped the box top back into place.

"Don't touch that," he said. "I'll finish the last piece in a week."

Of course, it had been a trap. Food provision, like food thievery, was a highly nuanced business in our family. As soon as she came home, my mother checked the refrigerator. She touched the Velveeta box, which yielded to her finger's pressure, and screamed. She demanded our presence before her. *I hope you two enjoyed your feast!* Philip ate no dinner that night. Neither did I, his ravenous sidekick.

But he got away—we both got away—with his cabbage operation. I remember that near the end of it, rapt in his work, Philip did drip a freckle of sauce onto the linoleum.

Like our mother, I raced to grab a paper towel, gasping instead of screaming. After I'd cleaned the floor, he winked at me. Then we tiptoed back to our room.

One Sunday morning in 1956, my father woke me and Philip by slapping our feet with a spatula. He wore his chefs apron, and stood between our beds with his right index finger pressed to his lips. *Shhhhh. Don't wake her.*

I'd never seen my father cook, and didn't know he could. He sold the stuff that other people cooked, he ate stuff that other people cooked, and I figured he had nothing to do with what happened in between. The apron, I thought, was only for when he served drinks before a dinner party.

Usually, we had Sunday breakfast at Toomey's Diner on Empire

Boulevard, then went to Prospect Park or Coney Island or the cemetery where my father's father was buried. But this morning it was raining, and he'd heard that Toomey's was closed all week because of a death in the family, and since we'd all be driving up to Connecticut later that morning to visit my mother's cousins, we couldn't do our usual Sunday outing.

"Breakfast in ten minutes," he whispered. "Get yourselves ready."

Soon there was an alarming smell from the kitchen. I looked at Philip and he smiled, raised his eyebrows, and rubbed his hands together. "Baloney and eggs!"

This was another revelation for me. I hadn't known it was possible to cook baloney, or to eat baloney with eggs, and survive. Besides, such a combination might be against the rules.

We weren't exactly Kosher in the house, though our father's was a Kosher market, its poultry slaughtered according to the rules. We routinely mixed meat and dairy at the same meal, and didn't keep separate meat and dairy dishes, or buy specially blessed foods, so I figured Kosher only applied when people visited other people's homes. I knew it didn't apply to meals eaten in restaurants, unless we were in a restaurant with family or friends who kept their homes Kosher. I knew about the restaurant exception to Kosher rules because we could have pork in restaurants. The truth is, I lived for ham: ham steak, country ham, Virginia ham, fried ham, sliced ham, ham with eggs, ham in baked beans. We could sometimes have pork at home, but only when our father brought fresh pork sausage from the Italian butcher next door to his market. Probably keeping Kosher, when it came to pork in the home, only applied when people got their food from strangers. At home, we ate only beef hot dogs or cold cuts, except when at Ebbets Field or when the grocery store had a special on bratwurst or braunschweiger, so the rules about pork also had something to do with sports and economics. Similarly, we ate shrimp and lobster in Chinese restaurants, but not at home, so I figured that the Chinese had special access to Kosher shellfish. To poultry as well, since their restaurants were my father's best wholesale customers, in which case it was all right to ignore the fact that their kitchens were contaminated, or *trayf*, as my parents called anything non-Kosher when we weren't eating it. Clams we ate only at restaurants located near the ocean, which led me to believe that clams were Kosher if consumed within sight of their homes. The rules were sometimes a little hard to follow.

But my shock over baloney and eggs wasn't about violations of rules. It was about the strangeness of eating baloney and eggs together, even if the combination was technically permissible. The smell, and the way the meat curled away from the eggs no matter how I tried to flatten it, certainly suggested they didn't belong on the same plate.

I was learning that most of my assumptions about food were false. Every time I thought I understood what we did and didn't do, something strange would occur. There seemed to be few guiding principles other than stealth and the violation of all rules. Eat what you want, especially what you're not supposed to, whenever the opportunity presents itself.

When my father sold his poultry market in 1957, we celebrated with a series of dinners. One for his employees and best customers at a restaurant in Red Hook. Another for his fellow butchers, bakers, and produce men on Union Street, where almost every guest had provided one of the menu's fresh items, from the mussels posillipo and garlic bread to the roasted meats and desserts. There was a dinner for the Skloot uncles and aunts and cousins, held at our grandmother's home because she was the one who had gotten the family started in the poultry business originally. We had dinner at the home of the Italian family who bought the market. And dinner for just the four of us, a final feast shortly before we moved away from Brooklyn, featuring poultry my father had killed and cleaned with his own hands. My mother, who had been urging him to sell his market for the last three years, burst into tears when she set the heaped platter down. She left the room for a minute or two, then as we were about to begin eating that last dinner, my father took off his glasses and wept. It was the only time I ever saw him cry, and it made me cry. My brother laughed, but then his laughter converted to crying too. We sat there, all four in tears, watching the pullet give off steam and sag into its bed of fennel.

Like so many families, we celebrated holidays, events, and achievements by eating. For us, though, as with the rules of keeping Kosher, these celebrations had fine calibrations governed by complex regulations. If I brought home an especially good report card from school, we would go out to eat, but not at an Italian or seafood restaurant, the most expensive cuisines we liked. Grades might be worth dinner at a diner, or a sit-down deli feast, but not fancy chicken cacciatore or fresh lobster. After the first week of my brother's new job at a clothing factory, we ate at a restaurant in the west end of town famous for its spare ribs, but we weren't allowed to order appetizers and skipped dessert. The end of a week of continual rain was worth a Chinese dinner, but only combination plates, not separate main dishes, which were proper for adult birthdays and certain holidays. When my mother got a singing role in a community theater production, we had steaks all around. Some visitors merited better meals than others when we went out together. My mother's brother and his wife, so successful in the garment industry, got the full Italian restaurant treatment. My father's eldest sister, a distinguished interior decorator, and her well-to-do husband, got to eat at Meyer & Kronke, which my mother called a four-star Manhattan restaurant stranded in Oceanside. But my father's middle sister and her traveling salesman husband, on the rare occasions we ate with them, got the small café with its burgers and sandwiches.

If we celebrated by eating, and entertained by eating, we also grieved by eating. Four years after my father sold his market, when we'd left Brooklyn and settled in a rented home on the south shore of Long Island, he died suddenly at the age of fifty-three. Only Philip and I were home when the phone call came, and our first act was to open the refrigerator and slap together roast beef sandwiches. A day later, family and friends returned home with us from the cemetery and shared a catered feast. Kosher, from the restaurant on Park Street, because my father's mother and eldest brother would be with us. Wearing a black dress and demure white apron, Hannah—the woman who helped my mother cook and clean—took me into a corner and whispered, "You Skloots is the eatin'est people I ever saw." Then she continued rushing through the living room, dodging mourners, carrying heavy trays.

She was right, and I've remembered her observation for forty-four years. We ate a lot, we ate meaningfully, and we ate recklessly. A family given to heart disease, strokes, and diabetes, we gorged on fatty foods, salty foods, sweets. We often ate with abandon, especially Philip and I down at our corner of the table, grabbing for dishes if they weren't passed quickly enough, snaring morsels from one another's plates, licking our fingers to lift a few final crumbs of bread.

Meals could be a time of peace, if the food satisfied in quality and amount, if everyone's mood was stable, if the stars were aligned. But meals could also be a battleground, every member of the family looking out for himself only, seizing what they wanted, hunching over the plate to guard their food like animals. Tempers could flare, the day's misdemeanors and insults and losses tossed into the mix as forks shoved food into mouths between accusations and recriminations.

Food mattered to us, to me, in ways that evolution may not have intended. It sure seemed to be the center of all attention.

"Don't get any on the seat," Philip said.

I leaned further outside the car and said, "Don't worry, I know what I'm doing."

"And don't get any on the door, either."

As usual, Philip and I were trading *don'ts* as we ate. We were hunkered back-to-back in his new, white 1961 Plymouth Valiant, eating ham sandwiches on loaves of crusty bread. The car's front doors were open wide, oil and vinegar dressing dripped down our chins to land between our feet on the asphalt, and bread crumbs exploded all around us. We didn't look around when we talked, and we didn't stop chewing, but none of that mattered because we didn't have to hear each other to conduct this conversation.

"Don't talk when you eat," I said. "You spray food all over the place."

"Don't be a wise guy. And don't forget, last week, there was mustard all over the floor on your side."

I leaned further out the door, held the sandwich at arm's length, stretched my neck like a goose in flight, and took another bite. "Don't distract me."

That sunny Saturday afternoon still lingers in memory because it was the one time my brother broke with his routine. Instead of the usual hero sandwich, he'd ordered what I'd ordered, ham and Swiss with extra lettuce and dressing.

"Don't kid yourself," he said as we neared the end of our meals. "This isn't a real sandwich, it's an *hors d'oeuvre*."

Lacking the proper variety of meats, containing only one kind of cheese, missing the pickles and tomatoes and onions and peppers, my regular Saturday lunch seemed like diet food to Philip. A semi-sandwich. But it was the kind I loved, the kind I'd even begun to dream about.

Halfway through lunch, he began the ritual quiz: "Okay, what's a hero sandwich called in Philadelphia?"

"A hoagie."

"In Boston?"

"Grinder."

"What about Chicago?"

"A sub."

"And why do they call it a sub?"

"Because it's shaped like a submarine."

He nodded. I could hear seagulls bugling as they circled above us, coming in off the bay just beyond the playground where we were parked. If one landed near us, hoping for a scrap of bread, Philip would roar like a walrus till the gull fled. We had just finished playing a doubleheader in a men's summer softball league. The rest of the team had gone home for showers, but we'd headed straight to the deli, as always. He'd ordered a ham sandwich, I believe, to reward me for having hit my first home run of the season. Even though, as he pointed out immediately after I'd reached the dugout, it was an inside-the-park homer and therefore not a REAL homer, like the kind he hit.

"Yonkers?"

"Wedge." I didn't know if his information was correct, but Philip had taught me the regional names for hero sandwiches and my job was to learn them as he instructed, not to challenge his data.

Names, I'd come to understand, mattered when discussing food. It was essential to know what you were talking about, even if correct names were as fluid as the rules that governed my family's diet. Maybe that's why our chatter was as packed with *don'ts* as a hero/hoagie/grinder/sub/wedge was with fillings.

"Very good. Don't put the napkin on the seat." *How did he know I'd wiped my lips?* "I'm done with my cream soda," he said, "let me have a sip of yours."

I was, thanks in large part to Philip, a serious student of food information. Not a scholar, not in my brother's league at all, but no slouch either. Even after our father's market was sold and he went to work for his brother-in-law in the garment district, even after he died, we felt it was our business to recognize fine culinary distinctions, particularly among meats and fish. To carry on the tradition. By the age of fifteen, as Philip left home to marry, I could differentiate between littleneck and cherrystone clams by taste alone, and knew that soft-shell clams really had hard shells and were best for steaming. I knew that head cheese was not cheese, but jellied meat from a cow's head, and that the baloney with pearly white chunks of fat scattered throughout was called Mortadella, which—since I'd taken Latin in school—sounded to me like Death Meat. I knew, of course, that the difference between a capon and a pullet had more to do with tenderness than gender. I knew that gefilte fish was made from pike or carp, which was like a Jewish version of scrapple, which was a Pennsylvania Dutch concoction made of boiled pig scraps and cornmeal. The connection, Philip had explained, was that both were garbage foods given fancy names to make them sound better.

Our teacher-student relationship regarding food was like our coach-rookie relationship regarding softball, where Philip was the team's founder, captain, and slugger, and I was the fourteen-year-old shortstop among men in their twenties, a slick fielder and a speedy singles hitter, learning the game. But as I sat there beside him, chewing and acing his quiz, I knew in my rebellious adolescent soul that the secret to a hero sandwich was the bread. Had to be crusty outside and chewy-soft inside. Philip said I was a fool, it was all about the proper mass and balance of ingredients. Which was why the plain ham sandwich we were eating did not hold up to a hero's standards.

As a high school football and baseball player, I somehow remained lean despite my family's eating habits. Maybe it was all the exercise I got, or youthful metabolism, or the fact that I had distractions that sometimes made me rush away from the table. Maybe, as I often hoped, not being fat meant I was not really my parents' child. My mother, barely five feet tall, weighed a hundred eighty pounds. My father, in the years shortly before his death, was all belly and jowl, a man only three inches taller than his very short wife and at least as heavy. My brother, the only one of us to grow taller than five-four, eventually topped out at five-nine and three hundred fifty pounds. Through college and into the early years of my first marriage, I held my weight at a hundred fifty. But then, at the age of twenty-five, I lost control. At my peak, I carried two hundred pounds spread over my sixty-four inch frame.

I still tried to play ball with my friends, but my knees and back hurt from carrying all those pounds. I wore polka dotted polyester suits to work that had belonged to my Uncle Saul, wore soft wide shoes to cushion the load, and spent my weekends in an vast ochre jumpsuit. I met people who hadn't seen me in a couple of years and barely recognized me. At a Skloot family picnic during the summer of 1974, a cousin joked that I was finally starting to look like a member of my family. One evening, dressed in undershorts and walking past a mirror in my den, I glanced sideways and saw that I was already shaped like my father in his final years. All I needed to complete the look was a fat Havana cigar.

Late that fall, I invented a diet that I thought I could manage. First, I focused on breakfasts, changing my morning habits but not worrying about lunches or dinners yet. No more breakfasts in restaurants. No sausage and gravy, ham and eggs with an extra order of ham, hash browns, buttered toast, side of pancakes. I ate a bowl of cereal at home, with my infant daughter beside me in her high chair sharing the same meal, both of us playing with our Cheerios and jabbering at each other. At work, when colleagues went out for midmorning coffee and snacks, I forced myself to stay at my desk. For a month, that was all I did about dieting. Then, when I felt in control of my morning eating, I worked on lunch. No more lunches in restaurants, I told myself, till I weighed 150 pounds again. No ham. I brought to work baggies filled with sliced carrot sticks and celery stalks, red pepper strips, rounds of cucumber, cherry tomatoes, apple slices. For protein, I brought a small chunk of low-fat cheese or a few almonds. At lunch time, I retreated to a disused vault in the state capitol building where I worked, and ate as I read the daily newspaper. Before long, and without saying anything about it, two friends began to join me. I hadn't realized they'd noticed what I was doing. Craig and Ruby said they wanted to lose weight too, but I believe they were actually trying to support me. Instead of going to the newsstand at mid-afternoon and buying a candy bar from the blind vendor there, I went for a quick walk with Craig and Ruby up the capitol's five flights of stairs. By early February, with my morning and afternoon eating mastered, I worked on dinner and evening snacks. Small portions of chicken or fish. Salad, green vegetables, no ham.

There is a photograph of me, taken just before my diet began, wearing a white T-shirt and bulging with fat all around my daughter's small form as she sleeps in my arms. A companion photograph, taken during our trip to Disney World in March, 1975, shows me in a pair of new shorts and a vertically striped polo shirt, fifty-two pounds lighter, seated beside her in a toy car in which I'd never have been able to fit five months earlier. Nearby, oddly enough, was a Disney World staffer dressed as Porky Pig. Ham incarnate.

It was late-September, 1984, the night before my second marathon, and I was carbo-loading with a group of fellow runners at an Italian restaurant in Portland. The atmosphere was businesslike, a half dozen skinny men and women too busy fueling themselves to joke around, argue, or brag about their best times. In lieu of chatter, silverware clanked. Huge bowls of pasta circled the table, followed by bread and a small plate of skinless, boneless, grilled chicken breast. We all ate at least two helpings. But if I weren't eating to fuel a twenty-six mile run, I'd have had less than half a serving.

Once I began running, in 1982, I also began evaluating my weight by the ounce. Childhood's dietary rules may have been complex, the parsing of minute distinctions among poultry or types of baloney fanatical, my history with food bizarre, but my mid-life weight management techniques verged on the pathological. I kept records of miles run and food consumed. Though I normally ran close to fifty miles a week, I would add more miles to compensate for the occasional large meals that accompanied social occasions. Though I weighed less at age thirty-seven than I'd weighed in junior high school, I talked and worried about my weight all the time. Diagnosed with high cholesterol despite the good diet and exercise, I took medication and became even more rigorous about what I ate. If I liked it, I avoided it, or found substitutes that would have made my brother weep, buying ham made out of soy, yolkless egg substance in milk cartons, sugar-free taste-free cereals and cookies.

I thought I had my diet under control. I thought I had broken all my childhood food habits and escaped the family's culinary grip. But the truth was that food was still the center of attention.

Then neurological illness, caused by a viral attack, disabled me in 1988. Once it became clear that I would survive, what terrified me most was that I might get fat again.

Because I couldn't run, couldn't exercise, because I was largely bed-bound for a year and walked with a cane for another fourteen years, I dreaded adding weight. For a few years after getting sick, I was as crazy in my restricted eating as I'd been when running. If the first half of my life was about obsessive excess around food, the second half threatened to be about obsessive diligence.

Gradually, I came to understand that I needed to ease my grip, that the stress I felt over diet and weight was making my other health problems worse. I needed to integrate everything I did into an overall strategy of consistent health management. I had to rest for several hours daily, lower my expectations about what I could accomplish, structure a life that was stable, balanced. Illness, it turned out, nudged eating from the center of my attention. It was, after all, acceptable to eat what I wanted. Oddly enough, I had grown to like such things as soy baloney and soy cheese, cereals sweetened with fruit juice, cooked vegetables, raw nuts. I no longer wanted the food of my childhood, so it was no longer necessary to untangle the rules that governed it.

Except for ham. I still have dreams about ham sandwiches. In last night's, for instance, I was wandering through an unknown city feeling hopelessly lost and disoriented. Then I noticed a pushcart in the distance, where a man was selling baguettes so stuffed with ham that they seemed impossible to eat. Sandwiches were stacked behind the cart's glassed front and drooped from its edges. More sandwiches dangled from the cart's roof like skewered fowl in a butcher shop while others peeped like flowers from wicker baskets on the ground. I approached the cart and realized that suddenly I felt at home, though I still didn't know where I was. I reached out, the vendor said *don't get any on the seat,* and I awoke just before touching the proffered sandwich.

I knew right away what the dream reflected. Earlier this summer, my wife, Beverly, and I had spent eighteen days in France. We were in Paris for the final week, where I taught at the Paris Writers Workshop, and it was there that feelings of dislocation surged. I was tired from the heat and the travel and the seven flights of stairs I had to climb to reach our apartment; I couldn't speak the language; I was homesick for our isolated, tranquil, country way of life back home; I got lost as I tried to walk from our apartment to the place where I taught. But one afternoon near the end of our stay, walking back from class to the apartment, I stopped at a boulangerie to buy a sandwich. The counter display was like the pushcart's in my dream: baguettes everywhere, stuffed with meats that stained their wax paper wrapping, and though I couldn't read the signs I had no trouble deciphering the choices. It felt as though Philip were over my shoulder, urging me to buy one that had the greatest variety of meats. But I chose the plain ham sandwich with lots of lettuce, *jambon et salade,* then walked happily—even jauntily—down the Rue de Sevres, eating amidst a shower of crumbs, feeling almost purely at home.

Surely this feeling wasn't associated with ham alone, with satisfying my hunger in a way that was so deeply rooted. I think it was associated with freedom, with a sense of Home as the place where I could enact my deepest desires because they were truly mine, not my brother's or mother's or father's. They were right for me, trustworthy. I could allow myself to eat and enjoy, guilt-free, a *jambon et salade* sandwich knowing it was something I could do in moderation. Besides, after so many years of slow neurological recovery, I was now capable of walking off the calories. The feeling of being at home was present, too, because Philip was there, alive within me eight years after he had died from complications of diabetes brought on by morbid obesity. He was yakking as usual about my choices. I listened to him, but I could make my own decision. And the bread in my dream, like the baguette in Paris, was perfect, crusty on the outside but chewy-soft inside.

Home Cooking

Chef's Homemade Secret

by Laura Taxel

from *The Cleveland Plain-Dealer*

Laura Taxel's down-to-earth food writing is a perfect fit for a newspaper with a name like the *Plain-Dealer*. In this essay, she cuts right to the heart of things, recalling an encounter that for her summed up the true culinary state of the nation.

WEDNESDAY, MARCH 15, 2006

In a grocery store recently, while scanning the shelves in search of a can of crushed tomatoes, I was approached by a woman in culinary distress.

"Excuse me," she said. "Can I ask you a question?"

I smiled and nodded in an encouraging way.

"Have you ever made real spaghetti sauce, from scratch?"

I had, many times.

"So, if I got home, say by three in the afternoon," she continued, "do you think I could have sauce ready by six PM?"

"Absolutely," I replied, "no problem."

"OK, great. I thought maybe it took all day." She looked relieved, even happy. I turned, ready to move on in search of some great northern beans and smoked turkey wings, gathering up ingredients for a hearty winter soup.

But she wasn't done with me yet.

"Would you mind explaining to me how to do it?"

"You mean how to make tomato sauce?"

"Yes, what do you do? I've only used the pre-made kind in the jar." She then explained about a sister coming, wanting the meal to be special, plus a few more details than I needed for the task at hand.

Recovering quickly from my surprise that someone who looked to be between 25 and 30 had never attempted this most simple and basic cooking effort, I commenced a midaisle tutorial. She listened attentively as we worked our way through the chopping and sauteing of onions and garlic, the addition of tomato puree and a splash or two of red wine—then, on to a discussion of seasoning options.

She didn't blanch when I mentioned upgrading, if she wished, with diced carrots and celery. (I did not use the word *mirepoix*, but the kitchen savvy among us know that's what I was describing to her.) I raised the issue of meat. She was definitely going the meatball route, so we took a conversational detour to discuss browning them, then adding them to the simmering sauce to finish so their beefy richness would infuse it with flavor. I mentioned leaving the lid off the pot, keeping the heat low, and promised that good things would happen as it reduced and thickened.

Time was marching on, but she wasn't going anywhere. She had questions, lots of them.

Grabbing a can of puree in one hand, tomato paste in another, and gesturing with her chin to the can of crushed tomatoes I was still holding, she wanted to know the differences between them and whether she could make sauce with any one of them?

I gave her a quick overview of each of these products and their particular properties, along with some personal commentary. Yes, various types of sauce could be made with any of the products. Paste needs to be diluted. Kids, in my experience, generally prefer a smooth spaghetti sauce without chunks and bits. I get best results with puree. No, you don't add water to puree.

The encounter seemed to be wrapping up. But not quite.

"If making tomato sauce from scratch is so simple," she demanded, "then why have I been buying all this prepared stuff?"

I couldn't really provide a genuinely satisfactory explanation for her years of ignorance, of course, so I took a broader, more cultural perspective.

"You've been duped," I said. "They didn't want you to know. It's business."

She commented on my vast knowledge and my uncanny ability to explain the required steps. So I 'fessed up and told her she'd picked the right person to ask because I was a food writer. She seemed pretty excited, though I must admit that she didn't ask for my autograph. In fact, she didn't even ask me my name.

And then my ego got the better of me. Unable to resist the impulse to further impress her, I offered to share A Real Chef's Secret.

She came just a tad closer. I looked around conspiratorially to be sure no one else was listening.

And then I told her about adding a couple of spoonfuls of the water in which the pasta had been cooked to the sauce at the last minute to thicken it. "All the restaurant chefs do it," I shrugged.

She was thrilled with this bit of insider information, effusive in her thanks and clearly ready to become a sauce-from-scratch master.

And me—I felt like the next Rachel Ray.

Laura's Quick and Easy Tomato Sauce

2 tablespoons olive oil
1 medium onion, diced
2 cloves garlic, minced
1 large (28 ounce can) tomato puree or crushed Italian plum
    tomatoes
1/3 cup good red wine
1/4 teaspoon dried oregano, or 2 leaves fresh oregano, torn
1 teaspoon dried basil, or 8 leaves fresh basil, torn
salt, pepper to taste
a pinch of sugar or a splash of balsamic vinegar if needed to
    finish

Sauté the vegetables: In a deep heavy pot, heat oil and saute onions until they begin to brown, about 5 minutes. Add garlic, stir to combine and cook another minute.

Combine, simmer ingredients: Add puree (or crushed tomatoes) including juice from the can, salt and pepper, wine, and herbs. Simmer uncovered, stirring often, about 20 minutes over low heat. Cook to reduce another 10 minutes or until thickened.

Finish the sauce: Remove from heat. When pasta is done, add 2 tablespoons of the water in which it was cooked to the sauce.

Variation: Stir in half of a diced bell pepper, green or red, added with garlic.

Variation: Stir in 1 cup fresh mushrooms, sliced, added with seasonings.

Variation: In a separate pan, heat 1 tablespoon olive oil, saute 1 stalk celery, diced and 1 carrot, peeled and diced until soft. Add 1 pound ground chuck or loose Italian sausage. Brown, drain, and combine with simmering sauce. Deglaze pan in which meat was cooked with a little red wine and add that liquid to sauce as it simmers.

SERVES 4

Macaroni and Lots of Cheese

by Julia Moskin
from *The New York Times*

Moskin's supple, sensuous prose style invariably makes me hungry. A perfect example is this handy recipe piece, in which Moskin investigates all the primal taste sensations that make macaroni and cheese the ultimate American comfort food.

Macaroni and cheese is just the kind of all-American, old-fashioned home cooking I was not raised on.

New York City in the 1970s was a hotbed of culinary radicalism. Food-forward parents like mine served dinners of homemade falafel, Mediterranean fish stew or stir-fried beef with broccoli. To me, dishes like spaghetti and meatballs, mashed potatoes with gravy and macaroni and cheese seemed exotic and unattainable.

Naturally, this is where my greatest passions lie as a cook. And after the frenzy of holiday cooking, a simple dish like macaroni and cheese is just what I want to make now.

Lacking a family recipe, I turned to cookbooks for guidance. A strange substance called "white sauce" cropped up again and again. Bread crumbs, Worcestershire sauce and alien cheeses like smoked gouda and parmigiano also kept finding their way in. None of the recipes came close to my fantasy of what the dish should be: nothing more than tender elbows of pasta suspended in pure molten cheddar, with a chewy, golden-brown crust of cheese on top.

While reading the following passage in a twenty-year-old cookbook called *Simple Cooking*, the problem became clear:

"A good dish of macaroni and cheese is hard to find these days.

The recipes in most cookbooks are not to be trusted . . . usually it is their vexatious infatuation with white sauce, a noxious paste of flour-thickened milk, for this dish flavored with a tiny grating of cheese. Contrary to popular belief, this is not macaroni and cheese but macaroni with cheese sauce. It is awful stuff and every cookbook in which it appears should be thrown out the window."

The book's author, John Thorne, still adheres to this position, but said that he has largely given up the fight. "Starting at about the turn of the twentieth century, there was a huge fashion for white sauce in America—chafing-dish stuff like chicken à la king, or creamed onions," he said last week. "They were cheap and seemed elegant, and their legacy is that people choose 'creamy' over everything else. But I maintain that macaroni and cheese should be primarily cheesy."

Marlena Spieler, author of a forthcoming book, "Macaroni and Cheese" (Chronicle), agreed that most recipes simply do not have enough cheese. "I believe in making a cheese sauce and also using shredded cheese," she said.

But she refuses to forgo white sauce altogether. "You need a little goo to keep the pasta and cheese together," she said. Having made a global study of the subject, she ticked off a list of alternative binders: mascarpone, crème fraîche, eggs, heavy cream, egg yolks, cottage cheese, butter and evaporated milk, which she deems a little too sweet but "delightfully trashy."

Like me, Ms. Spieler believes that macaroni and cheese, which is often served alongside fried chicken or barbecue, deserves pride of place as a main dish. "I love it so much that I want to focus on it," she said. A crisp green salad and a glass of wine turn mac and cheese into a meal, she added.

I first made Mr. Thorne's recipe, a step in the right direction: it combines a whole pound of cheddar cheese with half a pound of macaroni. But the method, which entails taking the dish out of the oven every five minutes to stir in more cheese, is tiresome. And so, armed with the knowledge that a seemingly outrageous 2:1 ratio of cheese to macaroni is indeed possible, I set out in search of the ideal recipe.

At cheese counters across New York City, complex blends of pungent, unaged, rind-washed and cave-ripened cheeses have been devised for makers of macaroni and cheese. Rob Kaufelt, who owns

Murray's Cheese in Greenwich Village, counsels a 30-50-20 blend of Swiss Gruyère, young Irish cheddar and Parmigiano-Reggiano, or a blend of English cheddars. At Artisanal, cooks are steered toward the softness of Italian fontina and Welsh Caerphilly.

These are all indisputably glorious cheeses. But they do not all belong in a casserole dish. An impromptu focus group of children living in my apartment building showed a strong preference for the cheddar family. Ultimately, I found, the dirty little secret of an honest macaroni and cheese is often American cheese.

American cheese is simply cheddar or colby that is ground and emulsified with water, said Bonnie Chlebecek, a test kitchen manager at Land O'Lakes in Arden Hills, Minnesota.

"The process denatures the proteins in the cheese," she said, "which in plain English means that it won't clump up or get grainy when you melt it. With natural cheese, it's much harder to get a smooth melt." The cheese industry and the Food and Drug Administration call a cheese "natural" if it has been produced from milk, as cheddar and mozzarella (and virtually all other nonindustrial cheeses) are.

Plain American cheese, labeled pasteurized process cheese, contains the most natural cheese and is the best for cooking. American cheese derivatives are made from cheese and additives like sodium phosphates (acids that promote melting), nonfat dry milk and carrageenan. In descending order of their relationship to natural cheese, they are cheese food, cheese spread (such as Velveeta) and cheese product.

Daphne Mahoney, the Jamaican-born owner of Daphne's Caribbean Express in Manhattan's East Village, makes a wonderfully dense version of macaroni and cheese that combines American cheese with extra-sharp cheddar. Macaroni pie is hugely popular in the Caribbean, especially on islands like Jamaica and Barbados that once received regular stocks of cheddar from other members of the British commonwealth: Canada, Australia and New Zealand.

"We put a little pepper in it to spice it up," she said. "But as long as you don't make the macaroni soggy, and you use plenty of cheese, it will be good."

The macaroni must not be slippery and soft, but firm and substantial. This is not the time to bring out your whole-wheat penne and artisanal orecchiette: elbow pasta is the way to go.

One of the most surprising recipes I tried called for uncooked pasta. Full of doubt, I mixed raw elbow noodles with a sludge of cottage cheese, milk and grated cheese. The result was stunning: the noodles obediently absorbed the liquid as they cooked, encasing themselves in fluffy cheese and a crust of deep rich brown.

The last decision—to top or not to top—is easily dispensed with. Resist the temptation to fiddle around with bread crumbs, corn flakes, tortilla chips and other ingredients that have nothing to do with the dish. When there is enough cheese in and on top of your creation, a brown, crisp crust of toasted cheese will form naturally. There is nothing more delicious.

The moral of the story: When in doubt, add more cheese.

Creamy Macaroni and Cheese

Time: 1 hour 15 minutes

2 tablespoons butter
1 cup cottage cheese (not lowfat)
2 cups milk (not skim)
1 teaspoon dry mustard
Pinch cayenne
Pinch freshly grated nutmeg
½ teaspoon salt
¼ teaspoon freshly ground black pepper
1 pound sharp or extra-sharp cheddar cheese, grated
½ pound elbow pasta, uncooked.

1. Heat oven to 375°F and position an oven rack in upper third of oven. Use 1 tablespoon butter to butter a 9-inch round or square baking pan.

2. In a blender, purée cottage cheese, milk, mustard, cayenne, nutmeg and salt and pepper together. Reserve ¼ cup grated cheese for topping. In a large bowl, combine remaining grated cheese, milk mixture and uncooked pasta. Pour into prepared pan, cover tightly with foil and bake 30 minutes.

3. Uncover pan, stir gently, sprinkle with reserved cheese and dot with remaining tablespoon butter. Bake, uncovered, 30 minutes more, until browned. Let cool at least 15 minutes before serving.

SERVES 6–8

Crusty Macaroni and Cheese

Time: 1 hour 15 minutes

3 tablespoons butter
12 ounces extra-sharp cheddar cheese, coarsely grated
12 ounces American cheese or cheddar cheese, coarsely grated
1 pound elbow pasta, boiled in salted water until just tender, drained, and rinsed under cold water
¼ teaspoon cayenne (optional)
Salt
⅔ cup whole milk.

1. Heat oven to 375°F. Use one tablespoon butter to thickly grease a 9 × 13–inch baking dish. Combine grated cheeses and set aside two heaping cups for topping.

2. In a large bowl, toss together the pasta, cheeses, cayenne (if using) and salt to taste. Place in prepared pan and evenly pour milk over surface. Sprinkle reserved cheese on top, dot with remaining butter and bake, uncovered, 45 minutes. Raise heat to 400°F and bake 15 to 20 minutes more, until crusty on top and bottom.

SERVES 8–12

The Pilgrims Didn't Brine

by Kim Severson

from *The New York Times*

Formerly at the *San Francisco Chronicle*, now *The New York Times*, Kim Severson is a crack food reporter who not only digs deep for details, but writes with warmth and flair. Here she puts a fresh spin on the traditional Turkey Day recipe piece.

I have done foolish things in pursuit of a delicious Thanksgiving turkey.

I have cooked them in the style of countries I've never visited.

I've dismembered them raw.

I have stood in a cold garage drinking beer while men I barely knew poked at one floating in a caldron of hot oil.

I've hunted down twelve perfect juniper berries and submerged them, along with a turkey raised more carefully than a Montessori student, in a tub of salted water overnight.

I've massaged butter into breasts and stuffed sage leaves under skin.

I've soaked cheesecloth in butter and flipped hot carcasses from one side to the other.

Several weeks ago, a friend gently suggested that serious cooks spend entirely too much time thinking about the Thanksgiving turkey.

Naturally, I thought about that.

Is the time and money spent on a gamy American Bronze heritage turkey worth it when most guests prefer the bland flavor of the Broad-Breasted White they grew up eating? Is 24 hours of preparation excessive, when that time might be better spent on traditional holiday pursuits like creating a spectacular pumpkin pie or actively ignoring your family?

On the Thanksgiving plate, turkey is never the star nor the most memorable dish. Turkey recipes are not passed down through generations, like your grandmother's cranberry relish.

No one remembers the turkey unless it is bad.

This year I set off to see how simply I could roast a turkey and still have good results. I wanted something neither dry nor taxing.

To start, I took a page from Barbara Kafka, who in her 1995 book *Roasting: A Simple Art* advocated a two-hour turkey in a 500-degree oven. But my oven is never pristine enough for that kind of heat, and the result—even with the cleanest of ovens—is a screeching smoke alarm and a greasy kitchen. I would go high, but not that high.

Next I called Harold McGee, the science and food writer who recently revised his encyclopedic *On Food and Cooking*.

"How simple do you want to keep it?" he asked. Very, very simple, I said.

The goal, he pointed out, is to get the leg meat to at least 165 degrees, when the connective tissue is cooked and the pinkness has just faded. But straight-up roasting would leave the breast dry at any temperature much past 155.

"The trick is to establish an unevenness in the temperature of the two different parts, the breast and the thighs," he said. The easiest way is to set the turkey on the counter and strap a couple of ice packs on the breast about an hour or so before roasting.

This year, Mr. McGee plans to increase the effect by starting the bird breast side down in a cold pan with cold vegetables and placing a sheet pan on the floor of the oven to slow the heat from the bottom. Then he'll flip the turkey halfway through cooking.

That didn't seem so simple. So I called Christopher Kimball, editor of *Cook's Illustrated* magazine. He has long advocated brining, an overnight soak in salted water. I have brined many times. Even with a mediocre, overcooked bird, the process makes the meat well seasoned and juicier.

But this year I didn't want to wrestle with plastic garbage bags and coolers and bags of ice. I wanted simple.

"You can buy a frozen, prebasted Butterball which is essentially brined and thaw the puppy out," he said. "You do have to butterfly it and rip the backbone out, but that's not too difficult. Shove it on a broiler pan at 450 degrees. That's about as painless as it gets."

I had hoped to avoid butchery projects. So I called Sara Moulton, the *Gourmet* magazine chef and television personality whose new book, *Sara's Secrets for Weeknight Meals,* is all about assuring people they can cook excellent food easily.

"I do the old 325 degrees," she said. "I don't do anything funny."

She likes a big turkey, maybe 16 pounds. She stuffs it, and prepares a separate pan of dressing to cook outside the bird. If the stuffing doesn't get hot enough (it ought to reach 165 degrees), she removes it from the bird, then puts it back in the oven.

"The biggest problem people have is that they follow those charts and they are the vaguest things in the planet," she said.

The key is a good meat thermometer. Some chefs take the turkey out when the legs hit 155, others at 165 degrees or 170 degrees. The U.S.D.A. says the thigh meat should be 180 degrees, which is insanely high but hospital safe. Ms. Moulton is not willing to buck the U.S.D.A. in print, but I am. Bringing the thighs to at least 165 degrees seems the best compromise between food safety and avoiding breast oblivion. The temperature will continue to rise as you let the turkey rest for 30 minutes before carving, another tip from Ms. Moulton.

Finally, I called my mother. She has been roasting turkeys for fifty years. It's always the same. A little onion and celery in the cavity, some salt and pepper and a constant 350-degree oven.

So, Mom, why were some of our family's Thanksgiving turkeys terrific and others, well, not so good?

"If you get a good turkey, you'll have a good turkey," said my mom, who always buys whatever is on sale. "If you get a bad turkey, it'll be a bad turkey."

So I tested three different turkeys. Since a kosher bird is already salted as part of the processing, I thought it might be the shortcut I was looking for. It offered juicy meat, but not so juicy to justify all the time I spent pulling feather shafts from the skin. Plus, depending on where you live, a kosher bird can be hard to find.

I tried a frozen supermarket bird. It was inexpensive, but I didn't like the taste or quality of the meat or the industrial-style methods used to raise it.

In the end, I settled on a fresh bird from Pennsylvania sold by my local butcher. For my money, any turkey that has been allowed to forage naturally and was raised close to where you live is the best option, both for flavor and politics.

As for cooking methods, I borrowed a little bit from everyone. I settled on a roasting temperature of 425 degrees, which seemed like a reasonable compromise between high-heat advocates and old-fashioned, slow-roasters. I started with a room-temperature turkey and I tented the breast with foil. No flipping, no basting.

When the thigh hit 165 degrees, I let the turkey rest for a half-hour, covered with foil and a slightly damp kitchen towel, to allow the juices to settle back into the meat.

For a 12- to 14-pound turkey, my method takes about two hours, which should leave plenty of time to do more important things this Thanksgiving. Like call your mother.

∞

Simple Roast Turkey

1 12- to 14-pound turkey, preferably fresh, giblets removed; if
    turkey was frozen, thaw completely in refrigerator (this can
    take days)
2 tablespoons kosher salt
1 tablespoon ground black pepper
1 large onion, peeled and quartered
3 stalks celery, each cut crosswise into two or three pieces.

1. A half-hour before cooking, take turkey out of refrigerator. Pat dry with paper towels. Place in large roasting pan and set aside. Place rack on lower third of oven; heat oven to 425 degrees. Higher heat speeds roasting without too much splattering and smoking.

2. Mix salt and pepper together and rub mixture all over skin and inside cavity of turkey. Stuff cavity with onion and celery. If you wish, tie legs together with kitchen twine and tuck wingtips under wing, but this will slow cooking time.

3. Put turkey in oven, uncovered. After a half-hour, remove turkey and place a sheet of foil over breast, crimping edges to side of roasting pan. Place pan back in oven.

4. After another hour, remove turkey from oven, take off foil and discard. Do not baste. Begin checking temperature by inserting a meat thermometer straight down into fleshiest part of thigh, where it meets drumstick. Check a second spot, then remove thermometer.

5. Place bird back in oven, checking periodically until thermometer reads about 165 degrees. Total cooking time should be 1½ to 2½ hours, depending on size of turkey. If bird is larger than 14 pounds, keep foil on longer.

6. Remove pan from oven and cover turkey with fresh foil and then a damp kitchen towel. Let it rest for a half-hour before carving. Turkey will continue to cook and juices will set into meat.

SERVES 6–8

A PLAN THAT LEAVES TIME FOR THE PARADE

Here are tips that will make roasting your turkey faster and easier.

• **PREPARING THE TURKEY** Don't wash it, although this might go against your better judgment. The heat of the oven will kill any surface pathogens, and rinsing only splashes bacteria around the kitchen. Better to take the wrapper off in the sink, put the turkey in the roasting pan and pat it dry with a paper towel.

• **TYING THE LEGS** Using a piece of cotton string to tie the legs makes a prettier bird, but for cooking speed, leave them untied. If you carve the turkey and put it on plates in the kitchen, the way the bird looks won't matter.

• **START AT ROOM TEMPERATURE** Allow the turkey to sit out for at least a half-hour before roasting. This will speed the cooking time.

• **TENTING** About half an hour into the roasting, cover

the breast with a foil tent. This will slow the heat and help keep the breast moist.

• **IF PAN SMOKES** Pour a little water or stock into the bottom of the pan if the juices start to burn.

• **BASTING** Resist the urge; the skin comes out crispy and bronze without it. Opening the oven door lowers the temperature and adds into the roasting time.

• **USE A MEAT THERMOMETER** About an hour and a half into roasting, begin testing the temperature. Insert a meat thermometer into the thigh, perpendicular to the pan, at the point where the drumstick meets the thigh. Test again in the meatiest part of the thigh, horizontal to the pan. Keep checking until you get a couple of readings of 165 degrees.

• **REST THE BIRD** When roasting is done, take the turkey out of the oven and tip it so that juices from the bird drain into the pan. Place the turkey on a platter, cover it completely with foil and place a damp kitchen towel over the foil to help keep in the heat. Let rest for a half hour. During standing time, the internal temperature continues to increase by as much as 10 degrees. Resting allows juices to set in the meat.

• **AFTER SLICING** Pour a small amount of warm stock over the sliced meat to moisten it before serving. This can help rescue dry white meat in particular.

Sometimes, Mother Knows Best

by John Kessler

from *Atlanta Journal-Constitution*

Former Atlanta dining critic, now an *AJC* food columnist, John Kessler has the food writer's equivalent of perfect pitch: time and again he reminds us that the best food is simply the food that tastes best, whatever the reason.

I was an adult before I realized that the dish my mother served company—cocoa van—was, in fact, the French recipe *coq au vin*. True, I had never actually tasted the cocoa in this saucy chicken, but I had assumed the word was figurative, like the "dog" following hot or the (presumed) "corn" preceding "beef hash." We didn't parse food.

My mother always browned the chicken in her big cast-iron skillet on top of sizzling, fat-pooling slices of bacon. Along the way, she factored in onions, garlic, red cooking wine and a heavy lid, under which the chicken gave up any hope of turning to rubber.

The white meat came out firm but not parching or chalky, and the dark meat had lost its gushy pockets of fat during the long braise. Also wonderful: the thin, oily sauce with its flavors of bacon smoke and sweet onion against a winy background. If each serving contained a wiggly piece of skin or boiled bacon, well, that was part of the charm of cocoa van.

The chicken was the centerpiece of an inviolate set entertaining menu. On the side came mushroom rice (Minute Rice with chopped mushrooms) and a congealed salad ring made with syrupy canned blueberries and lemon gelatin, then filled with an entire tub of sour cream.

Maybe it was the Jell-O that made me turn. Maybe my burgeoning Francophilia. But the first time I decided to braise chicken in red wine, I decided to make a "real" coq au vin. This effort meant—first and foremost—switching from slices of smoked Oscar Mayer bacon to lardons, or cubes of salt-cured pork.

The French don't cook with breakfast meats. But making a coq au vin also meant fresh herbs, veal stock and a finished sauce that clings to the meat rather than serves as a wading pool.

The coq au vin I developed was always good—very good—in a restaurant-food kind of way. And, so, I made it less and less over the years.

When I did, the veal stock would be replaced with canned broth, the fresh herbs with dried, the organic chicken with whatever bird Frank Perdue had to sell.

Then I finally stopped dicing pancetta or salt pork for lardons and took out the package of Oscar Mayer.

Bingo.

When I lift the lid and smell the smoke and fried onions, it's 1975, and people are coming over for dinner.

I look at those white-streaked slices of limp bacon and I might as well be looking into my mother's old cast-iron skillet and dreaming of leftover blueberry mold for a week.

Chicken Braised in Red Wine, aka Cocoa Van

HANDS ON: 30 MINUTES; TOTAL TIME: ABOUT 1 ½ HOURS

So this isn't exactly my mother's '70s party-dish recipe intact. I use good, cheap drinking wine instead of "cooking wine," cut down on the amount of sauce and create an extra step in re-crisping the chicken skin and bacon under the broiler. Oh, and I add carrots because I see no reason to spend an hour braising meat and not add carrots.

1 whole chicken, cut up
Salt and pepper
¼ cup all-purpose flour for dredging
4 slices bacon

1 tablespoon olive oil

1 medium onion, halved and thinly sliced

3 cloves garlic, minced

3 carrots, peeled and cut in thick rounds

1 tablespoon tomato paste

2 cups drinkable red wine

1 sprig fresh thyme or ½ teaspoon dried

1 cup canned chicken or beef broth (or water), as needed

If the chicken breasts are large, cut them in half through the bone with a large, sharp knife. Season the chicken and dredge it in flour; shake off excess.

Fry the bacon in a large cast-iron or other heavy skillet until crisp; set aside and do not drain pan. Add the oil to the pan and fry the chicken pieces over a medium-high flame until brown on all sides; set aside.

Add the onion, garlic and carrots to the pan and fry until onions wilt and carrots start to brown. Add the tomato paste and fry until it starts to brown and stick to the pan. Add the wine and the thyme and stir with a wooden spoon, loosening browned bits into the sauce. When the wine has reduced by half, put the chicken and bacon in the pan. Add enough broth or water until the liquid rises halfway up the side of the largest piece of chicken. Cover with a tight-fitting lid and braise over a medium-low flame for 45 minutes, turning chicken once in the sauce.

When ready to serve, arrange the chicken and vegetables in an oven-safe dish or casserole with the bacon slices across the top. Drain the sauce to a large measuring cup and let sit until the fat rises to the top. Remove fat and pour sauce over chicken. Broil 6 inches from element until the chicken skin and bacon re-crisp, about 5 minutes. If you spoon the sauce over the chicken a couple of times as it broils, you'll make a nice glaze on the meat. Serve with pasta or rice mixed with mushrooms. Blueberry mold optional.

4–6 SERVINGS

It Takes a Tough Man to Make Tender Tofu

by Henry Alford
from *Food & Wine*

I think of Henry Alford as a "food humorist": he not only writes funny, he has an unerring eye for life's absurdities. We've all had the experience of eating something delicious in a restaurant and longing to recreate it at home—but when Alford sets about it....

Before I became so enamored of fresh tofu that I started making my own, I thought of this benighted food as a consolation prize for vegetarians. But then I ate at New York City's En Japanese Brasserie, where the cooks make fresh tofu five times a night at regularly scheduled and advertised times—it's like Shamu the killer whale, without all the splashing.

Seated at a table near the edge of the reflecting pool in the middle of En's chic and cavernous dining room, I was presented with an elegant, black lacquered box of just-made tofu. I used a wooden ladle to carefully scoop some of the tofu into a beautiful jade-colored bowl, then poured a generous amount of *wari-joyu,* the restaurant's slightly sweet mix of soy sauce and fish broth, over it. I took a bite, and bean curd as I heretofore had known it ceased to exist. The combination of the delicate flanlike texture and the slightly beany, almost creamy flavor was as consoling as custard. It was like being handed a sweater in a snowstorm. Suddenly, five times a night didn't seem nearly enough.

I'm not alone in my enthusiasm. Tofu, as they say in the fashion industry, is having a moment. If sushi is now ubiquitous in America, the next distinguishing characteristic of a high-end Asian restaurant may be its fresh tofu. What's particularly surprising about the new trendiness of a food first made by the Chinese more than 2,000 years ago is the glamour quotient. The $15-a-serving tofu at New York City's Megu is made by the revered Japanese artisan Yoshimasa Kawashima, who sends shipments encased in lovely bamboo baskets twice a week. The new Beverly Hills outpost of Umenohana, a Japanese chain of tofu restaurants, serves its *yuba*—made from the skin of warm soy milk—in a martini glass, topped with caviar.

Yet it was not glamour, but shape, that was my first consideration when I started making tofu. While some people use a colander lined with cheesecloth, thus yielding tofu that is domed, I avow that many of life's greatest pleasures come to us in the form of rectangular slabs—chocolate, cream cheese, packs of cigarettes. And so I turned to the Internet in search of a "settling box," a small wooden contraption with a removable bottom and holes for drainage. I found a kit complete with ten packets of *nigari* (the seawater extract that is used as a thickener) for $48.95 from an Asheville, North Carolina, company called Natural Lifestyle.

Making tofu, I soon discovered, is not wildly dissimilar to making cheese. Using a recipe that came with my kit, I first soaked some dried soybeans overnight in water, then pureed them in a blender. I poured the batterlike puree into boiling water, cooked it for about 10 minutes and then strained it through a cotton cloth. Next, I thickened the resulting soy milk by adding *nigari,* which quickly caused the curds to separate from the whey. I ladled the curds into the cloth-lined box and weighted its moveable top to press the water out. The tofu firmed up in about 15 minutes.

What can be said of either godliness or mah-jongg can also be said of making tofu: It takes a minute to learn, a lifetime to master. While I found it fairly easy to produce something with the consistency of Cream of Wheat or ricotta cheese, it was very difficult to produce something flanlike—and, indeed, my first three efforts were mostly scrambled egg–like. But I soldiered on. My efforts suggested that, when it comes to texture, there are two crucial factors in the tofu-making process. Tofu gets firmer depending on how vigorously you stir in the *nigari* and how long and heavily you weight the lid.

A friend called me while I was consuming an early batch of too-soft tofu, and she gasped in amazement: "Artisanal tofu?!" She then opined that I should have a nickname redolent of honor and craftsmanship. I told her, "You may call me Small Batch."

At last I created tofu with a firmness I was pleased with. And yet, and yet . . . something seemed to be missing. Eager for inspiration, I headed back over to En. When I entered the restaurant and all the employees yelled hello at me in unison, it was the proud artisan within me who thought that surely this greeting was directed at Small Batch. I told my waiter, "I'm learning how to make tofu." His eyes widening slightly, he said, "Take notes." Some five minutes later, as I eagerly spooned tofu from my jade-colored bowl, I realized that, while my homemade tofu got good marks for taste and texture, it was a low-scorer in the third and possibly most important category. Heeding my waiter's directive to take notes, I took a pen out of my jacket pocket and wrote down one word on the back of an envelope. The word was *presentation*.

Back at home I rummaged through my cabinets and unearthed my best-looking piece of pottery—a brightly painted majolica saucer I'd bought in Italy: Yes, yes. I whipped up a batch of tofu and tried it out in this new vessel: Presentation City. Flush with success, I produced an extra-firm batch the next day, and steamed it and served it with sautéed shrimp in black bean sauce using a recipe from cookbook author Corinne Trang (see below).

And now, I knew, it was time to raise the tofu stakes: Not only would I serve some of it to someone else, but I would serve it to someone else who was in a somewhat remote location. And so I found myself on the New York City subway, making the 45-minute-long trek to my boyfriend Greg's apartment in Brooklyn. Seated, I carefully held in front of me a covered Tupperware bowl containing a fresh slab submerged in water. Would the delicate foodstuff withstand the rigors of mass transportation? I tried to anticipate the train's lurchings by gently bouncing my hands, a human bedspring. When an eight-year-old boy and his mother seated to my right started staring at the bowl—I think they were hoping to see goldfish—I sheepishly told the mother, "It's tofu. I make my own tofu." Slightly confused, she asked, "To eat on the subway?" Conscious that others were listening, I nervously mumbled, "No, it's . . . it's indoor tofu."

Once, uh, indoors, I uncovered the lid. Product intact! Product glistening with goodness! Removing my majolica dish and supplies from my bag, I prepared an appetizer: tofu spooned onto rice crackers, drizzled with soy sauce and topped with slivers of pickled ginger. I then placed the snacks on the all-important dish.

When my efforts were pronounced "Delicious," I smiled. Small Batch is forever humbled.

The Blowtorch Gourmet

by Chris Johns
from *enRoute*

Air Canada's inflight magazine, *enRoute*, features some excellent food writing. One of my favorites from this year is this droll piece by contributing editor Chris Johns.

I have dismantled and reassembled an entire pig's head, brined tongues for a week and fermented anchovies in a misguided attempt at making fish sauce from scratch. Child's play by today's culinary standards. Now that everyone's a gourmet, exciting jaded palates doesn't come easy. So, in a fit of hubris, I decided to take it one step further: cook an entire seven-course dinner party for twelve with a blowtorch and serve it in the penthouse at the Sutton Place Hotel, no less. Those sharp blue flames are all business.

Alas, the blowtorch rarely receives the kind of respect it deserves. Food stylists will use it to melt butter on a stack of pancakes, replicate grill marks on a steak, or crisp up a turkey. Even in most professional kitchens, the blowtorch gets stuck primping desserts like crème brulée and meringue. Only at select restaurants, like Vancouver's Shiru Bay Chopstick Café, is the torch finally getting a meaty role in dishes like their deliciously theatrical Hiaburi Shime Saba, in which the exterior of a marinated mackerel is torch-seared tableside. And chef Erin Fitzpatrick at Bar Carrera, in New York, uses the blowtorch to caramelize the sticky sugar on slices of cured pork belly.

While kitchen stores stock artfully designed little culinary torches, my soireé would require something more substantial. At my local hardware store I found a Benchmark propane torch with adjustable flame and trigger start. Above the massive Danger signs, the label promoted the torch as being suitable for soldering, heating, and lighting—by which I believe they mean igniting a barbeque, rather than creating ambiance.

My first experiment involved crisping up the skin on some leftover chicken, a task to which my new torch applied itself beautifully. Feeling confident, I tackled a dish by pioneering chef Ferran Adrià—egg yolk encased in a caramel shell—evidently created just to show off. Eight eggs and 75 minutes later, I managed to make a single perfect specimen. So the dish was replaced with another Spanish recipe: I sprinkled a bit of finely chopped chorizo onto a fresh oyster, added a splash of sherry vinegar and hit it with the blowtorch just long enough to warm the sausage, lightly cook the oyster, and coddle my ego.

Next up: house-made Jiffy Pop. I stood there waving the torch under my homespun foil bag, listening for any sign of life while trying to keep my eyebrows on my face. Eventually I thought I heard a pop and, in my excitement, let the tongs slip, sending hot, oily kernels across my kitchen.

Time to bring in some professional help. My first call was to chef Karen Barnaby. "I'm thinking caramelized endive," she said. "Cut the endive in half and dip it in sugar, then use the blowtorch to caramelize it." Check—a classic technique reinvented. Ditto for the lightly torched Atlantic salmon with caramelized apple taco offered up by Sam Mathison, chef at the Sutton Place Hotel Toronto. Pat Riley of Perigee Restaurant in Toronto suggested quickly torched mustard seeds paired with vodka-marinated watermelon, drizzled with balsamic vinegar. Double check; the heat would "pop" the mustard's flavor. Bruce Riezenman, personal chef to the Gallo wine family in California, envisioned some kind of sculptural mechanism from which food could be suspended and blowtorched—he is from California, after all. Pass (though I did serve his s'mores for dessert).

Heston Blumenthal, Brit chef of the three-Michelin-starred restaurant The Fat Duck and the man responsible for snail porridge, favors a blowtorch for searing meat in order to achieve the so-called Maillard reaction. When subjected to high temperatures, carbohydrate molecules and amino acids undergo a chemical change that results in a brown colouring and full, intense flavor. Hence the classic Japanese dish beef tataki. I marinated the raw beef, briefly seared it with the blowtorch, wrapped it back up and nearly froze it so it could be sliced paper-thin for the party.

Blowtorches, I also discovered, make ideal portable barbecues— great for torching the skins off peppers. I blackened some jalapeños with the torch, peeled them, stuffed them with cream cheese and then wrapped them in pancetta that I crisped up with the blue flame.

On the night of the party, do-it-yourself "Toolgirl" columnist Mag Ruffman arrived packing her own blowtorch, which she kindly used to light the candles before we sat down to eat (apparently, they *can* be used for creating ambiance). We started with the stuffed peppers, which were a hit. "I'm serving these at my next catering gig," declared my assistant, Heather Baker of The Cookworks school. The shiny caramel-coated endive trumped what usually passes for "salad," while the salmon got one last pass of the torch for a lustrous glaze. The vodka-marinated watermelon intermezzo was refreshing with added interest from the popped mustard seeds. But the big triumph was the tataki. The blowtorch had created a delicious crust on the exterior of the beef while leaving the centre deliciously raw. "What restaurant serves a dish this good?" asked entrepreneur Marcus Doyle.

The s'mores turned out to be the trickiest things to get right— one kiss from that wicked blue flame and the marshmallows went up like Roman candles. Lynn Crawford of *Restaurant Makeover* fame came to the rescue by suggesting we put a piece of tinfoil overtop to protect them. Following her lead, the guests got into the spirit and blowtorched their own. I had unknowingly engineered the first yuppie campfire.

The danger with cooking an entire dinner party with a blowtorch is not so much the possibility of self-immolation, nor is it the very real chance that dishes will be turned into coal. No, the biggest risk with a concept like this is that the chef is just a novelty act. The other problem, of course, is that you are now expected to do something even more impressive: volcano fondue, perhaps, or underwater sushi?

Anyway, that's for another day. Tonight, I'm ordering in.

WE'RE NOT SAYING DON'T TRY THIS AT HOME, BUT enROUTE IS NOT RESPONSIBLE FOR ANY BLOWTORCH INEPTITUDE. AND NEEDLESS TO SAY, YOU CAN NOT BRING A BLOWTORCH ON AN AIRPLANE WITH YOU.

Blistered Jalapeños

12 large, fresh jalapeños
½ bunch cilantro
1 pkg cream cheese
12 slices pancetta

1. Split jalapeños and remove the seeds and the white ribs (gloves are recommended). Line them skin side up on a baking sheet and, holding the blowtorch 3 to 5 inches away, cook until the skins blacken and bubble. Transfer to a bowl and cover with plastic wrap. Let them sit until cool or refrigerate overnight.

2. Chop a handful of cilantro and mix it into the cream cheese.

3. Peel the charred skin off the cooled Jalapeños and match up the halves as closely as possible. Fill both halves with the cream cheese mixture.

4. Wrap a thin slice of pancetta around each reassembled jalapeno and torch again for as long as feels good.

An Unexpected Kitchen

by Nikki Silva and Davia Nelson

from *Hidden Kitchens*

On their NPR radio series, the Kitchen Sisters explore some offbeat corners of the cooking world, with journalistic curiosity for the many paradigms that define cooking in this country.

Testing, testing, one-two-three," says Jeffry Newton into the microphone as we adjust the recording levels and ask him our standard warmup question. "What did I have for breakfast? I didn't have breakfast," he answers. "I don't have a kitchen."

Dressed in dark jeans and a warm hooded jacket, Jeffry shifts his weight from one leg to the other. He's got arthritis in both knees. All the homeless in Chicago have arthritis, he tells us. It comes from living on the cold pavement.

"The George Foreman Grill, yeah," he says. "That's the grill I had for a while under Wacker Drive. Me and a fellow named Smokey."

Jeffry Newton is fifty-seven years old. Until recently, he lived in a refrigerator box, part of a makeshift cardboard community tucked in around trash cans and restaurant loading docks hidden under Chicago's Wacker Drive. "You know, where the expressway goes through downtown, there's about thirty or forty refrigerator boxes down there. You take your box, mark it up, and put in blankets and pillows. That's going to be your home."

During the Great Depression, this lower stretch of Wacker, nicknamed the Catacombs, was home to thousands who sought out its rain-sheltered corners. "You don't get as much snow down there as on top," Jeffry says, "except that wind blowing in from the lake. But the refrigerator box is pretty sturdy. Once you close and lock it up and get in there and cover up, you're all right."

"Me and Smokey found the George Foreman Grill at the shelter," Jeffry remembers. Someone had donated it, broken, without a plug, so the two guys jury-rigged it. "Then you just get you a long extension cord and hook up. There's a lot of electrical plugs on the poles down there. You'd come home in the evening, and you'd fire up your Foreman. Some of us had jobs. Some of us had food stamp Link cards. You could put anything in that thing: bologna, hamburgers, grilled cheese sandwiches. We used to take an iron and do that too, press down, hot on the bread and cheese. You'd be inventive like that."

THE BOTTOMS, HOUSTON

George Foreman, two-time heavyweight champion of the world, Olympic gold medalist, former street preacher, and King of the Grills, is in a radio studio in Houston, Texas. His son, George—they call him "Three"—is with him. Each of George Foreman's five sons is named George. Foreman never knew who his father was, and he wants there to he no mystery about who theirs is. As "Three" settles things in the studio, we tell George what we've been hearing about his grill. The story hits a nerve.

"Whoa ... what a story! I've never considered it at all," he says, "how homeless people and low-income people, wanting to cook but not being able to, how that little grill afforded them a kitchen. I'm just happy that it's helped so many people. It helped me, of course.

"Growing up in Houston, my whole life was spent trying to get enough to eat. Having seven kids, and my mother raising all of us by herself, there just was never enough food for me. I always dreamed not about a car, not about a beautiful home, but about having enough to eat."

The Bottoms, that's what they called the Fifth Ward area of Houston, where George Foreman grew up, poorer than poor. Sometimes George's mother would come home with a cheeseburger and try to divide it among her seven kids. "I remember the taste of the mustard. It was the most supreme thing in our family when she'd come home with a burger."

During lunchtime at Atherton Elementary School, you could buy greens, vegetables, and meat for twenty-six cents. But even twenty-six cents was beyond George's wildest dreams. "I didn't even know what that looked like. I'd sit at the table, and it was so embarrassing. So what I would do is I'd get a greasy bag, blow it up on the way to school to make it look like there was a sandwich in it. Then I would get to my classroom and say, 'Boy, I ate my lunch,' so that they wouldn't look at me, and I wouldn't be embarrassed during the lunch hour. I learned to disguise my not having any food."

During the summer days, it was worse. Mothers would call their kids in for lunch and tell George to go on home to eat. "These people knew I had no food at home. I'd hide and peek through the window at the kids eating, and the parents would peel the crust off the bread, and I would just sit there hoping that they would throw it out the window for me."

George was always big and tough for his age, and when the school kept him back more than once, it made it harder and harder for him to fit in. "I think if you ever go to school hungry, it puts a chip on your shoulder," he tells us. "To go to school without breakfast, then without a lunch, it makes for a bad boy.

"I tried to conceal my lack of things by fighting all the time. Pretty soon I became an expert at fighting. But I never did get good at schoolwork."

George became a dropout and a mugger. "I actually mugged people. Took their money and ran away with it. I think hunger makes you angry.

"One night after mugging a guy, the police chased me. I crawled under a house to hide. I thought they were going to send out the hound dogs to find me. I covered myself with sewage from a busted pipe so the dogs wouldn't sniff me. And as I was laying there, a criminal hiding from dogs, I heard in my head what my cousin Rita had told me, 'George Foreman, you're not going to be anything. No one from this family has ever become anything."

THE TENDERLOIN, SAN FRANCISCO

Poverty and danger lived side by side in the Bottoms, where George Foreman grew up, and they are neighbors to this day in San Francisco's Tenderloin district, a borderline neighborhood of tourist hotels, soup kitchens, street people, junkies, and the homeless. Legend has it that the area got its name because the police who worked that beat in the 1920s got paid overtime in beef tenderloin for the risk they took patrolling some of the toughest streets of the city. Glide Memorial Church sits in the middle of all this, trying to deal.

We've come to talk to Pat Sherman, program coordinator for Glide's Walk-In services. When we arrive, Pat is leaning over her printer, ear pressed against it, listening to it lurch and gasp. It's on its last legs, and Pat is trying to coax one more job out of it before it gives up the ghost. The Walk-In program is a shoestring outfit—no fat, no margin. The sign outside Pat's office announces, "World Famous Glide Fried Chicken," today's offering for the lunch program that will serve some eight hundred free meals to the addicted, the hungry, and the homeless.

Not much fazes Pat, a calm, solid woman, with red dreads and dimples. Not the man darting in and out of the office as if he were being chased by something only he can see, not the phone that never stops ringing, not the steady stream of people she sees every day who need something to eat, somewhere to sleep, somewhere to work. She knows who they are because she used to be one of them.

"When I was in an SRO," says Pat, "I couldn't cook in my room. I mean, legally I couldn't. A lot of places don't have kitchens. So you have a Crock-Pot disguised as a plant holder, and you have a fry skillet that you know you're not supposed to have hidden in the closet. A toaster oven tucked under the bed. I'd get me a big bowl, put me some ice in it, and—voilà—that became my refrigerator."

SRO—single-room occupancy, no kitchen, some government-assisted, some one step away from a shelter. It is a life defined by eating out every day, which costs too much, or standing in food lines, where fights break out and where sometimes the food runs out altogether before you reach the head of the line. "Hunger pervades your whole life," says Pat, "and it's surprising what people come up with to fight it.

"I did the Crock-Pot thing for a while. I made it look like a flowerpot. I would take my flowerpot out, put my rice and beans in, go to work, come home, and have dinner. You need to use dry beans, because you can soak them and it doesn't look like anything. The water's dark, so if someone comes in to check out the apartment, they don't want to mess with that.

"The George Foreman Grill, that's the newest thing," says Pat when we ask her about the grill. "Doesn't set off the smoke detectors.

And since they come in colors, it just looks like you're getting real fancy in your room and decorating. It works well for people who have to live like this, because it doesn't take up much space. I've seen where people put a covering or cloth over it to disguise it so it looks like you have a nice tabletop in your room. It's your own kitchen. You make a kitchen for yourself so that you can survive."

TRAILBLAZING

Jeffry made a kitchen for himself on the street before he even got close to having a room. "Hey, I'm a great cook. Something I learned from my grandmother," Jeffry tells us. "I can cook and I can bake, but I just haven't had a kitchen. I've been homeless most all my life."

When Jeffry was a boy, his parents left him with his grandmother in Colorado. For most of his teenage years, he was in and out of reformatories and boys' homes. By age seventeen he was in prison. When he got out, at age twenty-one, he headed to Chicago, "land of opportunity," selling magazines on the road along the way. Just out of prison, newly arrived in Chicago, Jeffry got married. When that didn't work out, he turned to drugs and found himself scrounging on the streets.

"When you're homeless and living on the streets, you've got to look around. You've got to keep your eyes open in order to survive. It's called trailblazing. You've got to blaze the trail, you know." Trailblazing has taught Jeffry where he can get a free cup of coffee. He knows who will give him a doughnut and who won't and where they're giving free haircuts in the parks. On Sundays he knows which churches are serving and what the Salvation Army is offering for supper.

The winter pavement is blue cold in Chicago. Some nights Jeffry would slip into Cook County Hospital. "You go in coughing, you know, and they give you one of those little plastic bracelets. And when they call your name, you don't answer. And you got a hand around your wrist, so now you can sit there half the night and go to sleep or look for a hospital microwave to cook your Cup o' Noodles in."

Or your popcorn. Jeffry would go into office buildings downtown, sometimes looking for a job, sometimes not. "They'd say, 'Have a cup of coffee,' and I'd see there was a microwave in the lunchroom. I would never steal or anything like that. Mostly I just wanted a place to pop my popcorn. Sometimes I survived for days on popcorn."

THREE MEALS A DAY

In 1965, at age sixteen, George Foreman was headed for a life of crime, when he happened to be in the right place at the right time, watching TV. One of his heroes appeared in a commercial for President Lyndon Johnson's Job Corps program, part of the country's war on poverty.

"I heard about the Job Corps," remembers Foreman. "The great football player Jim Brown did a commercial. He said, 'If you're looking for a second chance to get an education, join the Job Corps!'" George Foreman decided to take him up on it—signed up and shipped out to Grants Pass, Oregon.

"It was the first time I'd been treated right. These people I had never met, they didn't look anything like me. I couldn't believe it. I had three meals a day for the first time in my life. It took me about two months before I realized, 'Hey, they're gonna have breakfast every day.' It changed my whole life. I started reading books, started doing my assignments."

In the Job Corps, George met an older boy named Richard Kibble, from Tacoma, Washington. "Sort of a hippie fellow. He listened to Bob Dylan. When I boasted about how I was going to fight somebody, he was not impressed. He said to listen to the music, 'Just listen to the words.' He explained every song. Bob Dylan, oh boy, I had never heard anyone sing songs that actually had meaning. I'd sit on the side of his bed and listen: 'They'll stone you when you're at the breakfast table, they'll stone you when you are young and able . . . But I would not feel so all alone, everybody must get stoned . . .' And he explained that song. In other words, everything that I was doing was physical and brutal and, to him, out of style. And I started to admire something about him."

But fighting was still in George's blood. One day the boys were all sitting in the dayroom, listening to the radio broadcast of the championship fight between Cassius Clay and Floyd Patterson, when one of them challenged Foreman. "If you think you're so tough, why don't you become a boxer?"

"I really didn't want to be a boxer," George remembers, "but I took that challenge that day in the dayroom, and here we are today."

IT WASN'T LEGAL AT ALL

When the city of Chicago put up fences under Wacker Drive and evicted the residents of the refrigerator city, Jeffry managed to get a room at the YMCA.

"For a while there, I was selling plates of food to the other homeless people. At the YMCA I had a microwave and a little stove—whatcha call it? You know, you hook it up, and it just warms up—a hot plate, there you go! A hot plate. I started cooking for everybody even though we weren't supposed to be cooking. I could take commodity food and do wonders with it—canned chicken, canned pork. Once you add some garlic and some bell pepper and some onion and tomatoes and get it all stirred up, you would be surprised with what you got."

Every Sunday Jeffry was cooking—fried chicken, mashed potatoes, string beans. "I had my door wide open. I'd turn the music on. They'd know once they hear the music on, Jeff's cooking. It wasn't legal at all."

But shelters have limits to how long a homeless man can stay, and low-income housing has waiting lists, so Jeffry's kitchen comes and goes with opportunity. At the shelter, there's no privacy, no place to store anything. Commodity canned food and boxes of Hamburger Helper sit stacked like small shrines by the beds. His day jobs vary. Sometimes he works for the Chicago Coalition for the Homeless, a job he got after sitting in their lobby every day for five years until they finally made him a member of their speakers' bureau. On occasion he also gets day work on setups and breakdowns at the Convention Center when a big convention hits town. Bur for the most part, he is unemployed.

On the rooftop of the Chicago Coalition building for the homeless, Jeffry has created a garden—eggplant, squash, and a few turnip greens and tomatoes. "I grow cherry tomatoes, peach tomatoes, purple tomatoes, green tomatoes. I got these tubs upstairs that are all filled with dirt and such, and every day I'm out watering. That's my little joy. I never knew I was a farmer, you know. I just like doing it. It eases my mind. Takes my mind away from the cares."

KING OF THE GRILL

"When I left boxing," remembers George Foreman, "I realized I didn't have any friends. People weren't pouring into my home anymore, but I noticed that if I barbecued something, they would come over. Even the guys, we'd go fishing, I wanted them to stay and come back so much, I would always clean the fish, do all the cooking. I found that more satisfying than even winning boxing matches, when people would lick their fingers and say my food was good.

"When I made a comeback in 1987, I was over 315 pounds and everybody made a joke of it. 'How can George Foreman, if he wants to be the prodigal son of boxing, do it when he's looking like the fatted calf?' And I'd gotten advertising sponsorships from all these companies— McDonald's, Doritos, Oscar Mayer weiners. A fellow I knew asked, 'Why don't you get your own product to promote?' And he told me about this little grill sitting up there, and no one wanted it. So I thought I'd just take a few grills and never see any revenues. You know, get the grills in my training camps because it really helped me with dieting. If I tell you I knew it was coming, I'd be lying. I had no idea this grill would be successful. There's over sixty million sold. It's the most successful electrical appliance in the history of England."

The Grill lets Americans grill indoors on a rainy day or in a college dorm, and it gives the homeless a way to have a hot bologna and cheese. It gave George and his brother Roy the means to open the George Foreman Youth Center. Foreman has never forgotten the central lesson of the Job Corps: All that most kids need is a chance. He still imagines what his life might have become, and so he holds out the same chance he got to kids who are hungry, and angry.

"I have these summer camps, put athletic equipment there, and these kids they can have three meals a day!" says George. "I've learned that any kid, any kid, if you give him a second or third chance, can make it. Never give up on anyone. Doesn't matter if you spend years in prison, or whatever. You never lose your citizenship as a human being because you're in trouble.

"I never forget peeping through that lady's window when she was serving lunch to her kids after she told me to go home. We've got to be there for those kids, no matter what. I'm pushed, I'm compelled, I'm motivated because of that. If there's a food bank, all they gotta do is ask George Foreman. If I can find a dime, I'm going to make sure you get it. I try to keep those little visions alive for myself. Feed them."

∞

Grilled Salmon or "Sir Loin"

When we asked George Foreman for his favorite recipe, the former heavyweight champion of the world said, "Oh, just give me a grill and plate. And salmon steak. That's my favorite. I can have it for breakfast, lunch, and there's nothing like a salmon dinner. When I do go for meat, there's nothing like 'Sir Loin' himself.

"Then you get out your garlic. I think that's the most exotic thing that you can have, is some garlic. You can't mess up; the room will smell nice, and you can smell it out the window. Then you get some lemon pepper, a wonderful invention.

"I cook both salmon and sirloin in the same fashion. Not too many exotic spices. I make a marinade with garlic, lemon pepper, black pepper, and balsamic vinegar. I use that with a little oil. I marinate the salmon or meat in the refrigerator, but not too long.

"Take that salmon steak or sirloin and put it on the grill so that the smell is there. Everybody loves smells. If you want to add other spices or ingredients, I just say go ahead. When you got ten kids like I do—five boys and five daughters—you can't go too far to the left or to the right with spices."

***

"Hidden Beans and Rice"

When Pat Sherman lived in an SRO with no kitchen and no cooking allowed, she came up with some ingenious clandestine Crock-Pot solutions.

"Beans and rice would probably be the best hidden kitchen recipe, because you can put your beans on in the morning, go to school or to work, and come home to a hot meal without anyone knowing. You soak 'em overnight and put them in your Crock-Pot in the morning before you leave (my personal favorite is pinto beans). Midday, you come back, throw your rice and spices in. (Now they've got these great 99 Cents stores. You can get a sixteen-ounce container of chile peppers, chili powder, onion powder and just spice it up!) Put your onions and your bell peppers in, if you want. Turn your cooker down—you start it off on high, then you turn it down. And then you come back—say, four or five-ish—and you have your beans and rice all ready for you. You don't have to do anything else but grab a bowl."

The Quest

by Jane Kramer

from *The New Yorker*

> Jane Kramer may be best known for her in-depth *New Yorker* reports on European politics, but she's also a passionate home cook—and like all passionate cooks, she has a love-hate relationship with her favorite cookbooks.

I read cookbooks. I am addicted to them. I keep a pile on the floor of my study in New York, knowing that if I manage to write a couple of decent pages I can treat myself to a $4.50 Chinese lunch special in the company of Richard Olney or Jasper White or Ruth Rogers and Rose Gray, thinking of all the succulent things I would cook for dinner if I didn't have to go back to work in the afternoon. I keep another pile on my bedside table, knowing that if I wake in the middle of the night I can pick one up and drift off into a soothing dream of Joël Robuchon's mashed potatoes or Claudia Roden's pumpkin dumplings or Marcella Hazan's red-and-green polenta torta, with a layer of onions, pine nuts, and ground pork between the spinach and the tomato. In my kitchen dreams, there are no crises. My books preclude them. The leg of lamb is never withering in the oven, waiting for a late guest. The chicken pot pie never collapses under the tug of its own crust. And I have sous-chefs—I think of them as husbands—standing quietly behind me, ready to shuck the oysters, stir the corn-meal, pit the olives, pound the pesto, grind the achiote, whisk the sabayon, or, at a nod, fly to my side, like angels, bearing sieves and spoons and spatulas, Thai fish pastes and fresh banana leaves and rare Indonesian spices and thick French pots so well calibrated that the butter browns without turning into cinders. My own husband, who is an anthropologist, finds my passion for cookbooks peculiar, something on the order of my addiction to thrillers and crossword puzzles. When we were first married, he would leave a copy of the "Tractatus" on my pillow, hoping that Wittgenstein would cure me. But Wittgenstein, of course, kept me up worrying about reality. My cookbooks are more like the lipsticks I used to buy as a tenth grader in a Quaker school where not even hair ribbons or colored shoelaces were permitted. They promise to transform me.

Some fifteen hundred cookbooks are published in America each year, and Americans buy them by the millions—no one knows exactly how many. Barbara Haber, who was the curator of the Schlesinger Library on the History of Women in America, at Harvard, for thirty years—and, in the process, invented the history of women and food—once told me that the sales figures for cookbooks are one of the real mysteries of the publishing business, perhaps because small presses with a cookbook or two in their catalogues don't always report those figures separately. But one thing seems clear: the only people who can touch us, when it comes to writing and buying cookbooks, are the British, and they are only just beginning to catch up. Until a few years ago, not even the French were much interested in cookbooks. The great professional chefs inherited the old French classics, but a Parisian bride, say, could expect to find one good copy of Escoffier, from a godmother or an aunt, among the wedding presents (brides in the South got "La Cuisinière Provençale," known in France as "that yellow book" because of its shiny yellow cover). And, for her kitchen, that amounted to the canon. Italians rarely admitted to buying cookbooks or, for that matter, to consulting the classics that were their—and their mothers' and grandmothers'—wedding presents. Those books had names like "Il Talismano della Felicità," or "La Scienza in Cucina e l'Arte di Mangiar Bene," which was written in the 1890s, and includes, in its section on *dolci,* a recipe for a Roman pudding said to be as "seignorial" in its pleasures as the puddings from Turin or Florence. (I think of those books as Italian versions of the Christian-housewife marriage manuals that used to advise women to greet their husband at the door at night wearing a black lace teddy and carrying a shaker of cold Martinis.)

But Americans have been buying cookbooks since the eighteenth century, and by now it seems as if half the people who ever read one eventually write their own. There are more new cookbooks in my local Barnes & Noble than there are new biographies or novels. There are seventeen thousand cookbooks listed on Amazon.com; sixteen thousand cookbooks in Barbara Haber's archives; and at least ten thousand in the splendid collection at the New York Academy of Medicine. More to the point, there are twelve thousand titles (not counting the used books) in stock right now at my favorite bookstore—the small, scholarly warren on the upper reaches of Lexington Avenue called Kitchen Arts & Letters. It has to be said that Kitchen Arts's cookbooks go back to a facsimile of a Mesopotamian cookbook in cuneiform on clay, and that Nach Waxman, who owns the store, is more likely to be reading up on the sixteenth-century Hindu shastra called the "Supa Shastra," which "treats of the arts of cookery and the properties of food," than settling into an armchair with the new Batali. In fact, his perennial best-seller isn't even a cookbook; it is a book called "On Food and Cooking," by Harold McGee, which involves a lot of biology and chemistry, and not a single recipe. Every man I know who cooks seriously owns McGee, but I am less interested in how things work than in how they taste and whether they taste perfect. And never mind the theories that would have me the victim of some late-capitalist delusion that it's possible—indeed, my American birthright—to put a purchase on perfection, or even of some embarrassing religion of self-improvement. It is *my* theory that American women started reading cookbooks because they had left their mothers behind in Europe and never "received" the wisdom that is said to be passed spontaneously from generation to generation, like the gift of prophecy, in the family kitchen. My mother could not cook. She had no interest in cooking, making her about as helpful for my culinary purposes as a mother I would have had to cross the Atlantic to ask, say, if it was all right to substitute Port for Madeira in the sauce for ham on a bed of spinach. Nor could my grandmother cook. I set up housekeeping without benefit of one of those frayed looseleaf notebooks or little black file boxes, filled with cards, that grandmothers supposedly gave to mothers and mothers copied for their daughters. What's more, I had married a graduate student—which is to say that we had no money for the Cordon Bleu. I learned to cook from cookbooks.

I bought my first cookbook on fieldwork in Morocco, mainly because I needed a recipe for *ras el hanout,* the spice mixture I use in couscous, that wasn't like my friends recipes—laced with hashish. (This was the late sixties.) My next cookbooks were the two volumes of *Mastering the Art of French Cooking,* written by Julia Child, Simone Beck, and (for the first volume) Louisette Bertholle, but quickly known to the world of would-be sixties and seventies cooks as "Julia." And the first important dinner I made from them was beef Wellington. This took me two and a half days, owing, among other things, to the fact that my kitchen was so small then that I had to scrub the hall floor in order to roll out the dough for the *pain brioché* after each rising. (There were two.) I made the beef Wellington for my husband in an effort to dazzle, or perhaps to convince him that, despite all evidence to the contrary, I was a doting, domestic sort of person, a woman who squeezed oranges in the morning and wrote discreetly in the afternoon while the foie gras softened and the dough rose. (About twenty years later, he said, "I was just wondering, why don't we have beef Wellington anymore?")

It wasn't long before I persuaded my mother that I could not survive without the "Larousse Gastronomique" for Christmas, and talked my Aunt Beatrice—who was just learning to cook herself and fed us chicken with rosemary and crème fraîche every Sunday—into handing over her new *Gourmet* cookbooks, two massive volumes in grainy brown bindings that turned out to be as grave and useless as a Britannica yearbook. I don't remember ever opening the "Larousse," but I did make a sweet-potato-and-walnut casserole from one of those old *Gourmets,* and never consulted them again. My addiction to cookbooks properly began a few years later, when I made a pilgrimage to Vienne to eat at Fernand Point's restaurant, La Pyramide. Point was the greatest French chef of his generation, and his widow had kept the restaurant open in tribute to what he had always referred to, modestly, as *"ma gastronomie?"* He had written one cookbook, and that, of course, became the title. The book, which I bought that night, was short, gracious, and taught me two extremely important things about cooking. The first was how much I didn't know—nap your lobster with a *sauce à l'américaine,* it said, but what was a *sauce à l'américaine,* and how did you make it, and was it really American? (Or was it Breton?) The second was not to be frightened of what I didn't know, because if making a *sauce à l'américaine* was so simple that, from the point of view of Fernand Point, it didn't even merit a recipe, then surely I could make one. Not exactly. It took me seven years and, of course, a cookbook. The book was *The Saucier's Apprentice,* the author was Raymond Sokolov, and the recipes were so satisfyingly complex that even Simone Beck, a notorious French snob when it came to Americans cooking, had been forced to admit, "This would be a useful book even in France." I made the sauce in two days of hard labor, preceded by a day of collecting veal and chicken bones from half a dozen butchers and calling neighbors who might be willing to drop by and kill an angry lobster with a chopping knife. But it was a sauce worthy of Fernand Point, and I had been determined to produce one. By now, I own more than a hundred cookbooks, and I am determined one day to turn a few plump oysters and some tapioca poached in cream, buried in sabayon, and topped with caviar into a dish worthy of Thomas Keller, whose *French Laundry Cookbook* actually tells you how to do this if you happen to have six hands.

I feel a certain affinity for Thomas Keller, despite the fact that he is the best chef in America (his "oysters and pearls" and his parsnip soup are hands down the best things I have ever eaten) and has real sous-chefs, and I am merely one of the two best cooks—my friend Juliet Taylor is the other—on the fourth floor of a Central Park West apartment house. We share a weakness for lobster rolls, Reuben sandwiches, hamburger joints, and Fernand Point. "So genuine, so generous, so hospitable" is the way Keller describes *Ma Gastronomic,* which he first read at the age of twenty, working for a classical French chef at a Narragansett beach club whose members, if my childhood memories serve, usually sat down to dinner three sheets to the wind and unlikely to taste the difference between a homemade demi-glace and a can of College Inn. I met Keller in May at his New York restaurant, Per Se, toward the beginning of what I am reluctant to call research. I wanted to talk to cooks who read cookbooks all the time, and to cooks who hated cookbooks, or claimed to. I had already discovered that a couple I know in Los Angeles read cookbooks aloud to each other in bed, as part of what could be called their amatory ritual; and that another couple, in Berlin, nearly divorced over an argument about which cookbooks to pack for a year in Cambridge; and that a friend in New York got headaches just by looking at the teaspoon measurements for thyme and garlic in a coq au vin. I had learned that some of my friends cooked only from recipes they had clipped from magazines and newspapers, and wouldn't touch cookbooks, and that others cooked only from hardcover books and wouldn't even touch a paperback, let alone a page torn from the Wednesday food supplement of the *Times*. Now I wanted to know if the people who cooked for a living, and whose food I loved, read cookbooks. Keller reads them as well as writes them. He had just bought three new cookbooks on the day we talked, and he keeps the classics in his restaurant kitchens, "for sous-chefs looking for inspiration." Not many of the great chefs admit to buying three cookbooks on their way to work, especially other chefs' cookbooks.

Keller began cooking mainly because his mother—who ran restaurants but whose culinary genes started and stopped at "spaghetti and onions tossed with cottage cheese"—handed him an apron when her cook got sick. (A few days later, I was pleased to learn that the mother of Judith Jones, the Knopf editor who had brought me Julia Child, Marcella Kazan, Madhur Jaffrey, and Irene Kuo, was no better at the stove than mine or Keller's; she owned one copy of *Fannie Farmer,* and had a bluestocking's horror of garlic.) Keller had never really read a cookbook before he drove to Narragansett, hoping to find a job that would float him through a season of America's Cup partying in Newport. He met his mentor, Roland Henin, on Narragansett Beach, and he says that what he admired most about Henin then was less his stock reductions than the fact that "he was six foot four, French, in his thirties, and had a great-looking girlfriend and his own jeep."

Jacques Lameloise, the Burgundian chef, tells a French provincial version of the same story. He started cooking only because his older brother, who was expected to take over the family restaurant and its three Michelin stars, got smart and went off to college and was soon running a business of seven hundred people. Jacques, however, hated school. What he liked was hanging around Chagny and playing soccer, and so, *faute de mieux,* the family consigned him to its famous kitchen. "At first, I cooked like I played *foot,*" he told me when I stopped at Lameloise, in June, to pick up his cookbook and treat myself to his *poitrine de pigeonneau rôti à l'émiettée de truffes, parmentier de béatilles*—something I wouldn't dream of attempting myself, though, of course, I have the recipe. "There was no sacred flame. It was simply a matter of learning that if you're going to cook it's better to love cooking and to cook well. This idea of genius is overblown." Lameloise rarely admits to reading cookbooks. Why would I do that? was the look he gave me when I asked. "What I adore is simple things," he said. "For lunch at home, I will make a lobster salad, then frog's legs, sautéed the way my father made them, then a *côte de boeuf,* then a crème caramel. Simple!"

When I saw Frank Stitt, the Birmingham restaurateur who wrote the cookbook "Southern Table," he told me that his recipe for squab—my favorite, with grits and a bourbon red-eye gravy—was "inspired" by eating at local diners where tired truckers would stop for a wake-up meal drenched in ham fat and coffee dregs. "It's the playful takeoffs I do best," he said, when I told him how much I loved that recipe, if not those last few minutes at the stove, known in the trade as "the assembly," when everything is supposed to come together. Stitt's first good cookbook was Richard Olney's "Simple French Food," and he bought it while he was studying philosophy at Berkeley and volunteering in Alice Waters's kitchen, at Chez Panisse. A few days later, he bought his second Olney, and after that it seemed quite reasonable to call his parents, in Birmingham, to say he was quitting school in the second semester of his senior year to cook. Eventually, he went to Provence to work with Olney, who was famously misogynistic and fired Stitt after his girlfriend "started dropping in with a suitcase." Today, Stitt reads food histories and old cookbooks. *Charleston Receipts.* The old Delmonico's cookbook. Compilations of New Orleans recipes from the nineteenth century. Not that he keeps them at his restaurants, though he will sometimes cut out a picture from one of Alain Ducasse's cookbooks—"things like how to cut a lemon"—and show it to his staff. "Remember, most of my staff have never eaten in a great restaurant," he told me. "So I'm more like a coach to them, or a team leader. I go to the market, see the food, and I click in. The dish comes to me, like a thought to an idiot savant, and I show them how to make it. I am totally unlike, say, Ferran Adria at El Bulli"—Adria being the Spanish chef with the gadget that turns everything to foam, and whose own cookbook, which comes with a CD, will set you back $350, plus the price of a laptop for the kitchen.

I divide my cookbooks into two categories: the ones I'm not worried about getting dirty—about spilling sauce or spattering fat on the best pages—and the ones like Keller's, which I tend to think of as coffee-table books, not only because of their size and their gloss and their four-color illustrations but because they seem to have replaced art books as the status offerings you find casually stacked in front of the couch in Manhattan living rooms. I don't keep cookbooks in the living room, but I treat them cautiously, like a new silk shirt that hangs in the closet for a month before I give in, risk the inevitable spot, and actually put it on. It took me at least a month, more like two, to move Keller onto my kitchen counter, ready for its first splotch and for the careless company of the books I think of as my work-horse cookbooks—homely, tattered affairs with awkward draw-ings of hands folding ravioli and boning capons.

In Paris this summer, I visited the French-cookbook historians Mary and Philip Hyman, who were hard at work on an *Oxford Companion to French Food,* and learned that there was nothing new about coffee-table cookbooks. The Hymans had shown me a few of the sixteenth-century workhorses from their collection—recipes lifted from the court classics and sold by street peddlers as soon as there were customers literate enough to read them—and those books were plain little things, like penny dreadfuls, no bigger than four or five inches, that could be carried home in a pocket or a small purse. Then they showed me the books they called the "here's what's happening at the table where you'll never be allowed to sit" cookbooks—the ones that probably never saw a kitchen. They lived in the libraries of the new rich, gold-tooled and bound in Moroccan leather, alongside the Virgil and the Voltaire and the folders of Veronese prints and the first editions of Diderot's encyclopedia. There was Taillevent's *Le Viandier,* written in the fourteenth century for Charles V and considered by the French to be the first major cookbook in Europe since Apicius; and La Varenne's seventeenth-century *Le Cuisinier François,* which, according to the Hymans, marked the beginning of modern cooking; and Vincent La Chapelle's eighteenth-century *Le Cuisinier Moderne,* in five volumes, written with a certain amount of borrowing from other chefs and filled with engravings of spectacular serving dishes and fold-outs of table settings for a hundred guests.

There wasn't a woman among the writing royal chefs, which may be why none of their books looked used. But by the nineteenth century, when many of those chefs had been reduced to opening restaurants or cooking family dinners in the kitchens of the bourgeoisie, some of them looked to the future and took to writing profitable, practical cookbooks—cookbooks for housewives—although their shame was such that they often published under women's names. Hence the irresistible Tabitha Tickletooth, an "English-woman" whose book was published under the title *The Dinner Question, or How to Dine Well and Economically.* ("Economically" was not a word likely to burnish the reputation of a male chef de cuisine, moonlighting from a precarious job at an English castle.) The women who actually did write cookbooks then were not important chefs. I like to think of those women as more like me: women who read cookbooks and learned to cook that way. The Americans among them often simply collected recipes from European books and translated them, adding a bit of cautionary down-home commentary. I own a tiny edition of Miss Leslie's *Domestic French Cooking,* which was published in Philadelphia in 1832 and stayed in print for the next quarter century, and which I cherish for its recipe for oyster stuffing and its maidenly shudder at the voluptuary French practice of fattening geese.

Authentic American cooking, in all its regional variety and ethnic influences, really came into its own when women's groups—book clubs, church groups, suffrage groups, daughters-of-this-or-that groups—started putting together "community cookbooks." Community cookbooks are a purely American phenomenon. They began to appear during the Civil War, written by housewives, North and South, who contributed their best and hitherto secret recipes, published them locally on a shoestring, and sold them to raise money for the hometown troops. And they outlasted the war by at least a century, because, for one thing, everyone covets a recipe so good that generations of your neighbor's family have refused to share it, and because, for another, they carried the imprimatur of charity and were considered a respectable womanly pursuit—not likely to produce a bonneted Martha Stewart, abandoning hearth and husband for fame and fortune in the big city. (I like to think that Miss Leslie, whose name was Eliza Leslie, assumed her literary "Miss" in order to reassure her readers that she was not sitting at a desk, neglecting some man's hard-earned household.) Community cookbooks still account for about half the American cookbooks published, though the ones you find in bookstores now are mainly regional or ethnic cookbooks, not charity books, and the women who put them together, and even the women who contribute recipes, usually want to make a few dollars for themselves. And why not? Charity aside, Mrs. Clarence W. Miles, who contributed "tomatoes brown" to the cookbook "Maryland's Way"—tomatoes brown are tomatoes stewed for hours in brown sugar, and they make a gooey treat—deserved to be collecting royalties.

It occurs to me now, sitting in a farmhouse in Umbria, surrounded by thirty new cookbooks recommended by my daughter—a screenwriter and fellow cookbook addict—and wondering when to start dinner, that there is a strong connection between women who write and women who cook and who love recipes. This is something anyone who has read *To the Lighthouse* knows. It is impossible to follow Mrs. Ramsay through her vegetable garden and into the kitchen for that long braising of the *boeuf en daube* and doubt that Virginia Woolf read cookbooks, though she was too crafty to say so. It is, however, possible to sit through twenty or thirty of Trollope's Sunday dinners and never know how the roast got to the table. Henry James never taught me how the Florentines made pasta, Proust never taught me how the cooks in Combray made madeleines, and I don't remember that Flaubert even mentioned what Emma Bovary made for the doctor on the maid's day off, let alone how she cooked it. I know how Hemingway grilled the fish he caught, but nothing about how he sauced them, or what he did for dessert. I do, however, know what Rachel Samstat cooked in Nora Ephron's roman à clef *Heartburn,* because the novel is full of recipes, surely making it the only saga to emerge from Deep Throat Washington whose revelations involve a stove. The list is long. Patrizia Chen's lovely Italian memoir *Rosemary and Bitter Oranges* sent me straight to the kitchen with recipes for Livornese fish soup and lemon tea cake. Even Frances Mayes—whose ubiquitous memoir *Under the Tuscan Sun* has two chapters of recipes—started cooking as a young poet, which may account for some of the poetic license in those recipes; I have yet to read a real Tuscan cookbook or enter a Tuscan kitchen where the olive oil was so often replaced by butter and heavy cream.

Maybe I am an anxious cook, like the woman who famously botched a recipe for "green onions" which she had taken so literally as to throw away all the white parts of her scallions. Not only do I keep buying cookbooks, I usually cook with three or four of them on my kitchen counter, open to different recipes for the same dish. But that is nothing compared with my psychoanalyst friend J.J. Dayle, who cooks from more than two hundred cookbooks, subscribes to (among other things) *Cook's Illustrated, Saveur,* and *The Rosengarten Report,* and stocks forty kinds of sea salt in his kitchen. J.J. Dayle is not his real name, but it's the name he is planning to use when he writes *his* cookbook, so that his patients won't associate their gentle shrink with the man who refers to a great therapy as "like a great dish—something you know, in the first five minutes, where it's going." J.J. once drove down the Mediterranean coast sampling the fish soup in every town, and he describes his own bouillabaisse by crying, "I am Samson Agonistes with my soups! God damn it, I have to wrestle them to the floor."

I was quite comforted by J.J.'s quest for the perfect fish soup. It reminded me of my quest for the perfect *sauce à l'américaine.* Usually, I try to avoid quests. Like most cookbook addicts, I buy a book, read it, and, if I'm lucky, find a couple of recipes that sound right, and forget the rest. I can always locate those recipes, because my books fall open to the pages I cook from most, and after ten or twenty years they even fall apart at those pages—which I find convenient. My old *Joy of Cooking* is split at the Bulgarian cucumber soup and again at the fruit preserves; my Craig Claiborne at the Yorkshire pudding; my *Silver Palate* at the salmon mousse; my *Julia* at the *choucroute garnie;* my Madhur Jaffrey at the shrimp curry with the best spices. This is something I wait for—the spine of my first River Café cookbook is just beginning to go, at the zucchini soup and at the *penne alla carbonara*—the way I wait for splotches. (My latest splotches are on the Circassian chicken in Roden's *Picnic* and on the boneless chicken breasts with lemon and capers in *Southern Table*.) But certain recipes elude me, and I go on quests. A few weeks ago, I almost went on a quest for calamari sauce. I had stopped at a small restaurant on the Lago di Garda called Nuovo Ponte, eaten a wonderfully inky pasta with calamari sauce, and asked the chef, Fiorenzo Andreoli, for the recipe. He wasn't at all surprised. He had once spent two years in San Francisco, working for an old friend with an Italian restaurant, and he said that the thing he remembered most—the one thing that always made him smile when he met an American—was how everyone in the kitchen besides himself and his friend "cooked with his nose in a cookbook." He told me that his calamari sauce "just came to me when I started cooking, because this is how calamari sauce is made on the Lago di Garda." A little *aglio*, a little *olio*, a little *basilico*, he said, when I asked if he couldn't be more precise.

I don't usually cook from books in Italy; my garden tells me what to eat and the butcher tells me what he's got, and I go from there. (Call it a vacation; to me, it's cold turkey.) But this summer I packed up my new cookbooks and sent them off—and was quite lucky to receive them, inasmuch as they disappeared for ten days and had to be dug out of the customs shed at the Milan airport, where they were held for commercial duty on the ground (roughly translated) that "no one person has that many cookbooks." think it was also the exotic titles—*Lulu's Provençal Table; Couscous; Savoring the Spice Coast of India; The Key to Chinese Cooking; Hot, Sour, Salty, Sweet*. Italians have no interest in foreign food, and as for their own food—a lot of my new books were Italian—it is considered an insult not only to your mother's kitchen but to your mother herself to suggest that anyone else's mother may have cooked better.

In the event, it was impossible to find any of the things I needed to savor the coast of India or make a proper couscous (for one thing, Umbrians do not eat turnips) or to unlock the door to Chinese cooking. In Italy, it is even impossible to sit down to a Provençal table. The one time I tried—I served braised rabbit on a bed of noodles to some Roman neighbors—they said, "Pasta is for before the meat," and scraped the noodles off their plates. (On their last visit, they arrived with a new black garbage pail as a house gift.) Italians today are arguably more broad-minded than they were in the fifteenth century, when a food-loving papal secretary named Bartolomeo Sacchi was thrown in jail by Pope Paul II as a "sectarian of Epicurus." (Under a nicer Pope, and using the pseudonym Platina, he produced the legendary cookbook *De Honesta Voluptate*.) But they do not willingly eat anybody else's food.

The quest I am on right now is for the perfect pot-au-feu—which is to say, a pot-au-feu as good as the one I ate this Easter, in New York, at the house of my friend Susannna Lea. Susanna is an English vegetarian who never cooks, so it stands to reason that she did not have a great recipe for pot-au-feu at her fingertips or, indeed, any interest at all in pot-au-feu. But she is also a Paris literary agent married to a French writer and, having moved to New York last fall, they wanted to serve something ur-French at Easter to their American friends. Susanna's pot-au-feu was, in fact, a kind of long-distance literary collaboration between three cookbooks she had bought for the occasion —Patricia Wells's *Bistro Cooking*, Anthony Bourdain's *Les Halles Cookbook*, and Guy Savoy's *Simple French Recipes for the Home Cook*—and one of her Paris clients, a novelist named Marc Levy whose first book, a romance involving a lonely architect and a young woman in a coma, sold so many millions of copies that he went out and bought a six-burner Gaggenau stove and grill and a couple of Gaggenau ovens and started "reflecting," as he told me himself a few months later, on reinventing pot-au-feu. His version takes at least two days, and he had walked Susanna through it by telephone, starting early on the morning of Good Friday and ending at noon on Sunday. It was very fussy. It involved not only hours of braising—not to mention of steaming vegetables, one by one, over meat broth; poaching marrow bones wrapped in tinfoil; and making a vinaigrette with riced eggs and capers—but also a hunt for beef cheeks, which are not easy to come by if you live in New York, where the only people who sell them are wholesale butchers and you have to buy them in frozen blocks of thirty pounds. Susanna had to give up on beef cheeks, but, even so, the work was worth it. I copied the recipe from the back of an old manuscript envelope by the phone on her kitchen counter. My quest began there.

I now own twenty-two recipes for pot-au-feu, if you count the Italian versions of *bollito misto,* and am halfway through the biography of a Paris film-world hostess whose own recipe was so renowned that the book is called *Le Pot-au-Feu de Mary Meerson*. What I am really doing is waiting for fall, because it is much too hot in Umbria to cook a pot-au-feu and, anyway, my butcher, who is hard put even to cut a chicken into four pieces, has never heard of anyone eating beef cheeks. He says it is "not Italian." (He means not within shouting distance of his own shop.) So I am concentrating on calamari, and if I succeed tonight I will not look at another cookbook until I am back in New York, making "oysters and pearls." My husband has offered to do the cooking while I recover. He is (his word) an "instinctive" cook and claims that cookbooks are a waste of time. He goes to the fish store, picks what's fresh, and makes it in fifteen minutes. It may be that the best recipe I ever got came from M. Picot, the *patron* of Le Voltaire, my favorite Paris restaurant. I was there in June, and ordered a sole meunière that was so buttery and delicious that I asked M. Picot how he did it. He smiled wisely, and said, *"Madame, il faut choisir le poisson."*

Lobster Killer

by Julie Powell

from *Julie & Julia*

In this engrossing, hilarious memoir, Powell
tells the Cinderella story of her yearlong
project to cook her way through *Mastering
the Art of French Cooking*—and the blog that
made her an overnight Internet celebrity.

Over a period of two weeks in late December of 2002, at the exhortation of Julia Child, I went on a murderous rampage. I committed gruesome, atrocious acts, and for my intended victims, no murky corner of Queens or Chinatown was safe from my diabolical reach. If news of the carnage was not widely remarked upon in the local press, it was only because my victims were not Catholic schoolgirls or Filipino nurses, but crustaceans. This distinction means that I am not a murderer in the legal sense. But I have blood on my hands, even if it is the clear blood of lobsters.

We had finally gone ahead and bought one of those sleep machines to drown out the roar of freight trucks that rumble past our apartment all night. It had a small speaker that fit under the pillow, and most nights it did the trick. But on the eve of my first crime, the lulling roar and crash of the "oceania" setting droned at me: "Lobster killer, lobster killer, lobster killer. . . ."

I was awake by dawn, worrying. It was Sunday in Long Island City—forget killing a lobster, how would I even get one, for God's sake? How much would it cost? How would I get it home? I peppered Eric with these questions, hoping that he would reply, "Oooh, you're right, that isn't going to work. Oh well—guess we'll have to save lobster for another day. Domino's? Bacon and jalapeno?"

He didn't say that. Instead he got out the yellow pages and made a phone call—the first fish market he called was open. The Bronco started, the traffic to Astoria was smooth. The fish store didn't smell fishy, and they had lobsters in a nasty-looking cloudy tank. I bought two. The stars fell into alignment, for fate had decreed these two lobsters must die.

I had been imagining lugging the lobsters home in a bucket, but the guy just stuck them in a paper bag. He said to keep them in the refrigerator. He said they'd be good until Thursday. Ick. I brought them back to the car and set them in the backseat—what were we going to do, cradle the creatures in our laps? On the drive home the back of my neck tingled and my ears stayed pricked for the sneaking crinkle of a lobster claw venturing out of a paper bag—but the lobsters just sat there. I guess suffocating will do that to a body.

Julia gets very terse in her description of Homard Thermidor. She always seems to go all Delphic on me in my times of need. She doesn't speak to the storage of lobsters, for one thing. Neither, to be fair, does the *Joy of Cooking,* but at least that tome gives me the hint that lobsters should be lively and thrashing when they come out of the tank. Hey. My lobsters didn't thrash. *Joy* said if they were limp, they might die before you cooked them. It seemed to think that was a bad thing. I peeked into the paper bag in the refrigerator and was faced with black eyes on stalks, antennae boozily waving.

I had read up on all sorts of methods for humanely euthanizing lobsters—sticking them in the freezer, placing them in ice water then bringing it up to a boil (which is supposed to fool them into not realizing they're boiling alive), slicing their spinal cord with a knife beforehand. But all these struck me as palliatives thought up more to save boilers from emotional anguish than boilees from physical. In the end I just dumped them out of the paper bag into a pot with some boiling water and vermouth and vegetables. And then freaked the fuck out.

The pot wasn't big enough. Though the lobsters didn't shriek in horror the second I dropped them in, their momentary stillness only drew out the excruciating moment. It was like that instant when your car begins to skid out of control and before your eyes you see the burning car wreck that is your destiny. Any second the pain would awaken the creatures from their asphyxia-induced comas, I knew it, and I couldn't get the goddamned lid down! It was just too horrible. My heroic/homicidal husband had to take things in hand. I'd have expected him to collapse just like me, he's not exactly the *Field & Stream* type, but some of those pitiless West Texas sheriff genes must have hit their stride, because he managed to get those bugs subdued with a minimum of fuss.

People say lobsters make a terrible racket in the pot, trying—reasonably enough—to claw their way out of the water. I wouldn't know. I spent the next twenty minutes watching a golf game on the TV with the volume turned up to Metallica concert levels. (Those Titleist commercials nearly blew the windows out.) When I ventured back into the kitchen, the lobsters were very red, and not making any racket at all. Julia says they are done when "the long head-feelers can be pulled from the sockets fairly easily." That they could. Poor little beasties. I took them out of the pot and cooked down their liquid with the juices from some mushrooms I'd stewed. I strained the reduced juices through a sieve, presumably to get rid of any errant bits of head-feeler or whatever, then beat it into a light roux I'd made of butter and flour.

When Eric and I start our crime conglomerate, he can be in charge of death; I'll take care of dismemberment. The same no-nonsense guy who brusquely stripped two crustaceans of their mortal coils had to leave the room when I read aloud that next I was to "split the lobsters in half lengthwise, keeping the shell halves intact."

But it was no problem, really. For once, a blithely terse turn of phrase by Julia was not an indication of imminent disaster. The knife crunched right through. It is true that all within was not as clear-cut as you might think. When Julia told me to "discard sand sacks in the heads, and the intestinal tubes," I was able to make an educated guess. The sacks full of sand were sort of a dead giveaway. But when she said to "rub lobster coral and green matter through a fine sieve," I got a little lost. There was all manner of green matter—what is "green matter," though, and why won't Julia tell me?—but the only orange stuff I found seemed to reside where a lobster's shit would go, so I decided not to risk it. After that was done, I pulled the rest of the meat out chunk by chunk, cracking open the claws, using a tweezer—carefully cleaned of all eyebrow hairs, naturally—to pull the strips of meat out of the legs. The sieved "green matter" got beaten into some egg yolks, cream, mustard, and cayenne, poured into the lobster broth/roux sauce, and boiled. I sautéed the meat in some butter, then poured in some cognac and let it boil down. Then I stirred in the stewed mushrooms and two-thirds of the sauce. I heaped the mixture into the four lobster half-shells, poured the rest of the sauce over, sprinkled with Parmesan and dotted with butter, and ran them under the broiler.

They were, I must say, delicious.

I stalked my third victim in Chinatown on a rainy evening one week later, inconspicuous amid the bustling Christmas shoppers picking up knockoff bags and the more obviously murderous umbrella wielders. (Umbrella wielders in Chinatown have the key advantage of diminutive stature. On a rainy day—and it's always a rainy day in Chinatown—one must step lively or risk losing an eye.) The creature stopped groping almost immediately after the guy in the shop tied it up in a plastic bag, dropped the plastic bag into a paper one, and handed it to me in exchange for six dollars. I was nervous about getting on the train with the thing, fearing it would thrash around and call attention to itself, but it just sat there like a bag of groceries.

When I got home I peered down at the lobster to see how he was doing. The inner plastic bag was sucked tight around him and clouded up. It looked like something out of an eighties made-for-TV movie, with some washed-up actress taking too many pills and trying to off herself with a Macy's bag. I tore open the bag to let in some air—so this underwater creature would breathe better?—before putting him in the freezer. Suffocating is worse than freezing to death is better than being steamed alive? Perhaps anticipation of my evening of bloodletting had addled my brain, but the philosophical intricacies of lobster murder were proving too much for me to rationally negotiate.

The second murder went much as the first—steamed in water spiked with vermouth and some celery, carrot, and onion. The rosy-red dead lobster was bisected in just the same way, its flesh removed, and again its shell was stuffed with its sautéed meat, this time napped in a cream sauce made with the lobster's cooking juices. I think I overcooked it a little.

I confessed to Eric as we sat down to our Homard aux Aromates that cutting lobsters in half was beginning to prove eerily satisfying. "I just feel like I've got a knack for this shit."

Eric looked at me, and I could see him wondering where was the finicky, soft-hearted young girl he had married. "By the end of this you'll be comfortable filleting puppies."

That chilled me. I lay low after that for a good long while, until after Christmas. I told myself it was because a transit strike was threatening, and I didn't much relish the idea of buying a lobster in a bag and then unexpectedly having to hike across the Queensboro Bridge with it, in the company of a hundred thousand grousing outer-borough shoppers and menial workers. But that wasn't really it. The reason was the next recipe, Homard à l'Américaine. For while I am sure that the argument can be made that any meat-eating person ought to take the responsibility once in her life for slaughtering an animal for food, that one ought to chop that animal up into small pieces while it's still alive, I am less certain of. And even more frightening was the thought Eric had planted in my head—what if I *liked* it?

My final victim was another Chinatown denizen. He was spryer than his predecessors, flailing around in his bag for the entire subway ride. Because shivving a dead lobster in the back would be no challenge at all.

I put him in the freezer for a while when I got home, to try to numb him, maybe make it go a little easier, but is there such a thing as an easy vivisection, really? After half an hour or so, while Eric retreated to the living room and cranked up the volume on the TV, I took the lobster out of the freezer and laid him on the cutting board.

JC writes: "Split the lobsters in two lengthwise. Remove stomach sacks (in the head) and intestinal tubes. Reserve coral and green matter. Remove claws and joints and crack them. Separate tails from chests."

"Well, gosh, Julia, you make it sound *easy*."

The poor guy just sat there, waving his claws and antennae gently, while I stood over him, my largest knife poised at the juncture of chest and tail. I took a deep breath, let it out.

It's like shooting an old, dying dog in the back of the skull—you've got to be strong, for the animal's sake.

"Oh, you've shot a lot of dogs in your time, have you?"

Go ahead.

"All right, all right. Okay. One. Two. *Three.*"

I pressed down, making an incision in the shell where Julia said I could quickly sever the spinal cord.

The thing began to flail.

"He doesn't seem to think this is particularly painless, Julia."

Chop it in two. Quickly. Start at the head.

I quickly placed the tip of my knife between its eyes and, muttering "I'm sorry I'm sorry I'm sorry," plunged.

Oh God. Oh God.

Clear blood leaked off the edges of the cutting board onto the floor as the lobster continued to flail vigorously, despite the fact that its head was now chopped neatly in two. The muscles in its chest gripped at the blade, so that the knife's hilt trembled in my hand. I sawed away at the thing, managing to get about halfway through before I had to leave the room for a bit to clear my head.

But I think perhaps I'm approaching a Zen-like serenity when it comes to crustacean murder, because when I reentered the kitchen to the sight of the giant thing pinned to the cutting board with a huge knife, still squirming, instead of being horrified by man's inhumanity to lobster, I just giggled. It really was pretty amusing when you thought about it.

Laughter through nausea is my favorite emotion, and after that, things got easier. In not too much time I had the thing cut into four pieces, plus detached claws. I cleaned out the intestines and "green matter," which looked more like an organ when it was unsteamed. The pieces of the thing kept twitching throughout, even keeping on awhile after I threw them into hot oil.

My final victim was sautéed with carrots, onions, shallots, and garlic, doused with cognac, lit on fire, then baked in an oven with vermouth, tomato, parsley, and tarragon, and served atop rice. I arranged the rice into a ring on a plate, as Julia asked. I've committed brutal murder for the woman, why not make a rice ring? I piled the lobster pieces in the middle and ladled the sauce over. "Dinner's served."

Eric overcame his momentary horror at being presented with a heap of mutilated lobster and dug in. "I suppose it's no worse to eat an animal you killed yourself instead of one they kill in the factory. Maybe it's better."

"It's true." I took a bite of lobster meat with rice. It was quite tasty. "Arguing the morality of slaughter will send you into a tail-spin of self-loathing every time."

"Unless you're a vegan."

"Uh-huh. But then you're a vegan, and you don't count. Hey, have you read about how they slaughter chickens? See, they hang them upside down on this conveyor belt with their little feet clamped in manacles, and—"

"Julie, I'm eating here."

"Or what about pigs? And pigs are way smart."

"*But*—" Eric jabbed his fork in the air rhetorically. "Does the intelligence of the creature have any bearing on its right and desire to live?" Eric had already finished his first serving of Homard à l'Américaine and was reaching for his second.

"George Bush would say no."

"So, the question is, is George Bush a vegan?"

"No, the question is—wait, am I turning into George Bush? Oh, God!"

"I think we're getting a little confused. Let's just eat."

"Oh, hey, I just remembered—I forgot to tell you about this *crazy* call I got at work today."

So sometimes I'm irritated by my husband, and sometimes I'm frustrated. But I can think of two times right off the top of my head when it's particularly good to be married. The first is when you need help with killing the lobsters. The second is when you've got an inspirational story to relate regarding a large African American woman who runs an S&M dungeon. I told it to him as we sopped up the last of the buttery lobster juice with some hunks of French bread.

"That's *great*."

"I know, I *know!*" I knew of no one else I could have told who would have understood the joy this story brought me.

"It just makes you happy, thinking about the *possibilities* out there."

He didn't mean the possibilities of getting naked ladies to clog dance for him, or at least he didn't *only* mean that. He meant that sometimes you get a glimpse into a life that you never thought of before. There are hidden trap doors all over the place, and suddenly you see one, and the next thing you know you're flogging grateful businessmen or chopping lobsters in half, and the world's just so much *bigger* than you thought it was.

So that night I made my New Year's resolution, better late than never: To Get Over My Damned Self. If I was going to follow Julia down this rabbit hole, I was going to enjoy it, by God—exhaustion, crustacean murder, and all. Because not everybody gets a rabbit hole. I was one lucky bastard, when you came down to it.

Dining Around

La Belle France

by Julia Child with Alex Prud'homme

from *My Life in France*

Although Julia Child died in 2004, this posthumous memoir—which she was writing with her grand-nephew Alex Prud'homme when she died—has all her trademark vigor, wit, and bracing common sense. This pivotal scene in 1948 was a turning point in her life.

At twelve-thirty we Flashed into Rouen. We passed the city's ancient and beautiful clock tower, and then its famous cathedral, still pockmarked from battle but magnificent with its stained-glass windows. We rolled to a stop in la Place du Vieux Marché, the square where Joan of Arc had met her fiery fate. There the *Guide Michelin* directed us to Restaurant La Couronne ("The Crown"), which had been built in 1345 in a medieval quarter-timbered house. Paul strode ahead, full of anticipation, but I hung back, concerned that I didn't look chic enough, that I wouldn't be able to communicate, and that the waiters would look down their long Gallic noses at us Yankee tourists.

It was warm inside, and the dining room was a comfortably old-fashioned brown-and-white space, neither humble nor luxurious. At the far end was an enormous fireplace with a rotary spit, on which something was cooking that sent out heavenly aromas. We were greeted by the maître d'hôtel, a slim middle-aged man with dark hair who carried himself with an air of gentle seriousness. Paul spoke to him, and the maître d' smiled and said something back in a familiar way, as if they were old friends. Then he led us to a nice table not far from the fireplace. The other customers were all French, and I noticed that they were treated with exactly the same courtesy as we were. Nobody rolled their eyes at us or stuck their nose in the air. Actually, the staff seemed happy to see us.

As we sat down, I heard two businessmen in gray suits at the next table asking questions of their waiter, an older, dignified man who gesticulated with a menu and answered them at length.

"What are they talking about?" I whispered to Paul.

"The waiter is telling them about the chicken they ordered," he whispered back. "How it was raised, how it will be cooked, what side dishes they can have with it, and which wines would go with it best."

"*Wine?*" I said. "At *lunch?*" I had never drunk much wine other than some $1.19 California Burgundy, and certainly not in the middle of the day.

In France, Paul explained, good cooking was regarded as a combination of national sport and high art, and wine was always served with lunch and dinner. "The trick is moderation," he said.

Suddenly the dining room filled with wonderfully intermixing aromas that I sort of recognized but couldn't name. The first smell was something oniony—"shallots," Paul identified it, "being sautéed in fresh butter." ("What's a shallot?" I asked, sheepishly. "You'll see," he said.) Then came a warm and winy fragrance from the kitchen, which was probably a delicious sauce being reduced on the stove. This was followed by a whiff of something astringent: the salad being tossed in a big ceramic bowl with lemon, wine vinegar, olive oil, and a few shakes of salt and pepper.

My stomach gurgled with hunger.

I couldn't help noticing that the waiters carried themselves with a quiet joy, as if their entire mission in life was to make their customers feel comfortable and well tended. One of them glided up to my elbow. Glancing at the menu, Paul asked him questions in rapid-fire French. The waiter seemed to enjoy the back-and-forth with my husband. Oh, how I itched to be in on their conversation! Instead, I smiled and nodded uncomprehendingly, although I tried to absorb all that was going on around me.

We began our lunch with a half-dozen oysters on the half-shell. I was used to bland oysters from Washington and Massachusetts, which I had never cared much for. But this platter of *portugaises* had a sensational briny flavor and a smooth texture that was entirely new and surprising. The oysters were served with rounds of *pain de seigle,* a pale rye bread, with a spread of unsalted butter. Paul explained that, as with wine, the French have "crus" of butter, special regions that produce individually flavored butters. *Beurre de Charentes* is a full-bodied butter, usually recommended for pastry dough or general cooking; *beurre d'Isigny* is a fine, light table butter. It was that delicious *Isigny* that we spread on our rounds of rye.

Rouen is famous for its duck dishes, but after consulting the waiter Paul had decided to order *sole meunière.* It arrived whole: a large, flat Dover sole that was perfectly browned in a sputtering butter sauce with a sprinkling of chopped parsley on top. The waiter carefully placed the platter in front of us, stepped back, and said: *"Bon appétit!"*

I closed my eyes and inhaled the rising perfume. Then I lifted a forkful of fish to my mouth, took a bite, and chewed slowly. The flesh of the sole was delicate, with a light but distinct taste of the ocean that blended marvelously with the browned butter. I chewed slowly and swallowed. It was a morsel of perfection.

In Pasadena, we used to have broiled mackerel for Friday dinners, codfish balls with egg sauce, "boiled" (poached) salmon on the Fourth of July, and the occasional pan-fried trout when camping in the Sierras. But at La Couronne I experienced fish, and a dining experience, of a higher order than any I'd ever had before.

Along with our meal, we happily downed a whole bottle of Pouilly-Fumé, a wonderfully crisp white wine from the Loire Valley. Another revelation!

Then came *salade verte* laced with a lightly acidic vinaigrette. And I tasted my first real baguette—a crisp brown crust giving way to a slightly chewy, rather loosely textured pale-yellow interior, with a faint reminder of wheat and yeast in the odor and taste. Yum!

We followed our meal with a leisurely dessert of *fromage blanc,* and ended with a strong, dark *café filtre.* The waiter placed before us a cup topped with a metal canister, which contained coffee grounds and boiling water. With some urging by us impatient drinkers, the water eventually filtered down into the cup below. It was fun, and it provided a distinctive dark brew.

Paul paid the bill and chatted with the maître d', telling him how much he looked forward to going back to Paris for the first time in eighteen years. The maître d' smiled as he scribbled something on the back of a card. *"Tiens,"* he said, handing it to me. The Dorin family, who owned La Couronne, also owned a restaurant in Paris, called La Truite, he explained, while Paul translated. On the card he had scribbled a note of introduction for us.

"Mairci, monsoor," I said, with a flash of courage and an accent that sounded bad even to my own ear. The waiter nodded as if it were nothing, and moved off to greet some new customers.

Paul and I floated out the door into the brilliant sunshine and cool air. Our first lunch together in France has been absolute perfection. It was the most exciting meal of my life.

Putting Le Bec-Fin to the Test

by Pete Wells
from *Food & Wine*

An editor at *Details* and a regular columnist
for *Food & Wine*, Pete Wells somehow comes
across as a foodie and an ordinary guy at
the same time—no mean feat.

All the arrangements had been made weeks in advance: the dinner reservation, the hotel room in Philadelphia and finally, crucially, the babysitter. After a volley of phone calls and faxes with the hotel concierge, I'd confirmed that a nanny would show up at 8 o'clock to watch our baby while my wife and I went out to eat. Around 5, just to double-check, I rode the elevator down to the lobby. "I'm sorry, Mr. Wells, but I don't see any record of your request," the concierge said. He checked with the nanny service; all their sitters were booked. "I can call my manager and see if we can help," he offered.

"Please do," I begged. "I've waited twenty years for this meal!"

Our dinner reservation was at Le Bec-Fin, a restaurant I've dreamed about since college. When I arrived at the University of Pennsylvania in 1981, the school's promotional brochures bragged about what everybody in town called "the Philadelphia restaurant renaissance." The greatest of the renaissance chefs, the Michelangelo of Walnut Street, was Georges Perrier, who learned his craft at La Pyramide in France and began cooking in Philadelphia in the late '60s as a young man. By the time I arrived in the city, his Le Bec-Fin was recognized, both by the nation's reigning food critics and by the locals, as the best restaurant in town, maybe the best in the country.

I never went. I had grown up in the suburbs of Rhode Island eating what every suburban American kid ate in the '70s. My favorite fancy restaurant was the Rusty Scupper, where I always carefully studied the menu, miraculously printed on a wooden oar, before ordering baked stuffed shrimp. In Philadelphia, I was introduced to such exotica as bagels, sushi, tandoori chicken, falafel, tacos, Italian sausage, pad Thai, Brie, Peking duck and porcini mushrooms. As for haute cuisine, I remained in the dark. Just off the Penn campus was a desperate stab at a French restaurant called L'Artiste Affamé. I hadn't been to France, but even I knew that there was something not quite authentic about a place where, if somebody ordered Champagne, the gum-chewing waitress yelled out, "Harry, get the bucket!"

Evidence suggested that Le Bec-Fin existed on another plane, but, with its $65 prix fixe, it was always out of reach to me. Through stolen glimpses and secondhand reports, however, I began to build my own mental replica of Le Bec-Fin. Anyone who loves restaurants knows this process. You read about a place, your friends talk about it, and soon you develop a kind of crush. As with the more common kind of crush, imagination quickly outstrips the real thing. Perhaps the never-ending busy signal keeps you away from the French Laundry until you believe it's the second coming of the Garden of Eden, minus the snake. Maybe a flight to Catalonia to eat at El Bulli just doesn't fit on your calendar, so you find yourself dreaming about what "apple caviar" might be. A restaurant that lives in your dreams can be anything you want it to be, and you never have to pick up the tab.

After pacing the halls of the hotel for an hour—I was too nervous to sit in our room—I got a call on my cell phone from the concierge. He'd talked one of the hosts from the front desk into babysitting. After explaining to the sitter what to do with Dexter in every emergency scenario we could think of, my wife and I set off for Le Bec-Fin. On the four-minute walk, we passed Striped Bass and Susanna Foo, two restaurants that muscled in on Perrier's block after I left town. The city has renamed the side street across from Le Bec-Fin "Georges Perrier Place," but the town fathers can't do anything to slow the advance of ambitious new competitors with a more modern outlook. These days, menus in French and domed plates aren't enough to make you the best restaurant in town.

The entrance to Le Bec-Fin was still as forbidding as I recalled, with a brass plaque instructing us to ring the bell for admittance. Ignoring it, I pulled on the smoked-glass door and it swung open. We were in the world's smallest lobby; it was barely big enough for the hostess to step from behind her station and take our coats. Another door was opened and we were led into the dining room.

I believe we gasped. The new room was all white and gold, like a bride. Restaurants with chandeliers and mirrors usually make me picture either dotty great-aunts or beefy men with pinkie rings. This didn't. It was the kind of room that made you feel smart, cultured and attractive just for being there. At the same time, I wanted to run my fingers across the woven silk wall panels.

This was not the same room I would have seen in my college days. Five years ago, the Mobil Travel Guide demoted Le Bec-Fin from its top five-star ranking down to a mere four. Now, I have never met anyone who based his dining decisions on the Mobil Travel Guide. Who cares what a gas station thinks about food? Well, Philadelphia cared. The day Le Bec-Fin lost the star, TV trucks parked outside the door. And Georges Perrier cared. Boy, did he care. He had a nervous breakdown, followed by severe depression. He huddled with his psychic. He launched an investigation into what went wrong and fired a waiter he deemed responsible. He fired *himself*, turning over command of the kitchen to a chef from Daniel in New York. He hired a new wine guy, who added 500 bottles to the list. Finally, he tore down the dining room, ripping out the flocked persimmon-colored wallpaper, the fleurs-de-lis carpeting, the wrought-iron banisters, several walls—everything but the chandeliers.

Our first three courses were all pleasure. Perrier was still serving one dish I could have ordered back in college, his *galette de crabe,* a high-end crab cake. Meanwhile, my wife had a sunchoke soup that took its smoky depth from bacon and its substance from sliced quail breast laid on the surface. She followed that with lobster in red wine sauce; in its copper casserole, it seemed more bistro than haute cuisine. The same was true of my meat course, a roast pigeon, and even of my wife's dish of sweetbreads and veal with blue-potato spaetzle. The food had the simplicity and depth of flavor you find at those casually thrilling restaurants opened by Paris chefs who've tired of dancing the three-Michelin-star rumba. Often, after ambitious restaurant meals, I leave feeling that too many hands mucked around with my food, and that despite all the fussing, the result wasn't even remotely satisfying. The cooking at Le Bec-Fin was of a different order; you didn't notice how much work had gone into it until you tasted it. But nobody was getting more pleasure from the restaurant than the Lone Gourmand at the next table. He was toting the program for a scientific conference, but his true purpose in coming to Philadelphia was obviously dinner at Le Bec-Fin. On top of his conference program, he set a copy of Perrier's cookbook to await the chef's signature. Before dismantling each course, he photographed it. When caviar appeared, he held his hands above the plate and wiggled his plump fingers in the air like a concert pianist getting ready to play a particularly delightful mazurka.

I'd always supposed that Le Bec-Fin would be full of solemn old snoots whispering behind their fish knives. Instead, the joint was jumping. In the corner was a man, his face pink from wine, who waved a waiter over and demanded, "Please escort my wife to the ladies' room!" Then he said thank you very loudly in Japanese, although neither he nor the waiter looked Japanese. On our other side was a richly dressed Latin American family: a dour father, a glamorous mother, three daughters with long, straight, black hair, and their suitors. They were all having the tasting menu and they were all cooing over it, even the old man. I'd never been any place so formal where people were so loose. It must have been the waiters. There seemed to be an endless supply of them in black tuxedos of varying degrees of elegance. There was the one who lit the candles and the one who refilled our water; the bread-basket keeper; the cheese tender; the wine steward; the other wine steward; the dessert sheer; the crumb scraper; and on and on. Because of the restaurant's layout, they bump and squeeze past each other in the center of the dining room, treating customers to a floor show.

A former dishwasher once told a reporter, "You're either here two days or ten years—nothing in between." This was evident on the floor. Certain servers seemed to have been picked up at the Greyhound station a half hour before dinner. The waiter who dropped off our *amuse-bouche* described it as "seared tuna with a black-olive tam-manna." A what? (That's the closest I can come to his pronunciation of tapenade; no alphabet on earth can do justice to the way he said *"amuse bouche."*) Other servers, though, were both confident and knowledgeable. When I asked the sommelier which of two rosé Champagnes he preferred, he decisively replied, "Definitely the Paul Déthune," as if he'd been hoping for just that question all night. Another waiter stopped by from time to time to drop some quick pleasantry, like the host at a cocktail party. When I told him how much I'd liked my fish course, a black sea bass fillet with pickled lotus root and huitlacoche sauce (I know, an assemblage this eclectic doesn't fit into my haute-bistro paradigm at all, which is why I didn't mention it earlier), he shared some huitlacoche facts. "It's corn must," he said. "A kind of fungus that grows on the ears of corn. The word comes from the Nahuatl, the language of the ancient Aztecs, and it means 'black excrement.' So—black shit." He flashed a grin and pirouetted away.

Without a doubt, many diners do not want to hear about excrement or any of its synonyms in the middle of a meal. But our waiter somehow knew, from a few moments' observation, that far from offending us, his bizarre remark would smash any inhibitions we might be harboring. It told us, succinctly, that we weren't in church. I wish my twenty-four-year-old self had been given the chance to hear a Le Bec-Fin waiter say "black excrement." It might have saved me from years of taking food too seriously.

It was lucky we were in such a giddy mood, because things were about to go downhill. After I'd chosen five tremendous cheeses and my wife had amused herself with a small salad that was perfectly— I mean perfectly—dressed, the sweet courses began. Sorbets were clumsy, studded with crunchy bits of ice. Le Bec-Fin's dessert cart is even more famous than the *galette de crabe,* celebrated for its sugary landscape of just about every dessert. Tonight, it held row after row of cakes and tarts. Clearly, the idea was excess, but not one of our four choices was worth the trouble of slicing it.

The time had come to go back to the hotel and relieve the babysitter, so I called for the check. With tip, the total bill came to just under $500. I'm still not sure I can afford Le Bec-Fin, particularly when the pastry chef seemed to have been nabbed in the same bus-station roundup that caught the tammanna guy. But we'd gotten something that's been absent from meals we've had in other elevated restaurants that were brought off without a flaw. My wife, with no preconceptions, and I, with decades' worth of expectations, had had more fun than we thought possible.

It's easy to forget that restaurants are human institutions. With rare exceptions, the great ones have a life span that is closely tied to the man or woman who made them great. By waiting twenty years to eat at Le Bec-Fin, I'd taken a giant risk. And, indeed, almost nothing had stayed the same. Butter and cream had fallen out of favor in the kitchen, nouvelle cuisine had been embraced and then rejected, the waiters who spoke perfect French and the customers who understood them were gone. But Georges Perrier has refused to go away.

In 2003, Le Bec-Fin got its fifth star back. Perrier owns three other restaurants, but he still shows up out of nowhere to torment the employees, parking his car across the street, on Georges Perrier Place. A portrait of Napoleon hangs in his office. Perrier is the reason that, thirty-five years after its birth, Le Bec-Fin was still around to show me a good time when I was finally ready. And he's the reason that the evening had surprised me at every turn, defying all my expectations. I was grateful for that. If things always turned out the way we pictured them, what fun would that be?

Vive Le Restaurant

by James Villas

from *Saveur*

Who in Manhattan still goes to old-school French restaurants like Le Veau d'Or? James Villas, for one—author of *My Mother's Southern Kitchen*, *Between Bites*, and *Stalking the Green Fairy*—and he captures perfectly their peculiar charm.

A dour middle-aged couple perch side by side on a banquette in a New York City restaurant, he grumbling about the sweetness of the sauce around his oeufs à la neige, she complaining about the table location, the limited menu, the wine prices. This is obviously their first visit. The owner, a gracious eighty-one-year-old Frenchman, tries politely to explain, to console, even to apologize, but the woman will not let up. Finally, the owner draws back his head in Gallic outrage, grabs the edges of his checkered velvet vest, informs the couple that there will be no bill, and tells them never to return to his restaurant.

"Well," the woman says at the door, "no wonder this place is almost empty."

"Madame," the owner retorts, "any fool can operate a full restaurant. But it takes a genius to successfully operate an empty one."

The restaurant in question is Le Veau d'Or, and the owner is Robert Tréboux, who, having once worked under Henri Soulé at New York's legendary Le Pavillon and later operated two other distinguished French establishments, also serves as reservationist, host, bartender, table captain, wine steward, cloakroom attendant, cashier, and raconteur par excellence. Located on a busy East Side street between Bloomingdale's on Lexington and the apartment houses of Park Avenue, this mostly forgotten bastion of French cuisine is virtually lost amid an array of anonymous storefronts. (Though it's more than sixty years old, few can agree exactly when the restaurant opened; Monsieur Robert bought it in 1985.) Just twenty years ago the neighborhood boasted countless classic French restaurants, but most have disappeared to make room for cacophonous faux bistros, trendy cloned Italian substitutes, and glitzy social playpens serving a hodgepodge of cuisines. Le Veau d'Or is a throwback that defies every social trend, every fashion, and every culinary innovation.

Inside the homey restaurant are a tiny mahogany bar, well-patinated woodwork, beveled mirrors, black-and-white photos of France, and a signature oil painting of a sleeping calf (*Le Veau Dort,* its title a pun on the restaurant's name, which means the golden calf) that's been on the same wall for well over half a century. It's true that Le Veau d'Or is never, ever more than half full and that most of the customers, myself included, are regulars who consider the place an exclusive club—or, to use the more precise French term, a salon—owned, operated, and supervised by an exacting but benevolent monarch who brooks no threats to his domain or his perception of what civilized dining should be about.

The ages of the slightly eccentric clientele range from perhaps thirty to ninety, and on any given evening there might be a party of priests tucking into a platter of choucroute garnie; a British real-estate bigwig whose hobby is carving wooden penguins; a couple who drink vintage port throughout the entire meal; a stylish lady who, in open defiance of the city's draconian smoking ban, reaches into her purse for a miniature porcelain ashtray before lighting up; and, almost invariably, a contingent of young European rakes accompanied by alluring damsels who decorate the room and cause Monsieur Robert's eyes to sparkle. Not long ago a tipsy gentleman sitting at the bar was approached by an attractive woman who wanted to say hello. "I'm sorry, but could you remind me where we met?" the man asked. "Well, you should remember," the woman snapped. "I was your second wife." They're the sort of customers who tend to be regulars at Le Veau d'Or.

• • •

I've been going to Le Veau d'Or ever since my father first took me there when I was a college undergraduate, in the early 1960s. Over the years, I've eaten the luscious poussin en cocotte "bonne femme," escalopines de veau, and tripes à la mode de Caen more times than I can count. I've dined with the likes of Bobby Short and Craig Claiborne. I've watched Tennessee Williams drink too much chablis. And I've nurtured a few dozen love affairs.

The strictly table d'hôte menu I know today (a three-course dinner averages about $28) looks and reads almost exactly like the one back in the restaurant's heyday, in the 1960s and early '70s, when Princess Grace, Orson Welles, Truman Capote, and Jackie Onassis made Le Veau d'Or their canteen and three-hour lunches of rognons de veau dijonnaise, roast duckling aux cerises, oeufs à la neige, multiple bottles of Chateau Talbot, and premium cigars were hallmarks of sophisticated, utterly adult dining and people didn't scrutinize, rhapsodize over, or pontificate about food and wine but simply relished what they ate and drank—or sent it back.

Order a Pernod here, and the whole bottle, a small pitcher of water, and a glass of ice cubes will probably be placed on the table. Why? For the same reason the sole waiter is required to don a formal tuxedo: because it's "correct." Can't decide between pâté and céleri rémoulade as an appetizer? If you're a regular, portions of each will be served on a single plate. Craving something not on the menu, like some French classic you simply can't find anymore? Make your wish known, and there's a good chance the dish will materialize. In all these years I've never once seen the kitchen or been introduced to the longtime chef, and, like other regulars, I can't remember when I did much more than glance at the menu. Nor can I imagine ever seeing a bottle of exotic mineral water, tuna tartare, foie gras "confit," rare-seared arctic char, or organic this or that prepared with heirloom ingredients on any table. Le Veau d'Or is not a restaurant for zealous foodies or even sophomoric ones. It is, blessedly, an eatery without culinary surprises.

I posit that neither Monsieur Robert nor his most loyal clientele knows or cares a whit that other restaurants exist. To my knowledge, the man has only a handful of true passions. Among them are his restaurant in all its faded glory, his grandchildren, vintage bordeaux wine, and beautiful women of any age. "Ah, l'amour, la passion, le coeur!" I've heard him proclaim more than once. On any given day or night after service is finished, it's entirely normal to find Monsieur Robert at the front window or at a corner table flirting with his favorite lady customers, among them his Egyptian princess, his beguiling fortune-teller, his African-American twins, his Singapore siren (she considers him her philosophical mentor), his buxom young friend whose family owns a vineyard in Bordeaux, and a socialite with whom he often goes out dancing after the restaurant closes on Friday nights. Most women, it seems, find the octogenarian irresistible; those upon whom he sheds special attention he refers to as "mes muses."

How does a venerable restaurant like Le Veau d'Or survive year after year when most in its class disappeared long ago and literally dozens of New York City's snappy upstarts go belly-up seemingly overnight? Yes, the traditional cuisine is good—often exceptional—but it is only part of the mystique. Yes, the gentle nostalgia that the restaurant conjures is comforting in a troubled time of world turmoil. Yes, most of the anomalous clientele make for a refreshing change from all the wannabes flocking to the latest hip eating arenas. And yes, there can be no doubt that Monsieur Robert is not only an inimitable character but perhaps Manhattan's last real restaurant doyen. Combine all these things, and it's not hard to conclude that what Le Veau d'Or has is a real, indefinable soul that transcends time and change and fashion. As one regular put it recently, "Le Veau d'Or is more a jaded spiritual adventure than anything else."

Over the past couple of decades, I suspect, there's not much that hasn't happened within the confines of Le Veau d'Or. But to my mind the most notable event is the annual birthday lunch that a wealthy collector of Chinese art throws for his golden retriever, Emma. For the festive occasion, the host invites a dozen or more guests, and he and the groomed dog arrive in a chauffeur-driven car. Tables are set with linen cloths, fresh flowers, and an array of wineglasses, and during cocktails Emma proudly assumes her place of honor on a red banquette. Afterward, while the guests partake of foie gras, steak au poivre, pommes lyonnaises, and other dishes determined in advance by the host and Monsieur Robert, the dog lies on the floor next to her water bowl gnawing a huge soupbone. There's a chantilly cream birthday cake, and Emma wolfs down her serving as everyone bestows best wishes.

How much longer Le Veau d'Or will exist in its present incarnation is directly dependent on Robert Tréboux's stamina and his determination to fulfill a stubborn vision that couldn't be more irrational—a vision that in the eyes of most outsiders no doubt seems downright insane. That the place might one day finally close or, worse, be transformed by some new wizard into yet another updated gastronomic rumpus room is a depressing prospect that regulars refuse even to contemplate. Most likely the restaurant will remain for some time exactly what it has been for nearly seven decades: a patently identifiable, perennial French sanctuary of comfort and conversation, quietly aberrant behavior, and intelligent cuisine that will still be around when all the vegetable froths and crudo conceits are long gone.

And why not? In today's erratic restaurant climate, where hype often seems more urgent than sound cooking and buzz more important than pleasure, New York needs Le Veau d'Or. Boston and Los Angeles and Chicago need a Veau d'Or. In fact, every major city in this country needs a venerable French restaurant like this—a place where yahoos get booted out from time to time, culinary integrity is measured by the precise preparation and presentation of a classic pot-au-feu, and customers are free to throw proper birthday parties for dogs.

My Parents Are Driving Me to Drink

by Chip Brown
from *Food & Wine*

> When literary journalist Chip Brown, author
> of *Good Morning Midnight* and *Afterwards,
> You're a Genius*, takes a tour of Long Island
> vineyards, he throws in one element that
> makes his *Sideways* road trip extra surreal:
> He brings his parents.

I f you exclude scrabble, wine is my family's only sacrament. All of my siblings are grown, but we still count on wine to enhance the harmony of holiday reunions—or if tensions are running high, to at least make reunions bearable.

In their younger years, my parents drank mostly plonk. Their sense of what a bottle should cost was cramped by genetic Yankee thrift, but they also had four kids to put through college. When you live in the valley of *vin ordinaire,* you appreciate wine summits that much more. My mother relished in-law dinner parties not because my dad's father served good wine but because my great-uncle Gordon stashed bottles of Domaine Romanée-Conti in the trunk of his car and would share them with any guests who had the sense to freshen their drinks in the driveway.

My parents are in their eighties now. Since many of the friends they once raised a glass with are gone, certain wines are imbued with ghosts. The name Château d'Yquem recalls the ardent spirit of our neighbor Mr. Reiss, with whom they shared a bottle not long before he died. These charged associations underscore something I've learned as I've gotten older myself: It's not soil or slope or climate that is the predominant element of a wine's *terroir*—it's memory.

With that in mind, I invited my parents to spend a couple of days last summer poking around the North and South Forks of eastern Long Island, where seven new wineries have opened in just the past two years. Historically, our family trips have been fiascoes, plagued by everything from eruptions of Oedipal tensions to infestations of sand fleas. But lately the shadow of mortality has made me prize the time I can spend with my parents. When I proposed the trip, they jumped. It had been a hard winter. They had traded the house they loved in Arizona for spots in an assisted-living village. In the midst of the move, my mother had lung cancer surgery. A week later her last sister died. They had not yet met my new baby, India, their first and only granddaughter, who was now five months old.

My parents arrived on a Friday afternoon at the house my wife, Kate, and I had rented for the summer in Sag Harbor, on the South Fork. Oliver, our six-year-old son, was outside trying to launch a foam missile with a burst of air by jumping on a plastic bladder. He dashed excitedly into the living room.

"The stomp rocket works!" he said.

"What?" my father responded.

"The stomp rocket works!"

"Oh, I thought you said, 'The stock market works.' My hopes soared."

Even if you're middle-aged with children of your own, it's always vaguely infantilizing to go out with your parents. At Almondito, a sleek new Mexican restaurant in Wainscott, a lot of sun-kissed women were stomping around in high heels; none had their parents in tow. Still, the baked striped bass, topped with chopped tomatoes, olives and jalapeños, was delicious. So was the 2001 Schneider Cabernet Franc, a North Fork wine with plummy fruit and soft tannins. When I'd tasted it some time before, it had come across as an oaky muddle. Did it seem better because my parents were enjoying it? They had advanced into the state of grace in which the temptation to find fault is eclipsed by the desire to praise.

On Saturday we drove to Wölffer Estate in Sagaponack, one of the wineries on the South Fork. Proprietor Christian Wölffer and winemaker Roman Roth met us under the chandeliers and barn beams of the elegant tasting room. Grapes were first planted here in

1988, Roth told us; now 50 acres of Chardonnay, Merlot and Cabernet Franc yield 16,000 cases annually.

Advised there was a ghost about, Oliver stayed close when we all descended the stairs to the cool gloom of the cellar. Many of the French oak barrels had been autographed by visiting celebrities like Billy Joel and Julia Child. We sat around a half-moon-shaped table tasting the top Wölffer wines. Everyone used the spit bucket except my mother. "I'm too old to spit," she said.

We moved from a Burgundy-style 2002 Pinot to the $40-a-bottle 2002 Cabernet Franc. "I like the Pinot more," my mother said. "The Cabernet Franc is out of my price range."

"The Pinot is $50 a bottle," Wölffer responded.

She gulped, first air, then what was left in her glass.

Wölffer opened a half-bottle of the 2001 Premier Cru Merlot, which lists for $125, the highest price ever for a Long Island wine. Among the Hummer-driving fat cats who have propelled Hamptons real estate into the stratosphere, it's something of a status item, or a least a fallback option if a California cult cab or some Bordeaux thoroughbred is unavailable.

"This is getting in your league," Wölffer said to my mother.

Alarmed, I realized he was right. Even my father, who for many years has had a diminished sense of taste and smell after cracking his skull on a birch tree behind our family house, seemed to be falling under a liquidate-your-IRA spell. I realized that if my parents were going to retain their financial independence, I had to get them out of there. Fortunately, after the seductive 2004 Late Harvest Chardonnay, which we sampled above ground under a vine-draped pergola, they were ready for a nap.

My parents rallied that evening for dinner on Shelter Island at the Vine Street Café, an unpretentious white-shingled restaurant overlooking a forested ravine. Chefs Terry Harwood and Lisa Murphy, who married after working together at Manhattan's Union Square Cafe, opened the place two years ago. Terry handles the savory courses and Lisa the sweet ones.

I had Prince Edward Island mussels in basil-saffron broth, while my father ordered seared diver scallops on a bed of sweet corn succotash with edamame and red peppers; both dishes paired well with a refreshing 2003 Peconic Bay Riesling. The dessert specialty was a fantastic pineapple tart that Kate had to guard from being pillaged by her dinner companions. The rustic setting and homespun barn ambiance were so far from the slickness of the Hamptons that it felt like going back in time.

On Sunday, my parents and I traveled by ferry to Greenport, on the North Fork. It's subtly different in growing conditions than the South Fork (the vines bud a week earlier in the sandier soils) and radically different in tone, with metal sheds and working boatyards, churches and roadside markets, and middle-class houses instead of gated mansions. That said, the wine industry has transformed the place like few others outside California. In 1995, there were only fourteen wineries on the North Fork. Now there are thirty-four, producing 450,000 cases a year. The pioneers who planted the wrong grapes in the wrong places and experimented with clones and trellis systems that were unsuited to the local conditions are now giving way to a new generation of wealthy owners who are investing millions to add acreage, upgrade facilities and bring in famous consultants. But perhaps the biggest reason for the area's growing reputation is that older vines typically produce better wine and many of those on Long Island have some age on them.

I'd been hoping to squeeze in visits to three of the best vineyards, Bedell, Macari, and Peconic Bay. But octogenarians can't be rushed. And my mother is a master of the art of the prolonged chat, which makes it hard to rip through a bunch of appointments. Thankfully, we started at the summit: Bedell Cellars in Cutchogue, whose wines are widely acknowledged as the benchmark of Long Island Merlots. Long Island's cool maritime climate produces reds like Bedell's that are more like Bordeaux's than California's; they're lower in alcohol and more food-friendly.

Kip Bedell began his career pumping heating oil for his family's business and made wine only as a hobby. He released his first commercial bottles in 1985. After an exceptional 1988 vintage and a string of well-received wines in the '90s, people began calling him Mr. Merlot. "At least now I can drink what I pump," he said. In 2000, Bedell agreed to sell the winery for $5 million to Michael Lynne, the co-chairman and co-chief executive of New Line Cinema, who the year before had bought nearby Corey Creek Vineyards for $2 million. Lynne promised Bedell he could stay on as winemaker, and Bedell is now collaborating with consultant Pascal Marty, who was director of wine-making at Baron Philippe de Rothschild.

In the tasting room, I noticed that my parents were happy to skip the lower-end wines, like the $14 Main Road Red, a fruity Merlot blend, in favor of the premium stuff—the 2000 Bedell Cupola, an elegant Bordeaux-style blend, and the 2001 and 2002 Reserve Merlot.

Bedell took a scrutinizing sip of the 2001 Reserve Merlot, the umpteenth time he'd tasted it. "I like this but it is not my favorite," he said.

"What's your favorite?" I asked.

He laughed. "For everyday drinking I really like the Main Road Red."

He suddenly reminded me of my parents and the values they'd embodied just two days ago, before they started touring Long Island wineries. I looked over and saw the astonishing sight of my mother, credit card out, springing for a case of the 2001 Bedell Merlot in half bottles.

"Mom, what are you doing?"

"Half bottles are the perfect size," she said.

Thank God the Reserve Merlot didn't come in half bottles. I spotted my father eyeing a Bedell Late Harvest Riesling at $39 a throw. How could I begrudge him a few bottles when a sweet wine improved his chess game so dramatically? The last time we'd played, the two of us had polished off a late-harvest Riesling from California, and I'd never seen him fianchetto a bishop so skillfully.

We'd already stayed an hour longer than I'd planned, mostly because my parents seemed so happy. We had a lunch to get to—and promises to visit two more wineries. Promises we would not keep. And I didn't care, because here was a memory I would have forever: my parents walking out of a winery together on a beautiful summer afternoon. They had altered the *terroir* of the Bedell Merlot, and I know whenever I drink that wine, I'll taste the day.

The Fish That Surpasses All Understanding

by Jeff Gordinier

from *Breathe*

Paying a fortune for one very special meal has an incalcuable value—or does it? Essayist Jeff Gordinier takes us along on his long-desired evening at Manhattan's most expensive restaurant.

I f you told the average person that he was about to experience the greatest meal of his life, he would probably be happy. Joy is a logical response when good things are about to happen. But if you had spotted my brother, Curt, and me walking through Central Park on a warm spring evening not so long ago, you wouldn't have picked up a lot of joy in our facial expressions. Watching from a distance, you would have seen two young guys—one an uncombed "creative type" with a motormouth and a thoroughly unnecessary black umbrella, the other a quiet and conservatively cropped money manager with the compressed muscle mass of a gymnast—checking their watches every 30 seconds. You would have seen furrowed brows and stiff shoulders. You might have figured we were headed to a funeral.

But Curt and I were, at that moment, basking in a state of exquisite good fortune: We had a reservation at Masa. Technically speaking, Masa is a sushi bar, but calling it that feels sort of like calling the moon a rock. Masa is the luminous, otherworldly ideal of what a sushi lair is supposed to be. Run by the master chef Masa Takayama, wedged like a chapel into the fourth floor of Manhattan's teeming Time Warner Center, and recently garlanded with four stars from *The New York Times,* Masa is where Japanese concepts like *shibui* ("simplicity devoid of unnecessary elements," according to the Masa Web site) and *umami* ("basic essence of flavor inherent in each ingredient") are expressed in everything that your eyes, ears, hands, and tongue encounter. It's a place that makes you forever ashamed to eat another Fantastic Spicy Elvis Roll, and, for that privilege, it is celestially expensive: By the end of the evening, one of us would be autographing a bill for $1,200.

But the cost was not the primary source of our anxiety. We were nervous because we are nervous people. We were nervous because we really, really wanted the dinner to go right. Everybody likes things to go right, but members of my family have a tense, gnawing need for it, especially when we're in restaurants. We love restaurants, we talk about them the way some people talk about opera or the Yankees, we've had the best times of our lives together in restaurants, and yet restaurants frequently turn us into puddles of stress. The problem is anticipation. There is always That Thing That Could Go Wrong. In fact, the international psychiatric community has diagnosed this response as Gordinier Restaurant Indulgence Paranoia Disorder, or GRIPD. People with GRIPD have such a Howard Hughesian obsession with food, and with the presentation of food, that each course, each rich bowl of ribollita or platter of roasted branzino, each molten pot of cassoulet or Taco Bell breakfast burrito, acts as a potential trigger for giddiness or frustration, euphoria or despair. Those afflicted with an acute case of GRIPD want so badly to enjoy everything that sometimes, in the end, they can't enjoy anything. A Buddhist might refer to this as a classic example of *samsara.* If Zen has an opposite, it's GRIPD.

Which partially explains why, even though we had made a reservation at Masa for 6 P.M., Curt and I showed up in the Time Warner Center at 5. (A standard symptom of GRIPD: punctuality stretched to a pathological extreme.) If you want another reason why Curt and I were tense, the short answer is: we're brothers. We know how to make each other laugh. We get on each other's nerves. We know how to make each other angry. We have, upon occasion, thrown things at each other. Because I love my brother, I still feel bad about chucking a hammer at him when he was seven, and there are times now when it feels as if a cloud of negative energy hangs between us and every word or gesture is tagged with misinterpretation. You might say we have a fraternal-fireworks variation on That Thing That Could Go Wrong. Both of us are men who remain stubbornly attached to our rituals; Curt, a natural athlete, sticks to a daily workout schedule, while I, the flabby family egghead, guard my reading hour like a starved pit bull. Both of us have a habit of chafing when one of these day-to-day ceremonies is subjected to the slightest disruption. A spilled cup of coffee can turn into a scene from *High Noon*. Ironically, this friction is the very thing that leads Curt and me toward a more sympathetic understanding of each other: Since we are, underneath it all, equally caught up in our Prussian craving for order, That Thing That Could Go Wrong has the potential to unite us.

So as we wandered the western edge of Central Park on that spring evening trying to kill time, we each knew intuitively that our appointment with Masa Takayama was a chance to chow down like kings *and* a chance to make some emotional progress. Even a couple of control freaks can recognize an exceptional opportunity to let go.

In fact, if there's one thing a control freak admires, it's that rare individual who has achieved such a supreme, all-encompassing, Kenobi-like state of control-freakery that his work feels as effortless and sedative as an ocean breeze. Meaning: A man who doesn't *try* to control things, he simply *does*. Masa Takayama is that man, and from the moment Curt and I entered his sanctum we knew we had no choice but to give up and give in. Our first impression, after attendants had whisked away our shoulder bags, was stillness. The room, which seats only twenty-six people, felt so hushed that the silence itself was almost tactile; it was as if Masa's team had fine-tuned the acoustics to allow us to hear the air in between the sound waves. (The only other time this kind of stillness has surrounded me in Manhattan was, ironically, around midnight in Times Square—on a night when the city was muffled by a massive blizzard.) Being geeks, Curt and I had arrived at the restaurant before anyone else, and the maître d' seated us in the center of the sushi bar. Every single review of Masa makes a point of mentioning that the bar is made of light-colored wood from the Hinoki cypress and that the wood is sanded by the restaurant's staff each morning. This sounds like some kind of sinister *dathun*-master's mind game until you actually sit there. At the risk of slipping into skin-flick self-parody here, it's true: The wood has a kind of powdery softness, and you can't resist rubbing your hands up and down its surface.

Once seated, the first choice we made—in fact, the only choice we made—had to do with what to drink. After we'd stared at the sake menu for a few clueless seconds, Curt, in his wisdom, said something along the lines of "When you're going for it, you might as well really go for it." With that, we ordered a small, cold bottle of Kakunkou Junmai Daiginjou, which would pixie-dust our tab with an extra $118. The sake came; an attendant poured each of us a tiny glass; we passed the sake under our noses and took a sip. It was delicious, and yet it was beyond delicious: It was new. Like almost everything we tasted at Masa, the sake was possessed of a flavor that came across as both sublime and synaptically trailblazing. We had never tasted anything like it. If it's possible to extract and distill the nectar of exotic flowers, I suppose it might taste something like that Kakunkou.

Past this point, we had no input into our own feeding. We forfeited control. Whatever joy arose in the next two hours (and there would be a whole lot of joy) would be the product of a mapless and inexorable adventure. Masa has no menu. As Frank Bruni put it in his *New York Times* review, "You pay to be putty," and that, for a couple of toaster-oven micromanagers like Curt and me, can feel like liberation. Masa Takayama appeared in a workmanlike steel-gray shirt, greeted us with a gruff, professional nod, and set to work with his bone-handled knife. Within a few minutes it dawned on us that being a geek has its advantages: One of the most prominent and inventive chefs in the world, the Cezanne of Japanese cuisine, was standing right in front of us—at this moment exclusively at the service of two working stiffs from the suburbs—and conjuring our meal by hand. In the words of the great sages Wayne and Garth, all we could think was: *We're not worthy.*

And yes, the meal was mind-blowing. If the entire dinner added up to 100 bites, about 90 of them ranked among the most amazing things my mouth had ever been exposed to. In nearly every nibble Masa introduced us to a texture or a seasoning that was new to us— flavors so far removed from our Western sugar-salt continuum that we felt like we were dining at the top-rated restaurant on Jupiter.

There were cool, white, gossamer fish noodles zested with shavings of *sudachi,* a green Japanese citrus fruit that hits like a cross between a lime and a kumquat. There were moments of blissful oddity (a semi-sour, crunchy "ocean eggplant") and pure, turbo-charged luxury (a bowl full of toro tartare generously crested with caviar). There were peace treaties between the familiar and the extraterrestrial: When a tempura course arrived, Curt and I realized that what had been deep-fried with a perfect balance of crispiness and softness were unidentifiable sprigs of flora that we'd never see on the menu at Teriyaki Boy. "Mountain vegetables," Masa explained, sort of. Between each course, members of the staff would, with movements that barely registered as a whisper, delicately move our utensils: the sake glass would go seven millimeters to the west, the chopsticks four hairbreadths to the north. I can't say for sure whether these micromovements were supposed to unblock our chi, but I have to admit that I started to feel an underlying logic with each change of scenery. Somehow it all made sense.

After the preliminary courses came the sushi. Masa sliced each piece of fish, rolled it with a handful of slightly warm and slightly loose rice, dabbed it with freshly grated wasabi, basted it with sauce, and placed it on a small round plate in front of us. "Pop in mouth," he said. He told us to use our fingers. There was fluke and *shima-aji* and toro crisped on a grill, and a wonderful shiitake mushroom charred on the open fire and clamped around rice, but beyond that my memory is fuzzy, because Curt and I were now heading for a level of euphoria that seemed to exist a few Himalayan crampons past the plateau of verbal communication. At first we fell back on the sort of standard male exchanges that we've always relied on, as most brothers do when searching for points of agreement—references to the majesty of Heidi Klum, the power of The Clash at the Hollywood Palladium, the memory of an especially godlike series of waves one afternoon long ago in Newport Beach—but by the time we had progressed to a consciousness-expanding rally of raw seafood (sweet shrimp, red clam, squid) the two of us were reduced to expressing ourselves with prelingual grunts. Really, we just shut our traps. The meal unfolded like a meditation, with all of our stray thoughts, grievances, and fixations gradually loosening and floating off.

Upon the delivery of a cold and invigorating cup of grapefruit *granita*, Curt and I happened to detect, without a word, that we weren't nervous anymore. We weren't worrying. We weren't coiled in anticipation of That Thing That Could Go Wrong. In fact, everything was going right, but that wasn't the point: Masa had somehow satisfied, and then subverted, our innate rage for order. We were simply enjoying each other's company. This was new too. As my friends know, I'm not much of a smiler, but after polishing off the iced grapefruit I caught myself in a mirror and saw a ridiculous and unfettered grin—the kind of grin that you tend to see on the faces of little kids with melty ice-cream cones. No, a person shouldn't and doesn't have to pay $1,200 to approach that kind of joy, but I guess something about the insane cosmic splurge of the whole thing, coupled with the extreme aspiration of Masa Takayama's culinary art, made it difficult to feel anything other than clear, open gratitude. Extremity itself, whether positive or negative, has a way of stopping you in your tracks.

A server with a look of mercy in her eyes brought us the bill, and we both glanced at it. Curt said, "Let me get this," and I let him, and we laughed. I have never been adept at accepting gifts, but this time I didn't flinch. We thanked Masa Takayama and said good-bye, and as we stepped into the honking frenzy of Columbus Circle, Curt and I seemed to be carrying along with us a box full of the stillness that we'd encountered in the restaurant; it was almost as if all of those tiny adjustments in the placement of the chopsticks and the sake glasses had brought about minute recalibrations in our brain chemistry. We talked, and then we stopped talking, and even our silence was shot through with a kind of present-tense alertness. We'd eaten a lot, but we didn't feel the slightest bit weighed down; we felt lighter, energized. As Curt and I walked east along Central Park, we found ourselves doing two brotherly things that we hadn't done in a while: First, we raised our arms in the air and exchanged a high-five, and then we veered right, down Fifth Avenue, planless and open to the Great Whatever. For the next couple of hours, until I caught my train home, I don't think we checked our watches once.

Ho Chi Minh City

by Brett Martin

from *Bon Appetit*

Travel writer Brett Martin lays bare the culinary soul of a city that, for Americans at least, was long off limits. He brings to life not only the Vietnamese city's sights and sounds, but—more important for hungry travelers—its smells and tastes as well.

A surefire sign that a city is serious about street food is that every resident has an opinion. Just ask a New Yorker where to get the quintessential slice, a Parisian for his favorite crepe, or a resident of Saigon about the best version of *pho,* Vietnam's famous noodle soup.

As the unofficial dish of Vietnam, *pho* is ubiquitous in Saigon (now named Ho Chi Minh City, though nobody outside of the airport seems to call it that). On the way in from the airport, my taxi driver swung blocks out of his way to show me his favorite *pho* spot, watching carefully as I wrote down the name. But *pho*—which, in its ideal form, is deep, bright, meaty, and floral all at once—is by no means the only street dish to inspire such strong proprietary emotions.

My notebook quickly filled with tiny maps hand-drawn by people directing me to, say, the perfect *banh mi* (a French break sandwich traditionally eaten for breakfast) or an exemplary *banh xeo* (a light, crisp crepe folded over chopped pork, shrimp, mushrooms, and mung beans). A Sofitel PR executive who had two restaurants of her own to promote urged me to visit a back-alley cart that served *bun bo hue,* a spicy beef soup from her home city of Hue. Everybody in

Saigon has a favorite dish—and it was my futile quest to try every one of them.

It's no secret that Vietnam, in the midst of its exuberant blossoming, has become the food-minded traveler's dream destination. Anthony Bourdain is moving there to write a book. Respected Vietnamese chefs like Michael Huynh of Bao 111 in New York and Mai Pham of Lemon Grass Restaurant in Sacramento have been leading cooking tours through the country with students from The Culinary Institute of America—a kind of CIA infiltration that would have been unfathomable here a generation ago. The world is coming to Vietnam to eat, and where it eats best is on the streets of the culinary capital of Saigon.

Navigating those streets is another question entirely. Saigon is divided into 17 districts, which may have once made sense to a colonial administrator homesick for Parisian arrondissements but now form a dense, chaotic spiral emanating from District 1—the tourist and business center bordering the Saigon River. On my first morning in the city, I stood for a full ten minutes at an insanely busy traffic circle across from Ben Thanh Market, trying to figure out how I could ever cross to the other side. The answer, I realized—after watching an elderly woman toddle across while the sea of trucks, bicycles, and motorbikes parted around her—was to take a deep breath and wade in. To hesitate would be the most dangerous thing of all.

And that's an equally good approach to the vast universe of Saigon street food. The most important Vietnamese phrase to learn is *Cai do la gi?* ("What is that?"), followed by *Toi muon mot* ("I'd like one"). This philosophy was imparted to me by Graham Holliday, a hearty thirty-six-year-old British expat who writes the blog noodlepie.com, an entertaining and exhaustive digest of "scoff and swill in Saigon." Holliday does not pretend to be an authority on Vietnamese cuisine. Rather, he is an enthusiastic pointer and taster—and thus, the perfect guide.

When I tagged along with him on an excursion, we stopped first at a restaurant called Quan Co Tam for *banh phoi suong,* a dish of sliced pork and herbs wrapped in thin rice pancakes. We crouched on brightly colored plastic baby furniture as the accoutrements for nearly every Vietnamese meal were set in front of us: a dish of pickled radishes and shallots, a bowl of salty and mildly pungent fish sauce called *nuoc nam,* and an enormous basket overflowing with bright green herbs. "You just chuck in a bit of whatever you like," Holliday said.

In Vietnam, the climate giveth and taketh away; luckily, both sides of the equation benefit the food lover. On one hand, the hot climate produces an astounding bounty of ingredients, and on the other, the same conditions mandate that everything be served at the height of freshness, since things spoil fast where refrigeration is scarce. It's one of the reasons that eating on the street—where you can observe the quality of the ingredients and watch everything being made—can be safer than eating at a fancy restaurant with a closed kitchen door.

"The Vietnamese are serious about their food," Holliday told me. "If something is crap, they're not going to stand for it."

We hopped in a cab that took us to my Sofitel lady's *bun bo hue* spot for a sinus-clearing meat broth perfumed with lemongrass and served with banana flower, herbs, and sprouts, and then across the street for another Hue specially—*banh canh cua,* a thick, greenish soup filled with fat noodles, cilantro, and flecks of fresh crab.

By the time we headed over to Ben Thanh Market, I had given up all illusions of even scratching the surface of Saigon's gastronomic variety. "Oh, that's very interesting," Holliday said as he spied a variation on *banh mi* that substituted beef patties for the traditional pork. "I've never seen that."

For all of the welcome this sexy, cosmopolitan city is extending to the world, an American is bound to wonder: How exactly did we get from the Vietnam War to this? In fact, the "American War" is one chapter in a century that saw conflicts with the Japanese, French, Chinese, and Cambodians, and then a period of forced collectivization, re-education camps, and real hunger. The Communist government's adoption in the mid-1980s of the open-market policy known as *doi moi* set the stage for the remarkable moment Saigon is now enjoying: Thanks to a peacetime baby boom, there are more than 83 million people in Vietnam, a country slightly larger than New Mexico, and their median age is just 25. Millions are now coming of age in a brand-new middle class, too busy partaking in one of the world's fastest-growing gross domestic products to dwell on the past.

One night, I took a whirlwind motorbike tour of Saigon with a near perfect representative of this new generation. Vy is twenty-five and an accountant at a booming construction firm. She carries a cell phone that comes complete with two Vietnamese/English dictionaries. Her parents, she told me, eat out maybe once or twice a year, but she and her friends spend their evenings socializing in bars, restaurants, and coffee shops around the city.

I held on for dear life as we sped through the streets, zipping down Nguyen Tri Phuong street toward District 5. We spun past neon nightclubs and sidewalk restaurants, open-air billiard parlors and late-night vegetable markets, stalls selling *pho* in steaming bowls and grassy median strips where young couples come to flirt and make out on their bikes. For all of capitalism's growing pains and the lingering oppression of a state that still controls many aspects of daily life, Saigon is simply bursting at the seams with the happiness of being alive. By the time Vy dropped me at my hotel, I was like a lad stumbling off a roller coaster: exhausted, shaky, but wanting to go again.

Peace and prosperity have had practical effects on food, too, allowing a free flow of ingredients into Saigon from all parts of the country and from all over Southeast Asia. "It's difficult to say what is typical Saigon food," Sakal Phoeung told me. "It's a fusion of Hanoi, Hue, Cambodia, Laos, everywhere." Phoeung is the Cambodian-born, French-trained executive chef at the Sofitel. But it was after-hours, and he and his Saigonese pastry chef and kitchen manager were hitting the town.

We were in District 5, at Phung Vy Restaurant on Nguyen Tri Phuong street, which is lined with late-night seafood restaurants. Sidewalk tables were filled with raucous families and groups of men, metal buckets of beer in ice at their feet. Cooks threw shrimp and crabs, still kicking, onto blazing charcoal grills. At the table, we dipped the sizzling meat into a paste of salt, chiles, and lime, throwing the shells into the gutter. Before *doi moi,* such freshness was an all but unattainable luxury, but now decent roads allow a daily flow of seafood from the coast and produce from the fertile Mekong Delta and Dalat regions.

• • •

On my final day in Saigon, Holliday took me to a focal outdoor market near his house in District 10 for a final bowl of noodle soup, this time *bun mam,* an intense Mekong Delta specialty flavored with purple fermented shrimp paste. The market was the length of a single block and featured at least ten food vendors, each with his own specialty. At the moment, there are probably a hundred markets like it tucked away on side streets in Saigon. But there's no telling how long before more fancy restaurants, gleaming skyscrapers, and Western franchises change the face of Saigon yet again. (For now, the sole representative of Fast Food Nation is KFC, and it's impossible to ignore the striking resemblance between Colonel Sanders and Ho Chi Minh himself.)

"My concern," said Holliday, "is that as the Vietnamese get richer, they'll want to appear richer, and that might mean sweeping all this food off the street. And once some of these recipes go back behind closed doors, they may not come out for a long time." Already, street vendors have been forced off two avenues in District 1.

All of which is to say: Go. Go now.

Eating Space

by John T. Edge

from *Oxford American*

Author most recently of a quartet of books about iconic classic dishes—Apple Pie, Fried Chicken, Hamburgers and Fries, and Donuts—Edge is a dogged and delightful investigator of the highways and byways of Southern food, relishing quirkiness and sense of place.

I once ate dinner at Lusco's—an elegantly shabby, Depression-vintage restaurant in the Mississippi Delta town of Greenwood—with my pants down. Two companions, both men, were similarly disrobed. I recall one filleting a pompano while his khakis pooled on the floor. The other, after cutting into a T-bone, cursed the sauce that splattered his boxers. Our lone female compatriot was demure: Her skirt remained on, but she wriggled out of her black brassiere, extracted it though the armhole of her blouse, and left it dangling on a lamp.

Our waiter, a dignified man whom I summoned to our curtained private booth in the accustomed way, by pushing a wall-mounted buzzer, made no notice of our attire. He simply brought ice for our highball glasses and asked if the onion rings were to our liking. I told him that they were. And, with a rustle of chintz, he was gone, back down the dim hall, bound for the lime-sherbet foyer, flocked with stuffed and mounted mallards, turkeys, and deer.

This was back in 1996. We were, by varying degrees, mature adults in our early thirties. Dinner at Lusco's was my suggestion. I tempted my friends with praise of Lusco's tempura-battered onion rings. I spoke of swabbing fries in the buttery *jus* that puddles their magnolia-rimmed steak platters. And I warned of the tiptoe heat of Lusco's shrimp sauce. But what I really pledged—and what Lusco's delivered—was, in the patois of my graduate school days, less text than context.

We traveled, not for prime steak or day-boat fish, but to cloak ourselves in the gone-to-seed glamour of the onetime cotton capital of Greenwood, to revel in the peculiar architecture of its most storied restaurant. Our grail was to make good on the no-tell motel promise of those trademark booths, and, like generations of Lusco's diners, to shamble toward bliss.

I recognized then, and can verbalize now, that resonance of place is integral to dining. The pattern of a pressed-tin ceiling, the window bank by which sunlight knifes through the afternoon gloom, the geometry of people at table in a well-proportioned room, these architectural elements—and others both structural and decorative— have defined the tenor of my restaurant meals.

While in graduate school, I became a student of dining. I learned to ferret the value bottles from a French wine list. I earned the confidence to eat asparagus with my fingers. At Galatoire's in New Orleans, Highlands in Birmingham, and, yes, at Lusco's, I came to know restaurants as places of possibility, where the simple act of calorie-taking is transformed and capitalists make good on Brillat-Savarin's observation that "the pleasure of eating is one we share with animals," while the "pleasures of the table are known only to the human race."

The spaces lulled me. The crackle-paned casement windows and sinewy balustrades and incised pediments won my favor and loosened my purse. I was an easy mark, for most of my experience in public dining had come during bright-light-of-day cafeteria meals and pass-the-biscuits-to-a-stranger boardinghouse feeds. In other words, I was not to the damask-draped table born—to say nothing of a damask-draped table set in a cloistered dining compartment, well-disposed to all manner of randy thought and deed.

Lusco's is not a grand restaurant. Not in the traditional sense. The facade is a plane of bricks, offering little to passersby but the blank stare of oblique windows. By the grace of entropy, the church and business that bookend the single-story building have remained intact, although the sign in the window of L.C.M.C. Memorial Garden, the one that read, WE MAKE HEAD-STONES, has disappeared.

The interior exudes a gravitas that comes not by design, but by dint of benign neglect. Step from a booth through the rear vestibule up into the stoop-ceilinged rabbit hutch that passes for the men's privy, and you glimpse an interior courtyard–cum–oyster midden, no longer active but suggestive of past bacchanals. Eye the threshold that separates the front vestibule and the booth-lined central hallway, and you can envision a day when strong drink was best consumed out of sight and a member of the Lusco clan stood guard, passing judgment on all who wished to pass. Ponder the tight confines of booth three, and you can imagine a time when family members Marie and Philip Correro lived on premises and claimed that claus-trophobic rectangle as their bedroom.

It's been more than a decade since Lusco's underwent a major renovation. Back in 1989, fourth-generation family proprietors Andy and Karen Pinkston scraped the pressed-tin tiles free of the residue from hundreds of butter pats that diners, in a long-standing tradition, catapulted ceilingward on bent knives. The cleaning process was exhaustive. And the finish, an application of swimming-pool lacquer—as well as the placards, declaring butter-pat flipping to be malicious mischief—announced a kind of finality.

In the intervening years, the Pinkstons have made small modifi-cations, the most notable being a touch-up of the Coke sign that ribbons the front window. Now, as before, they safeguard the restau-rant's integrity, managing the modest warp of change with learned economy, not studied purity, for Andy and Karen are business-people first, stewards of place second.

Time spent at table in Lusco's is spellbinding. And awareness of this effect is important to the budding gastronome. Put another way, while my meals with the Pinkstons have been invariably good, if you carry a Lusco's steak home in a polystyrene box, expect illusions to fade as gristle hardens, as butter reveals itself to be margarine.

• • •

Since my strip-down debauch, I have eaten at Lusco's a dozen or more times. Thanks to the restaurant's brown-bag policy, my dining companions and I have been, by mid-meal, invariably drunk. (Once, my host, a local swell, tumped over in his chair while at table in Lusco's and was whisked from our booth with such dispatch and aplomb that I did not note his leaving.)

On a recent visit, I declined a lonesome booth in favor of taking my meal at the four-top counter. I stayed clear of the fog of drink. Sobriety offered me the opportunity, between bites of shrimp, to rifle through an old file, compiled while in graduate school. I redis-covered that, although I had come to prize the enclosed booths at Lusco's as signature, they are not unique.

According to my notes, the tradition of private dining in public spaces dates back to at least 1782, when the Grande Taverne de Lon-dres opened in Paris, France. American institutions followed suit, among them Musso and Frank Grill, a favorite of William Faulkner's during his Hollywood sojourn, and Fadich Grill, a San Francisco seafood house, famous for sand dabs. Closer to home, private booths remain elemental to Henry Terry's Highway 41 Fish House, a cin-derblock throwback south of Pontotoc, Mississippi, and Giardina's, the crosstown Greenwood restaurant which likely borrowed its seating configuration from Lusco's.

The traditional restaurant serves as a stage on which mun-dane and intimate acts become public theater. Private booths queer the paradigm, insuring that indulgence remains covert, that the Falwell Baptist neighbors may know you walked in with a fifth of Jack but can only guess at the consequences of its emptying. Whatever propriety might stay your hand in public when reaching for a sixth onion ring—or your date's thigh— vanishes. That's the plan, the promise.

Today, restaurants in Charlotte and Atlanta and other capitals of New South industry feature private dining rooms, enclaves where egos are stroked, menus fetishized, deals done. They are not places of possibility but conceits of exclusivity, bulwarks against the rabble. And yet these simulacra with chef's tables and ten-course tasting *cartes* may prove to be, by default, inheritors of the tradition.

That realization put no damper on my dinner, for, seated as I was, beneath that lacquer-coated ceiling, within sight of various stuffed woodland creatures that, in the right light, might be mistaken for gargoyles, I could swivel around and see the booth where I ate in the almost altogether. And I could take solace, knowing that, ten years hence, the food will be no better and no worse, the curtains on the booth fronts will be shading toward threadbare, and a naked bulb will shine bright, wanting for the cover of a black brassiere.

Mama's House

by Jason Sheehan
from *Westword*

Almost in the tradition of the late great Hunter S. Thompson, Jason Sheehan puts a high-voltage gonzo spin on his Denver dining reviews. This one could almost be subtitled *Fear and Loathing on the Ghanian Restaurant Trail.*

Mama T is leaving.

She's moving to Cincinnati, where her husband is working a factory job now, where there's another apartment waiting, another community expecting her. She's going with her son Rafael, and she's taking her pots and pans. She's taking her living-room set with the white lace doilies. She's taking her recipes and her traditions. And after she goes, there will be nowhere for Denver's tight-knit community of Ghanaian immigrants to eat.

Mama runs a house restaurant—a semisecret, unlicensed eatery that operates out of her crowded two-bedroom apartment in Aurora. "I talked to her on the phone yesterday," my friend Mark says. "Just to make sure she was still cooking today. And she said yeah, from eleven o'clock *through*."

Mama's kitchen doesn't take reservations. Dinner is catch as catch can. You knock on the door and maybe Mama's there, maybe she's not. *Through* means there will be pots on the stove, but it does not necessarily mean that anyone will be there watching them.

Mama has been running her house restaurant, in a variety of homes, for six years. Mark had eaten at her last spot, but he's not sure where she's cooking now. "When I called, I asked her where she was," he says, skidding his old Volvo to a stop on Parker Road. "And I don't know . . . she speaks good English, but sometimes it's still hard to understand her. Or hard for her to understand me."

He reaches into the back seat, pulls out a camera case and digs around in the pockets for a scrap of paper that has assorted address permutations scratched on it. "Side of Florida and Dayton," he says, mimicking Mama, his voice slowing, tongue thickening. The accent is strange and almost Caribbean—one that makes "Florida" into three distinct syllables and "Dayton" into *Day-tone*. "That's what she said to me, but the address? I don't know. I wrote down a couple, so we'll see."

Mark spent three years in Ghana as a teacher with the Peace Corps. He loved the country and wants to get back there someday, maybe open a bar or a school of his own. His Peace Corps work is his connection to Denver's Ghanaian community, the community his connection back to Ghana, and as he drives through the snow, we talk about the people, the culture, the diaspora that sent tens of thousands of displaced Ghanaians to the United States (roughly 3,000 call Denver home). Mostly, though, we talk about the food, about what he ate while he was there, what he misses most and what he now has to go to Mama's to get.

In Ghana, the men don't cook, he tells me; the women do. But that isn't to say they just stay home, chained to stoves, tending to home fires. Rather, they run restaurants.

"If you were to get a job managing, say, a gas station in Ghana—which would be a very good, very respectable job—your wife would immediately find a place close by to start selling food," Mark explains. This might be as simple as a charcoal grill set up by the side of a road, where she'd sell grilled meats or plantain or kabobs. The next step up would be a couple of chairs, a screen so others passing by can't see those eating. After that, a roof. After that, walls.

The fanciest restaurants in Ghana are Chinese—rice being a special delicacy in the starch-obsessed food culture—and fried-chicken places. Mark tells a story about a Ghanaian who got a job managing a Kentucky Fried Chicken in Germany. The industrious fellow stole everything that wasn't nailed down—menus, recipes, signage, banners, kitchen equipment, what have you—and had it all shipped back to Accra. When he returned home, he opened his own quasi-KFC, but because no one in Ghana would understand what "Kentucky" was, he called it Kiki Riki Fried Chicken. "It's a very famous restaurant in the north," Mark insists. "Ask anyone, and they'll probably know it."

But aside from Kiki Riki Fried Chicken, Ghanaian food hasn't been corrupted by colonialism or degraded by the influences of immigrants (except for the Chinese and their ever-present takeout operations). Today it's essentially unchanged from what it was centuries ago. At roadside stands, in shacks and "chop bars" and gas-station parking lots, the people eat beans and non-native corn. They eat fish and rice balls and risen, raw starch dough called *fufu*, which is made from pounded plantain and cassava root. "You'll see these guys who are just all biceps pounding the cassava," Mark says. "They use what looks like a whole tree trunk and just pound the shit out of this stuff until it's like a paste."

The meat is primarily goat, although the Ghanaian diet also includes chicken and fish. And because the Ghanaians like their meat prepared in very specific ways, they've found unusual sources here in Denver. The goat, for example, is specially processed by a rancher out near the airport, with the animals butchered whole with their thick skin and subdermal fat left on, their hair taken off with a blow-torch. "If you're not cutting bone, you're not cutting meat," Mark explains. "That's what they say. And the goat is cooked skin and bones and all."

American food horrifies most Ghanaians, so the community feeds itself out of necessity. There are African markets that sell pre-pared foods—prepared, always, by someone's wife or sister—and a few Chinese restaurants that cater to the immigrants. But because most of them are men who've left their wives and families behind to come work here and send American dollars back home, there is also Mama's, where they can gather to gossip, argue politics and eat.

"With Mama leaving, this is a very big deal," Mark says. "Everyone is trying to figure out who'll cook after she leaves, whose wife will take over. Everyone has been talking about it, saying, 'What about your wife? No, what about yours?' If someone has a wife who comes here and just wants to be a housewife, they say, 'No! You can't just be a housewife in America. You have to work!' But really, they all just want to know where they'll be able to eat what they like."

Tonight, though, is Mama's last night in business. Tomorrow is her going-away party at the Knights of Columbus hall. After that, she'll be gone.

"Hey, this looks promising," Mark suddenly shouts, pointing across the dashboard at a block of cookie-cutter apartment buildings that look just like every other block of apartment buildings we've passed. "Can you see the address?"

I can, and though it doesn't precisely match the number Mark has written down, it does share four of the five digits, in tumbled order.

"Let's try it," he says, and slowly guides the Volvo in.

We find a building number that matches and an apartment number that's close. Mark knocks.

No answer.

"This doesn't look good," he says. "Usually you'd hear voices, music, people inside. I don't know."

He knocks again. I smoke a cigarette and watch the snow fall, watch it haloing around the parking lot lights. It's quiet for a Saturday night. Mark says it's possible that Mama has stepped out and will be back momentarily, that she's tired and just not answering the door. Of course, this could also be the wrong place entirely.

We decide to continue looking, cruising through townhouse developments while Mark makes phone calls, trying Mama's number and getting no answer, calling a friend at Air Afrik who he thinks knows a guy who might know the right address.

It suddenly occurs to me that I've had a lot of nights like this one. Nights spent looking not for goat bones, but for girls or The Man. The messages that Mark leaves have that same edgy expectancy I remember from nights spent hunting for eight-balls or trying to run down the weed guy on a Friday night. And that guy who knows a guy? Jesus, how many nights have I wasted chasing him?

"Okay," Mark suddenly says. "I've got an idea. We're going to go see Francis."

Francis works at Kantamanto Market, maybe even owns Kantamanto Market, I don't know. More important, Francis knows Mama, so he's our man.

Kantamanto is a small African grocery that sells fresh produce, canned goods and staples like fufu flour, hairnets and gum. In the cooler, there's Guinness Malta (a nonalcoholic health drink made by the same company famous for selling a similar, very-much-alcoholic health drink to generations of Irish); on the shelves are cans of fish paste, international calling cards and DVDs. The market is invisible from the road, shoehorned into a tiny space behind a liquor store off Havana—one of those places you just have to know about before you can find them.

We step inside, into the crowded warmth and close-set shelving, and the first thing I notice is the smell. It's indescribable—not bad, but totally alien, earthy and thick, made up of the skins of vegetables I've never tasted, herbs I couldn't name on a bet, powerful cologne, cardboard boxes that have traveled halfway around the world, machine oil, earth, and blood. It hits me like a punch, the way stepping into a greenhouse does, the way stepping into a Whole Foods or Cost Plus World Market never will. It is both the smell of food up close and life far away. In a place like this, even the air is foreign.

Conversation stops when Mark and I step inside—in that awkward moment of trespass, crossing a very real social border between one world and another. Kantamanto Market exists to serve a specific community, and it's one that Mark and I are not a part of (not on the surface, anyhow). It's a color thing, of course. It's also a language thing, a culture thing, a taste thing. But in this first instant, we're just a weird curiosity: two white guys coming in from the cold on a Saturday night.

But that passes quickly. I'm instantly entranced by the food and start fondling the giant yams, the dusty baggies of cola nut and crystallized ginger, the tiny African eggplants called "garden eggs," no bigger than golf balls, each carefully wrapped in tissue paper. And Mark just starts talking, his voice doing that trick again—slowing and thickening and taking on an accent so natural, he might as well own it. He's comfortable here, and since Francis is busy inside the little glass booth where the register is (taking money from customers through one slot, talking through a circle of holes like you see in gas stations in bad neighborhoods), Mark drifts over to a group of young men who are just standing around and asks about the weather. He asks their names, where they're from, how they ended up in Denver, how they like it and why they left Ghana.

The answer to that last one is always the same. Jobs. American money. A better life. A chance to return to Ghana someday as very rich men.

Mark talks about the Peace Corps, asks them about their wives, their girlfriends. Somewhere in the back, a band saw starts up—the sound unmistakable—and shortly after, a young kid passes by pushing a cart loaded with big, bloody, raw hunks of goat meat bound for the coolers. A half hour passes before the negotiations really start, before Mark says, "So, do any of you guys know Mama's new place? My friend and I want to eat Ghana food tonight."

Immediately, there are raised voices, hands waving in the air. No, they say. Mama is leaving. Mama's not cooking anymore. Mama is gone.

"No," Mark replies. "I talked to her yesterday. Yesterday she tells me today is her last day. Today she would be cooking from eleven o'clock *through*."

"Through?"

"Eleven o'clock *through*," Mark insists.

The men convene a conference, all speaking in a language that Mark understands only a little, and me not at all. Francis comes out of his booth to talk to Mark, then to the men. A consensus is reached that it's *possible* Mama might be cooking tonight. Now Mark just has to figure out where.

Ghanaians are not, apparently, a people who care much for addresses.

Finally, two of the men—K.B., who's big and quiet, and Akwesi Hanson, who's short and talkative—decide to take us to the place where they think Mama may or may not be. "Come on," Akwesi says. "You follow us. We'll find her." Akwesi holds open the door, and the four of us are washed back out into the cold on a wave of alien smells and reggae music.

Fortunately, the drive is quick. A couple of turns, a moment of hesitation at the intersection, and then Mark and I follow K.B. and Akwesi right back into the parking lot of the first apartment complex we tried, the first door we knocked on.

"Isn't this—" Mark starts.

"Yeah," I say. "It is."

Again we climb the stairs. Again we knock on the door. And again there's no answer.

"She's not home, I think," Akwesi says, shrugging his big jacket with the fur hood close around his thin shoulders.

K.B. pulls out a cell phone and retreats to the car. He's only been in the country a short time and doesn't like the weather. Akwesi, though, has been here for years. He, Mark and I stand out in the cold talking about Ghana, where it is seventy degrees every day and the sun never stops shining. Akwesi tells me that his name means "Sunday-born," and how everyone in Ghana is named after the day of the week on which they are born. He has no idea where the name Hanson came from.

After a few minutes, K.B. calls Akwesi over to the car.

Mark starts apologizing. "I'm sorry this has taken so long," he says. "I'm sorry she's not home. I wish I could have planned this better."

How can I explain to him that this is what I wanted? Exactly this, with all the confusion and the waiting, the anticipation and disappointment. That I would gladly trade a hundred nights at places with actual addresses and menus for this, the car and the cold and the company we've found. That this—all of this—is what I've been looking for since I started this job: an experience not just of food, but of the culture that food nourishes and the people that culture serves.

I say it just like that, I suppose—and do.

Akwesi shouts from the car and calls us over. We're going back to Kantamanto, he says. They have a plan.

At the market, K.B. shops for me. He opens a green plastic cooler set at the head of one of the aisles and takes out two plastic-wrapped tubes that look like fat tamales wrapped in banana leaves. This is *kenkey*—fermented cornmeal dough a lot like masa that's left to ripen in the sun. He sniffs one, nods his head, tucks both into the crook of his arm and then, as an afterthought, grabs two more that don't have the banana-leaf wrappers. He picks out a tomato, an onion, roots around on the shelves until he finds a can of *sheto*, a herring, shrimp, and vegetable paste cut with a wicked dose of red chile. He gathers everything, brings it to the counter, taps the pile of supplies with one hand.

"This," he says. "This will make you dinner. Just in case."

Meanwhile, Mark and Akwesi have been talking with more men at the market, and it seems that someone has heard about our plight and knows someone who knows someone who knows where Mama might be: at a strip-mall salon a few blocks away, getting her hair done for her going-away party.

"We go there and we see," Akwesi says. "If she's there, maybe she'll cook for you."

"Probably she cook for you," K.B. adds. But if not, he's made sure that we have dinner covered.

Mark and I follow K.B. and Akwesi to the salon, where we find women in chairs, women under dryers, women having their hair sculpted into any number of improbable geometric configurations. Akwesi asks after Mama, then Mark asks after Mama. At first, no one will even admit that Mama is there.

K.B. starts explaining how to prepare the kenkey. "You chop the vegetables very small," he tells me, bringing the edge of one hand down into the palm of the other. You pinch off a piece of the kenkey, make a dent with your thumb, use that to scoop up the chopped tomato and onions and the sheto. There's a Chinese restaurant that caters somewhat to the Ghanaians just down the way, he adds, pointing, "a little that way." It's one of those buck-a-scoop places that I can never understand how it stays in business. Now I know.

"Go there," he says, "and you ask for the tilapia, fried." It's not on the menu, of course. "Before they cook it," he continues, "say add salt, okay? Extra salt. There's salt already in the batter, but you want more."

"And that tastes just like Ghana food?" I ask.

"Just like," says K.B., smiling.

Mark returns with good news. "Mama's here," he says. "She's in the back. They're getting her."

I ask if we still have a chance at getting dinner.

Mark shrugs. "At first they wouldn't admit she was here," he says. "This is such a Ghanaian thing, for her to say she's cooking, you know, eleven o'clock *through*, and then just leave to get her hair done. Maybe it was slow, or she just didn't feel like cooking anymore. We'll see."

And then Mama herself comes out, shorter than I expected, younger—prettier, even—with her hair slicked down with whatever it is that the stylists use to work their magic. She has a cape draped around her shoulders, and it's obvious that she's in the middle of a process, but when she sees Mark, she smiles and comes right over. "Mark!" she says. "How are you?" She takes his hand and leans in close between us, the classic conspirator's pose. "You want me to cook for you? Okay. But could one of you drive me back here when we're done?"

And just like K.B., just like Akwesi, Mama is only too willing to interrupt her life and her Saturday night in order to see the two of us fed. Anxious, even. She's halfway to the car with the goo still in her hair and the cape around her neck before we both insist that she should finish with her hair first. We can wait.

"You're sure?" Mama asks.

We're sure.

"Okay, then maybe nine o'clock I will be done. Then you can eat."

"You'll be cooking at nine?" Mark asks.

"Yes," Mama says. "Of course. Nine o'clock *through*."

We shake hands with K.B. and Akwesi in the parking lot, offer to stand them to dinner for their help.

"Not necessary," Akwesi insists.

"It's okay," K.B. says, reminding me again about the Chinese restaurant and to ask for extra salt.

Mark tells the guys that they should at least take a couple of beers. We have four bottles of Gulder Ghanaian lager in a bag in Mark's car. He offers them each one. They discuss it, refuse again, are asked again, agree to take one. Total.

"My friends," Mark says, "there are two of you. What will you do with one beer?"

More talking. An accord is reached, with K.B. and Akwesi taking one beer each for the road, followed by smiles and handshakes and sincere thank-yous all around.

"So it looks like we're going to get dinner after all," Mark says. "You ready?"

I am. I've been ready for years.

When we finally arrive at Mama's, it's nearly ten, but Mama welcomes us warmly into her home, takes our coats, seats us in her small living room dominated by couches and a huge TV showing an old rerun of *Fresh Prince of Bel-Air*, then gives us our options for dinner. She has some rice balls, but maybe not enough left to make a meal. She has soup, kenkey (of course), goat. There's a bottle of wine unopened on the sort of filigreed silver server I haven't seen since Christmas at my grandma's house, and gin in a plastic jug turned cloudy and brown by the spices, leaves and bits of bark steeping at the bottom. We ask for some of this, please, and please, a little of that. I let Mark do most of the ordering, because for the first time in a long time, I have no idea what I'm asking for and even less of what might eventually arrive.

Mama works fast in her little kitchen, almost silently—a model of professional efficiency going through motions she's made a thousand times before. For six years, Mama has cooked almost every night, throwing what amounts to an impromptu, nonstop, round-the-clock dinner party for an unknown number of guests. You show up and she just cooks whatever is on hand, serves it on the same plates she uses to feed her family. Over the years, she's gotten so good at it that what would be a nightmare for any normal hostess is just her routine.

"You could show up at two in the morning hungry, and if she was there, Mama would cook for you," Mark had told me earlier. K.B., Akwesi, Francis, the girl behind the desk at the hair salon—they'd all said essentially the same thing. Mama is a hostess in the truest sense of the word, a restaurateur stripped of all but the most essential character.

And we are her final table.

When dinner begins, we eat fufu, of course. Huge blobs of it, risen and smooth-skinned and yellow, served in big bowls. We eat *banku* and soup. We eat with our right hands only, as is the custom, pinching off a wad of the cassava paste and using it to scoop up mouthfuls of smooth, sweet peanut soup, okra broth or light soup with a slick of palm oil floating on top. Eating meat on the bone one-handed is a trick to learn, eating soup with no spoon impossible to do delicately. Mark just sinks his hand in to the wrist and slurps from his palm, packing his mouth with fistfuls of banku, and I take my cue from him. My broth—the light soup—is spicy but smooth, the burn mounting then fading away like that of a perfectly made posole or menudo. It's good and undeniably rustic, with a balance and precision of taste that comes only with long practice in the kitchen. The goat skin tastes charred and earthy, the meat is as chewy as boiled chicken, and the fat has a slick musk to it that lingers on my tongue and fingertips for days.

"Check this out," Mark says, lifting his dripping hand from the bowl. "A nipple."

He's right: goat-nipple soup. He pops the thing into his mouth with a grin and goes right back to eating.

No matter how intimate or authentic, the restaurant experience is an essentially isolating one. There are special rooms in which to dine, people paid to be accommodating to my needs, plates and pots and silver and glassware all made for the business of selling me on the vision of a chef or owner. In ethnic restaurants—especially those that operate almost exclusively to serve a specific community the raw fish or pigeon or calves' brains or yucca they can't get at an Olive Garden or in a Happy Meal—there's the added bonus of being served a taste of someone else's home, a slice of their memories of comfort and strange latitudes.

But here, I *am* home—in Mama's home—and she serves me on her own plates. The giant, battered stock pots that line her stovetop and the floor of her tiny renter's kitchen are the same ones from which she takes her own meals and serves her own family. I am offered the silverware out of her own drawers, a seat at her table and a meal unlike any I will probably ever have again. When I look over at Mama in the kitchen, she's smiling, watching us eat. There's a goat leg poking out of a stock pot, more pots stacked up everywhere, more rolled kenkey, more swollen mounds of fufu. Should anyone show up in the middle of the night looking for dinner, Mama will be ready.

But no one does. It's after midnight by the time I push back from the table, hand her a few crumpled bills and thank her for one of the best nights I've had in longer than I can remember. She smiles, nods and sees us to the door, just happy to be doing what she loves—even if this is the last time.

Someone's in the Kitchen

Two Cooks

by Adam Gopnik

from *The New Yorker*

In this deft dual portrait, Gopnik follows two chefs with almost diametrically opposed philosophies—the carnivorous traditionalist Fergus Henderson of England, and his French colleague Alain Passard—with an almost ascetic determination to cook strictly from his own garden.

On an overcast, gray-to-white London summer morning, the British chef Fergus Henderson is standing and staring reverently at the edge of Smithfield, the great meat market in the East End. If it is still reasonably early by restaurant standards, it is late in the day by those of a wholesale market; though Smithfield, an arcaded nineteenth-century affair of bright-painted cast-iron arches and venders' stalls, is beginning to close for the day, it still hums with a sense of sociable business ritual. Wholesalers in straw hats pack up their bacon and chops and trotters, some in Cryovac, some in shiny brown butcher paper.

Henderson's relationship to Smithfield these days is largely spiritual—he gets most of the meat for his nearby restaurant, St. John, from private country suppliers and small boutique slaughterhouses— but it is still an enchanted place for him. "It's a bit of a closed society, with its own customs and traditions," he says. "And it represents a certain tradition that began before pink-in-plastic." ("Pink-in-plastic" is Henderson's dismissive name for supermarket meat.) "For centuries, using the whole beast was the common sense of the market. Embrace your carcass and you'll be richer and happier."

Fergus Henderson is a man in love with meat. He even looks like an English butcher. His face is florid, with the raspberry blush that one associates with the kind of all-right-then-dearie butcher who might appear in a Boulting Brothers comedy of the fifties. Since he opened St. John, in 1995, he has become famous for his devotion to the odd bits of ordinary animals. Ox tongue and tripe, lambs' brains and pigs' heads, stuffed lambs' hearts and rolled pigs' spleen: St. John has returned them to the repertory of the world's "high" cooking, while Henderson's book "Nose to Tail Eating"—which for a long time had to be bought in the United States on a gray market of sec-ondhand copies, where prices could sometimes reach a hundred dollars—has become the "Ulysses" of the whole food–Slow Food movement, a plea for the fullness of life that begins with a man eating innards. (It has at last been published in America, under the slightly cosmeticized name of "The Whole Beast.")

Henderson starts walking the block and a half back to his restau-rant. "The *squirrels,* I suppose," he says, after a moment's pause. He has been asked if any particular adventures in heterodoxy caused com-ment in London. "Squirrel is delicious—like an oily wild rabbit. We had some that had been trapped by keepers in the country, and I decided to do a whole plate of them. Re-create the forest floor: wilted greens, to suggest the bosky woods they come from. Rather poetic, the whole thing. But somehow serving squirrels created quite a stir."

St. John, a converted nineteenth-century smokehouse, has two rooms: a twenty-foot-high sky-lit, cathedral-ceilinged front room, where the bar and bakery are, and the dining room, just beyond. The dining room is large and whitewashed; a row of knobs and hooks for coats goes around the room, giving it the air of an eighteenth-century eating house or tavern, though the open space is unlike any actual eighteenth-century tavern—it's more Saatchi collection than Cheshire Cheese, a hint, perhaps, that archaism and modernism are in more complicated relation here than is evident at first glimpse, or smell. The kitchen seems to be visible from the dining room, but, as Henderson says, "It's a very tricky kind of openness. You can't actu-ally see inside. It's the Mt. Fuji principle borrowed from Japanese prints. You should never see the whole of Mt. Fuji, you know." Hen-derson shows off the restaurant's tiny, cool larder. Inside a steel drawer, a suckling piglet lies waiting to be eaten, its feet curled up comfortably, its eyes closed, its face smiling. It has been specially ordered, and will be roasted and served later that week, nose to tail.

Over Hobbit-like elevenses (seed cake and Madeira), Henderson begins to talk about the ascent that has turned him, at forty-two, into a public figure widely viewed in his homeland as a cross between Jamie Oliver and Sweeney Todd—an image that he sustains with a complex and comic irony. "Isn't the approach to lunch the most wonderful time of day?" he asks. "Lunch is a choice, a decision of a sort. At dinner one must eat, but at lunch one chooses to eat well. There's a certain excitement in lunch." An assistant brings him the day's menu, and he looks it over. Though he no longer works in the kitchen, he still oversees each day's choices. Today's menu, written a little defiantly in nothing but English (only "crème fraîche," an adopted phrase, breaks the Anglo-Saxon attitude), is a calm, squirrel-less document: there is to be Middlewhite—a kind of northern pig—and also deep-fried tripe, veal-tail broth, devilled kidneys, and ox heart with beetroot and pickled walnut. The desserts are English, too, or Englishy, Eccles cake and Lancashire cheese, and even something called Eton Mess, which some people have suggested is not food at all but a succinct explanation of the sex lives of many British politicians.

In spite of his matey, Ealing Studios manner, Henderson is actually a former architect, with almost no formal training as a chef. "My mum was a good cook and my dad was a big eater," he recalls, "and both of them were architects"—well-known second-generation modernists, in fact. "I trained as an architect, but I found lunch in architectural offices discouraging. People ate at their desks. Then, with a friend, I began doing big peasant dishes over in a restaurant in Covent Garden when it was closed. We did cassoulet or pot-au-feu and would have forty or fifty people come and sit at a common table. That led to my finding work as a chef, even though I didn't have the training. I became the cook in a couple of places—I was lucky not to have to work for other people—and then I met my business partners. We found this place, and I began cooking here. We opened, got warm reviews, and, very quickly, turned the corner. I don't know what that corner was, but we turned it." (Henderson opened St. John at the height of the B.S.E. scare, which makes him modify his menu slightly; to this day, lambs' brains are out.)

Henderson had always liked innards, but it was only as he began to cook that he came to recognize the absurdity of our usual meat eating, which clings to a few square feet of animal muscle near the skeleton, as timorous natives might cling to a few square feet of coast on an island while avoiding the volcanic mountains inland. "There were all these wonderful, splendid bits of the animal being wasted, thrown out, while we were eating nothing but the filet," he said, pronouncing "filet" in the English manner, with a hard last consonant. "It seemed positively insulting to the animal that one had raised to treat it with such contempt. So many wonders there. Spleen! Spleen is a very fine, perfectly framed organ. In fact, your spleen swells when you're in love! How can you resist an organ that does that?"

He believes not only that animals should be made happy by being raised well, slaughtered humanely, and eaten entirely but that you can taste the emotional state of the animal on your plate. He senses this with hares. "Rabbits, when they're wild, have a very different temperament, which is expressed in their muscles. Welsh rabbits used to have a certain . . . tension. You could *taste* their tension. Now we've been using more relaxed Yorkshire rabbits, which are splendid in their way, but not as tense and interesting as the Welsh rabbits."

Henderson's devotion to the bits of the animal that other people tend to throw away or make faces at is partly a revivalist aesthetic, a tribute to peasant traditions, but it is closer to certain weird outer ends of conceptual installation than to anything nostalgic. The more time one spends with him, the more inclined one is to think that certain of his American devotees can miss an edge of irony and po-faced British wit in his approach. This is not to say that he doesn't think that tails and heads and spleens are good to eat—he does think that, absolutely—but he also thinks that the *idea* that noses and tails and feet and spleens might be good to eat would be interesting even if they weren't as good to eat as they are. He grasps that even sincere gestures in the kitchen become social symbols on the plate—that the idea of eating rolled spleen and pig's tail has resonances and challenges apart from the taste of rolled spleen and pig's tail in the mouth. He is, as an ironist, close to Damien Hirst, an inventor who plays on the line between display and disgust, and yet Henderson steps soberly over that line to the constant edge of delight.

His attitude to the Englishness of his food is complex. Despite that menu written almost entirely in English, and English English, at that—no ricotta ravioli, no noisettes—the wine list is exclusively French. ("Of course, there's the Aquitaine connection," he says.) Yet when pressed for his influences he cites Marcella Hazan, and his favorite experience of eating is the walk in Paris through the Palais Royal toward the Grand Véfour on a sunny afternoon. The book that lurks behind his approach is Elisabeth Luard's "Sacred Food," an eccentric polemic for a kind of universal home cooking, a transformational grammar of whole beasts and comforting puddings, rooted in the conviction that a restoration of this kind of cooking, in each of its regional guises, is essential to the recovery of a whole civilization.

The most famous dish that Henderson has created is a study in the invention of English tradition through multicultural wit: a salad of bone marrow, parsley, and capers, which, though it seems today to be as rural and English as Eccles cake, occurred to him a decade ago after watching a French film, *La Grande Bouffe*. "It has that scene where the man delights in marrow bones," he recalls. "And a friend had come in and all I had left were the marrow bones and the parsley and some capers. I thought that they would make a splendid marriage. I love the idea of food in which you participate. The singe is very important, getting the right singe on the bones. And the parsley. Vegetables these days are chopped into tiny grass. We *discipline* the parsley, so that it's chopped, yet still parsley. And capers are so important. They're the 'Nyeh!' factor in the dish." He makes a kind of complaining, whinnying noise. "You always need a little 'Nyeh!' on the plate. Pickled walnuts do the same thing for ox heart."

He sighs and looks over at the kitchen. "I wish I could stay in the kitchen through the service, but I'm not really trustworthy with this ropy left side of mine," he says. For the past few years, Henderson has been struggling with Parkinson's disease, which courses through his body like a lightning storm in summer, sending his left arm and hand into paroxysms of uncontrolled movement. He is neither melodramatic about it nor showily brave. "It was a bad day," he says of the moment he learned from his doctors about the disease. "My hand had been moving steadily to my chest, John Wayne in a Western movie, and I thought, How odd! And then it turned out to be this. I sat down and had a good lunch and felt somewhat better."

His wife, Margot, and his three children, he says, have come to accept his "ropiness," and, later this year, he will have experimental surgery that will place electrodes in his brain to try to control it.

"Disgust is always rooted in a perception of asymmetry," he says suddenly. "Geometry cures it. Take the haggis, for instance. It's made of sheep's stomach and sheep's lights, but people will eat it because it's comfortably round. Sausages have always been allowed in, because of their shape. People are somehow reassured."

Disgust, the psychologist Paul Rozin has suggested, may be a kind of optimal strategy for solving what he calls the "omnivore's dilemma": animals that can eat everything have to be especially cautious about what parts of other animals they eat. The default assumption seems to be that all animals are disgusting, and we have to learn an item-by-item list of what's acceptable. In this way, we enclose our children in our own double wrapping, composed of both common sense and collective neurosis. Yet it is also obviously true that the mind overgeneralizes its fear of the unshaped, and knows it. So along with the "Don't eat it!" impulse comes a "Dare you to eat it!" impulse, and it is between these two impulses that Henderson dances.

By now, lunch has progressed through many meats, with various quick detours into the vegetable world—St. John serves leaves, and even excels at them—and there is the promise of an unequalled dark-chocolate ice cream ahead. Henderson finishes off his ox heart with pickled walnuts. "The heart is the most expressive muscle in any animal," he says as he cleans his plate. "It's amazing, a muscle that works so endlessly and tirelessly to keep us alive. And yet it emerges tender and distinctive. Each animal heart is resonant with its animal. Ox heart has an honest beefy quality, lamb's heart rubs up against you. Each heart tastes like the animal that depended on it."

In Henderson's own heart there is, one senses, a harmony between man and his food that comes from eating all of the animal there is to eat, a mysticism rooted in fatality and the fact of our being, head to toe, animals, too. We are all meat, trembling and fresh, dying and spasming, and we enter into our humanity, as we leave it, by way of our animalness. We are beasts eating beasts, and the real bestiality, he suggests, lies in avoiding the truth of it. "Taste that!" he says, pressing a bit of fatty Middlewhite on his neighbor. "It comes from a happy pig. You can taste the difference. People eat meat. You

can be an unhappy carnivore, and eat pink-in-plastic, or a wise carnivore and eat the animal with care and respect. To eat the whole
beast is to accept existence. Embrace your carcass! It's simply
common sense."

On a hot, white-and-gold French summer afternoon, Alain Passard is
standing in his kitchen garden on the grounds of the Château du Gros
Chesnay, in Fillé-sur-Sarthe, about two hundred kilometres southwest
of Paris, near the racing town of Le Mans. A few years ago, Passard, the
owner and chef of the restaurant L'Arpège, on the Rue de Varenne, in
Paris, which since 1996 has had three stars in the Michelin Red Guide,
bought the château in order to create a *potager,* an organic vegetable
garden. He bought it through a uniquely French practice, in which a
younger person buys the property of an older one while the old
person is still alive. This gives the older person a cash infusion, and the
new buyer gets at least a little use of the property while he or she waits
to get it all. The practice can create a situation as intensely delicate as a
Roman imperial adoption, since the buyer becomes nearly a son or
daughter of the house as he begins to occupy it, or bits of it, while, by
ancient French cynical conviction, the sudden onset of money combined with the power of spite extends the life of the older person out to
the demoralizing edge of immortality.

Passard, fortunately, had bought the place from Mme. Baccarach,
an impeccable French grande dame whose family has owned the
château for centuries but who, as it happens, lived for thirty years in
Grosse Pointe, Michigan, and with whom he has a perfect long-term
relationship: she loves to mind the house while he is content to work
the grounds. While Madame prepares a table in the dining room, he
begins the tour of the *potager,* with one of his gardeners,
Mohamadou, a severe Frenchman of African origin.

"It is an organic garden but not merely an organic garden,"
Mohamadou says. "It's a vegetable garden controlled by the beasts.
Do you know a garden only by its sights and smells? No. You know
it, too, by its sounds. Listen!" The visitors cock their heads in the
gasping heat and hear: the sounds of birds flying to nests specially
provided for them in the orchard; the distant croaking of frogs in the
pond that Passard has had dug in order to have natural predators for
crop-eating insects; and, off in the further distance, a lovely, slightly

ominous buzz of bees. The garden has a set of wood-frame hives; the bees make honey for the restaurant. "Those are the sounds of a true garden," Mohamadou says. "We're bringing the birds back, and vipers to eat the mice, and frogs to eat the bugs . . . It's a balance."

Alain Passard is a man in love with vegetables. For most of his career, though an infinitely inventive cook, he was famous for his roasts: particularly roasts of veal and lamb, cooked for six or seven hours *sur la plaque,* on the stove. Then, five years ago, he startled his diners, and his staff, by announcing that he would no longer cook red meat in his restaurant, and that he might phase out animal protein entirely. Today, though he will still throw a few *moules* or langoustines into his dishes, and there is usually fowl available for the incorrigible, the menu he prefers is made entirely of vegetables.

His garden in Sarthe is a showpiece of "permaculture," a system of intensive small-plot rotation that is intended to preserve the energies and resources of the soil. All the planting, for instance, is prepared traditionally, by horse-drawn plow, in order to prevent the soil from being torn up too deeply, as happens with tractors.

Mohamadou looks at Passard. "I saw you on television, chef," he says. "I approved of what you said about the single gesture." On a television program the night before, exploring the new, rococo cooking of the Spanish chefs, Passard had said that a single gesture on a plate was the right direction for the future of cooking, that one properly sliced tomato was a higher accomplishment than a tomato confit, that to get the single gesture right was harder than to make a set of gestures on the plate.

"I believe it," Passard says. "I believe it utterly. One sincere action from the garden is worth six skilled actions in the kitchen. When I'm in my kitchen, I shut my eyes and think that I'm here." He points all around. "And, by seeing myself here, I see what I want to do with the gardens." Passard is a handsome man, light on his feet, younger-looking than his forty-odd years, with a French schoolboy's face: hair *en brosse,* expression intensely earnest and open. "The other day I made a plate of tomatoes—just these tomatoes, sliced the right thickness, salted, and with a dab of balsamic. It was perfect."

The gardener nods seriously. "Of course, one gesture on the plate demands a thousand acts here in the garden," he says, and Passard nods in response.

Passard offers a comprehensive embrace, taking in the garden and the frogs and the birds and the budding vegetables. "I chose this place for many reasons," he says as he walks through vine-covered trellises. Off in the distance, golden cattle low. "It was important to be here in the Sarthe, in part because the soil is promising, neither too sickly rich nor too poor, and in part because it gave us excellent access to the TGV. That means we can pick vegetables at seven in the morning and have them in the kitchen to start making lunch at ten-thirty, and on the diner's plate at noon." He shakes a finger beside his nose, impressed by the efficiency of his own system. "They don't have to be refrigerated for their journey and they lose nothing, or nearly nothing. This fall, we're going to start selling what we don't use for the restaurant at a little counter at the Grande Épicerie at the Bon Marché, so that people who can't eat at the restaurant can still have an experience of true garden vegetables."

Passard continues his tour. "It's an experimental garden, too. We're trying to revive some of the great heirloom varieties of tomatoes and potatoes. We're trying to see what might happen. The beet, for instance, has never been completely appreciated." He leans down and gently brushes the dirt from a fat, dark beet. "We're raising larger, richer beets, and they have a potential that is vast! Enormous!" The new beets have inspired Passard to make an imposing *plat* in his kitchen: the beet is cooked in a crust of *gros sel,* as duck and lamb have been for centuries, and then the crust is broken with a flourish and the beet is delicately sliced and served, with a light *jus,* as the main course.

For lunch, in the château, Passard prepares a few single-gesture plates from the garden outside: tomatoes, potatoes, and a fine Comté and a bit of country bread from his city restaurant, with a red wine from the Gascogne country, on a table that Madame has set beautifully with old china and etched glass and white linen.

"It was many things," he explains earnestly to Madame B. and his visitors, talking of his conversion experience, five years ago. "There was the fear of B.S.E. And for years I had been seeing new dimensions in vegetables when I cooked: green beans with peaches and almonds. Seeing them, but not seeing them all. But, especially, it was because I no longer wanted to be in a daily relationship with the corpse of an animal. I had a moment when I took a roast out into the dining room, and the reality struck me that every day I was struggling to have a creative relationship with a corpse, a dead animal! And I could feel inside me the weight and the sadness of the *cuisine animale*. And since then—gone! All the terrible nervousness and bad temper that are so much part of the burden of being a chef: that was gone with the old cooking. I entered into a new relation to my art, but also to my life. Everyone in the kitchen commented on it. And the lightness of what I was doing began to enter my body and my entire existence, and it entered into the existence of the kitchen. Digestively, yes, of course, but also spiritually, a new lightness of step and spirit that entered my life. It was like a light that I saw, and a door that I walked through. One day, I found myself regarding a carrot in a different light, and I saw the *cuisine végétale* ahead of me through an open door."

"Of course, we have always had many beautiful vegetables here in France, as they do in America," Madame B. says, in the classic style in which mannerly French people search for polite consensus while still speaking the truth. "But in America vegetables were always horribly overcooked. There would be this, and then that, with special utensils to fish them out."

"There have been great vegetable dishes in France," Passard says. "But no great vegetable chefs."

"Very true!" Madame says.

Like all classically trained French chefs, Passard has the sensitive, quick-turning eyes of one who learned at an early age, and from tough masters, that the world is not always easily at your service. (Passard apprenticed as a chef when he was fourteen, and subsequently worked for Gaston Boyer in Reims and, most important, for Alain Senderens at the old L'Archestrate, whose premises L'Arpège now occupies.) He therefore takes his preëminence as a chef seriously, but almost egolessly: that he has something special to contribute to French cooking is a fact independent of his desires, not so much an accomplishment as a grace. "It is the good fortune of vegetables to have at last found a great chef at the height of his powers to explore them," he says. He isn't being immodest, just truthful.

A typical *cuisine végétale* menu at his restaurant these days might include a tomato gazpacho with mustard ice cream (Passard makes the mustard himself); a gratin of white Cévenne onions with black pepper and baby lettuce; a langoustine bisque with a speck-scented cream; a consommé of cucumber with ravioli stuffed with lemon-grass; a light soup of mussels with yellow flowers, ginger, and coriander ("The cuisine of flowers has hardly been touched, even by me," he said later); and a plate of summer root vegetables—carrots and new potatoes and small golden beets—dusted with couscous. For dessert, he offers a chocolate-and-avocado soufflé, the dark chocolate swirled into the rich and slightly eggy avocado, and a simple black-currant sorbet, made from black currants that were just in season in Sarthe.

In his new style, Passard has achieved a level of cooking that surpasses his earlier excellence, a fact that can be acknowledged even by those who think it prudent to eat an entire *côte de boeuf* the night before having lunch at his place. If some people will never quite get his cooking, his stature in France is indisputable, and with good reason. Cooking is both an expression of the essence of the ingredient and an attempt to turn it into something else; it's both melodic and harmonic. The old French cooking was all harmony, with the chicken breast or the sole treated as the bass note, and everything coming from what went on top. The new cooking, which has spread from America and Australia out into the world, is almost purely melodic: the unadorned perfect thing, singing the song of itself. Passard is among the few to cook both ways at once; one is intensely aware of the thing on the plate, and intensely aware of the mind of the chef that gets it there. The very best of what Passard is doing—say, the cucumber broth with herb ravioli—is as straightforward as a vegetable garden and as complex as the system that makes it run. (And not cheap, either, of course. Lunch costs a couple of hundred dollars per person—not surprising, given that the beet on your plate took the TGV to Paris that morning.)

He sharply distinguishes his *cuisine végétale* from vegetarian cooking. He is not a fan of raw vegetables, or of a health-conscious cuisine. "The real malady and unhappiness of vegetables has always been the vegetarian restaurant," he says. He sees cooking vegetables as an aesthetic challenge before anything else. "The white of chicken, or even a fillet of fish, cooking these things can be taught. But sautéing white onions, or a pan of turnips—that calls on every bit of the wisdom and knowledge and skill that a chef has accumulated in his training. Everyone in the kitchen has to pay attention in a new way. My team is alert and awake now in a way that it could never be before."

Passard's sense of purpose is undiluted by irony; if the objects of his cooking are beets and roots and tomatoes, the subject of his cooking is France. It is the French cooking tradition, the great tradition that began after the French Revolution and that he embodies. When, at L'Arpège, the single beet comes out of its crust of salt, or the cauliflower emerges from under a silver bell, where once there had been a rack of lamb, there is no conscious parody, but there is certainly an element of play, of a quiet joke—not at the expense of the old grand style but about the wit required to continue it by other means.

Cooking, we are told, ought to be a sensible craft, a peacemaking practice, a human act of reconciliation and repetition, like gardening or popular song, rather than a place for experiment and extravagant imagination. Yet there is another kind of cooking, whose point is to press borders, turn corners, suggest extremes—extremes not merely of possible palates we might possess but of possible positions we might yet take. It is in these extremes, Carême's edifice-building or Escoffier's encyclopedism, that cooking touches the edge of something more. Both Henderson and Passard speak in conversation the language of realism: of the sensible, the healthy, the logical, the natural. But one feels in both, finally, an adherence less to a moral logic than to an aesthetic illogic: Passard was once Henderson, Henderson could easily become Passard; their real morality is that of the extreme case taken seriously. So perhaps one may be forgiven if one feels, in their single-mindedness, not common sense at all but something of that appetite for perversity which is at the root, and forces the flowers, of art.

Southern Exposure

by Todd Kliman

from *The Washingtonian*

Kliman's profile navigates all the cultural crosscurrents as it follows an Italian-American chef from New Jersey, taking a crash course in Charleston's Lowcountry cooking—and then updating it for a trendy DC eatery.

I. LOOKING FOR A MODEL: COLLARD GREENS

The waitress knows what's coming. She remembers him eating everything he could get his hands on when he worked at the restaurant some months back. The Jersey guy, he sure did love him some Lowcountry.

Even so, she can't help raising an eyebrow when Bryan Moscatello orders half the menu one busy midweek afternoon at lunch.

"Anything else?" she joshes.

"I didn't forget the collards, did I?"

The collard greens. It's one of the big reasons we're here, jammed into a small booth at a modest little spot east of downtown Charleston called Boulevard Diner—small, at least, for the feast that hits the table minutes later: five entrees, five side dishes. A chair sits at the end, the seat supporting a plate of black-eyed peas that couldn't be squeezed onto the table. Bryan Moscatello tries a little of everything, then returns for seconds of each dish on the table. The food is great, but that isn't why the beefy, baby-cheeked chef is helping himself to seconds.

This is his second trip to Charleston in a month. In December and January, he worked on the line at a number of kitchens in the city, unpaid work called *stages*. The *stages* were intended to give the Jersey-born chef—acclaimed by *Food & Wine* as one of the ten best new chefs in the country in 2003, when he manned the stoves at Adega in Denver—an insider's familiarity with the techniques and traditions of Lowcountry cooking.

The idea behind this refresher trip, his final tour of the city's kitchens before Indigo Landing opens in April on Daingerfield Island north of Old Town Alexandria, is to burn the precise details of certain staple dishes into his memory.

What Moscatello is after is what Dan Mesches, who runs the group that owns Zola and Red Sage and now co-owns Indigo Landing, calls "base flavors"—the building blocks of the cuisine.

At first glance, Lowcountry would seem largely indistinguishable from Southern cooking. In fact, Mesches tells me, he ate Lowcountry for years as a graduate student in the '80s in Columbia, S.C., "without knowing that I was eating Lowcountry."

In part, that's because John Martin Taylor hadn't yet written *Hoppin' John's Lowcountry Cooking,* the 1992 compendium of folklore and recipes that *Gourmet* recognized as triggering "Charleston's culinary resurgence."

Taylor, who now lives in DC, wrote in his introduction, "Nowhere in America did the cooking of master and slave combine so gracefully as it did in the Lowcountry kitchen. . . . It is not European, African or West Indian dishes specifically that characterize Lowcountry cooking; rather, it is the nuances of combination and a respect for the past that make the cuisine unique."

Scan a typical Lowcountry menu, and you'll find the collard greens and shrimp 'n' grits and even barbecue that are common throughout the South. The differences are in the details. Lowcountry lacks the spicing and intricacy of much of Creole cooking, and it draws its methods more from Africa than France. The long braise, the slow-simmered stew, trumps the quick sear—slow cooking to match the gentle, loping rhythms of the culture itself. To be sure, pork and its endless by products finds its way into everything from biscuits to side dishes, as is the case generally in every kitchen that lies below the Mason-Dixon line, but fish and seafood, owing to the great abundance of piscatory life that gathers in and around the peninsula, dominate the restaurant menus in Charleston.

Like much of Southern cooking, the food is heavy, rich, and incomparably fattening (all that butter, all that cream, all that lard), but what fascinates Moscatello are not the big, heavy bass notes that makes the cuisine so comforting and irresistible, but the trebly top notes that reveal themselves the longer you study it: "The vinegars, the acids. You need that, with food this rich."

He points to the dish of collards.

"Right on," he says, "in terms of vinegar, acidity. Right on the path of where I want to go."

I mention the leaves, their integrity still intact. They've retained their green.

Moscatello smiles. "That's what you don't want," he says, then cites the truism he has come to live by. "You can either have green collards, or you can have good collards."

He has me dip my spoon into the braising liquid, also called the pot liquor—sometimes spelled "pot likker." "You should be getting something with a depth of flavor in it."

Until he was hired last fall as the new restaurant's chef, Moscatello had never heard the term. Then one day he was paging through an old cookbook and saw a recipe: "baked bread with pot likker." Pot likker! He was like a kid who'd learned a new curse word; he couldn't stop using the term.

If the wording was new, the idea was not. Every Sunday in Jersey, his mother would make a pot of escarole and white beans, which she cooked slowly in the rendered fat of pepperoni. Connecting the tastes he'd grown up on to the flavors he was now immersing himself in, he realized that what had made the dish so good was the braising liquid that resulted, fortified by the smoke and spice and fatty richness of the sausage. It excited him to think that he'd grown up eating something analogous to the food he'd spent months researching and cooking. The Jersey boy was not so far out of his element after all.

Lunch has barely had time to settle, but no matter: We're back on the road for more, crossing the Cooper River bridge into Charleston. We pull into the parking lot of a pink-colored cinderblock shack called Martha Lou's Kitchen. It'd be hard to find a restaurant that's further from the vision that Mesches and Moscatello have for Indigo Landing than a roadside diner that looks to have once been a strip club.

No sooner does the food hit the table in two heaping styrofoam containers than Moscatello spears a forkful of the collards. They're a lot less green than what we just ate, more broken down. To the uninitiated, they resemble the sort of grayish, wet dishes you find on a buffet table. But Moscatello is nodding as he chews.

"The more you cook collards, the more the flavor develops. They're also less chewy than what we had at Boulevard. A little earthy, a little smoky."

He likes the soulfulness of the greens, the unmistakable quality of home cooking in the pot. But it's not his model, not the memory he wants to retain. Too down-home. On the other hand, the collards at Peninsula Grill aren't his benchmark either. Peninsula Grill is an upscale Lowcountry restaurant, as Indigo Landing hopes to be. But in a city in which every chef serves up collards, Chef Robert Carter can afford to depart from script, slicing the large, flopping leaves into thin ribbons and giving them a quick sauté.

Moscatello knows he must hew to tradition. Elsewhere on the menu, he can chance experimenting a little, putting his own spin on things, but he recognizes that the restaurant's ability to invoke the spirit of the Lowcountry will be measured, in part, by how authentic its collard greens are. It's a foundational dish.

What he wants is "something almost like a smoky leaf."

What he wants is the collards at Fleet Landing, a former Navy debarkation center with a view of Ft. Sumter. Tromping through the kitchen with chef Jim Epper, Moscatello rubs his hands together in anticipation. "Man," he says, "I can smell those collards."

What he smells is pork. It fills the kitchen, a thick perfume of smoke and liquified fat. Epper renders two quarts of bacon fat, an entire case of ham hocks, a dozen smoked pig feet, and five pounds of sausage before his collards ever touch the bottom of a 40-pound kettle drum. After thirty minutes, the leaves are soft, but "they don't have any flavor." Epper aims for a "solid five hours." That degree of patience, of giving the food time to develop its flavors, is one of the reasons Epper calls Lowcountry "comfort food, soul food, love food."

We dig into his collards. They're terrific. Not brilliantly green but not gray, either, a bit of chew, and full of such smoky, bacony flavor they leave a residue on the tongue. The pot liquor is addictive, managing to be all at once salty, smoky, a little bitter and slightly sweet, too. I spoon it up like a soup.

Moscatello is moaning over how good it is, even as he's rattling off a bunch of mental notes about what he wants to remember: The sense of balance in the dish. The amount of vinegar. The smokiness. The way the pork fat permeates every bite of the leaf.

Epper adds one more: The simplicity of it. "You can't get too upscale with this food," he says, as if he were sending Moscatello away with a warning to keep the cuisine rooted in the culture.

Moscatello nods, dutiful.

II. Lightening a Tradition: Shrimp 'n' Grits

Hank's Seafood Restaurant is housed in a 100-year-old warehouse in downtown Charleston. Its sun-blasted exterior evokes a fish house on the water. Inside, the handsome dark leather booths and polished wood floors capture the stately classicism of old Charleston. It's hard to believe it hasn't been around longer than seven years, just as it's hard to believe that such authentically good shrimp 'n' grits comes from the kitchen of an Irishman with a brogue as rich and lilting as any Dublin barman's.

"Hey! Bryan!" Frank McMahon strides into the dining room, wiping his hands on his apron before commencing a long, hearty handshake with his one-time volunteer.

A former sous chef at the four-star Le Bernardin in New York, McMahon is proof that with enough study and desire and command of technique, an outsider can pass for an insider. As such, he is as much a model for Moscatello as Epper's collard greens.

When McMahon arrived in Charleston twelve years ago, he might have known everything there was to know about seafood and fish, but he didn't know the first thing about Lowcountry.

"Grits to me was alien—'What's that, pig gruel?' Can't they make a polenta?' It was coarse, not smooth at all."

He roars at the memory of his ignorance.

Moscatello begins with an advantage, having cooked with them for as long as he's worked as a chef—in one memorable dish, stirring heaping spoonfuls of epoisses into his grits at Adega.

His problem is not that he will be an outsider trying to pass for an insider in Washington. His problem is that he will be cooking largely for other outsiders.

Regarded as a Southern backwater only a couple of generations ago, today DC is a city that is culinarily neither North nor South, conservative in its tastes but evolving. The city is full of chefs who draw from many regions and serves a smart but fickle dining public that craves simplicity even as it demands sophistication. Whip us up a heaping plate of shrimp 'n' grits. But can you do something to cut the fat?

To hear Mesches talk about Indigo Landing as "the kind of restaurant you visit once a week, not once a month," and to hear Moscatello stress the need for "lighter, more refreshing" dishes than those of the Lowcountry, is to hear an acknowledgment of the predicament they find themselves in as a Southern-themed restaurant in a city that is straying farther and farther from its Southern roots.

Establishing authenticity is important; so is competing in a marketplace of small plates and stylish, well-tailored dining rooms.

Thus, with the shrimp 'n' grits, they have set themselves the difficult task of evoking the past while simultaneously updating it, of turning a guilty pleasure into a weekly staple. How to deliver the coarseness of the grits, and the warming, spoon-it-up runniness, and the bacony essence that gives the dish its unmistakable backtaste while also contemporizing it, lightening it?

The question is fraught with implications. For some, lightening and contemporizing is code language for yuppifying and upscaling.

Moscatello says he doesn't want to sacrifice the character of the dish, merely tamper with its rib-sticking effects.

But as he returns to Peninsula Grill to talk with Carter about the grits he uses, he's finding it hard to shake the assumption that he aims to use the flavors of Lowcountry as a starting point, the way a jazzman might use a melody to create new sounds.

As they sift through a plastic container of white stoneground grits from Carolina Plantation Grits, Carter, a burly man with a scraggle of blond beard and a rascally glint in his eye, interrupts to ask, "You're gonna be doing an upscale Lowcountry thing, right?"

It's frustrating, if understandable. Of course a celebrated Yankee chef is going to summon his fancy tricks and turn an identifiable, warming cuisine into something unrecognizable.

The truth is, Carter has more freedom to experiment than Moscatello will, because in Charleston there can be no confusion about his point of reference. He can remind his well-traveled diners that polenta is really just grits, pairing them with sauteed wild mushrooms and reinforcing the bond between an unpedigreed American staple and an Italian country classic.

Cooking out of context and for an audience unaccustomed to the flavors and meanings of Lowcountry, Moscatello is forced to work within an existing structure.

He's already made a few decisions. He will use white grits instead of yellow grits. He will use a coarse, stone-ground grit instead of the cheaper instant grits. The difference in cooking time? An hour rather than ten minutes. But it's worth it to him, because you can taste the difference. He doesn't want thick, clotted grits, the kind that clump like mashed potatoes on the plate. He wants soupy grits, soft, almost runny.

"Wet, I like to call it."

We're sitting at brunch at Jestine's Kitchen, a bustling diner popular in Charleston with both locals and tourists. There are lots of dishes on the table, among them is a version of shrimp 'n' grits that appears to meet with his approval.

"Love that soupiness," he says, "love that looseness. Good flavor." But in the end, they're too creamy for him, too cheesy—too much about the cheese and the cream.

Cream is the X factor. Solve for cream, and he completes the equation.

He's seen it in nearly every version he's tried, from the crummiest dive on up to the swankiest restaurants. And now, on this second go-round, it's becoming obvious: There are no models to copy.

Though he adores Epper's collards, regarding them as the embodiment of Lowcountry tradition, Epper's shrimp 'n' grits are problematic.

Oh, the grits are properly "loose." They're also intensely creamy, in the same way that many cream soups are intensely creamy. Moscatello pointed to the "shine" on them. They looked ready for their close-up, glistening under the lights of the kitchen.

Like a detective sniffing out a case, Moscatello asked, "What are you using in here? All cream, right?

"100% cream," Epper replied.

The goal, Moscatello says now, is not to eliminate cream entirely from the equation. The goal is to reduce its impact. And he doesn't want to rely on the obvious answer: chicken stock or veal stock.

"Why put a meat stock in there when it's the corn you want to bring out the flavor of?"

Here, again, he finds himself reaching back into his own past for a solution. At Adega, he always kept a corn stock simmering on the stove. In most high-end kitchens, where the aim is intensifying the flavors of meat, and where chicken stock and veal stock are predominant, a generic, all-purpose vegetable stock has to suffice for everything that is not meat.

A corn stock, made from corn cobs and fresh, shucked corn, would impart an almost floral sweetness that would intensify the corn taste of the grits. It would also reduce the need for so much cream.

Half cream, half corn stock. No loss of bacon, no loss of flavor.

It's his best hope of bridging the divide between a dish that is authentically rich and heavy and a dish that nods halfheartedly in the direction of tradition.

III. INVENTING: ROASTED GROUPER WITH GREEN RICE AND MUSSEL-SMOKED BARBECUE SAUCE

The next time I see Moscatello, he's in his chef's whites in his new kitchen. The restaurant, three weeks before opening, is still under construction. Plastic wrap covers the chairs and booths, and workmen troop through the debris-strewn dining room affixing wrought-iron fishing nets to the leather-covered walls. Inside the kitchen, there's some of the same sense of buoyancy and anxiety that attends a theatrical troupe in the lead-up to a play as Moscatello and his crew send out a parade of dishes for the newly hired staff to try. I'm taking tastes, too, intercepting plates as they head out the door.

Moscatello slides a plate across a metal workstation: a square of roasted grouper, perched atop a mound of green-flecked rice, the whole thing ringed by an ochre-tinted yellow sauce.

There's no immediate reference point for this dish; it looks like nothing I saw in all of our many tastings in Charleston. I stick my fork in.

Delicious. But what compels me to keep tasting is the ochre-tinted yellow sauce. I can't identify it; it's not a mustard sauce, exactly, although it's got a pronounced tang. And there's a smokiness whose source I can't place. It's mystifying.

"Smoked mussel barbecue," says Moscatello, with a big, sly grin.

No bacon? No ham hock?

"Nope. But you still get the smoke and the acid, right?"

For months he'd looked in vain for the one herb, the one seasoning, that would unlock for him the essence of Lowcountry. As tarragon is to French cooking, as red pepper is to Creole cooking . . . he couldn't complete the analogy.

He'd been fixated on pork. He loved the way the ham hock flavored vegetables, loved the way it bathed them in its juices. He loved the variations of surf and turf he'd come across, the way certain dishes would marry shellfish and pork, fish and pork. Pork was a flavoring agent. It was a main course. It was in the background of a dish, it was in the foreground. No part of the animal was wasted, everything was used. Entire dishes in the repertoire had been invented just to exploit the enormous potential of certain tasty joints of the pig.

"If you don't eat pork," he says, characterizing the attitude of nearly every Charlestonian, "see ya later."

Returning to Washington from Charleston the first time, he was toying with the idea of a dish that would pay homage to the barbecue joints of the Lowcountry, with their sweet mustard sauces. He tried it with grouper.

At a tasting, Ralph Rosenberg, the wine guru and director of operations for Zola and Red Sage who would also be creating the wine list for Indigo Landing, wondered where the smokiness was. "When you say barbecue," he told Moscatello, "you want smoky."

Smoke. That was it.

It was more than simply a case of loving the taste of bacon, the incomparable richness it brought. It was the smoke, too.

Smoke and acid, the one a byproduct of curing or slow-roasting the pig, the other a means of countering its fattiness.

It wasn't the first or second thing you thought about when you thought about Lowcountry. But it was there—in the collards, in the shrimp 'n' grits, in nearly every dish he tried.

Back to the drawing board. Moscatello tried the sauce again, only this time with a ham hock to flavor it.

The ham hock provided the smokiness, but although it solved one problem it created another: a menu in which every single fish dish includes pork fat. Much as he might like to "celebrate the hog" in every plate he puts out, "when you consider what we are and where we are," says Moscatello, "we need to make sure we're accommodating."

"How do you get the smoke in there," the chef asked himself, "if you eliminate the bacon or ham hock?"

The question dogged him. And the more he thought about the dish-in-progress, the more he realized it also lacked the sharpness it needed.

One day he remembered that he'd done a smoked mussel vinaigrette at Adega—the clue, as before, right there for him in his own back pocket.

He set to work, prizing the mollusks from their shells, then laying them on the tray of a stove-top smoker with what the French call *mirepoix*, a dice of carrots, celery and onion that provides the basis for soups and sauces—a light smoke, just enough to give the mussels and veggies an extra layer of flavor. Then he ground them up in a food processor, adding yellow tomatoes, yellow bell pepper, mustard and vinegar. Smoke and vinegar.

No one in Lowcountry would look upon a smoked mussel barbecue sauce as authentic, and he can't recall using a vinaigrette for much more than a salad in the kitchens he'd worked in, but in another sense, wasn't he being true to the spirit of Lowcountry as he understood it?

Out comes a bowl of collard greens. The smell is unmistakable. Smoke and vinegar.

"Five hours," says Moscatello, anticipating the inevitable question about how long they'd cooked, "and not a minute less."

The dish is a near-replica of Epper's, except for the insistent saltiness—a result, perhaps, of the Virginia bacon Moscatello is using.

A plate of shrimp 'n' grits follows. The shrimp have been grilled, not sauteed, and their char is strong, perhaps too strong, as though he were determined to inject some smokiness in there any way he can. The grits, cheesy and runny, could have come straight from

Boulevard Diner. They're a lot coarser, though, harkening back to those he made and ate at Peninsula Grill—though he's opted to break with Carter in using grits from Hoppin' Johns, not Carolina Plantation. There's a sweetness there, too, that amplifies the taste of the corn. If I didn't know better, I'd have guessed it was Silver Queen sweet corn.

"That's the corn stock," says Moscatello proudly.

Anything seems possible right now. But then, business doesn't begin for three weeks. Sustaining that excitement, and sustaining the sense of invention and exactitude, will be a challenge. So will sustaining the sense of Lowcountry tradition in a city that has little connection to the culture. For now, though, the countless studying and the endless experimenting appears to have paid off: The journey from Denver to the Lowcountry to Washington is complete. The Modern American chef has reinvented himself as a chef of the South.

"Hey, Hoppin' John called me the other day," Moscatello says, sweat beading his face. Moscatello has read his book from cover to cover. He invited the author to drop on by the kitchen sometime.

"He's like—'Moscatello? That's not Lowcountry.' I said, 'No, it's not. It's Jersey.'"

The Romantic Ideal

by Michael Ruhlman

from *The Reach of a Chef*

In *The Soul of a Chef*, Michael Ruhlman cast Thomas Keller as the new celebrity chef; this more recent book uses the same fly-on-the-wall technique to watch several "hot" chefs as they each chart a different course toward money and fame.

Melissa Kelly arrives [at Primo] at 9:00 AM in her white T-shirt and navy blue overalls with the white pinstripes—the commis pattern in French kitchens—rolled high above her clogs to reveal thin, saggy white socks. Melissa is five-foot-four, dark hair pulled tightly back in a ponytail, and if you walk into her kitchen at most times of the day before service, you're likely to see her in this position: straight over a cutting board, neck cocked to hold a phone, talking to a purveyor, the press, family, or someone begging a reservation at the height of the season. Melissa is thirty-nine years old, was first in her class at the CIA in 1988, won the Best Chef Northeast award from the Beard Foundation in 1999, and became a media darling after she put the Old Chatham Sheepherding Company Inn, the Relais & Châteaux B&B and restaurant in upstate New York, on the map. She and Price Kushner—they're married in all but the technical sense (never had the time or a strong inclination to make it legal)—have owned this restaurant in the Victorian house since 1999. And while Price is nominally the pastry chef—his culinary background is breads and pastry—and he does *oversee* and often cook that side of the menu, he spends the majority of his time running the nonkitchen parts of the business and in the evening leads the front of the house. Melissa is the force of the kitchen, 9:00 AM to 1:00 AM, seven days a week in the summer. Most of the remaining hours of the day, she's dead asleep amid piles of cookbooks and notepads, which cover the bed and surrounding floor in their home nearby.

When I asked when her next day off would be, she said without thinking, "Labor Day." Her last day off had been Independence Day and before that Memorial Day. "We close for all the barbecue holidays," she says. Summers are busy in Maine. If you're not busy here in the summer, you've got a problem. Capacity summers are the only way to get through winter.

"You could shoot a gun down Main Street and you wouldn't hit anyone for three towns," says Price of the winter population.

But even those months, January through March, Melissa likes to stay open five days a week, despite the fact that they consistently lose money—she does it to keep her staff employed. Otherwise, she's afraid, they'd have no choice but to leave her. Also, I suspect, she's happiest in a kitchen.

"I'm not a groundbreaking chef," Melissa says. "I like to cook . . . I *cook*. That's what I do. That's what I've done my whole life. Food is it. I'm not a photographer, I'm not an artist, I'm not a boatbuilder, I'm not anything else. I'm a cook, that's who I am."

And so she's most likely to be in her kitchen just about any nonsleeping hour—not dressed for a photo shoot, in the office on the phone with her brand consultant, or scouting new restaurant locations—dicing the onion and peppers for the peperonata, a base for a grilled swordfish–mussels–saffron gnocchetti, or mixing yolks and flour in the KitchenAid for the hand-rolled spaghetti, served with Nicoise olives, capers, and ricotta salata, as well as eggplant, basil, and tomatoes from the garden out back.

"I don't know why I do it," she says in her slightly nasal, slightly Long Island voice and without looking up from her board. "I enjoy it, I enjoy the routine, the sense of accomplishment. Even last night going through the cooler and getting everything organized makes me feel really good.

"I love the circle," she adds, "the cycle of cooking. It is a life cycle, it has its own life." The finest moments of the day are when she's got four or five pots and pans going, she's stirring a risotto, butchering the lamb, dicing the onion for the sauce, throwing the onion ends into the stock, every act and every scrap propelling her and the food toward the finished dishes, moments when one movement works toward several different ends, and all those different ends fulfilling a singular goal. "I love when there's that full circle, to me that's the best feeling."

Tuesday, August 3, 2004, is a typical summer day at Primo. Melissa arrives at 9:00 and begins her lists. Even before she knows what she has she writes on a legal pad:

Soup:
Stock:
Butcher:
Prep:

And it's the "Prep" that typically fills up quickly (pea soup, herbs, mash, gnocchetti, peperonata, chix jus), and the priorities marked with an asterisk. She's moved through every inch of the walk-in cooler, to check to see what they have and what they'll need, and has brought out the striped bass to begin butchering them. Lucy will wander through the kitchen in jeans and a tank top, sweat already beading at her temples, and drop off her "harvest list," all the items she'll be taking from [Primo's] garden. Today's list includes zukesla (a type of zucchini), zucchini blossoms, calendula, nasturtiums, tomatoes, eggplants, gooseberries, micros, one artichoke, cucumbers, fresh garlic, and tetragonia. Also available to pick, but not required today, are red leaf, pea shoots, young chard, young leeks, Genovese basil, an herb called cutting celery, and parsley. Of all the produce they use, about 60 percent of it they grow and harvest themselves during the summer months.

Melissa can usually bang out several items on her list before its time for the daily menu meeting with her sous-chef, Rob Holt.

Rob is an affable thirty-five-year-old who carries a few extra pounds, is balding appropriate to his age, keeps his remaining light brown hair clipped short, and sports a trim beard and mustache. Originally from Dallas, Rob started out playing in a band years ago, then moved into cooking. It's always nagged him that he doesn't have a proper culinary education. He learned as he went along, as many cooks still do, but he doesn't know what he's missed or what he's lacking. And now he feels he's too old for school, thoughts that fellow cooks who have been to school (everyone else on this hot line has a culinary degree) thoughtfully concede. He's been here less than a year, having come from San Francisco, most recently the kitchen of Boulevard, Nancy Oakes's restaurant, where he did exclusively stocks, sauces, and soups. He liked that focus and after two years there decided to make a change. He moved with his girlfriend, Monica, across the country to work at Primo. Monica is a hostess here.

Kitchens are like families—but adoptive families, with distinct personalities. Sometimes you feel comfortable in them and sometimes you don't. Rob has never quite felt comfortable here, it seems, much as he likes his colleagues and the restaurant itself. And Maine in the winter he found to be deadly dull. He's given his notice and intends to head back to San Francisco to start work the first week of September.

This is fine with Melissa. She likes Rob—he's been good and dependable—but also recognizes it's not the right fit. Furthermore, she's really missed the line. She's eager to get back in there cooking. She loves to cook. It drives her crazy that Rob toward the end of service begins to flag, and when big orders come in late, she feels like an expectant father: "Push!" she says through the service shelf at her puffing sous. This is physical work and you have to be in good shape—it gets hard. I've heard many chefs after they hit forty say, *I just can't do this anymore.* But she's lean and mean and loves it—*loves* it.

Service is a long way off. A lot has to happen over the next six hours in order to be ready, and writing the menu is first on the list.

Melissa and Rob sit in the dining room where it's cool, each with a pen and a copy of yesterday's menu. The room is quiet. The old wooden chairs creak. The framed photograph of Primo looks down on his granddaughter, as does a gallery of other black-and-white family portraits.

"Are we getting chanterelles in today?" Rob asks.

"Yeah," says Melissa. She looks over her list and the menu. "Skate—gotta finish butchering that. That's going on." She slumps over the menu, just staring. Minutes of silence pass. These are her least active, least intense moments of the day, as if when she's sitting, her whole body takes advantage of the break. "We're going to use the rest of the confit on a pie," she says. "We sold twenty-five pies last night. That was *hard*. Our record is twenty-nine, so he was right up there." Joe was on pizza last night, which also serves some appetizers and the *amuse*—he'll tell you how hard it can get. An order for five pies is called followed by three pies—it becomes a space issue as much as a time issue. He's got to spin and stretch each dough ball, then garnish the twelve-inch disk (with duck confit and fig for the "chef's whim"; or artichokes, olives, ricotta, and basil; or mushrooms and roasted garlic and thyme and radicchio), and then fire it. But it's hard to find the space and hit the cooking time just right on all of them because they take only a minute. Plus he's got the wood-roasted oysters topped with Jonah crab, and Rob or Aaron beside him firing numerous roasted whole dorade. That station is either a killer or a breeze, rarely in between.

"We got tuna tonight for the ap," Melissa says, then scans the menu, and Rob does the same, for a quiet minute. *How should I do the bluefin?* she thinks. Melissa says, "I just talked to Jess. He's got some nice swordfish, and littlenecks from Prince Edward Island, and they're the size of mahogany clams. We'll use those for the dorade, and he's bringing some lobsters for Lindsey." *(Chilled Garden Pea Soup with a salad of lobster, mint, and preserved lemon.)*

Melissa will buy only large swordfish, telling all her purveyors this, sending the message that she'll not bring in any that haven't had a chance to breed.

"Swordfish from here is amazing," Rob says, hungrily. "It's like butter, the best I've ever had."

"Whey and milk are coming," Melissa continues. "We'll make sheep's-milk ricotta tomorrow. She's bringing two animals."

"We're gonna do lamb two ways?" Rob asks.

Another long pause scanning the menu, the dining room is quiet.

"I'm gonna verbal out the quail," Melissa says, meaning it will be a special described by the server, "and I'll put the tuna on. I'm not sure about the blossoms."

More pondering. Melissa's still in the aps section of the menu and suggests doing arancini. Rob grins, he loves arancini—"Street food in Sicily," he says—risotto croquettes: flour, egg, bread crumbs, and fried, often with different additions to the fillings. Melissa will wrap sticky cold risotto around mozzarella and anchovies, deep-fry them, and serve them on tomatoes from the garden.

"That's gonna replace the blossoms, we need to accumulate some. We usually do those every other day, and we've done them the past two days."

The squash blossoms—flowers filled with ricotta, fried, and served on a bed of grilled squash, red onion, cherry tomatoes, and a pesto vinaigrette—are an irony: they don't sell well when they're written on the menu, but when they're verbal they sell like crazy.

Rob, whose attention on the menu is now on the pasta section, says, "No more pappardelle, need more eggplant and sauce, and I can pick some nice basil for that."

"Agnolotti for the scallops tonight," she says.

"We have enough gnocchi," says Rob. "We need to wrap salmon." *(Salmon fillets wrapped in grape leaves, grilled, and served on green beans, roasted peppers, and couscous with cumin-spiced eggplant sauce.)*

"Fingerlings?" she asks.

Rob says, "Yeah, I'll do a little bit more." Those for the strip steak, and then for the striper entrée, he needs more coulis, saying, "Red pepper for the bass."

"I don't know about the fennel," Melissa says. "She's picking more today, we have to check it out. Also ratatouille. . . . We'll wait to put sword on tomorrow to get rid of the dorade and halibut." She runs down the menu. "Ten plus two verbals, that's good."

"You still want to go with marjoram for the lamb?" Rob asks.

"Yeah, it was in the braising liquid," she says. Then, remembering, she says, "We used to do a lamb at American Place"—Larry Forgione's seminal New York restaurant—"the saddle. We put a crust on it with cheese and brioche bread crumbs. It's a little bit of a pain. It's a great dish and that'll really make it sell. But one crepe, make it more blini."

"Squarish," Rob says.

"Yeah, that'll make it a really nice dish." *(A double chop with a goat cheese crust, grilled, served with braised lamb shoulder in a spinach crepe, called "Crespelle" on the menu, and baby vegetables from the garden.)* "Oh, I got black-eyed peas in today," she says.

"Are you getting chicken in tomorrow?"

"Yeah."

"Maybe do black-eyed peas with that."

"Yeah."

"Quail?" he asks.

"Yeah, have to order. . . . We've got beans, she's picking leeks today. Squash, lots of squash, eggplant. It's hard when you've got a lot of the same stuff coming out of the garden. You want each dish to have its own personality." She fiddles with her pencil, staring at the menu, sighs. "We could do something with citrus and radishes." Long pause. "Skate, I think of citrus and beets, but also capers." Pause. "Need to go with the citrusy direction." After a few quiet moments she reverses herself, says, "Keep it Italian with panelle, with fried chickpeas, preserved lemon in the salad. Piccata—capers."

"Maybe segment some lemons, parsley," Rob says, referring to the herb salad that will go with the skate.

"I was thinking tarragon."

"Lovage."

"Chervil's good, fines herbes." She thinks. "Tarragon, lovage, arugula, maybe chervil, preserved lemon in the salad with the skate."

"For the steak do you want a vinaigrette with that?" Rob asks.

"Yeah. We can go with the red wine with that."

Melissa looks back up and sees her note to put tuna on the menu. The citrus and radish will go with that. She writes in the margin of the menu, "Tuna—salad radishes citrus cooked on plane in wood oven."

The meeting often concludes not when they're finished, but when they sense they simply need to get into the kitchen and start working.

Rob stands first and as he's heading in, asks, "Do you have the panisse recipe?"—the chickpea flour that's cooked like mush, then poured onto a baking sheet and cooled till it's set, then cut into shapes and reheated at service, a bed for the skate.

"It's just like the polenta," she says. "Four cups chickpea flour, nine cups water, salt and pepper, cook it for a long time, till it starts to pull away from the sides." Rob nods and departs. She makes some finishing touches to the menu to give to Monica to type up.

The day's routine almost never varies. Morning prep is followed by the menu meeting with Rob, followed by about four more hours of prep—all afternoon and up until service the kitchen is a hive of activity, and work space becomes territorial, especially when service arrives and begins the sidework, wiping down silver and glasses and stacking plates, folding napkins. At 4:15, Melissa writes the day's specials, the verbals, on the dry-erase board.

At 4:30, the servers, usually about ten of them during the summer, gather in a wallpapered Victorian dining room hung with old black-and-white photographs of Melissa's family. They busily scribble the contents of the board into their pads. Melissa waits quietly, apparently relaxing, taking advantage of this time off her feet. No hurry. If you work in the kitchen, the pre-service meeting, a ritual in virtually all good restaurants, is a time of strange calm.

When Melissa senses the servers are nearly finished, she begins: "The first turn looks hellish on paper, the second turn looks spread out. We have a hundred and nine." The night before, they did 131 covers—served 131 customers—which is almost exactly two turns in this 65-seat restaurant. They're likely to do the same tonight, with walk-ins and people eating at the bar.

She then begins at the top of the two-by-three-foot board. "Duck-sausage pie"—each day there's a "chef's whim" pizza, this one using duck confit and figs, same as yesterday.

"How much is that?" a server asks.

"Fifteen," Melissa says. "The antipasti is a fried-squid salad. Quail is wrapped in serrano and wood-roasted, served on a salad with red onion, a quail egg, and mustard vinaigrette . . . The beet salad has our roasted beets with an orange-pistachio vinaigrette . . . The duck confit is served on the bone with an arugula salad, a champagne vinaigrette. The duck is cooked with allspice, cloves, bay, thyme, garlic, and white pepper . . . The salmon is wrapped in fresh grape leaves, not the brined ones we've been buying. They've been blanched and it's grilled, so they get a little charred and crisp. That's served with fresh beans . . . The bass tonight is served with a ratatouille of summer squash and eggplant—that's from our garden . . . The duck is served with potato gnocchi . . . We have seven orders of the leg of lamb with couscous, mint, peas, and Thai basil."

There is no real order of events here—it's a general group meeting. Price, sitting to the side, says, "Everyone did a great job with the verbals yesterday." Price, age thirty-three, is an energetic presence. His five-foot-six frame is compact and athletic. He's got dark hair that hangs in curls, and he's got a bright and ready smile. He's an easygoing guy, happiest when he's out on the lake in a flat-bottomed skiff with his huge Newfoundland, Otis, on his way to a little island at low tide to pick sea beans for one of tonight's seafood dishes. "People really change—it's August," he says to the servers. Everyone knows that August crowds tend to spend less, are more demanding, and are generally less savvy than off-season patrons. "So do your best to maintain your composure."

A server says, "The green zebras were a little hard yesterday, and I noticed some people were leaving them."

"Do you think that was because they were green?" Melissa says. "Sometimes people think the green zebras just aren't ripe."

"No," the server says. "They were a little hard."

Melissa nods OK.

Melissa scans the board, set on a table beside her, propped against the wall. "There are two changes on aps tonight. The oysters tonight are Pemaquid; they're roasted with a tomato-fennel glaçage, which is kind of like a hollandaise, but not really—it's whipped egg yolks, with a reduction of Pernod, shallot, dry vermouth, and tomato. We're folding some whipped cream into that, and that's spooned over the oyster. We'll have a little fennel sauce on there as well. The glaçage will get a little brown on top when it comes out of the oven. It'll get toasted bread crumbs with toasted fennel seeds ground into them."

"What's the best way to describe that to the customers," a server asks, "kinda like a hollandaise?"

"No," she says, "it's more like a gratiné with fennel and tomato."

"And it's called glaçage?"

"Glaçage—it's a classic preparation. And we also have a house-made sheep's-milk ricotta. The sheep's milk came from Perry Ells's farm and we got whey from Apple Hill Farm. They're making a sheep's-milk cheese as well. We used the whey and milk to make the ricotta here this morning. So it's house-made, served warm on a lightly toasted baguette, with a little arugula, Black Mission figs, and extra-virgin olive oil. Very simple."

The servers are eager to know how Melissa worked the magic on the whey. Melissa describes the process and also notes the difference between this ricotta and ricotta salata, which is salted, pressed, and baked. The nature of the curds that define ricotta is that they don't fall apart under heat—they don't melt. Instead, they simply dry out. Melissa likes to use ricotta salata, in strips using a vegetable peeler, grated, or in chunks on pizzas and pastas. The servers listen intently, many taking notes, presumably for their own use.

The easy discussion goes on in this manner until all the servers have asked everything they need to know, or addressed any issues, for the night ahead. Then Melissa at last stands slowly and returns to the kitchen, finishing prep, then cleaning up for service.

Unless she hears someone whistling. Once, while seated in this dining room toward the end of the pre-service meeting, she heard whistling and was out of her seat like lightning. "Who's *whistling?!*" she shouted, the only time I heard her raise her voice. *"Jesse?!"* She bolted for the dish station where the new dishwasher was merrily hosing down plates. Melissa is superstitious: Whistling in a kitchen means death to the chef, she said. Jesse agreed to refrain.

My Dinners with André

by Gael Greene

from *Insatiable*

Longtime restaurant critic for *New York* magazine, Greene reviews a lifetime of dining adventures in this delectable (and often downright sexy) memoir. Here's her fond portrait of the great Lutece chef-owner Andre Soltner.

He is the John Wayne of *beurre blanc,* defending the fort long after the rebels have hoisted the flag of radicchio," I wrote in September 1993. André Soltner, ruler of a tiny world on East Fiftieth Street, in a dollhouse castle eighteen feet wide by one hundred feet long, shepherd of America's most celebrated restaurant for decades, struck me in the hebephrenic nineties as our town's one pure chef—fearless in his conviction, immune to flash and fad, dedicated to his idea of perfection, endearingly modest. "I'm just a cook," he liked to say. His streak of naïveté was refreshing, though one might also see it as stubbornness (like refusing to upgrade the house's bland French roll when the city was rich with young American baking talent). "He is simply what he is, no apology, no pretension, proud of his faith," I wrote.

Sirio Maccioni might phone a dozen strayed customers every morning to woo them back for lunch. André had never called one. It would never have occurred to him. Unlike the gallivanting playboys of the American range and the Bocuse mileage-plus gang, he famously never strayed from the kitchen. "We are cooks, not ambassadors," he liked to say. "I missed just four nights in thirty years," he told me proudly. Knee surgery forced two of his absences from the kitchen. Asked to join his confreres in a splashy tasting dinner to benefit Citymeals-on-Wheels, André agreed to send dessert. That way, he could rush over to take his bow after his Lutèce clients had been sufficiently cozened and fed.

There were no Technicolor drawings in his sauces, no layered pyramids, none of the flying buttresses on the plate, technical tics of the nineties. "*Cook* means what it means—to cook the food, not to architect it." Unlike Sirio, who could always create a table at Le Cirque if an unexpected VIP suddenly materialized, André rationed out his tables judiciously but never had one left for the last-minute big cheese or friend of the house. One night, he had to send his one-time boss and partner, the creator of Lutèce, André Surmain, to Le Cirque for dinner. "I will call Sirio myself," Soltner offered. "He will have a table for you."

In 1975, I took a look at Manhattan's top French restaurants—rating them not with stars or Michelin boutonnieres but with mouths signifying "culinary excellence" and hearts for "total pleasure" quotient. Lutèce led what I described as "the frozen-in-amber crowd" with five mouths and four hearts. "Lucullan appetites have one extraordinary hero," I wrote. "André Soltner never stops inventing, perfecting, rethinking, improvising.

"In a world of so few eternal verities, there is Lutèce. The neighbors change. New gaudy awnings confuse. But there it is, two steps down to the narrow town house with its unassuming beige door, circa February 16, 1961." That was the day André Surmain opened what he brashly promised would be "the best restaurant in the world." He would be the first to serve on bone china and Baccarat crystal, he insisted, first to bring in Christofle silver, first to use Irish linen napery. ("We gave that up when we couldn't find anyone to iron it properly," he said later.) Everything would be fresh, a radical concept at the time. "Dover sole and freshly smoked Scottish salmon was flown in from England daily," he told me. And it was he who tasted the filet mignon Wellington at a Parisian restaurant named Hansi and persuaded the twenty-seven-year-old chef, André Soltner, to bring himself and that pastry-wrapped hunk of meat to New York and run the tiny kitchen of Lutèce. "A miracle on Fiftieth Street," as Surmain billed it, thrilled when his young chef returned home to compete and win France's coveted Meilleur Ouvrier award a few years later. I loved it with an ingenue's exuberance from my earliest review in 1970, though I knew that Craig had dissed it crankily in the *Times*.

Claiborne, swayed by his admiration for Henri Soulé as the arbiter of fancy French dining—red velour banquettes, sketchy murals, cold striped bass with sauce gribiche in tempting display—found Lutèce sorely lacking. Surmain, in his country squire tweeds and suede Hush Puppies, was slammed as both rude and rudely dressed. And the pen in his pocket. To the ever-proper Craig, that was unforgiveably barbaric. Later, Craig admitted to me that he'd let Souléism blind him to André Soltner's grace, and he bowed and threw in a few more stars in a later assessment.

Dizzy and genuinely thrilled by the high-wire acts of younger chefs, I would go often to Lutèce in the early nineties for a calming déjà vu. I would nod to Madame Soltner, the unsmiling Simone, tucked into her cloistered crib, tracking the bills. I'd walk past the scrawny Pullman kitchen with its pass-through eye on traffic, then into the parlor with its luxury of space, and sometimes into the trellised garden, where affection and expectation retracted the daylight. Always the same. There would be roses in a silver pitcher, the famous Redouté print of the rose on the menu, a museum piece with its retro foie gras en brioche, the venerable mousse of pigeon with juniper berries, that *ancien* relic of the sixties, *mignon de boeuf en feuilletée*—the signature beef Wellington by any other name. Habitués, of course, never saw the menu. We ate the plats du jour. Those who ordered "whatever André feels like cooking" ate best of all.

It was only after the day in 1972 when André Surmain, in a fitful midlife crisis, packed up his wife and four children and sailed his own boat across the Atlantic to Majorca, leaving the chef behind to buy him out, that Soltner was forced to emerge from the kitchen to do the dining room rotation that had been Surmain's routine. "Smiling, eyes tilted up at the corners, Soltner stood, one hand on his hip in his laundry-issue whiteséno custom embroidery here," I wrote, in 1993. "There are chefs working six weeks and they must wear their name. Not me. I don't need it. People know me anyway," he said.

He would take the order. "What do you suggest?" we would say.

"Meat, fish . . . chicken?" he would ask. Not altogether graceful in this verbal rap, but never mind. How they loved him. Newcomers were thrilled by his attention. The devout (regulars) fairly gushed: "It's like eating at home. He does dishes for us he wouldn't cook for just anyone."

His Alsatian mother's *baekoffe*—layering lamb shoulder with onions and potatoes—was a rustic nostalgia prepared only for special friends. With that famous Soltner grin, he would deliver a portion of calf testicles— *"amorettes,"* he called them when we asked. Once I requested something lemony for dessert. Not to seem too sycophantic, I suspect, he ignored the lemon part and created a complex masterwork—what I came to call "the Sunshine Tart"—with fresh orange segments caramelized on top, a thin layer of genoise underneath to capture runaway juices, so as not to dilute celestial Grand Marnier–spiked crème pâtissière below in its buttery crust. "This is the best I could do," he offered. "I spent the day with the tax man." I begged him to put the Sunshine Tart on his menu, but he just laughed. Indeed, he never made it exactly that way again.

But witnessing the kitchen revolution abroad during his August *vacance,* he began to experiment. When Lutèce regulars raved about the specifics of a thrush mousse they had tasted at Troisgros, he nodded with interest. One week later, he served them tiny egg-shaped ovals of creamy pigeon mousse spiked with juniper berries gathered at his upstate retreat near the ski trails of Hunter. He had clearly succumbed to a taste epiphany at Frédy Girardet in 1979 and began to do what seemed like daring tricks for Lutèce. Just barely cooked *rouget* flown in fresh from the market of Rungis, outside Paris, appeared as the plat du jour. And French scallops with bright blushing coral still attached thrilled house loyalists. His new vegetable terrine was held together with its own juices, and there was a shocking presence of cilantro. But he was proud of thrifty improvisation, too. Every day at lunch, there was a different soup. "Try my chicken soup," he urged. And when I complimented him, he confided triumphantly, "For this, the ingredients, it costs me ten cents to make it."

André started offering tasting dinners—a forty-five-dollar parade of hors d'oeuvre and entrées with a Gewurztraminer marc–doused lemon ice in between and then two desserts. He began cooking fish noticeably less, though he still nursed old-fashioned notions. I begged him to do my venison rare. Just the thought of it made him screw up his face in distaste. Even now he likes to tell people how misguided I was to demand my chicken "pink" when I am sure what I said was, "Less cooked, André." It was the squab I wanted rare. He acquiesced, and it was the best squab I'd eaten to date (in 1980), faintly gamy, with threads of celery root and rather punky spatzle. He came by to watch my reaction and was skeptical: "It's not too bloody?"

He was almost sixty-one and complaining about his cartilage-ravaged knees the day in 1993 when I asked if he could do two tasting dinners for the four of us—a challenge for the finale of what I didn't know would be my final review of André Soltner's Lutèce. That evening's new dishes were surprising in their complexity. And the simplicity of his mellow signature tarte flambé was stunning in its perfection. There were flaws and I listed them, too, of course.

"My affair with Lutèce mirrors scenes from a long marriage," I wrote at the end. "The first storm of passion. The deepening of love. Affectionate familiarity. A certain ennui. The seven-year-itch. Irritation at the other's inability to be anything but what he is. And now, admiration and tenderness for exactly that."

How long could he fly down those stairs to the prep kitchen? I wondered. Who would take over? The Soltners were childless. He had told friends that Simone longed to go home to France. The staff was family (with pensions), and even the busboys had been there for twenty years. He could not simply leave them, he said. He'd brought in chef Pierre Schutz and a maître d' for a six-month trial marriage, hoping they'd decide to buy the place. But Schutz found it an impossible dream. "Lutèce is André Soltner," he told me. "No one can replace him."

The choice was painful. To let Lutèce survive without its soul or to sell the town house minus its name . . . and see the legend disappear forever. A year later, Michael Weinstein was thrilled to add Lutèce to the mostly pop-feeding ventures of Ark, and the Lutèce family of regulars went into mourning. André's kitchen staff scattered. Eberhard Müller, the first chef de cuisine of Le Bernardin, took up the fallen whisk. André and Simone bought a retreat on the Riviera but decided to stay in New York, living above the store as always.

"I always check the kitchen before we go to bed at night, to be sure the oven is off," André reported. I thought that the compulsive workaholic would pine away in retirement. But he surprised us by joining the faculty at the French Culinary Institute and becoming a celebrity regular on the luxury-cruise circuit . . . seeing the world gratis in exchange for a few demonstrations. He would disappear for weeks at a time with the constantly radiant Simone smiling . . . yes, always smiling now. I like to think they float on gentle seas in a buttery pool on an endless honeymoon.

Pasta-Maker

by Bill Buford
from *Heat*

Reading *Heat* is almost like witnessing a religious conversion, as writer Buford, apprenticing himself to Mario Batali, falls more and more madly under the spell of the kitchen life. In this excerpt, he's even traveled to Italy to find Mario's old mentors.

The next day Betta was in the kitchen when Mark and I arrived. She was resolved: today she would tell us how to make tortellini, although, before she began, she renewed her conditions.

I understood them. I will not tell Mario.

"Do you promise?"

Mark and I looked at each other. (We said nothing, but what was communicated between us was unmistakable: this, we agreed, is very weird.)

I promised.

"Okay," Betta said. She was solemn. "This is what goes inside. There are four meats: pork, chicken, prosciutto, and mortadella." The measurements were in etti. "You start with two etti of pork, ground up."

"Any cut?" I asked.

"The shoulder or butt," she said, indicating her own shoulder and butt, that cook's thing of pointing to the cut in question as though it had been butchered from your own body. "A lean piece."

I repeated the quantity and wrote it in a notebook. Two etti is about eight ounces.

"About half as much chicken. The breast. Also ground up. You cook both meats together in a pan with butter."

I wrote a formula: Maiale + polio = padella con burro. Pork + chicken = pan + butter.

"Next. The cured meats. Half an etto, or fifty grams, of the prosciutto and mortadella. You grind these up, too." Fifty grams is about two ounces. Prosciutto is found all over Italy but is at its most refined in the Po River Valley, the heart of Emilia-Romagna. Mortadella—a fatty pork mousse in a casing—is another specialty associated with Bologna (thus "baloney," the bastardized name of a bastardized version). These were the tastes of the zona; you won't find them in a Tuscan preparation, even though Tuscany was so close I could see it from the kitchen window.

"You add your ground-up prosciutto and mortadella to your pan. Cook them slowly. You want the flavors to mingle." In all, there was about a pound of meat. "Let it cool, and add two eggs, some parmigiano . . ."

"How much?"

"Enough to thicken it. And some grated nutmeg . . ."

"How much?"

"A little." She bunched her fingers together. "You mix it with your hands. That's the filling."

The result—like grainy sand before the eggs, cheese, and nutmeg are added; like a gray mushy toothpaste afterwards—wasn't much to look at, but, since it was about to be tucked inside a piece of dough, what it looked like was irrelevant. The smell, however, was powerful. What was it? The Bolognese meats? The combination of the raw and the cured? I stuck my head in a bowl and my mind said: pizza toppings and eggnog and a barbecue on the Fourth of July. It was all my holidays in one. My mind also said: This is not a smell you know. It wasn't of the mountains, which I'd now come to think of as damp and mushroomy brown. It was different. Appetizing, certainly, and wintry, and, somehow, highly specific. This was a taste I knew I would encounter nowhere else in the world. An urban medieval perfume, I concluded. This, I wanted to believe, was the fragrance of a Bologna kitchen, learned by someone in Betta's family, preserved and passed on until it had reached the aunts in Vergato.

Betta wouldn't show me the next step—preparing the complex pasta engineering that encased her filling—until I met a new condition. I would have to return later in the summer, my third trip. It was,

I concluded, a test of my promise that I wouldn't reveal the recipe to Mario: if enough time had elapsed and she got no reports of her tortellini on the Babbo menu, she could assume the coast was clear.

If you're a boy, your principal difficulty in making tortellini, I discovered (because of course I returned), is your fingers, which, alas, really need to be a girl's, and not just any girl's, but an elfin girl's.

Your fingers need to be small because all the action occurs on the top of the smallest one, the pinky—in Betta's case, the tiny top of her very petite pinky—where you place the puniest square of pasta. You then pack the puny square with largest amount of filling possible and fold it, corner to corner, to form a miniature but bulging triangle. You next tip the top part of the triangle forward, as though it were bowing in an expression of gratitude, and then (the crucial step) pull the other two corners forward, as though securing the bowing head in a headlock. You then press it all together to form a ring. When you turn the pasta over, you'll be astonished by what you created: a belly button. (What can I say? It's wildly erotic.)

Each infinitesimal tortellino takes a *long* time to make, and during the whole delicate process I found myself always on edge, hoping against hope that I wouldn't crush the fuckers. (I crushed many fuckers.) And, given how *little* time it takes to eat the peanut-sized little bastards, you come away with an understanding of what they are: munchkin food made by people with a lot of time on their *tiny* hands. And yet, for all that, it is an angelically yummy munchkin food. You simmer it in a clear broth, turn off the flame, and let it sit for a while in the pot, doing that back-and-forth thing that a good pasta does, taking in the broth's flavors, releasing its own starchiness, until it is tender and floppy and bloated with taste and can then be served, smelling fragrantly of Christmas.

The truth is, Betta was right. You learn pasta by standing next to people who have been making it their whole lives and watching them. It seems simple, and that's because it is simple, but, characteristic of all Italian cooking, it's a simplicity you have to learn. My advice: Go there. Make Betta a star. Isn't it about time? You'll have to put up with Porretta—very authentic because very ignored, and characterized by the temperamental irritability of a place that feels it has been abandoned (don't even think about getting change for a parking meter) and stay at an overpriced hotel with no bathroom, occasional water (sometimes hot), plastic walls (although wood-colored), no windows (you think there's a view?), and a dysfunctional telephone that works from noon on Sunday to early on Monday morning. And then, once you've settled in (hah!), wander down to the bottom of the valley, listening for the River Reno, and, near the old aqueduct (now housing a sewer—you'll smell it), watch out for a sign, painted by hand, virtually illegible and probably fallen down. It says "Capannina." There will be an arrow. Follow it, and after half a mile, where the river bends around itself, a peninsula of Emilia-Romagna surrounded by Tuscany, you'll find the pizzeria. Betta gets in at about four. Good luck.

After leaving Porretta, I became a tortellini student. I was curious to see if I'd find Betta's recipe elsewhere. I didn't. But I can't say there's a lot of difference between hers and, say, the twenty-five other recipes I came upon. Since the sixteenth century, the filling of this tiny folded pasta has almost always involved a bird (capon, chicken, or turkey), a cut of pork, a cured meat (or bone marrow and cured meat), cheese (almost always parmigiano), and occasionally herbs. And, since forever, it has been cooked either in broth or with cream *(panna)*. But the quantities of these ingredients vary from recipe to recipe, even if only minutely, and these variations are what one generation passes to the next, always as guarded secrets, each family convinced that its recipe is the definitive one. The arguments about what constitutes a genuine tortellino were so passionate that, in 1971, a convention was held, La Dotta Confraternita del Tortellino, the Learned Confederation of the Tortellino, to determine once and for all the correct preparation. With considerable ceremony, the preparation was published three years later, on December 7, 1974, and then locked away in a vault in the Camera di Commercio di Bologna, the city's chamber of commerce. Today you can find it on the websites of various agricultural and official-sounding institutions, introduced by appropriately solemn injunctions about the dangers of not following the instructions precisely, but the effort is to miss the point. The Learned Confederation cannot tell you the one recipe because it doesn't exist, and to go looking for it or to experiment with the many variations until you persuade yourself that you've arrived at the definitive one is to miss the intimate ideology of the dish. There is not one recipe; there is only the one you've been entrusted with. "You are not to tell Mario this recipe," Betta instructed me again. "This is my gift to you."

I honored the terms of the gift and didn't pass it on to Mario, while knowing that he had no use for it anyway and that the injunction would have baffled him and made him sad. Would he have understood the resentment implicit in it? Gianni and Betta have long been accustomed to not getting their due. They're mountain people. There is a hardship in their cooking. In their eyes, they took in a man they genuinely believed couldn't cook (probably because they themselves understood only one way of cooking) and taught him what they knew. When he returned to America, he became rich and famous, telling the story that he'd learned everything from his "second family" in the mountains. But Mario hadn't come here to learn a region's cooking in order to reproduce it faithfully, as though from a textbook. I find myself thinking of the Mississippi Delta and the visits made by students keen to learn the mournful lyricism in the music that you can still hear in the juke joints there. Mario is forever making food his own way, not just griddle pizza or a porky linguine alle vongole or carbonara with raw eggs on top, but his whole approach, that nightmare display of contorni that I worked with at the grill, the secret sauces, the ingredients never revealed on the menu, the squirter bottles of syrups and acids and juices, the performance: like a musician.

For my part, I'd come for the textbook and was glad to have it. Betta's tortellini are now in my head and my hands. I follow her formula for the dough—an egg for every etto of flour, sneaking in an extra yolk if the mix doesn't look wet enough. I've learned to roll out a sheet until I see the grain of the wood underneath. I let it dry if I'm making tagliatelle; I keep it damp if I'm making tortellini. I make a small batch, roll out a sheet, then another, the rhythm of pasta, each movement like the last one. My mind empties. I think only of the task. Is the dough too sticky? Will it tear? Does the sheet, held between my fingers, feel right? But often I wonder what Betta would think, and, like that, I'm back in that valley with its broken-combed mountain tops and the wolves at night and the ever-present feeling that the world is so much bigger than you, and my mind becomes a jumble of associations, of aunts and a round table and laughter you can't hear anymore, and I am overcome by a feeling of loss. It is, I concluded, a side effect of this kind of food, one that's handed down from one generation to another, often in conditions of adversity, that you end up thinking of the dead, that the very stuff that sustains you tastes somehow of mortality.

A Mentor Named Misty

by Gabrielle Hamilton

from *Food & Wine*

> The chef/owner of Manhattan's Prune restaurant, Hamilton is as talented a writer as she is a cook. Her secret? Never forget that you're cooking for people; have a novelist's curiosity about your diners and your staff.

When I met Misty Callies, my reluctant mentor, who inadvertently shaped me into the chef I am now, I'd left New York City, paradoxically, to escape from cooking. After soldiering through nearly twenty years in second-rate kitchens, starting as a twelve-year-old dishwasher at a tourist restaurant in my Pennsylvania hometown, I had somehow gotten a spot in the master's program in fiction writing at the University of Michigan. So, in 1995, I packed a U-Haul and rolled into Ann Arbor to start a new, clean-fingernailed life.

I unpacked the U-Haul, registered for classes and immediately took a part-time job cooking to help pay the rent. When Misty hired me, she was grilling boneless chicken breasts for a U of M tailgate party, wearing a stained V-neck T-shirt. Not more than ten years my senior, she was the tired, taciturn, slightly beaten chef of a perfectly decent catering company in a university football town where grown men wear maize-and-blue parkas and golf socks and will not venture beyond salmon and filet mignon, cooked to death and preferably covered with melted cheese.

At the time, I knew nothing about academic fiction-writing obsessions like "narrative strategy" or "diction," but about food and cooking I thought I already knew everything—knives, burns, 20-hour days, gold leaf in Champagne flutes, ring molds, braziers, butter rosettes and blowtorches. Working quietly across from Misty under the fluorescent lights, I had, I estimated, nothing to learn from her. She was not French or male or wearing a toque or blowing sugar into fragile candy shells to be filled with mousse. She was, rather, assembling rigid, odorless domestic cheese platters for university functions. I had a 25-pound knife kit brimming with tweezers and Q-tips, fish spatulas and needle-nose pliers. I had cooked for the king of Thailand.

But Misty had a couple of tricks of her own, which aren't found in a knife kit. Most importantly, she knew the difference between what she did for a paycheck and what she did at home. At her farmhouse, which is part of a land conservancy started by her husband, Bill, and some friends and neighbors, Misty was her real self as a cook; there, she was an organic gardener on a scale just two mules shy of farming. At work, she communicated in vaguely disapproving grunts (I have never met a person who could not talk the way Misty could not talk), but at home, she eked out full sentences. With my first invitation to dinner at her place—brined chicken, barbecued on a charcoal grill and served on the sunporch with some excellent rose—I began to feel the stirrings of a remote past, of a someone I had meant to become a hundred restaurant kitchens ago. The second meal, with grilled sardines and rhubarb from her garden, transported me to a place I hadn't been to in so long, I didn't even remember it existed: my own home in my own childhood. Misty's bumpy, misshapen tomatoes ripening on the back steps, her cabbages shredded and broken down with salt, her hunks of pork swimming in smoky, earthy juices—all of these began to revive in me the girl I was when I first learned about food, when my family ate rustic, simple dishes that connected to our rural French heritage.

At Misty's house, and by her example, I relearned how to cook for myself, purely for pleasure and not for commercial consideration. Together we ate dark, oily fishes like bluefish and mackerel. She made duck prosciutto and confit. Every fall she emptied the garden and pickled and canned enough to fill a room in the cellar with hundreds of Ball jars. We made cornichons with the tiny yellow blossoms sometimes still attached, and Concord grape juice. She deep-fried with as little hesitation as you or I might brew coffee. The artisanal cheeses she ate at home sat out on the counter unwrapped and stank and oozed. And always, always, she offered guests a well-made cocktail.

At work, Misty and I continued to grind out salmon pinwheels and balsamic-glazed chicken breasts, and she maintained a taciturnity of impressive measure. At school, I found myself in the mostly unbearable company of pale academics, who sat around the grad-student lounge endlessly discussing "post-Hegelian moments" and "Barthesian tropes." I was gunning the motor of my car to get off campus each day and get to my job as a cook, which I was distinctly starting to prefer.

And then she left. In 1996, Misty walked out the door of the catering company and, with her brother as co-chef, opened Zanzibar, a pan-tropical restaurant with dishes from countries around the equator. To get her hands on new ingredients, and to read incessantly about unfamiliar dishes and cultures, gave her demeanor a brightness that made the stained T-shirts she still wore seem almost clean. Within weeks, she was happily exhausted rather than hopelessly worn down; she was almost *talkative*. I quit the catering company and ran after her. For the first time I tried *picadillo*, the slightly sweet ground meat hash popular in Spanish and Latin countries; and chimichurri, the green Argentinean sauce with chopped herbs; and asafoetida, a pungent, sulfuric Indian flavoring. I was deeply impressed not only by being exposed to new things, but also by how thoroughly Misty had done her homework, with her piles of books marked with yellow tabs. We tested dishes over and over until we got them right or as close to right as Misty could get. She found a local tortilla maker, and she persuaded the famous Michigan store Zingerman's to make chipotle challah for her rock-shrimp club sandwich.

Working with her at Zanzibar taught me how to run a restaurant. It was the first time in twenty years I'd heard a chef say "I don't know, let me look it up." It was the first time I'd seen a chef solicit the opinions or ask about the experiences of her staff. If the dishwasher's mother made posole for every family reunion, Misty would ask him about it. She ran her kitchen without insults or humiliations or fraternity-like hazings.

The restaurant flared, but then sputtered, and now smolders along like Pennsylvania's great Centralia coal-mine fire, which still burns more than 40 years after its first spark. Misty is still the chef, but Michiganders, it seems, were not ready for such unfamiliar foods, and within a year, Zanzibar's owners made Misty "reconceptualize." Although she was able to refuse to sell nachos, she had to cave on the Zanzibar Caesar salad with chipotle challah croutons ($5.95; $9.95 with grilled chicken breast, crab cakes or salmon).

In 1999, I returned to New York City with my new degree and ditched it. I opened a restaurant, Prune, and started cooking all of—and only—the foods I wanted to eat at home: trickless, gadgetless and pretenseless. I feature in my restaurant everything I grew up eating—the duck-crackling omelet for dinner, the calves' brains with brown butter, the Swiss chard from the garden, the lumpy tomatoes still warm from the sun. And all of the food goes directly from the stove to the plate, cooked by one person, using tools no more complicated than a spoon and a sauté pan and a pair of clean hands. I run my kitchen much as Misty runs hers; Prune is everything she reconnected me to.

I can hear Misty's protesting, self-effacing grunt every time I even try to introduce her as my mentor, but she remains the person I look to and listen to most. I visit her at the farm about twice a year for delicious dinners and to exchange new ideas or dishes, like *manti,* the tiny Turkish ravioli. These dinners can last well into the night, with fluid, effortless conversation as the Michigan breeze rustles the Concord grape vines, under which I have buried my 25-pound knife kit and my university degree.

An Encyclopedia of Seafood Cookery

by Molly O'Neill

from *Mostly True*

Though Molly O'Neill's engaging memoir isn't totally about food—it's also about growing up the only girl in a family of baseball-mad brothers—her coming-of-age as a cook is one of its most charming strands.

L ike most people who grew up landlocked in America during the 1950s, I was deeply suspicious of any piece of fish that was not rectangular, boned, breaded, and deep-fried. Unlike most Midwesterners, however, I'd spent my toddler years confiding in a mermaid named Karen, and the briny fishy smell of my new hometown [Provincetown, Massachusetts] moved me. In the fog before dawn, I pedaled my racing bike down the pier to watch the day boats, the scallopers, and the draggers leave the harbor. Whenever I could, I also rode back for their return, an empty pail swinging from my handlebars.

The fishermen gave away "trash fish"—the monkfish, goosefish, and dogfish, the eel and squid, the tinkers and herring and occasional "cull," or one-clawed lobster, that they couldn't sell. I had no idea what to do with any of it. In my kitchen in the west end, the writhing contents of the pail made me gag. Determined to be a local, I resolutely studied A. J. McClane's *Field Guide to Saltwater Fishes of North America* and his *Encyclopedia of Fish Cookery*. I spent hours imagining recipes that would conceal the flavor of the often hideous, slimy, and flopping fish I was given.

I shared the basic misconception of many young would-be Escoffiers. I thought cooks were conquistadors: I thought that my

mission was to triumph over my ingredients. My coworkers, however, did not share this vision of our vocation. They didn't lie in bed
at night imagining what an ingredient could become; they just
tried to cook their dishes fast and well and to do no harm. Alex
appointed himself my teacher, countering each of my gourmet
innovations with lessons in the anatomy of seafood and drills in the
simplest cooking technique appropriate for any given species.

When, for instance, I presented my colleagues with fluke poached
in tomato sauce with anchovy and olives and enough garlic to
frighten a vampire, Alex countered, "I can't taste the fish." He used
his fork to unravel the tomato skin that I'd formed into a rose garnish, and said, "Let me show you how to clean a sea urchin."

"What do you think?" I asked when, after weeks of reading and
recipe development, I served him gray sole fillets stuffed with
shrimp and crabmeat and blanketed with a champagne cream sauce.

"Shrimp are not local," he said. "Have you ever had bone squid?
The size of a thumb, so tender, too good for customers. Let me show
you how to fry them, *fritto misto.*"

In the face of flounder in dill cream sauce on a bed of cucumbers,
Alex offered a lesson in sautéing scallops with roe. My flounder with
Nantua sauce brought a lesson in steaming clams the size of a
quarter, and my flounder Florentine with spinach and béchamel
earned me a lesson in deep-frying whitebait and serving it—to
cooks only—with homemade tartar sauce.

"Too good for customers," said James A. Madison, dipping a tiny
fried fish into the pickle-spiked mayonnaise.

"Did you use olive oil in the tartar sauce?" asked Petey Boy
approvingly.

One night, Alex decided to teach me how to make a perfect pan-
fried sole and, for the duration of the Red Sox pregame show, we
made sole à la meunière again and again. I learned to season milk
lightly with a fleck of Tabasco sauce, to soak the flounder fillets for
two minutes, to season flour with salt and pepper, to dust the fish
with the flour and to shake it off. I learned the sight and sound and
smell of the moment when a slick of butter is hot enough to seal the
fish, and the sound and smell of the instant the fillet needs to be
turned over. The staff ate well that night.

"Do it with your eyes closed," said Alex, and then, handing me tiny wads of paper towel, "OK, now put these in your ears, close your eyes, and do it again."

I obeyed. "Out, out, out," he cried less than a minute after I flipped the fish. "Get it out of the pan! Now hit the pan with lemon, OK. A chunk of fresh butter. No! Not on the fish, not yet. Now the secret! Open your eyes," he said, and when I did, I saw that his fingers were poised twelve inches above the fish fillets. He released a delicate rain of sea salt.

"It brings the flavor of the fish and the flavor of the sauce together in the mouth," he said. "Call the waiter before you put the fillet in the pan. Hold the salt and the sauce until he's standing in front of you. OK. Now you do it again. Close your eyes."

As I learned from my colleagues to cook by my senses, I also absorbed their antipathy for the clientele. These attitudes and habits seeped into my pores and lived in my body, just beneath my rational mind: I began preferring the company of cooks. After all, customers were the other—the tourists, the day-trippers, the Philistines, the rubes. Cooks were us. We worked harder and we knew more. We had substance and we had moral fiber. This lesson was brought home to me on the night of the full moon in June, when the striped bass were running.

As the moon waxed, the bass had begun to run, and commercial and sport fishermen alike brought their catch to the restaurant. The fishermen wore shorts and tall black boots and they bargained with Chef Gun for cash, drinks, and dinner. Using shiny metal hooks, they lugged their fish in heavy wooden boxes behind them. Sometimes they were iced; more often, the creatures were still flopping and writhing. One or two would regularly escape the boxes, which were deposited in the trash area outside the kitchen door.

During lulls in the kitchen, Gun would send me out to clean and steak the fish. He wanted enough bass in the freezer to last the entire summer. I still had the lowest rank in the kitchen and, having mastered flatfish, I was ready to learn about the oily species. The lesson was hideous. But rather than blame the chef, I blamed the patrons for my assignment. If there weren't so many of them, after all, I wouldn't have to clean so many fish.

"Customers," I huffed as I arranged two garbage cans four feet apart and heaved a length of butcher block between them to form a counter.

"Customers," I groused as I reached into the gills of one of the bass and heaved the huge fish onto this counter.

I stared at the big, beautiful fish and the fish stared back at me. I memorized its head, the shape and size of it, and its relationship to the butcher block counter. Then, grasping the wooden handle of the cleaver with both hands, I raised it above my head and slammed it into the sloping indentation between the fish's skull and the first vertebra of the spine. Its glistening blade whistled in the cleaver's terrible descent. I made a noise that was part scream and part grunt. I sounded like Amazonia teaching karate.

"*Ay!*" I gasped.

I blamed the customers for making me murder the fish and I blamed them, too, when my aim was imperfect. When I hit the right spot, the cleaver met the table with a dead and final chunk. If I missed the mark, there was a slushy, splintery sound followed by a splatter of fish blood across my white apron. The fish's body jumped a little and then flattened against the wooden plank. I used the back side of the cleaver to push the fish's head into the five-gallon bucket that I'd placed near one end of the execution table.

I then exchanged the heavy cleaver for a fillet knife to gut the fish and cut out the fins after removing the head and tail. Then, taking an aluminum scraper, I scraped the scales from the bodies. The bass ranged in weight from five to thirty pounds and were, at this point, sometimes still moving.

After scaling the fish, I used the tip of a chef's knife to locate the sweet spot between each vertebra then, using a rubber mallet, I cut the body into a series of steaks. There were nearly a hundred steaks that night. Later I would wrap each in plastic and freeze it. Later still, the bass steaks would be thawed, marinated in Italian vinaigrette, broiled, and served with a lemon crown.

"Their fish is always soooo fresh!" I could hear one customer tell another as a group of them crunched the shells in the alleyway that ran past the trash area and led to the restaurant's front door.

How stupid they were! Naugahyde palates! Beneath the stockade fence that shielded them from my murderous activities in the trash area, I could see the tiny rounded toes of their Pappagallo shoes, the errant ties of their Top-Siders. I was close enough to smell the balsam from their shampoo, while my own hair was caked with fish blood and scales. But at least my coworkers and I could tell the difference between fresh and frozen.

We knew the sweet, briny flavor of a fish that had still been alive when a serving was cut from its frame. We knew the faintly acrid flavor of fish that had died after writhing frantically on dry ground before being butchered. Our tongues could tell what a fish had fed on, whether it was male or female, and whether it was young and lean, or older, fatter, and spent. We knew good from bad. We knew everything. We had taste.

After the first rush, the cooks joined me in the killing area to smoke. "So fresh," said Alex with the sort of reverence he normally reserved for his Red Sox. Taking my fillet knife, he cut bites from the center of the bass on my counter. He balanced the small triangle of meat on the tip of his knife and squeezed a single drop of lemon on it. Standing around the execution table, my colleagues and I watched silently as the flesh winced under this acid. Closing our eyes and opening our mouths, one by one we each accepted the tip of the knife. The cold weight of it against our tongues was metallic. The still-warm flesh was sweet and faintly briny. It quivered and winced in my mouth.

Seafood was my tabula rasa, the medium on which I honed basic cooking techniques, the food that taught me about the symmetry between the nature of the ingredient and the feel of the day. The bass, I soon learned, were followed by the bluefish that swam in their wake, mouths wide open, eating indiscriminately, which made their oily flesh taste disturbingly unpredictable, fish to fish. A brutally quick cooking and an acidic accompaniment—mustard, lemon, vinegar, or tomato—was the answer. These bold dishes were also an antidote to the swath of rainy days that often followed these fish. The swordfish of July was a different lesson, a simpler fish. Cut into steaks, the fish was as firm as the pectorals of the young men who danced bare-chested to Gloria Gaynor late at night, their T-shirts bobbing from their back pockets like tails. The fish steaks needed a dose of olive oil or compound butter and a quick turn on the grill. Likewise, the tuna of August wanted nothing more than a fast, hot romp.

It made sense that the mackerel came when the tourists left and life turned inward. Mackerel was harder to handle than the big, easy boys of summer. It needed more fussing—a slow, cool smoke, for instance, a light pickle, or, like the cod and other fish that appeared in the fall, a pungent poaching, a simmer or slow bake. I walked the breakwater and picked mussels in September. I played God, experimenting to see which aromatic improved and which detracted, honing my timing as I steamed the mollusks to capture the moment between a juicy life and a dry, tough death.

In October, there was a scallop bonanza on George's Banks. I got scallops in forty-pound muslin sacks and cooked them until they were gone. After a year, I could pick up a piece of seafood and know whether it wanted to be cooked fast or slow, if it wanted liquid or oil or to be cooked dry. The taste of my fingers after touching its flesh told me whether to underscore its richness, it herbaciousness, its sweetness or its brine, and how to offset these flavors. One can build a life around knowing one thing well.

Meet David Bouley

by Dan Barber

from *Don't Try This at Home*

> Though today he himself is a top chef—running both Manhattan's Blue Hill restaurant and its sibling Blue Hill at Stone Barns—Barber recalls vividly a night in the kitchen with David Bouley, and a lesson that has stuck with him ever since.

You're not talking to your fish," moans the chef. I hear the moan from the other side of the kitchen.

There is mayhem all around. A nonstop circus of people appears and disappears through swinging doors. The expediter yells, "Ordering; two hamachi, three skate, a bass, and a halibut à la carte. Ordering: one crab salad—make that two—*two* crab salads, two sardines, and a finnan haddie *on the fly* . . ."

Cooks are everywhere, spinning, dodging, and impossibly stretching their way across vast distances to reach plates, spoons, garnishes. Chef's whites suddenly blur into a mountain of vanilla ice cream. I'm rushing now, fumbling for pans. I refuse to be licked.

But the expediter will not stop: "Waiters, pick up table seven. Hello? Waiters. Here we go, waiters!" he screams in a tattoo of insistence that cuts through the kitchen's screech and hurry. "One snapper, two veal, three is a duck—I'm holdin' a duck. I need a duck, please. Where the fuck's my duck? Where's my goddamn fuckin' duck, *please?*"

I am witness to an unfolding madness: a night in the famed kitchen of David Bouley. It is my first time cooking here, but I have heard stories of the intensity and the confusion, of the six-course tasting menus ordered by two hundred or so customers every night—twelve hundred plates of food flowing out of the kitchen in a matter of hours.

The sweat trickles from behind my kneecaps, down my legs. I am working on the fish line, and the chef has a hand in nearly every plate. Few chefs believe this is possible. Bouley, though, has made a career of confounding expectations. Years ago, no one in the culinary establishment believed that a self-proclaimed country hick from Connecticut, a mercurial dreamer, would be able to survive in the best (and toughest) kitchens of the world, as Bouley had done, some of them so abusive and demanding that Bouley himself can only describe them as "numbing."

"I said you're not speaking to your mackerel," repeats the chef, now incensed. I look dumbly at the stove. Could he possibly be talking to me? He's all the way across the kitchen. I've spread a dozen small saucepots on the searing heat of the flat top. Sauté pans align themselves like train cars. I season furiously, dropping and flipping fish, basting, and seasoning again.

The expediter bellows orders from the pass, the window through which dishes travel from the kitchen to the dining room. Around him there is an orbit of madness. Are there twenty-eight cooks or have I counted the bread warmer twice? Here a cook lunges to sauce a naked scallop, as another picks sprigs of lemon thyme from one of the twelve herb plants standing at attention by the door; here a dishwasher waltzes through a sea of cooks, plates stacked so high as to obstruct his face.

Why all this confusion, I wonder. "Forget confusion," a cook tells me at the end of service. "Chaos. He wants the chaos. He *needs* it."

Another cook tells me about one evening's service when the orders were coming in slowly. Chef was unhappy with how relaxed all the cooks were during the first seating. "Changed the menu," the cook tells me, his eyes widening in shock and awe at the memory as though it were unfolding before him all over again. "Never said shit, neither. All of a sudden the second seating arrives, tickets come in, and the dishes ordered no one had prepped for. Totally nuts, man. He's four goddamn stars one night and Dirty Harry the next. Taught me a big lesson," he says, still wide-eyed, though he doesn't explain what the lesson was.

Steve, the philosopher-cook of the brigade, sums it up: "The qualities that mark Chef as a lunatic-genius are his absolute fearlessness, and his profound, unabashed enjoyment of his own strangeness. That's the sort of dementia these cooks respect, and perhaps even share."

The lunatic-genius's gaze intensifies in my direction, and cooks are beginning to look my way as well. I am scared, and losing control. I realize I'm the only one cooking mackerel, and that the chef, who was at the Fulton Fish Market after last evening's service until 4 AM, who went home to "nap and shave" and return by 8 AM, and cook straight through the day, a day so utterly exhausting that by the end of it you will often find him holding his left hand to the left side of his face—holding up his collapsed cheek so cooks can make out what he's mumbling—is, from a hundred feet away, in the midst of a crush of crazed cooks, talking to me about not talking to my mackerel.

Chef appears to be garnishing a plate of raw tuna from across the kitchen, but his eyes are somehow also locked on me. I have read that David Bouley's shyness is his most striking quality, that he relies on observation, rather than inquiry, to understand things.

This moment—our first "meeting"—confirms that assessment. He seems to be soaking up nuances and details. It isn't a hostile gaze, but it isn't exactly empathetic. He can have a big smile, an actor's guffaw at even the slightest quip, and act like he knows you well. And he's studied you so closely that you are sure he *does* know you well. The awkward thing is that you hardly know him, if you know him at all.

"Get that mackerel out of the pan," says the chef, mingling directive and threat. The kitchen falls suddenly silent as he appears next to me and pulls me close. Just as quickly, the noise roars back up. Everyone around us has resumed the whirling, except for Chef and me. We are in our own world. I hear the expediter: "Chef: table six—old man—he's fading. He won't last—he needs his food, he needs it now."

"Be cool," says the cool chef, with one hand pulling the fated mackerel from the flame, the other pulling me close to him. "You're not talking to your fish." He pauses for effect, bracing my neck against his forearm. We stand together and gaze at the mackerel. I'm about to introduce myself when he interrupts the thought. "I *always* talk to my fish," he says, staring at the sizzling mackerel.

"How else would I know when she's done?" In the observation of great Hollywood scriptwriters, the best endings must be surprising and yet inevitable; and the best of Bouley's pronouncements take this same shape.

"How else?" he asks again.

The expediter yells—there are twenty tickets on the board. I tense, trying to push free. Chef squeezes my neck with his bicep. Sweat is pouring from my face, and I find myself quickly, almost imperceptibly, rubbing my wet temple into his crisply starched chefs jacket.

"I'm going to tell you a story," he says.

"I need some tables, people. I need tables," yells the expediter.

"No time for stories," I mumble halfheartedly.

"Two bulls," Chef says, ignoring me, tightening the grip. We're still standing side by side, Chef's arm tightly wound around my neck as the kitchen blazes before us. I wonder if I might faint.

"Two bulls standing on a small hill, an older and a younger bull, overlooking a field of beautiful lady cows," he says to me.

"Oh, man," yells the expediter. "I need table six. I need that table."

The chefs lips are now only inches from my ear. "The younger bull looks up to the older bull: 'Hey, hey, you know what I'm gonna' do? I'm gonna' run as fast as I can right now, as fast as my legs will take me, as fast as I can run down this hill, and I'm gonna' get me one of those lady cows and make her my own.'" He pauses now, as if to let me marinate in the genius. "Do you know what the older bull said back to the younger bull?"

As I shook my head no, that I did not know what the older bull said to the younger bull, I lifted my eyes from his arm and peeked around. Chaos of the sort I had never seen. Cooks were yelling at busboys who yelled at dishwashers who yelled at each other.

"I don't know, Chef," I muttered.

He put his nose in my left ear and leaned heavily on me. I felt the heat of his breath as he held me there. "Well, the older bull paused for a moment," and here too the chef paused. "'Son,' said the older bull, 'I'm going to slowly walk down this hill, and I'm going to make them *all* my own.'

"Don't rush what you do here," he said, and let me go.

Life on the Line

by Francis Lam

from *Gourmet*

The chaos of a major restaurant kitchen running at full dinner-service throttle—the adrenaline rush of being "in the weeds"—is such that only a trained cook can survive the experience, yet only a talented writer can capture it in prose. Luckily, Francis Lam is both.

From the moment I started culinary school, I heard talk about the "externship"—the time when, halfway through the program, you get thrown into the world, out to the wolves, to fend for yourself and make good on the promise of your brand-name education.

For the hothead line cooks—the ones who'd been slinging pans for years in steamy kitchens, waiting for the day when they'd get to scream at hapless lackeys who cut themselves and burned their food—a high-profile extern site with a name like Boulud or Bernardin was a much-desired mark of pride.

But for the more—shall we say—recreational students, "extern" was a constant source of worry. For as great as culinary school is, it can't teach you a cook's instinct—the ability to just get it done, even if you have no time, no space, and the handle just fell off the last sauté pan in the place. That instinct you get only through experience, and in school you have three hours to make ten simple plates. What would it be like in the real world? Could you go from a classroom to working the line on a Saturday night? And would the wolves like their externs medium-rare or medium?

One day at school, I worked with a student who'd spent the last five years as a sous-chef in Omaha. We had a good time, making *feijoada* and talking about Nebraska and halibut and girlfriends and rock and roll—real brothers-in-arms stuff. But there was something about the way he held his knife, the way he attacked that piece of kale, that said, "Man, I'd do this to you, too, if you got in the way of me and my plate." He was a good guy, but he was a good cook first. He wasn't worried about extern.

Later that day, while washing pans at the sink, another student pointed at something hanging on the wall and asked me, with a casual curiosity, "Hey, man, what's that thing?"

"What's what thing?" I asked back.

"That thing right there, the thing with the holes."

I looked at him to see if he was serious. "You mean the colander?" He wasn't smiling.

"Hey, dude," I started, handing him a saucepan to dry, "so where are you going on extern?"

People kept telling me about a place in Oregon called Higgins. Since my friend scored the cushy food-magazine externship I wanted, I decided to look into it.

For years, I learned, Greg Higgins had been a champion of sustainable food practices, someone who respected not only food but the people who produce it. To me, the only thing as important as how food tastes is the community it builds. At Higgins, it seemed this went beyond sharing a meal with friends: It meant understanding where the food comes from, supporting farmers and artisans, creating economies of scale.

I was excited. I gave them a call. They had an opening. I packed up my car with knives and flame-retardant pants and headed to Portland.

By the end of my first shift, my knees were sore, my back ached, and whenever any feeling other than exhaustion got through to my brain, it was either shame or confusion.

Higgins, it turned out, was indeed an awesome restaurant. Yes, the philosophy and the politics were important, but the main thing was this: The food at Higgins was mind-blowing. But what this meant was that I became incredibly intimidated. I had never cooked at such a high level before, using products of such quality and such preciousness, and for a chef of such renown and skill.

I started doing the Scared Guy Thing.

I hovered over the burners, cooking three gallons of squash a handful at a time for fear of messing it up, until one of the other cooks grabbed the bucket, dumped it into the pot, and told me to find something else to do. There's nothing wrong with working thoughtfully, but if it means standing around and getting in someone's way before screwing something up, the fact is you're better off screwing it up quickly. Because no one likes the Scared Guy Thing.

Still, I learned a lot. I learned, for example, that a great way to feel like you don't belong is to be the new extern at a restaurant that packs nine cooks into a 9- by 27-foot kitchen, playing pinball with hot stockpots. I clumsily trudged through as everyone else danced around each other with a familiar grace. I watched Scotty tap Rich gently on the back, saying "Hot, behind you," slip by him with a side step, duck into his oven, and spin back around, pan in hand and plating the order. I felt like a hippo in a tutu, bumping and breaking and burning. And I was the smallest guy in the place.

On my third day, I met Aaron, the burly, goateed sous-chef with a handshake like a test and a black T-shirt that read "I Am An Arrogant Bastard."

He handed me a recipe for crab cakes and sent me off. It looked easy enough: Dice a few vegetables, prep some crab, zest a couple of lemons, gather up some spices. I jumped at it, eager to show some basic ability. But in the same way that trying to demonstrate your wit is really just asking to show off your idiocy, I got overanxious and forgot a basic kitchen rule: Don't do anything until you know what to do next. I started dicing vegetables before getting the water to cook them in hot. I started gathering spices before getting a bowl to toss them in. Then I overcooked the vegetables.

And that's just how the day began. After that, I made some rice cakes. "Make these again, tighter this time." I scooped out the crab cakes. "Make these again, bigger this time." Aaron kept shaking his head, not angry, just disappointed. "Do you know how to cut chickens?"

I perked up at this assignment. Back at school, butchering chickens had been a hobby of mine; before class, I often went down to the meat room, reveling in its strangely sweet smell, and asked for a box of birds to break down. (Yes, I was a cooking school nerd.)

But of course these chickens were twice the size I was used to, and I was working with half the space I was used to, and they wanted them cut a totally different way than I was used to. An hour later, Aaron was shaking his head again, this time with a mixture of pity and terror. "That's way too big. And what happened to the skin on that one? Just go home, Francis."

Twenty-five degrees Brix. I hadn't had much interaction with Greg Higgins, because whenever he was in the kitchen, I basically stepped aside and watched him cook food better than me. Greg can make something, show you how to make it, walk you through it step-by-step, and still, his will just be . . . better. Smoother, crisper, more tender, more flavorful. Every time. It would have made me feel bad, if it hadn't been for the 25 degrees Brix.

During a lull in service one night, I decided to purée a carrot-habanero mixture to freeze for a *granité,* but I didn't know how it was supposed to look in the end. And one thing I had learned was never to finish something and then find out how it was supposed to look in the end.

I turned to ask Scotty, who'd become my man for advice in everything, from hot rods to tattoos to *granité,* but he had just gotten busy with a few orders. I looked around. Everyone had just gotten a few orders. There was only Greg himself, meditatively sharpening his knife. "Uh, hey, uh, Greg? Do you have a minute?"

He turned calmly, and saw what I was doing. He smiled. "Go get an egg," he said. When I returned, he had a cup of warm water. "First, you have to get that egg to room temperature," he said, dropping it into the cup. "Let's start puréeing."

As the blender smoothed out the crossing-guard-orange mixture, throwing its sharp tartness into the air, Greg explained, "For a *granité* to freeze up correctly, you want it to be about twenty-five degrees Brix. Brix is a measure of sugar in a liquid, like in wine. To know if it's right, you drop that egg in here and watch it—the part that sticks up above the surface should be somewhere between the size of a quarter and a nickel. If it's sinking too far, you need to add more sugar. If it's the other way, you should thin it with more water or vinegar."

I reached for the cup. He dipped a spoon in the purée, tasting it. I plopped the egg in. "That's about right. It tastes good." The egg floated back up slowly in the dense mix, showing between a quarter and a nickel. "Nice work," Greg said.

• • •

You know you're getting deep into a culture when the language starts to make sense to you. One night a few weeks into my stint, while plating poached-halibut napoleons, I paused for a moment to listen to the strange words being tossed about. "Drop that gratin," said one of the cooks, meaning to heat it in the oven. "Put a taste on that!" commanded another, meaning I should taste something before sending it out so that I'd know it was right. "Fire table!" the servers said to Rich, who then shouted "Pick up!" to the crew, meaning that it was time to get cooking.

When Scotty, sweat dripping from his brow, called, "I'll take a two on two-two," he meant, "Will you please inform me when you have two minutes remaining before your completion of table twenty-two's order? I, too, have items for that table and it will take me that amount of time to prepare and present those items in the tastiest and most attractive manner possible." When I called back, "Two on two-two," he heard, "Yes, I will comply, as we share a mutual interest in satisfying our guests." And when Rayna sang the gentle phrase, "Francis, please," it was to say, "Come hither, boy, for there is a task that is distasteful and beneath me." I was, after all, still the extern.

One of the things that strikes me most about kitchens is the sound. I thought about that one night while we were getting hammered by guests, the ticket wheel churning away, order after order. It's a pedestrian sound, really—the clacking type and paper-feed wheeze of a computer printer. But depending on the night and on how many tickets you already have hanging in front of you, that sound can be sickening.

Another night, Greg was just coming in to eat dinner when walk-ins started showing up out of nowhere and my supply of mushroom strudels began to dwindle as if the servers were giving them away. It was my fault. "Oh, man, I styled you out on those," the guy from the lunch shift had said, line cook-ese for "I made lots and lots and lots so you won't have to worry about them." I didn't check. A half hour after opening, I had three left. Cursing and cursed at, my partner and I tried frantically to throw some together on the fly, taking us away from the implacable ticket machine. CLACK–CLACK–CLACK–CLACK–CLACK, it went, taunting us as we fell behind. "I styled you out," I kept hearing the lunch guy say. CLACK–CLACK–CLACK. "Greg's here in ten minutes! What do you mean, you have no strudels?!?" CLACK–CLACK–CLACK.

"Oww!" My partner had nipped the hot oven door while trying to bake our last-ditch tray. She dropped it, spilling mushrooms and dough all over the rubber-matted floor. CLACK–CLACK–CLACK–CLACK. That sound was killing me.

But that was months ago—when I was still working my way around the Scared Guy Thing, when Aaron and his T-shirt still terrified me.

Tonight, the ticket wheel's sound is pure music, and our little team of line cooks dances to it, singing in our own language. Cam taps a duck breast with his long, bony finger to check its doneness, twirling his tongs and mapping out the meat and fish on his grill—salmon on the hot side, steaks cooking slowly on the other. Scotty reaches in and out of ovens, pushing and pulling sizzling sauté pans, tongs and towels never leaving his hands even as he spins from burner to plate, his apron a blur over leopard-print pants. Rich orchestrates from the middle, his body set taut watching his ticket wheel, spindly arms finishing plates, matching orders, putting them in the window as he calls for servers. Aaron pops in, every time as if on cue, to style us with freshly cut fish or jars of foie gras mousse whenever supplies look grim. Behind me, Rayna works our tiny oven, swinging the door open and shut, shuffling and piling pans to conserve our precious space, laying down plates with a rhythmic clang for us to sauce and serve.

And all night I dance along, my tongs clacking in time with my partners', my plates getting there when their plates get there, hitting the marble of the servers' window with a punctuating ring. Forget the hippo in a tutu; tonight I'm James Brown.

So when the music finally ends, when the buckets of hot water come out and we start to feel the soreness in our knees and the tightness in our backs, we all look at one another, and we know we've done good. We know it, because we don't have to say anything —we've all been dancing to the same music.

It's my last night before going back to school to finish my program. On his way out, Aaron stops by my station. "Hey, you know, Francis," he says, "I was a little worried about you when you started here. I thought you'd be the kind of kid from culinary school that knows who Escoffier is but can't put a salad on a plate to save his life. But I was wrong. You're a good guy, man. You might even be a cook someday."

New Year's Meltdown

by Anthony Bourdain

from *Don't Try This at Home*

Ever since his best-selling book *Kitchen Confidential*, Tony Bourdain has practically owned this bit of literary turf: the surreal tragicomedy of a big-time kitchen on the brink of spectacular disaster.

In my long and checkered career I have been witness to, party to, and even singularly responsible for any number of screwups, missteps, and overreaches. I am not Alain Ducasse. The focus of my career has not always been a relentless drive toward excellence. As a mostly journeyman chef, knocking around the restaurant business for twenty-eight years, I've witnessed some pretty ugly episodes of culinary disaster. I have seen an accidentally glass-laden breaded veal cutlet cause a customer to rise up in the middle of a crowded dining room and begin keening and screaming with pain as blood dribbled from his mouth. I've watched restaurants endure mid-dinner-rush fires, floods, and rodent infiltration—as well as the more innocuous annoyances of used Band-Aids, tufts of hair, and industrial staples showing up in the niçoise salad. Busboy stabbing busboy, customer beating up customer, waiters duking it out on the dining room floor—I've seen it all. But never have I seen such a shameful synergy of Truly Awful Things happen, and in such spectacular fashion, as on New Years Eve 1991, a date that surely deserves to live in New York restaurant infamy. It was the all-time, award-winning, jumbo-sized restaurant train wreck, a night where absolutely everything went wrong that could go wrong, where the greatest number of people got hurt, and an entire kitchen bowed its head in shame and fear—while outside the kitchen doors, waiters trembled at the slaughterhouse their once hushed and elegant dining room had become.

Like Operation "Market Garden" (the ill-fated Allied invasion of the Netherlands) or Stalingrad—or the musicals of Andrew Lloyd Webber—responsibility for the disaster that followed rests, ultimately, with one man. In this case it was a talented and resourceful chef we'll call Bobby Thomas. Bobby had the idea that he could create an ambitious menu—as good as his always excellent à la carte menus—and serve it to the 350 people who would be filling the nightclub/restaurant we'll call NiteKlub. He also felt confident enough in his abilities that he could pretty much wait until the last minute to put the whole thing together: little details like telling his staff what the fuck they were going to be serving, and how. In his visionary wisdom, Bobby did not share his thinking or his plans with others. Like the strategic braniacs who thought invading Russia to be a good idea, he was undisturbed by useful details ("Mein Fuhrer? Are you aware winter is coming?"). Those who might have pointed out the obvious warning signs were not included in Bobby's conceptualizing of what could well have been a spectacular success—for a dinner party of twenty. Bobby was, after all, a kind of a genius. And it's often the geniuses who put us in a world of pain.

I arrived at NiteKlub at about a half hour before the shift, the other cooks trickling in after me. We pulled on our whites, cranked up the radio, and, as usual, stood around waiting for someone to tell us what to do. Our leader had characteristically neglected to entrust us with a prep list. So we did what cooks left unbriefed and unsupervised tend to do, which was stand around gossiping.

The lobsters arrived first. There were cases of them, so many that they reached to the ceiling, 125 of the things, skittering around under wet newspaper and heaps of crushed ice. Since I was de facto quartermaster, and the guy who signed for such things, the cooks—Frankie Five Angels, Matt, Orlando, Steven, Dougie, Adam Real Last Name Unknown, and Dog Boy—all stood there expectantly, looking at me, waiting for instructions as a puddle of water grew larger and larger from the rapidly melting ice. What do we do with them? Who knows? Bobby hadn't left a prep list. Do we blanche them? Cook them all the way? Whack 'em into wriggling chunks? Shuck them, split them, or turn the damn things into bisque? We don't know. 'Cause Bobby hasn't left a menu.

The game arrived next. Boned-out *poussin,* duck breasts, bones, a case of foie gras. We cleaned up the duck breasts nicely, put on stock with the bones (that didn't take much to surmise), and laid out the *poussins* on sheet pans and got everything in the walk-in for when Bobby showed. We wanted to start in on the case of foie gras —whole loaves of the stuff!—but were we making terrine, which would require us to open them up and start yanking out veins, or were we leaving them whole for pan-searing? We didn't know. And once you tear open a liver, you can't untear it. So we left those alone. When the meat order arrived, we cleaned up the tenderloins, but left them whole, not having any idea of portion size, whether we were making filet mignon or tournedos or chateaubriand or beef fucking Wellington for that matter.

Oysters! There was a collective moan from the team, as not even a madman would want to put oysters on a menu for over three hundred. Perhaps we could crack them open ahead of time. But should we? What if . . . what *if* Bobby had planned oysters on the half shell? In which case I'd be cracking oysters to order all night, since the customers, for the $275 per person they were paying, would prefer them moist and fresh. It was too horrible to contemplate. Out of the corner of my eye I saw Steven peel off out the back door—which meant he was probably going to score—and from the way Frankie was working his jaw muscles, half the cooks were well into the coke already and likely looking for a re-up.

When the produce order came in, it was getting toward panic time. Two cases of oranges, a case of lemons, ten cases of mache (lamb's lettuce)—which, at least, we could clean—Belgian endive, fennel, wild mushrooms, the ubiquitous baby zucchinis, yellow squashes, and pattypan squash and baby carrots that Bobby so loved. Dry goods followed, an impenetrable heap of long-haul purchases: fryer oil, salad oil, vinegar, flour, canned goods. There was no way of knowing what was for today and what was for next week.

We peeled the carrots. It was two o'clock now, cocaine and indecision grinding the heart right out of the afternoon. And still no Bobby.

Truffles arrived. Nice. Then the fish. Not so nice because it was Dover sole—a bitch to clean and an even bigger bitch to cook in large numbers. Orlando, Frankie, and I got down on the sole with rubber gloves and kitchen shears, trimming off the spines. Matt and Dougie cut chive sticks and plucked chervil tops and basil flowers and made gaufrette potatoes for garnish, because we knew—if we knew anything—that we'd be using a lot of those. Dog Boy was relegated to fiddling with the dial on the radio. A new hire, Dog Boy was a skateboarder with a recently pierced tongue and absolutely useless for anything—he could fuck up a wet dream—so it was best that he was kept safely out of the way. Adam, at least, knew we'd need bread, so he stayed reasonably busy balling dough and putting loaves in the oven—which was ironic, really, as Adam was usually the last person to know what was going on about anything, and here he was, currently the best informed person in the kitchen.

By four o'clock, with still no evidence of Bobby and no word, the mood was turning ugly. Dougie's neck and cheeks were red, which meant he'd been hitting the sauce somewhere. Frankie was retelling, for the umpteenth time, the story of how he had communicated the plot to *Cliffhanger* to Sylvester Stallone during a three-second near-telepathic encounter by the men's room of Planet Hollywood, his previous employer. He'd as good as written that movie!—despite the fact that he couldn't even pronounce it, calling it *"Clifthangah"*—and one of these days, he'd get paid for it. That's if Sly's "people" didn't "get to him first." Frankie, while high on blow, was often under the impression that various "agents of Stallone" were "watching him" as he clearly "knew too much." When we all started laughing (and how could we not?), the by now manically high, dangerously paranoid Frankie began to tweak. This was not good. As Frankie was taller and bigger and stronger than all of us (over six foot six) and a vicious hockey player sensitive to criticism, things could get really crazy.

"Fucking Bobby," muttered Dougie again. Dougie, at least, wouldn't get violent. He was more of a sulker. But he might very well just disappear if discouraged. He'd done it before—just walked out the door and disappeared for a few days.

I nervously looked at the clock and debated doing exactly that myself. Happily, when I looked back, Matt was doing his pitch-perfect Frankie Pentangeli imitation from *The Godfather II:* "Oh . . . sure, senator . . . sure . . . that Michael Corleone . . . Michael Corleone did this . . . Michael Corleone did that," which always gave Frankie the giggles. Violence, for now anyway, seemed to have been averted.

Time passed. We continued to set up as best we could. At five thirty, Bobby finally rolled in. I say rolled in because he was (not unusually) on Rollerblades, wearing a new *Blues Traveler* tour jacket he'd scored off a private client and that charming little-boy smile that had so successfully helped convince a legion of hostesses and floor staff to come into close contact with Bobby's genitals. We, however, were not so charmed.

"Uh . . . Bobby? What's the menu?" I said. "We'd really kind of like to know."

Bobby just smiled, gave us the Ronnie James Dio "devil horn" hand sign, skated back to his office, and emerged a few moments later in his whites, bearing the fatal document:

The NiteKlub New Year's Eve Menu 1992

Oysters Baked in Champagne Sauce with Beluga Caviar
or
Pan-Seared Foie Gras with Apricot Chutney, Port Wine Sauce,
and Toasted Brioche
or
Beggar's Purses of Diver Scallops and Wild Mushrooms
or
Truffle Soup

followed by
Dover Sole with Citrus Beurre
Lobster in a Shellfish Nage with Fennel
Chestnut and Truffle Stuffed *Poussin* with Foie Gras
Sauce
Chateaubriand "Rossini" with Baby Vegetables
and Chive Mashed Potatoes

> followed by
> Harlequin Soufflé
> New Year's Parfait
> Lemon Tart
> Profiteroles

To be honest, my memory is not perfect on the exact menu choices. I approximate. What *is* burned permanently into my brain, however, is the simple fact that this was a killer menu to do "à la minute" and seemed heavily skewed toward the sauté station. Which was not, tactically or strategically, our strongest point. The hot app station appeared overladen with dishes as well, and as Frankie Five Angels was already, at this early hour, quietly having an amusing conversation with himself, the prospects of a smooth night in that area seemed . . . unlikely. Our fearless leader, though, brimmed with insouciance that we took for confidence. My muttered concerns were dismissed—understandably, given my pessimistic nature, and my kitchen nickname of the time: "Dr. Doom."

Bobby curtly gave us our prep assignments and a brief rundown of how he expected us to prepare and present his creations. To our credit, we quickly put our stations together, set up our *mise en place,* dug in, and by seven we were loaded and ready for the first orders.

It should be pointed out that I had, basically, nothing to do but crack oysters—which I sensibly did in advance (given they were to be baked)—and help Adam plate desserts. Everything else was coming off hot appetizer (Frankie and Dougie), grill (Matt), or sauté (Steven and Orlando). Dog Boy was sent home after a less-than-grueling half day.

Half an hour later, there were still no tickets. The little printer hooked up to the waiters' computer order systems lay silent. Our two runners, Manuel and Ed, informed us that the guests were arriving, the dining room filling, and all of us hoped that they'd start getting the orders in fast, in comfortably staggered fashion, so we could set a nice pace without getting swamped all at once.

"Tell them to get those orders in," snarled Bobby. "Let's knock down some early tables! C'mon!"

But nothing happened. A half hour passed, then an hour, as our now-full house of New Year's revelers sat at their tables, admired each others' clothes, drank Veuve Clicquot, and presumably pondered their menus. It would be a long night.

The first order came in at eight thirty. *Clack clack clack . . . dit dit dit . . .* "Ordering! . . . One oysters, two foie gras . . . a scallop . . . followed by three sole . . . a lobster . . . one chateau and a *poussin!*" crowed our chef. *Clack clack clack . . . dit dit dit.* The sound of paper being torn off. "Two more oysters . . . two more foie . . . followed by three Dover sole! One lobster!" *Clack clack clack . . . dit dit dit . . .* and already I'm getting worried because they seemed to be hitting the sole hard. Each order took up a whole pan—a whole burner—meaning we could cook only four of the things at once. And sauté was also plating oysters because the lone salamander was on that station; so while I'd popped the hinges on three sheet pans of the things, the sauté guys still had to set them on rock salt, nape each oyster with sauce, brown them under the salamander, plate them, carefully top each one with an oh-so-delicate little heap of caviar (of which there was a limited amount), then garnish before putting them up in the window. The beggar's purses were inexplicably coming off that station too, with only the soup and the foie gras coming off Frankie's area.

The machine was printing full-bore now, paper spitting out end over end, and Bobby calling it all out and stuffing copies in the slide. So far we were keeping up, racing to drill out what we could before it really hit the fan.

Two big tables—a ten-top, and a twelve, one after the other—and still no main courses had been fired yet; I looked over and saw that sauté was already in the weeds, that Frankie was spazzing out on all the foie gras orders, and that the truffle soup—which was supposed to be a layup—was not cooking as quickly as anticipated. Sure, the heating-the-soup part was a breeze, but the part where Frankie stretched precut squares of puff pastry dough over the ovenproof crocks was taking a lot longer than hoped. Frankie was fumbling with the dough, which either broke because it was too cold from the refrigerator, or tore because it had been out of the refrigerator too long, or tore because Frankie was so high he was shaking—and Frankie wasn't so good at keeping a lot of orders in his head anyway, so the combination of minor frustrations and all those foie gras and the fact that the little crustless pieces of brioche that were supposed to accompany it kept burning in the toaster was taking its toll, pulling down the pace . . . already the oysters were stacking up on one end, getting cold waiting for the foie gras orders that were supposed to go with them, and Bobby (highest standards *only,* please) was sending them back for reheats and replates, which was causing some confusion as good became commingled with bad. And the printer kept clicking and the stack of orders that Bobby had yet to even call out while he waited for sauté and hot-app stations to catch up kept getting bigger and bigger (getting mixed up with the orders that he'd already called out and had yet to post in the slide), and it was clear, a half hour in, with not a single main course served—or even fired—that we were headed for collision.

Bobby's reaction to the ensuing crisis was to urge on Frankie. Forcefully. Some might say, considering Frankie's known pathologies, too forcefully: "Where's that FOIE, you idiot?! What the FUCK is up with that fucking FOIE!? What's WRONG with you, Frank? FRANK? Where's that fucking FOIE GRAS?"

Poor Frankie. He was spinning in place, trying to do ten things at once, and succeeding at none, eyes banging around in his skull, sweat pouring down his face, a dervish of confusion, the little four-burner stove full of melting foie gras and over-reducing sauce.

The runners' faces were starting to take on worried expressions as more time passed without anything coming up. A lone four-top went out—and was quickly returned as cold, causing Bobby to scream even more. Bobby tended to blame others in times of extremis. "You *idiots!*" he'd yowl at the runners when yet another order of oysters was sent back, making our already-stressed-out runners even more jumpy. And the printer, all the while still clicking and clacking and going *dit dit dit . . .*"

The first of the front waiters appeared, inquiring fearfully about app orders, which made Bobby even crazier. There were easily fifty tables' worth of orders up on the board, God knows how many in Bobby's hand, and a long white strip of them curling onto the floor that Bobby had yet to even acknowledge—and nothing was coming out of the kitchen. Nothing. Bobby finally managed to slap cloches onto a few orders of oysters and foie and send them on their way; and when he finally began to take stock of what he had in his hand, and what was still coming in, and how, by now, the sauté station had come to a complete standstill, I think his brain shut down. The next waiters who came in asking about food got shrieked at.

"Just GET OUT! GET OUT OF THE FUCKING KITCHEN!!"

The constant clicking from the computer, the background grumbling and swearing and cursing from the cooks, the back-and-forth questions necessary between line cooks working together like "Ready on Table Seven? Ready on those oysters and that scallop?" and the occasional whispered request from a runner combined was too much noise for the chef. He shouted: "SHUT UP! EVERY-BODY SHUT THE FUCK UP! NOT A SINGLE FUCKING WORD! I WANT TOTAL SILENCE!"

He then issued orders for Matt to move some of the foie orders over to sauté, put Dougie in exclusive charge of the toaster, told Orlando and Steven both to get out of the way, and took over the sauté responsibilities himself, while abandoning expediting responsibility to me.

The pile of intermingled dupes I inherited was discouraging. The board itself—meaning the orders that had already been begun, or fired—was a mess, with orders already dispatched mixed up with stuff still to come. I had no idea what had been called and what had yet to be called. Fortunately, the printer had calmed down. There was silence, *real* silence, as Bobby stepped into sauté and began putting together orders, running back and forth between hot-app station and his own to personally make sure tables were complete before putting them in the window.

We managed to get some apps out, and some more, and even a few more—before runners started whispering in my ear that they needed entrees, like *now*. The printer was strangely silent still, and I was thankful for it, figuring they were backed up at the terminals downstairs, or that maybe, just maybe, between all the orders in my hand and the ones that I was slowly feeding onto the board and the pile I was getting ready to call out, maybe we'd actually got the whole dining room in. I called out a few fire orders for mains but Bobby just screamed: "SHUT UP! I DON'T WANT TO HEAR IT!" He was cooking foie gras orders now, in addition to doing the oysters, and the beggar's purses, and dealing with the sole, and though a very fine line cook, he was biting off way more than he, or any cook alive, could chew. Alone in his head, out there on the edge all by himself, ignoring me, ignoring the waiters, ignoring the other cooks, he was slinging pans at high speed, just trying, as best he could, to knock down some of those hanging tickets, to get the food out. So I just kept my mouth closed and clutched my stack of dupes and held my breath.

The printer. Something was wrong with it. I knew it. It was too quiet. It had been too long. Not a click or a clack for twenty minutes, not a single fire code or dessert order. I checked the roll of paper. No jam. The machine seemed plugged in. Jumping on the intercom, I called Joe, the deejay and techie who knew about such things, and asked him discreetly to check and see if there was a problem.

Apparently there was. Suddenly the machine came alive, clacking away like nobody's business, spitting out orders in a terrifying, unending stream, one after the other after the other, faster than I could tear them off: twenty-five minutes of backed-up orders we hadn't even heard about. Worried front waiters entered the kitchen, took one look at what was going on, and retreated silently. Nothing to be done here.

It was clear to all of us by now—except maybe Bobby, who was still in his own ninth circle of personal restaurant hell, cursing and spitting and doing his best to cook, plate, and assemble orders, elbowing us out of the way as he ran heroically back and forth between stations—that we were now involved in a complete disaster. The situation was beyond saving. We could dig out . . . eventually. At some time, yes, we might feed these people. But we would not bring honor to our clan tonight. We would not go home proud. There would be no celebratory drinks at the end of this night (if it ever ended), only shame and recriminations.

Then I looked over at the kitchen doors and saw a particularly dismaying sight: three or four waiters clustered silently in the hallway. I hurried over to confer, away from Bobby's hearing. When waiters stop complaining, it is an unnatural thing. What were they doing out there? Things were bad in the dining room, I knew, but shouldn't they be down on the floor, putting out fires? Comping champagne? Reassuring their tables with self-deprecating apologies and offers of free cognac and port?

"What's up?" I inquired of the most reasonable of the lot, an aspiring playwright with many years of table service experience.

"Dude . . . they're drunk out there," he replied. "They've been sitting out there without food for an hour and a half. Drinking champagne. They've got nothing in their bellies but alcohol—and they're getting belligerent."

Veronica, a chubby waitress with (we had heard) a rose tattoo on her ass, was red faced and shaking. "A customer choked me," she cried, eyes filling with tears. "He stood up and put his hands around my neck and fucking *choked* me, screaming 'WHERE'S MY FUCKING FOOD?!' . . . It's out of control, Tony! I'm afraid to go out there. We all are!"

I rushed back to the kitchen, where Bobby was successfully putting out a few tables of appetizers. But orders were still coming back. There was more stuff coming back than going out, and with all the replates and refires, the caviar supply was running low.

"Bobby," I said, carefully. "I think we should 86 the oysters."

"We are *not* 86ing the fucking oysters," snarled Bobby.

The kitchen doors swung open. It was Larry the waiter with tears running down his face. Now this was about as bad a sign as you could see, as Larry only moonlighted as a waiter. His day job was as a cop in the South Bronx. What, on the floor of a restaurant, could be so bad, so frightful, so monstrous as to cause a ten-year veteran of the force, a guy who'd been shot twice in the line of duty, to become so traumatized?

"They're beating the customers," Larry wailed. "People are getting up and trying to leave—and security is beating them! They're going fucking nuts!"

"It's out of control," moaned Ed, the runner. "It's a nightmare."

NiteKlub, it should be pointed out, usually operated as exactly that once the dinner shift was over. Consequently, we employed a security staff of twenty-three heavily muscled gorillas. These folks, though quite nice when not frog-marching you out the front door or dragging you down the steps, were employed to deal with the more rigorous demands of keeping order in a busy dance club: organized posses of gate-crashers, out-of-control drunks, belligerent ex-boyfriends—many of them potentially armed. They were frequently injured, often for giving a momentary benefit of doubt, for instance, to some barely-out-of-adolescence knucklehead half their weight denied entry to the VIP area, who promptly sucker-punched them or cold-cocked them with a beer bottle. This kind of thing gave our average security guy a rather shorter fuse than most ordinary restaurant floor staff. That this was a tonier crowd was a distinction security could hardly be expected to make. Especially as the customers were drunk and outraged at having spent hundreds of dollars for nothing, and heading for the doors in droves. Though they were said to be dealing out beat-downs to middle-aged couples from the suburbs who'd only wanted a nice New Year's Eve and some swing music, they could hardly be blamed for following the same orders they had been given every other night.

"I'm not going back out there. For anything," said Larry.

We tried. We did the best we could that awful night. To his credit, Bobby cooked as hard and as fast as he could until the very end, pretty much doing everything himself, unwilling or unable to trust anyone to help him out of the hole he'd put us all in. It was probably the wisest thing to do. Between my calling and his cooking, there was a nice, direct simplicity, less chance of confusion. We served—eventually—a lot of cold baked oysters (many without caviar) and undercooked foie gras, leathery Dover sole and overcooked lobster, lukewarm birds, and roasted beef.

1991 slipped into 1992 without notice or mention in the kitchen. No one dared speak. The word "Happy" in relation to anything would not have occurred to any of us. At twelve forty-five, in what was perhaps the perfect coda to the evening, a lone, bespectacled customer in a rumpled tuxedo entered the kitchen, wandered up to the sauté end (where Bobby was still doing his best to get out entrees), and, peering back at the stove, asked, in a disconcertingly bemused voice: "Pardon me . . . but is that my appetizer order?"

He'd been waiting for it since eight forty-five.

I thought he'd showed remarkable patience.

At the end of the night, as it turned out, management had to comp (meaning return money) for $7,500 worth of meals. A few overzealous security goons had (allegedly) incited a few of our guests to file lawsuits claiming varying degrees of violent assault. And the effect on the kitchen staff was palpable.

Dougie and Steven quit. Adam became a titanic discipline problem, his respect for his chef declining to the point that it would, much later, lead to fisticuffs. Morale sank to the point that cooks arrived high—rather than waiting until later. And I got the chef's job after Bobby, wisely, went elsewhere.

And I learned. Nobody likes a "learning experience"—translating as it does to "a total ass-fucking"—but I learned. When the next year's New Year's Eve event loomed, I planned. I planned that mother like Ike planned Normandy. My menu was circulated (to management, floor, and every cook), discussed, tested, and retested. Each and every menu choice was an indestructible ocean liner classic—preseared or half-cooked hours before the first guest arrived. There wasn't an oyster in sight, or on any of the many New Year's menus I've done since. Just slice and serve terrine of foie gras. Slap-and-serve salads. *My* truffle soup the next year (it had been a good idea, actually) sat prebowled and precovered in a hot bain, ready to toss in the oven. I spread dishes around evenly between stations, imagining always the worst-case scenario. As, of course, I'd lived through it. My tournedos were preseared and required only a pop in the oven, some reheated spuds, a quickly tossed medley of veg, and a ready-to-pour sauce. My lobsters took a swift pop under the salamander. I'd be proud of the fact that *my* New Year's went flawlessly, that *my* full dining room of customers went home happy and content, and that I, unlike the vastly-more-talented-but-less-organized Bobby, brought honor and profit to my masters.

But the fact is, I could have served the following year's menu with a line crew of chimps. The food was nowhere as good as it could have been. My food arrived fast. It arrived hot. It arrived at the same time as the other orders on the table. But it was no better (or worse) than what a bunch of overdressed drunks dumb enough to eat at our club expected. Having tasted total defeat the previous year, when my last entree went out at eleven thirty, leaving only the mopping-up operations (aka desserts), I was ebullient. Not a single order had come back. I jumped up on the stainless-steel table we'd used to stack assembled dishes and beat my chest and congratulated one and all. We turned up the music, peeled off our reeking whites, changed into our street clothes, and I ordered us up a few pitchers of Long Island Iced Teas and beer. We drank like champions. And felt like champions. We went home exhausted but proud.

Sometimes, you just have to make compromises to get the job done.

Formal Dining Be Damned

by Sara Deseran

from *7 X 7*

Does every chef dream of succeeding with a high-end, four-star restaurant? Maybe so, but as Sara Deseran discovered in these conversations with five San Francisco–area chefs, once you've made it you may long for something quite different.

I'm having lunch at Aqua with chef and restaurateur Laurent Manrique, a man who has spent his career creating magical moments like this. The mammoth vase next to us holds a jungle of crimson snapdragons threatening to take a bite out of my shoulder. The ceilings are high and the banquettes are low, forcing me to sit up straight to reach the table. No aroma comes from the kitchen, no sound of meat hitting a hot pan. Gorgeous food simply floats to our table with nary a fingerprint on each oversize porcelain plate. The gossamer fan of salmon carpaccio in front of me is scattered with micro-cilantro and impossibly square croutons the size of pinpricks. Although it would be much more enjoyable to eat it with my hands, I do what's proper—going for the heavy silverware, selecting the correct fork.

The next course comes, and the server, with no cheat sheet visible, tells us what we're about to enjoy: "You'll be having oven-roasted Alaskan halibut served with an English-pea purée, English peas and king trumpet mushrooms. Over the fish itself is a black-trumpet mousse and brioche crust, all finished with a mushroom mignonette." Manrique barely listens. He already knows what she's going to say—after all, he's been the chef at Aqua since 2003, when he took over from Michael Mina—and his mind is elsewhere, reminiscing about what he ate last night with his friend Gerald Hirigoyen. "I had a confit of duck with lentils. We opened an incredible bottle of wine." He sighs contentedly, practically rubbing his belly and propping up his feet. "That is what it is about."

When he says it, Manrique is certainly referring to life in general but especially to his new venture, Café de la Presse, the decidedly casual Parisian-style cafe a few blocks from Union Square that he and his business partner, Charles Condy, bought in order to remodel, change its menu and make their own. (They plan to open this month.) Lately, Manrique, who has headed the kitchens of such high-end institutions as Campton Place and New York's Peacock Alley at the Waldorf-Astoria, has been thinking seriously about soups, sandwiches, and salads. Not that he seems to mind. In fact, he seems liberated. "Café de la Presse is going to be the food I like to eat when I'm with some friends," he enthuses. The server clears our carpaccio. I ask him if this is the kind of food he likes to eat regularly too. He shakes his head. "Never. No, never."

Here's a dirty little secret: Even the finest of chefs prefer to eat like mere mortals. While the dining room is full of couples clinking glasses of Champagne over a painstakingly composed mille-feuille of foie gras, the chef is backstage, polishing off a PB&J, gnawing on a hunk of cheese or, even more commonly, skipping dinner altogether. And when they get off work, they don't sit down to enjoy their own creations. They head straight to places like the fluorescent-lit Yuet Lee in Chinatown for a plateful of deep-fried, mindlessly enjoyable salt-and-pepper squid.

The same chefs also like to cook mindlessly enjoyable food. You don't have to pry too hard to get them to admit that, at times, they harbor dreams of losing the brunoise, the mise en place, the tower of food that takes a staff of twenty to execute, in order to do something homespun. Melissa Perello of the Fifth Floor told me that she's long had designs on her own breakfast joint. But how many are willing to give up the glory of it all—not to mention the financial stability—to make French toast?

More than you'd think. In the past year or two, numerous executive chefs in SF, at the height of their careers, have been acting on their cheap-eats impulse, making their next project the kind of place where you can bring your toddler and read the newspaper. Traci Des Jardins, the chef-owner of Jardinière and a recent winner of the Food Network's Iron Chef America competition, went from truffles to tacos last summer when she opened Mijita, a taqueria located in the Ferry Building Marketplace and inspired by her Mexican heritage. Hubert Keller, who's about to celebrate the twentieth anniversary of his iconic restaurant, Fleur de Lys, sheepishly admits that he's been having a hell of a lot of fun with Burger Bar, the burger-stravaganza he opened in Las Vegas. It quickly became an industry hangout for such chefs as Jean-Georges Vongerichten and Bradley Ogden.

While Manrique, Des Jardins and Keller are still very much involved with their original restaurants, others have given up fine dining cold turkey. Chad Callahan left behind eleven years at Masa's to open an upscale seafood shack on the docks of Sausalito called Fish, where, in flip-flops, he serves up the likes of fish-and-chips (as well as a killer grilled-salmon Saigon sandwich). And after doing his time at such conservative establishments as Rubicon, Dennis Leary said no to a well-paying gig at a hotel in Shanghai in order to open Canteen, an itsy-bitsy coffee shop next to the Commodore Hotel in the TenderNob. There, Leary cooks haute diner food for breakfast, lunch, and dinner and relishes his freedom to play Motorhead on the sound system.

Maybe the dip in the economy put all of this in motion, but it also provided a good excuse for chefs to free themselves from the pressure that comes with the stars. Every chef I speak to laments the vicious circle of prestige and the constraints of formal dining.

"The one thing I despised at Masa's was people lifting up the flatware to see what kind it was," says Callahan, who now serves wine in mason jars to guests sitting at picnic tables. "When someone drops five or six glasses here, I don't have a cow. I wonder if they're OK . . . I don't want to be a guy that's white-tablecloth-this and fancy-china-that. I want to cook for everybody, and here we can cook for everybody."

Still, diners expect magic from this level of chef, even if slinging hash, so to speak. Keller, who created Burger Bar while he waited for his second Fleur de Lys to be built as part of the Vegas Mandalay Bay resort, was worried that the press would think that one of the most reputable French chefs in San Francisco had lost his mind—"that the whole thing would backfire." When Manrique's regulars hear about the cafe, they want to know, "What's the trend?"

But Leary's the one who's truly under the lens. He's had diners come into Canteen, brandishing the rightfully glowing three-star *Chronicle* review, and attempt to order every Bauer recommendation (the wild mushrooms spooned over a goat cheese clafouti, the homey blanquette de veau) while scrutinizing his every move— something that's easy to do in a 300-square-foot space with an open kitchen. Leary, whose goal is to create a community meeting place instead of a destination restaurant, doesn't mince words: "I don't really like catering to people who come into a restaurant with a chip on their shoulder or want the food to save their lives or something. I don't have the patience for them. Fortunately, now that I'm an owner, I don't have to put up with any shit."

The customers might be demanding, but the chefs aren't exactly letting their high standards slide. At Burger Bar, more than forty toppings are available. The burgers start at $8, but for $60 you can get an all-Kobe beef patty with foie gras and black truffles. "Fleur de Lys in Las Vegas—we put two years into it. But Burger Bar—we put four months into it and it's a success in the sense that people just love it and they have the same smile on their face as when they leave Fleur de Lys," says Keller, who's smiling too: Burger Bar does almost 3,000 covers a month. And as it turns out, he feared the press needlessly. VH1 is to stop by soon, as is Rachael Ray, the suspiciously happy favorite of the Food Network.

Manrique, who at the time of our Aqua lunch has just had the exterior of Café de la Presse painted a bold red, is still pondering how to make a classic frisée aux lardons less greasy. For his pan bagnat, he refuses to use seared tuna instead of the traditional canned, but of course, that doesn't mean he's serving Starkist. He wants to can it himself, a two-day process. "It's funny," he muses. "Sometimes with the simple dishes, you have less room to hide. So you can't mess up."

Des Jardins and Callahan, on the other hand, don't just serve casual food; they each have an altruistic agenda focusing on San Francisco's favorite dinner-table topic: sustainability. Mijita might look like a relatively average taqueria, but the meat is from Niman

Ranch, the workers receive a fair wage and the thick corn tortillas are pressed by hand. Callahan switched his life priorities after a near-fatal car accident. At Fish, the seafood has been harvested in environmentally friendly ways, and he makes a concerted effort to support local fishermen. Callahan, who now spends his mornings doing things like cleaning 30 pounds of squid, thinks back to his days at Masa's: "It wasn't until my rehabilitation that I realized, Shoot—I really sold a lot of caviar that I knew was gray market or black market even though the demand was there. I can't imagine doing that now. I believe that we really need to start taking care of home."

Depending on how you look at it, chefs are experiencing either a revelation or a reverse midlife crisis, giddily acquiring the keys to a station wagon after years of driving a Porsche. Manrique explains, "You see how chefs work so hard all their lives to make a public career, and sometimes—just by the snap of the fingers—they're forgotten. And sometimes, pushing themselves to be number one and to be on the cover of magazines, in the end they wonder, Is the food I'm cooking making me really happy?" If I were a therapist, I would counter this question with a question: But is it really about the food? Would making chicken noodle soup at a place like Aqua be more fulfilling? The real issue seems to be that once they reach a certain level, chefs hunger for the basics again, a true connection. The artifice of fine dining requires that the human side—the nurturing part of food—remain hidden. To top it off, an executive chef, whose days on the line are most likely over, functions more as a director than a cook, only appearing to shake his or her customer's hand right before the petits fours arrive with the check. Callahan says, "When you work at places like Michael Mina and Gary Danko, you're doing your art, but then what? You have to do it because it brings you joy and I gotta tell ya, it's pretty joyful to see families coming here with their kids."

Leary concurs. "I like meeting people. At Rubicon, I never got to meet anyone. And the people that I did meet were from one thin slice of demographic. Super-rich."

When I hook up with Leary at Canteen on his day off, it's almost as if he's produced a scene to illustrate this point. There he is, leaning over the kelly-green counter, making small talk with a sweet elderly woman named Ruth who's come by herself only to find Canteen closed. She has no idea that she's having a private lunch cooked by a former *Chronicle* Rising Star chef—which is exactly how Leary wants it. Enjoying a Niçoise salad spiked with romesco sauce, she doesn't have any of the expectations that come with fine china. In her eyes, Leary's just a nice young man who happens to be an excellent short-order cook. In this moment, it's all there: The connection, the food, the community. What even the finest chef is looking for, and some have finally found.

They Got Game

by Joe Yonan

from *The Boston Globe*

> What do chefs do on their (rare) days off?
> Yonan trailed along on a bonding experience
> with five Boston chefs to see how they
> play—and eat—when they've hung up the
> toque for a day.

W hen one of the first mallard ducks tumbles from the sky, having been shot once by a chef named Tony and then again by another chef named Tony, the low branches of a tree catch it like a pop fly.

Shooting ducks, pheasants, quail, and partridges, though, is not the only point of a day at a hunting preserve in New Hampshire. When five Italian chefs from Boston are the hunters, the prey will end up as dinner, maybe tonight.

But first they have to get into position. Four of the chefs Tony Susi of Sage, Tony Ambrose of Blackfin Chop House and Raw Bar, Antonio DiCenso of Rino's Place, and Pino Maffeo of Restaurant L rendezvous at dawn at Caffe Graffiti in the North End, then drive their SUVs north to meet the expedition's organizer. The fourth Tony, Anthony Caturano of Prezza, has killed bear, buffalo, and mountain lion in the wilds of British Columbia, Alaska, and Montana, but also hunts in tamer conditions near his second home on New Hampshire's Sunrise Lake. It's a crisp fall day in the middle of pheasant and duck season, but the rules of permits, seasons, and limits don't apply here at Green Mountain Kennels game preserve.

On the drive up, Ambrose's mind is already on that night's meal, imagining that the group might pick up pattypan squash and Amish butter. They might find wild rosehips they could make into jam, spiked with the Grand Marnier that Ambrose has packed along with Chartreuse, sweet late-harvest wines, and a thirty-year-old Bordeaux. They might run into some hen of the woods mushrooms by the side of the road.

In fact, Maffeo, 36, has brought wild mushrooms, along with pickled eggplant and even a pheasant, "just in case we don't shoot one." That's an unlikely prospect since the birds are stocked and released right before the hunters set out with guns and dogs. DiCenso, 37, has packed quail and spiedini, skewers of ground lamb.

And Susi? "These guys brought enough food. I've got the ammo."

Once they arrive at Green Mountain, the day starts with a series of shooting-clay stations, sometimes referred to as golf with guns, that let the guys practice not just their shooting but their quips and digs, most of them aimed squarely at the only non-Tony. When DiCenso sees a mushroom on the ground and asks whether it's edible, Susi, his cousin, says, "Have Pino eat one, see what happens."

Guides Rocky Aliberti and George Olson coach the chefs on technique and caution them on safety. Then it's time to move to real prey. The five change into camouflage gear and split into two groups, with Ambrose and Caturano going with Olson, the others with Aliberti. Each group trudges out to a duck blind, a collection of greenery and branches leaned against wooden posts, in front of a decoy-filled pond. The preserve has raised the mallards from chicks, feeding them in large pens; the day before, workers withheld the ducks' food. When they get released, "the first thing they think about is water," says Aliberti. "Hopefully they'll at least fly over the pond."

"Put a bowl of pasta in there, they'll come," Maffeo says.

At 11:15 AM, a horn sounds the start of the duck hunt. Olson starts blowing into his duck call, making a sound something like Huey, Dewey, and Louie breaking out into laughter. Soon enough, a mallard wings its way over. "Coming in low," says Olson, and Caturano raises his shotgun and turns the bird from animate to inanimate, dropping it into the pond. Olson sends his five-year-old yellow Lab, Mesa, to fetch it.

After a half-hour, Olson's radio crackles with a signal that the hunt is over. Ambrose, at forty-three the oldest of the group, picks up his cigar as Caturano says, "My gun's a little hot."

"I guess so," Ambrose says, impressed with Caturano's aim and speed. "I thought it was on auto load."

Purists may scoff at the idea of hunting in a stocked preserve, but it comes with some conveniences such as an ammo shop and meat-cleaning services that the chefs can't resist. Plus, "it sure beats sitting on a pond in Kingston all day waiting for [birds] to fly over," Ambrose says.

"You could wait a lifetime and not shoot that many ducks," says Caturano, 32.

They bag sixteen in a half-hour. The other guys get nine, blaming the difference, somewhat unconvincingly, on the wind.

Over a lunch of cheese-steak sandwiches and potato salad, DiCenso remembers hunting wild boar as a child in Sulmona, Italy. "We would just shoot out the window at night and then go out in the morning and see what was there," he says.

"If it's brown, it's down," says Caturano.

They pull on neon orange vests and hats for the afternoon pheasant hunt, when the dogs will do more than retrieve. Ambrose's dog, Oliver, is trained to point at a bird in the brush. The Green Mountain guides, though, use Labradors trained to flush the birds into the air, hopefully close enough that the hunters have clear aim when the birds take flight. Aliberti starts his group off with Isabella, his black Lab.

Izzy soon gets "a little birdie," Aliberti says as the dog pulls her head back and stiffens her tail to indicate a bird is nearby. Sure enough, she flushes out a Hungarian partridge. Susi bags it and then a chukar partridge, which DiCenso takes down. Izzy retrieves the "Hun" but not the chukar, so Aliberti sends her into the woods, eventually using whistles and hand signals to direct her into a swamp. "Back! Over!" No luck. "I hate losing a bird," Aliberti says.

Eventually, he has to change dogs. Caleb, a chocolate Lab, flushes birds far ahead of the group. They manage to shoot a pheasant or partridge every several minutes for a while, but by 2 PM birds and shots are few and far between. Tony, Tony, and Pino are getting antsy.

"Find us a bird, doggie," Maffeo tells Caleb.

"Find us a big [expletive] rooster pheasant," says Susi, 36. Then he puts on his best Homer Simpson voice: "Mmm, pheasant."

A half-hour later, after trudging along a swamp line, Maffeo and DiCenso light up cigarettes, and DiCenso sings out at the top of his lungs: "Daniel Boone was a man. He was a big man!"

They break to unload fifteen birds: six pheasants, seven Hungarian partridges, and two chukars. Should they keep at it? "If you say it's beer-thirty, we'll go have beer in the lodge," Aliberti says. "If you want to hunt till sundown, we hunt till sundown."

"I want to hunt," Maffeo says. They trudge ahead. But even with both dogs working, it's all wandering and no shooting. Shortly after 3, Olson radios to say he, Caturano, and Ambrose are back in the lodge with thirteen birds. Maffeo and the other two Tonys decide to call it a day, too.

"It's fun, right?" Caturano says when they meet up. "You get to walk around, shoot some birds, give each other a hard time."

And plan dinner. "We're just going to throw some burgers and dogs on the grill, right?" Ambrose says.

"Yep," Susi replies. "Maybe microwave some soup."

After settling their bill back at the lodge (about $500 apiece), they head off to Caturano's cabin in Middleton with the bird meat cleaned and packed into coolers. Inside the house, a stuffed mountain lion crouches on the wall above the dining room table, a buffalo looms over the fridge, a black bear stands in one corner, and a 15-point elk stares down onto a bed upstairs. Caturano killed them all. There's also a shiny new Wolf stove, a Lavazza espresso maker, an orchid plant in the middle of the dining room, and an iPod wired to the stereo and playing ZZ Top. "A little bit Daniel Boone, a little bit Martha Stewart," Ambrose says.

As Buster, Caturano's mild-mannered nine-month-old Rottweiler, snakes around the room, Susi pulls out some cheese and Maffeo takes out a bucket of mushrooms: maitake, hen of the woods, and cinnamon cap.

"Wanna make a risotto with them?" Caturano asks.

"Sure," Susi says, dropping them in a cast-iron skillet sizzling with olive oil.

The bearish Caturano has changed into sweatpants and a T-shirt that says "I Beat Anorexia." Susi has taken off his jacket to reveal a

.45 pistol strapped to his hip. "It's a great little carry piece," he says, "just in case one of you guys gets funny."

Ambrose plates cheeses, then pushes Susi's mushrooms to one side of the skillet to make room for toasting bread. Caturano brings out sopressata. "Where's the bread?" Maffeo asks.

"One thing about southern Italians you gotta know this is Pino is that they cannot eat without bread," Susi says. "Loaves and loaves of bread."

Caturano reaches into his freezer and takes out gnocchi and caribou Bolognese. After helping DiCenso fire the Weber grill outside, Maffeo opens a jar of pickled eggplant, his mother's recipe, and Ambrose adds it to the antipasti platter. Grillside, DiCenso and Maffeo argue over quail marinade. "Easy, easy on the pepper. Ah, these Abruzzesi!" he says, referring to the Abruzzo region in mid-Italy where Susi, Caturano, and DiCenso are from. "You're cooking like you're high now."

Ambrose tosses potatoes with garlic, rosemary, sugar, salt, and sliced onions, and then, over a peppery 1989 Cascina Bruni Barolo, they talk about scars and sous chefs. When Maffeo comes in to pick at the antipasti platter, he has one complaint: "The thing you have to know about the Abruzzesi," he says, "is that they never bring enough bread."

Susi scoops mushroom risotto onto a big plate and shaves Parmesan over it, while Caturano opens a 2000 Il Borro Toscana. Ambrose carefully pulls out the crackling cork from his 1975 Petrus Pomerol, the Bordeaux that he considered putting on his restaurant menu for $1,200. "We're gonna have this next, before we're too drunk to enjoy it," he says.

As the wine breathes, Maffeo drizzles olive oil onto the grilled quail and spiedini, and the four dig in, talking about hockey versus basketball, Caturano's bear-hunting girlfriend, and the hot tub and pool table that await at a neighbor's house. The conversation falls silent once Ambrose pours the Petrus and they start swirling it around and sniffing it. It's very cloudy, with lots of sediment, a huge nose, and a flavor like prunes macerated in old cognac. "This is lovely juice," Maffeo says.

Ambrose, who closed one of his two Blackfins this year, counts on his fingers: "It's '75, '85, '95, 2005 that's thirty years old. See how I had to figure that? Now you know why I had a bad year—I'm not much of an accountant."

After the Petrus is history, Caturano throws the gnocchi into boiling water, pulls them out as soon as they float, then tosses them in the Bolognese sauce. He takes yet another pan from the fridge, rabbit in the traditional agrodolce (sweet and sour sauce), and slides it into the oven.

"My girlfriend wanted rabbit last night, and I figured I'd make more in case we needed food," Caturano says.

"Let me get this straight," Susi says. "You've got a smoking hot girlfriend who hunts bear and eats rabbit? If you don't marry this girl, I will."

Any plans to cook the day's duck and pheasant fly out the window as the night goes on and the wine (and later, grappa) keeps flowing. Besides, Susi says, the meat will be more tender after it relaxes for a day or two.

Moreover, they're beat well, some of them are. By 10 PM, Ambrose is snoring on the couch, followed closely by Susi. The three still up have other ideas. "Who wants espresso?" Caturano asks.

The Restaurant Biz

The Egg Men

by Burkhard Bilger

from *The New Yorker*

Though Las Vegas has transformed itself into a gourmet dining capital in the past few years, Bilger—an adept anthropologist of our eating ways—finds fascination in a crew of cooks who toil in the less glamorous kitchen of Vegas.

Las Vegas is a city built by breakfast specials. Sex and gambling, too, of course, and divorce and vaudeville and the creative use of neon. But the energy for all that vice had to come from somewhere, and mostly it came from eggs. In the early days, when depositing your savings in machines designed to cheat, you still seemed a dubious proposition, the casinos offered cut-rate rooms and airfares. And eggs, always eggs. "They used to line up down the hall for the ninety-nine-cent special," a cook from the old Lindy's café in the Flamingo told me. "One time, so much grease built up in the ceiling that it came down the walls and set fire to the flat-tops. Pretty soon, the hood caught on fire and the extinguishers went off with that chemical that looks like smoke, and then the Fire Department came in. Everybody just kept on eating. They said, 'Does this mean my food will take longer now?'"

The ninety-nine-cent special has been lost to history: the new Vegas rarely stoops to giveaways. The empty stretch of desert where Bugsy Siegel built the Flamingo in 1946, has become the center of the Strip, home to America's thirteen largest hotels. (The MGM Grand, which has 5,044 rooms, is the largest; the Flamingo is eighth, with 3,545.) Up the street, at the Wynn hotel, which opened this spring, two eggs can cost $11.50, and a caviar breakfast for two with Dom Perignon is $350 from room service. Even Lindy's has had a makeover. It calls itself the Tropical Breeze Café now. Its nicotine-yellow walls have been repainted a sunnier shade, and it looks out on a water garden populated by turtles, koi, and some disgruntled-looking penguins from southern Africa.

Still, a good egg, honestly cooked, is what brings in most customers, and they eat them in staggering quantities. Last year alone, the cooks at the Tropical Breeze cracked well over a million of them. As a woman at the local Culinary Workers Union put it, "Egg cooks are worth their weight in gold in this town."

At six o'clock on a recent Saturday morning, a few early risers and ashen-faced all-nighters were already gathered in front of the café hostess. Scott Gutstein, the café's head chef, could hear the white noise of their chatter picking up volume, like the leading edge of some oceanic weather system. "You can feel it building," he said, sitting in his cramped office next to a walk-in refrigerator. "I worked swing shift last night. Busy. When I came out at midnight, the streets were packed." He scanned the inventory list on his computer one more time—on an average day, the Tropical Breeze consumes some 300 pounds of bacon alone—then buttoned up his white, double-breasted jacket. He checked the pocket on his left sleeve for his kitchen implements, which were color-coded for quick access: blue thermometer, red paring knife, black pager, yellow highlighter. Then he leaned over to read a handwritten sheet taped on the door by his assistant chef.

"O.K., here's the lineup," he said. "We've got Martin, the omelette man, and Joel on over-easies. René is doing pancakes and French toast—he's so strong, he just pushes it out—and we have Debbie on the eggs Benedict. I'm not used to watching women cook in high-stress situations, but she's surprised the shit out of me. She kicks ass. Frankie will do the steak and eggs, and Edgar will fill in for whoever is taking a break." He grinned. "You can't hurt these guys. I mean, I've been all over the country in all kinds of kitchens. I've worked in New Jersey. I've worked in L.A. I thought I saw the best, but these guys? *Nasty.*"

Gutstein, who is thirty-eight, was born in the Bronx and raised in Yonkers, a loyal Yankees fan even in their most fruitless years. He keeps a dusty Don Mattingly mug on his desk and a picture of Joe DiMaggio at spring training on the wall, and likes to think of his cooks as their short-order equivalents. When he describes their feats at the grill, his voice grows clipped and overheated, like an announcer's on AM radio: "I thought Bally's was busy next door. This place annihilates it. By a thousand covers a day. With less people." Gutstein has a round, eager face that's perpetually flushed, with pale eyebrows and fleshy earlobes. He has wide brown eyes and short, sausagy arms, and the over-all demeanor of a very large and very precocious toddler, given to bursts of impatience and spleen, but mostly just happy to be there, watching things flip and whirl around him.

Saturday morning is zero hour for short-order cooks. The café, which prepares some 2,500 meals on an average weekday, may serve an extra thousand on weekends, with the same cooks. As Gutstein made his way down the long galley kitchen, between the line of grills, griddles, and deep fryers against the wall and the stainless-steel serving counter, with its hot lights and warming trays, his cooks were entrenching themselves for the breakfast rush. They plunged quadruple baskets of chopped potatoes into hot oil, prepoached three dozen eggs, and mixed hash in a tub the size of a baptismal font. Busboys squeezed past with stacks of plates two feet high. Runners jogged in with carts of diced peppers and onions, mushrooms, bacon, and shredded cheese. "They're bringing the troops ammunition," Gutstein said. Then he looked around with a satisfied smirk. "The best term for it is 'controlled chaos,'" he said. "It gets crazy. I love it. Grown men come out of here crying."

I first heard of the short-order cooks of Las Vegas nearly twenty years ago, when I was working at a breakfast place in Seattle called Julia's 14-Carat Café. By then, I'd cooked at a half-dozen restaurants and hamburger joints, and spent two months as the chef at a nursing home, making dishes like American Soufflé. (Take two loaves of white bread, slather each slice with oleo, douse with egg substitute, and bake.) But those were just summer jobs, for the most part. Julia's was full-time work, and it wasn't clear that I had anything better waiting for me. I'd been out of college for a year, and frying eggs had begun to seem suspiciously like a career choice.

The classic short-order career began in the Army or the Navy, where kids who had never cooked were suddenly ordered to feed thousands. The military taught speed, volume, sanitation, and the rudiments of American comfort food, and the best cooks carried their skills into civilian life. Well into the 1950s, short-order cooking was a huge, informal guild with its own peculiar Cockney ("dog soup" for water, "moo juice" for milk, "nervous pudding" for Jell-O, "zeppelins in a fog" for sausages and mashed potatoes). By the 1970s, though, the craft had seriously declined. Fast-food franchises had replaced most diners, and "point of sale" ticketing systems—in which servers send orders from terminals in the dining room straight to printers in the kitchen—had helped silence the old diner slang. What was once a skilled profession was now largely the province of part-timers and students on summer break.

Julia's was a throwback. A hippie coffee shop in the Moosewood mold, it made everything to order, from scratch: sourdough pancakes, alfalfa-sprout omelettes, toast with the texture and density of prairie sod. If all those wheat berries had any fibrous benefits, they were more than offset by the pounds of butter and bacon fat we used, but people didn't seem to mind. The café was always full. A few local celebrities had made it their favorite hangout, including the cartoonist Gary Larson, who used to sit in the corner by the window while I made his breakfast. Julia's had a high ceiling, heavy wooden tables, and an open kitchen that jutted into the dining room so that customers could witness a cook's every oafish move. In the early weeks, I ruined several hundred eggs learning to crack them one-handed and flip them in the pan. I took comfort by imagining myself in future "Far Side" cartoons, having mordant exchanges with a chicken across the counter.

But mostly I just tried to keep up. The waiters scrawled out their orders in shorthand ("oe" for over easy, "sunny" for sunny-side up, "pot" for fried potatoes), clipped them on a revolving rack, and spun them around for the cooks to see on the other side of the serving counter. As business picked up, the wheel spun faster, till tickets filled its perimeter and began to double up. There were only two cooks per shift, and I once heard that we made an average of 350 meals every morning, which seemed an astonishing number. Yet the other cooks never seemed fazed. They cracked eggs two at a time without breaking the yolks and kept four, five, or six pans going simultaneously. They moved with such unvarying precision that some suffered from repetitive-stress injuries. One of them, a scrawny black man who lived on a houseboat with his son, had developed a kind of tennis elbow from handling frying pans; another, whom I'll call Jack, had thrown out his hip after years of pivoting from the stove to the serving counter.

When I called Julia's recently—it's known simply as the 14-Carat Café now—the owner told me that she had fired Jack years ago. "He was a worthless human being," she said. "All he did was sit and eat coffee cake all day long." But he was the fastest cook I'd ever seen. Tall and paunchy, with stringy brown hair and a drooping mustache, he managed to look crisp and light on his feet in the kitchen. His cooking was a seamless sequence of interchangeable tasks, reduced to their essential motions: crack, flip, scoop, pour, crack, pour, flip, scoop. It reminded me of an athletic performance in its unhurried intensity, its reliance on muscle memory. It reminded me of my mother. She had gone to cooking school in Switzerland, but her true skill wasn't preparing gourmet recipes from a book; it was making the same beloved dishes—*Spätzle, Reisbrei, Bratkartoffeln*—perfectly every time. It was getting four or five of them hot to the table simultaneously, though they all required different cooking times, and doing so while phones rang and children squealed and pets wound their way between her feet.

I tried to explain this to Jack one morning, in somewhat less personal terms. We were leaning against the counter waiting for the place to open, watching the waitresses take chairs down from tables while customers gathered on the sidewalk outside. Before I could finish, he grunted and shook his head. "This is nothin'," he said. "You want to see the real masters, you've gotta go to Vegas."

The coffee shop at the Flamingo has been open day and night, weekends and holidays, for so long that its employees, like its customers, can't always tell the difference. "This is my Friday," a server will say on Monday, meaning that she has Tuesdays and Wednesdays off. The Tropical Breeze serves breakfast twenty-four hours a day and diner food with a trace of the islands—Caribbean pot stickers, Polynesian seafood salad. Its role at the Flamingo, like the Flamingo's role on the Strip, is to appeal to the common palate, to give comfort to the outpriced and overstimulated. "The more daring we get, the more complaints we get," Gutstein told me, pointing to a vat of shredded cabbage. "We went from coleslaw that was creamy to one that was tropical, with pineapple and vinegar. They can't stand this shit. So now we're going to go back to the old way. It's a blue-collar place, this coffee shop. We don't cater to these trendy customers."

By 7:30 that morning, orders were coming in once a minute. There were five egg and grill cooks and twenty waiters for close to 300 diners, and tables were turning over about every 38 minutes. The breakfast rush had yet to begin. Gutstein stood in the center of the kitchen, across the serving counter from the cooks, banging covers on finished orders and stacking them five high for the waiters to carry off. He was still a little cranky from a Yankees loss the previous evening. "I did the numbers the other day, and I figured that for every pitch Randy Johnson throws he gets four thousand dollars," he was saying. "Could be a ball. Could be a strike. Could hit the batter. Four thousand dollars." He might have added that his cooks work more than six weeks to make that kind of money, but then the printer spooled out four new orders. He smacked his meaty hands together and grinned. "Let the games begin!"

Gutstein is the college boy who took a short-order job and never left. He is the one who, instead of feeling trapped by the grinding routine, found it liberating. "I never in a million years thought I would be doing this," he says. His father was a travelling salesman who studied trumpet at Juilliard; his mother was an office manager and a part-time caterer. In high school, he played defensive end on the football team and was good enough to earn a scholarship to Holy Cross. But he went to the University of Massachusetts at Amherst instead, played intramural basketball, and majored in political science, vaguely intending to become a lawyer. "I wasn't looking to do more work than I had to," he says. After graduation, he spent six months trying to launch a landscaping business, but customers were so scarce that he had to find other work in order to pay the rent. "So there was a job cooking kosher lunches at a yeshiva in Longmeadow, outside Springfield. Two hundred dollars a week. Next thing I knew, I was feeding a hundred and fifty little Jewish kids. That's when I caught the bug." The work was hot and fast and deafeningly loud, but the time went by like this, he says, snapping his fingers. "I just found myself."

Gutstein went on to apprentice at a French restaurant, starting out in the laundry and working his way up to chef de cuisine. After that, he took a series of jobs at larger and larger hotels in Hartford, Newark, and Los Angeles. By the time he came to Las Vegas, five years ago, he was married and had a six-month-old daughter, Hannah Brooklyn Gutstein. ("I went through all the other boroughs and none of them sounded right. Hannah Bronx, Hannah Yonkers . . .") He says that he couldn't get used to the newness of the place at first—the rectilinear streets and bulldozed desert plots; the jagged rim of mountains on the horizon. But real estate was cheap and the casinos needed chefs. So he bought a house in one of the stucco subdivisions south of town. Then he bought a newer, bigger house nearby and rented out the first. He had two more children, bought a charcoal-gray Mustang convertible, and slowly began to feel at home. "I was, like, 'Holy shit,' " he says. " 'You can make it in this town.' "

When Gutstein arrived at the Flamingo, in 2002, after two years as a chef at Bally's, Lindy's was still there, like a Vegas burlesque of a greasy spoon: the servers were mouthy and demanding, the kitchen cramped and grimy. "Dude, it was a fucking nightmare," Gutstein says. "I'm not kidding you. It was brutal. The cooks back there were losing their minds." Several years earlier, a section of the floor in the kitchen had collapsed when water from a broken pipe eroded the ground beneath it. The servers simply skirted the pit until someone laid down a piece of plywood to cover it. The plywood stayed there for months.

Gutstein spent his first few weeks walking around the hotel with a legal pad, just trying to grasp the scale of the place. The Flamingo has more than 4,000 employees, 1,100 of whom work in food service. Its ten restaurants and eleven bars cover every major theme in American dining—Chinese, Japanese, Italian, steak house, fast food, buffet—like a carpeted, air-conditioned version of a Midwestern downtown. The coffee shop's kitchen is half the length of a football field, and it's only the tail end of an intestinal tangle of prep kitchens, washrooms, and walk-in refrigerators that are shared by the restaurants and that coil around and beneath the casino. Go down one service corridor and you emerge in Pink Ginger, a pan-Asian restaurant that looks like the inside of a young girl's jewelry box. Go down another and you're in Margaritaville, where the booths are like fishing boats and a woman dressed in a mermaid suit slips down a water slide into a giant margarita blender.

Like the restaurants in the casino, the hotels on the Strip are just subsets of other corporate megastructures. The Flamingo used to belong to Caesars Entertainment, which also owned Caesars Palace, Paris Las Vegas, Bally's, and fourteen other properties. Then, this past June, Caesars Entertainment was bought by Harrah's Entertainment, which owned twenty-five casinos. For the Flamingo, all this merging and acquiring has meant, for instance, that the onion soup, turkey gravy, beef broth, marinara sauce, clam chowder, and chili served at the Tropical Breeze and its other restaurants are made in giant steam kettles at Paris Las Vegas, where they're pumped into two-gallon plastic tubes, loaded onto carts, and distributed around the Strip.

The newest hotels are designed for such economies of scale. (The juice room at the Wynn squeezes ten kinds of fruit daily; its bakery makes sixty kinds of bread.) But the Flamingo was built in stages, like the Vatican. Its pink glass towers stand on the ruins of a low-slung 1950s pavilion with a neon column that bubbled like champagne. Beneath that lie the elegant remains of Bugsy Siegel's supper club and riding stables, from a time when horses could still be hitched in front of stores downtown. The result is a maze of ramps, stairs, and blind corridors that crisscross behind the hotel's sleek new interiors, like something from an etching by Escher. "This is why they implode hotels," a former head of food service at the hotel told me.

Two years ago, when the Flamingo began renovating Lindy's to make the Tropical Breeze, Gutstein helped redesign the kitchen. He gave it larger cooktops and better flow, revamped its inventory system, and reorganized the staff. To keep his part of the casino's vast mechanism in gear, he knew that he had to understand it in all its particulars. He had to know that the average meal takes five minutes to make and fifteen minutes to serve. He had to know how many pounds of corned beef, diced papaya, Cap'n Crunch, and kosher pickles the café consumes in a week, and how those numbers change if a convention or a sporting event is in town. (When NASCAR came to Vegas in March, sales of chicken-fried steak went "through the roof," Gutstein says.) And he had to extrapolate from those numbers how many cooks and servers he would need on any given shift. But what he needed most he already had: three good egg cooks.

• • •

Martin Nañez Moreno, the omelette man, grew up on a small farm in Villa Lopez, Mexico, six hours southeast of El Paso. He came to Las Vegas eleven years ago with his brother-in-law. His three older brothers are all cooks in Los Angeles. Joel Eckerson, the over-easy man, was reared in an orphanage outside Seoul, South Korea. He was adopted at the age of eleven by a Christian couple from Duanesburg, New York, and joined the Navy seven years later, where he first worked in a kitchen. When he arrived in Las Vegas, in 1985, he took a job as a cook's helper at the Flamingo and never left. Debbie Lubick makes all the poached-egg dishes at the Tropical Breeze. When she was growing up, her parents owned a fleet of eighty lunch trucks in Houston and San Antonio. Her father taught her to crack eggs one-handed when she was ten; by the time she was sixteen she was running the kitchen.

Standing shoulder to shoulder at the griddle that morning, they looked as oddly matched as three champions at a dog show, and just as self-possessed: Martin was dark and slender, with a debonair mustache; Joel was short, angular, and efficient; Debbie was tall and matronly, with a pale, sweet face edged with melancholy. Like almost everyone at the café, they'd come to Vegas from someplace else—I counted eleven Mexicans, three Salvadorans, five Filipinos, a Peruvian, an Iranian, a German, a Canadian, and an Englishman among the employees on one shift—but the egg cooks shared certain basic traits. They were all in their forties, all married with children, all deeply unexcitable souls at the heart of a hyperactive environment. They were the still center at the eye of the Tropical Breeze.

The Flamingo is a union house, like most of the large hotels in Vegas. Cooks start at about $15 an hour—servers make $10, and generally collect another ten in tips—and work their way up the pay scale by seniority, from runner to cook's helper to fry cook to broiler cook to saucier to sous-chef to banquet cook. Martin and Joel were sauciers. They made a dollar an hour more than fry cooks, and had the privilege of working the day shift from six to two. (The swing shift was from two to ten, the graveyard shift from ten to six.) Debbie was just a fry cook, after nine years at the Flamingo, but even that made her a rarity in Vegas. Most women in casino restaurants get shunted into waitressing, hosting, or composing fruit and salad plates in the pantry. When they do make it to the line, they're not always welcome. "There are male egos involved," Debbie told me one day in the break room, with a tight smile. "The guys will die before they let me come over and help. They don't want to be shown up by a girl." That's fine with her, she said. "I have the easiest station on the line. Now I just tell them, 'You don't want the help? O.K., die.' "

The rush began at about ten o'clock. Or, rather, the first of a series of rushes: on weekends, customers come in waves, like Cossacks. When I arrived at the line, the heat seared my lungs—the griddle, at about six hundred degrees, was wreathed in steam from cooking pots and egg pans. Martin had ten omelettes on the griddle and was swigging something called SoBe Adrenaline Rush from a thin black can. Next to him, Joel had five pairs of eggs going and a hubcap-size pan of scrambled eggs. Debbie was fishing poached eggs from a roiling pot, while an assistant chef sliced red onions at a furious pace beside her, filling the air with a stinging mist.

"I need a four on two, sunny and scrambled, both wearing sausage!" a grill cook at the next station shouted. Joel nodded. The grill cooks usually made their own eggs to go with steaks or pancakes, but they sometimes needed help: "four on two" meant four eggs on two plates. Joel ripped a spool of new orders from the printer and tucked them under a clamp above the counter, then started cracking eggs into pans two at a time. When he was done, he had ten pairs of eggs cooking: five from previous orders, two from the grill cook's order, and three from the new orders. He finished the five original orders first. He put a pair of sunnys under a broiler and used his forefinger to break the yolks on a pair that had been ordered over hard. Then he flipped the eggs in that pan and those in three other pans that had been ordered over easy—one, two, three, four. He pivoted back to the counter, set five plates on it, and garnished them all with potatoes and bacon or sausage. He then flipped the over-hards and over-easies again, slid them onto their plates along with the sunnys from the broiler, and placed all the plates under the hot lights above the counter.

The whole sequence took about three minutes. Meanwhile, four new tickets had printed out, the potato bin needed refilling, the last five orders were ready to flip, and Debbie had asked for some over-easies to go with a chicken-fried steak. On Martin's side, the omelettes were multiplying—there were fifteen now, all with different ingredients—nearly crowding the egg pans off the griddle. He pivoted and flipped them in one motion, catching the omelettes in the pan as it reached the counter, ignoring a small commotion that had broken out over at the grill station.

"Would you eat that?" a barrel-chested black waitress named Rose was yelling. "Would you?" Apparently, she'd asked Frank—a hulking young grill cook who had been there for only five months—for an order of pancakes with a side of over-easies, but by the time the eggs were done the pancakes were cold. Frank had made a second batch, but Rose had left them sitting so long that they'd gone cold again. "You need some manners," Frank complained in a small voice, like a bike horn that had lost its squeak. Rose put her hand on her hip and cocked it to the side, then flung a flapjack across the counter as if it were a Frisbee. "I ain't servin nothin' I wouldn't eat!"

Gutstein, being a cook, mostly blames the servers when things break down at the café, which they rarely do. "They aren't bad people, but their nature is 'I want, I want, I want,' " he says. "They get spoiled. They put in an order and want it within three or four minutes. So the cooks start sandbagging—preparing things ahead of time." He went over to quiet Rose down but soon gave up and wandered back to his station. "Why can't we be friends?" he sang in a gruff baritone. Behind him, a tall, buzz-cut waiter named Eric made a gesture as if bending a stick. "I can almost hear it snapping," he said. "It's bowed. It's not broken. But it's just about to snap."

Short-order cooking is like driving a car: anyone can do it up to a certain speed. The difference between an amateur and a crack professional isn't so much a matter of specific skills as of consistency and timing. Most diner kitchens are fairly forgiving places. You can break a yolk or two, lose track of an order, or overcook an omelette and start again without getting swamped. But as the pace increases those tolerances disappear. At the Tropical Breeze, a single mistake can throw an entire sequence out of kilter, so that every dish is either cold or overdone. A cook of robotic efficiency, moving steadily from task to task, suddenly slips a cog and becomes Lucy in the chocolate factory, stuffing candies into her mouth as they pile up on the assembly line.

On early mornings, well before the first rush, Gutstein would let me work at the over-easy station for an hour or two. After a few days, I could crack seven or eight eggs in a row without breaking a yolk—good enough for Julia's but not for a rush at the café. When Joel cracked eggs, his fingers were as loose and precise as a jazz guitarists'. He held one egg between his thumb and his first two fingers, another curled against his palm. He rapped the first egg on the rim of the pan, twisted it into hemispheres, and opened it as cleanly as if it were a Fabergé Easter egg. As the spent shell fell into the trash, he shuttled the second egg into position, as if pumping a rifle. He was proud of this little move. It saved him about a second versus having to grab an egg from the bin. If he cracked six thousand eggs a week, the move saved him about an hour; in a year, it saved him more than a week.

The egg flip had to be equally flawless but allowed for more personal flair. I often wished that I had a slow-motion film of the different cooks doing it. Edgar Lopez, the sassy Salvadoran who filled in for those on break, liked to throw his eggs high into the air, like salsa dancers, catch them at the top of their arc, and let them slide vertically down the pan. Joel gave his eggs a quick little jerk, so that they stood up on edge and swung over like a door on a hinge. Martin barely moved his pan at all. His eggs just seemed to roll over on command. As for mine, they'd catapult up and turn an eager circle in the air, but every fourth or fifth pair would bellyflop in the pan and spring a leak.

"The hard part isn't flipping them," Debbie said. "It's catching them." But cooking a dozen egg dishes at once, while filling supplies and fielding side orders, is above all a feat of timing. Even if your technique is perfect, everything in the kitchen conspires to throw you off. The customer wants crispy bacon, so you have to root around in a warming tray or toss some slices into the deep fryer. The trash hasn't been taken out, so you have to dump your shells at the next station. A batch of eggs have been stored so long that their yolks are weak and more likely to burst. To keep track of every dish, you need a dozen egg timers in your head, all set to trigger alarms at different intervals.

Warren Meck, a neuroscientist at Duke University, has identified the neural circuitry that allows the brain to time several events at once. As it happens, short-order cooks are among his favorite examples. They're like jugglers, he says, who can keep a dozen balls in the air at the same time. He calls them "the master interval timers."

Whenever a cook sets a pan on a griddle, Meck says, a burst of dopamine is released in the brain's frontal cortex. The cortex is full of oscillatory neurons that vibrate at different tempos. The dopamine forces a group of these neurons to fall into synch, which sends a chemical signal to the corpus striatum, at the base of the brain. "We call that the start gun," Meck says. The striatum recognizes the signal as a time marker and releases a second burst of dopamine, which sends a signal back to the frontal cortex via the thalamus—the stop gun. Every time this neural circuit is completed, the brain gets better at distinguishing that particular interval from the thousands of others that it times during the course of the day. An experienced cook like Joel, Meck believes, will have a separate neural circuit set up for every task: an over-easy circuit, an over-medium circuit, a sunny-side-up circuit, and so on, each one reinforced through constant, repetitive use.

Meck has yet to put a short-order cook in a brain scanner, as he has done with musicians, but he suspects that the results would be similar: their oscillatory neurons will have grown far more synapses than those in the average person's brain. If they are asked to time certain events, more of their brain will light up. His description reminded me of something that Michael Stern, the co-author of *Roadfood,* had told me about one of his favorite short-order cooks: "It's like part of his brain is developed that I don't even have."

The servers at the Tropical Breeze like to say that they have the busiest coffee shop in the world, or at least that's how it feels. Customers sometimes ask them if they actually live in Las Vegas, as if no one could really stand this pace or lifestyle for long. "You can't raise children here, can you?" they say. But the truth is, if everyone seems to come to Vegas from someplace else, no one ever seems to leave. The average length of employment among the workers I polled was a little more than ten years, and Clara, who made salads and fruit plates, had been there for thirty-six. "Sometimes it feels like it's the only coffee shop in the world," Inge, a seventy-three-year-old hostess from Berlin, told me.

We were sitting in Bugsy's Backroom, the Flamingo's employee cafeteria, deep in the netherworld backstage of the casino. Steve, a former high-school social-studies teacher, who turned fifty-eight this year, stubbed out his cigarette and nodded. "They say that if you can work here as a server you can work anywhere," he told me. "None of us have easy jobs." He jerked his thumb at Patty, the brassy buffet hostess beside him, who had dyed-blond hair and heavy-lidded eyes. "I mean, she's only twenty-six, and look at her."

Patty broke into a loud, throaty laugh. "And I just had a facelift," she said. She pointed to her powdered cheek. "This is my ass."

All around us, groups of other casino workers were hunched over Formica tables in their gaudy uniforms, picking at food or watching TV on overhead monitors. There were craps dealers with gold shirts and flaming-sunset collars and cuffs; middle-aged cocktail waitresses wearing coat dresses with plunging necklines; gangs of scruffy young waiters from Margaritaville in Hawaiian shirts. In the far corner, under the cool fluorescent lights, a quartet of blackjack dealers with slicked-back hair were playing cards with a distracted air. "It has been __ days since our last worker's compensation accident," a sign near the entrance read. "When we reach __ days accident free there will be a reward."

Why do they all stay? I wondered. What keeps them here, of all places? For most, the answer seemed to lie in the union buttons on their shirts. Las Vegas is a city where a waiter can still spend his whole career in one restaurant without being laid off or relocated. The casinos, for better or worse, are stuck in the desert with their employees. They can't outsource their jobs to Bangalore. They can't drum up an army of minimum-wage replacements overnight. So they pay a living wage, provide health insurance and pensions, and give their employees a certain leeway. Not long ago, a couple of workers told me, a Flamingo employee stabbed another worker with a ballpoint pen. She's still working at the hotel.

"You have to fire yourself, just about," Patty said. "It's a trap, but it's a good trap. For those of us getting older—I'm really fifty-seven—it's a godsend."

Still, that didn't quite explain why the egg cooks stuck around. Joel had worked at the Flamingo for nineteen years, Martin for eleven. They were the fastest cooks that most of the café's servers had ever seen—"It just shocks me, what those guys do," one waitress told me. "My husband's a cook, and they just run circles around him." As sauciers in the union hierarchy, they could easily have shopped their skills around: Las Vegas has become a city enamored of fine dining. The new Wynn hotel alone has twenty-two food and drink outlets, ten of them run by three- and four-star chefs. Why were Joel and Martin still cooking eggs?

One evening, a few hours after the café's breakfast crew had gone home, I walked up the Strip to Corsa Cucina, one of the Wynn's flagship restaurants, to see how the other half cooked. Stephen Kalt, the restaurant's executive chef, is a burly forty-nine-year-old with a bald pate and a lively, incisive mind. With his sleeves rolled up and his apron on, he looks like an Italian butcher but talks like an epicure— a perfect fit for the new Vegas. Before apprenticing at Le Cirque, in New York, and training with such culinary stars as Thomas Keller and Wolfgang Puck, Kalt owned a couple of pizza parlors in Tennessee with his younger brother. Watching him work is like seeing short-order set to opera.

The dining room at Corsa Cucina is long and dimly lit, with red leather banquettes and an open kitchen along one wall, like a lavishly appointed diner. Kalt stands at the center of the serving counter, facing an enormous red-tiled oven, in a circle of light cast by four pendant warming lamps. With his back to the dining room and his eyes fixed on a row of tickets on the counter, he cues his cooks one by one, as if conducting musicians from a score. "Fire one lamb, a halibut, and a tuna," he'll say. "And give me a side of spinach, a side of whipped." The food that emerges a little later shares Kalt's robust sophistication, a world away from fried eggs: lamb-shank tagine, poached halibut with buttered cockles, seared tuna with prosciutto-wrapped figs. To make sure the meal is perfectly paced and presented, Kalt sends runners out to spy on diners and inspects every dish as it goes out, wiping away stray flecks of sauce or butter. "The finer the dining, the more constraint there is," he says. "If one of these guys smacks a plate down too hard, I'll tell him, 'You can't do that.' "

And yet, from a cook's perspective, the difference between Corsa and the Tropical Breeze is largely a matter of ingredients. Many of the dishes are grilled, deep-fried, or sautéed, just as they are at the café. Most are assembled quickly out of previously prepared elements. Instead of bins of shredded cheese, chopped ham, and bacon, Kalt's cooks have bins of black-truffle butter, olive confit, and salt-cod brandade. Instead of tubs of sausage gravy and refried beans, they have squirt bottles of tamarind-honey sauce and Thai-basil puree. The cooks at Corsa have to execute a few recipes flawlessly. They have to know how to build a veal sauce and how to keep a beurre blanc from breaking. But they rarely make more than three dishes at once. The real feats of timing—coördinating multiple courses, sequencing orders so they're done simultaneously—are all left to Kalt.

"If I was recruiting, those guys who can handle fifteen pans, that's who I'd want," Elizabeth Blau, a restaurant consultant and one of the impresarios behind the gourmet movement in Las Vegas, told me. "Forget French culinary technique. It's not rocket science. Whether it's cooking an omelette or cooking a beautiful piece of fish, it's about precision. They can do the job." Still, few of the cooks at Corsa came from short-order kitchens. Many were young, white, and male. Some had gone to culinary school; others were "homegrown," as Kalt put it; most probably wouldn't stay for more than a couple of years. They'd grow bored with cooking the same dishes and move on to the next restaurant, the next chef, hoping to run their own kitchen one day.

I asked Kalt what separated them from the short-order cooks at the Flamingo. "That's a different animal," he said. "That is a guy who grew up seventeen generations on a farm in Mexico. He isn't raised, like us, to think that he's going to be the President of the country. He's raised to think about his next meal." He shook his head. "Look, I've had guys from a little farm in Pueblo who were some of the best chefs I've ever seen. Phenomenal. Anything you taught them they could learn, and do. And yet they were happy where they were. They didn't need to be striving for the next thing. I can get a guy like that to make the same chopped salad for me the same way for ten years. Never been happier. Because that's the culture, that's the rhythm—you put seeds in the ground year after year. You get an American kid, he would jump off a building already."

It's easier to turn a short-order cook into a chef than it is to turn a chef into a short-order cook, Kalt said. I wasn't so sure. The cooks at the Tropical Breeze didn't seem resigned to their jobs so much as addicted to them. Joel had been offered higher pay for easier work at one of the Flamingo's gourmet restaurants, yet he'd stuck with the eggs. "I like it fast-paced, boom, boom, boom," Joel said. "You don't get bored." After a few years at the café, kitchens like Corsa Cucina seem to move at quarter-speed. On the Saturday night that I was there, Kalt's nine cooks prepared about four hundred meals. That same day, Joel and Martin alone made eleven hundred.

"I've tried to promote Joel," Gutstein told me one night at his house, over some crab cakes he'd made. "I've given him the opportunity to be a manager, to get out of that bullshit five-hundred-degree heat for eight hours. I'm, like, 'Come on, Joel, you're better than that!' But he doesn't want it. Straight up? He's in such a comfort zone that it's hurting him." Yet Gutstein wasn't so different. When I asked if he would ever work at Pink Ginger, the Flamingo's Asian restaurant, his shoulders shook as if a spider had scurried down them. "I wouldn't be able to stand it," he said.

If someone gave Gutstein a million dollars tomorrow, he'd probably quit the Tropical Breeze and open a bed-and-breakfast—"Like Martha Stewart," he said. "Real homey." But, in the meantime, he knew better than to doubt his good fortune. Growing up in Yonkers, he used to watch his father change jobs every few years. "I love my dad, but nothing was ever good enough for him," he said. "And he's still busting his ass. I think he's selling those life-alert systems now. Before that it was Craftmatic adjustable beds, before that window-shade treatments, before that light bulbs. He changes jobs like I change underwear." Now that Gutstein has a family of his own, he has vowed to stick to what he knows. "Because of the way my dad was, I'm pretty much Steady Eddie."

As he talked, there was a scuffling sound at the front door and three children came tumbling through, hot and sandy from an excursion to Lake Mead, the vast reservoir behind the Hoover Dam, half an hour from Vegas. When Hannah Brooklyn Gutstein saw her father, she ran across the room and into his lap, dropping her towel along the way. She was as round and red-faced and freckled as her father—baked pink by the desert, as he had been by the kitchen. He handed her a crab cake. "We're doing good," he said. "We work hard, but we're very lucky. I'm not after the golden egg."

The Business of the Restaurant Business

by Steven A. Shaw

from *Turning the Tables*

Dining reviewer and proprietor of the egullet.com culinary website, Shaw knows so much about the restaurant industry; he is the natural choice for writing this comprehensive, entertaining user's manual for getting the best out of your evenings out.

In Wilson, North Carolina, Ed Mitchell is presiding over his new "pig bar," one of several barbecue concepts he hopes to franchise in the coming years. The pig bar looks like any bar, anywhere, right down to the beer taps, dark wood, and television screens playing sports programming, but where you'd normally find liquor bottles on the back bar there is, instead, a bathtub-sized multicompartment apparatus holding different cuts of pit-roasted pork. Customers at the pig bar point to what they want, and the pig-bartender makes up a plate. "People eat with their eyes," comments Mitchell. "And this will get them hungry."

I met Ed Mitchell in New York City at a block party. He and his crew, including his brothers Aubrey and Stevie and his son Ryan, had driven up to Manhattan from Wilson in a semi truck filled with barbecue equipment in order to participate in the Big Apple Barbecue Block Party. There were several other participants in the event—pitmasters had come from as far away as Texas—but two things immediately struck me about Ed Mitchell: first, he was the only African-American pitmaster at the event. All the others were white, as are most barbecue restaurant owners in the South despite the genre's largely black roots.

Second, he was the only one barbecuing whole hogs. The rest were cooking ribs, pork shoulder, and other small-by-comparison cuts of meat.

At a panel discussion on the meaning of barbecue, Mitchell sat quietly on the dais with the other pitmasters. The others had plenty to say but, like a professional poker player, Mitchell just watched. A bear of a man, he cut quite a figure in his overalls, baseball cap, and massive white beard. When the rest of the crew was all talked out, Mitchell finally leaned forward toward his microphone and said, "May I add just a couple of comments?" At which point the crowd was treated to a quiet, intensive lecture on the social history of barbecue. Mitchell, among other surprises, has a master's degree in sociology. I knew then that, one day, I'd have to visit Mitchell on his home turf.

Mitchell's Ribs Chicken & BBQ, home to the pig bar, rises out of Wilson, North Carolina's spartan landscape like a secret government research hangar. With few surrounding reference points, the scale of the operation isn't entirely clear until you're standing right in front of it: Mitchell's barnlike structure is large enough to accommodate a large herd of cattle or a small shopping mall. By 11 A.M. the parking lot is filling with cars and tour buses—what are people doing on tours around here anyway?—and over in a far corner of the lot's expanse is the same semi truck I had seen in New York City the previous summer.

It didn't start out this way. Although as a boy he had assisted his father at many a pig roast—he recalls every occasion being transformed into an excuse for a pig roast, from birthdays to the birth of a favorite hunting dog's litter—Ed Mitchell never intended to run a barbecue restaurant. His G.I. bill–funded studies ranged from sociology to economics, and he spent seventeen years as a manager for Ford in Boston. It wasn't until his father took ill, and he came back home to help care for his family, that the barbecue idea was hatched.

The current Mitchell's site used to be the Mitchell family grocery. Like most small stores of its kind, Mitchell's grocery eventually came under pressure from chain supermarkets and evolving tastes. With Mitchell's father unable to work the store, the pressure on his mother was almost unbearable. One day, as Ed Mitchell was helping his mother open the store, she began to cry on account of the mounting pressure of a dying husband and a struggling business.

"What can I do to make you feel better?" he asked.

"Make me some of your barbecue," she answered, "like you used to make."

So Mitchell, a dutiful son, went out and bought a baby pig and spent the day barbecuing it. Near closing time, it was ready.

Mitchell recalls eating the barbecue behind the counter with his mother, when a customer walked in. "Oh, Mrs. Mitchell, you've got barbecue now?" The rest was history.

Ed Mitchell sees his restaurant—now more than ten times the size of the family market—as a research laboratory. Rooted in the Southern barbecue tradition, Mitchell is nonetheless a modernist, and his goal is to unite the old methods with contemporary business acumen to create a barbecue empire that can expand and replicate itself beyond Wilson, and beyond Mitchell's lifetime. "I'm doing this for my son," he said several times during the day I spent with him.

And so, unlike most Southern barbecue establishments, Mitchell's is decidedly high-tech. At the drive-through window, the employees wear wireless headsets and utilize the same computer point-of-sale ordering systems as Kentucky Fried Chicken. At the main service line, Mitchell has inverted the traditional barbecue kitchen by putting all the food out in the open: customers line up cafeteria-style and point to whatever they want, and the staff builds each person a plate. "People eat with their eyes," was another of Mitchell's oft-repeated comments. The cafeteria line also allows Mitchell to service easily in excess of a thousand customers a day. "We've never even tested the limits of this thing." Yet despite the streamlined look and feel of Mitchell's, everything in the back of the house occurs with old-fashioned rigor. Hushpuppies are shaped by hand (most barbecue places, even the most traditional ones, now use a machine), desserts are made from scratch, and vegetables are prepared according to old Mitchell family recipes.

"I'm developing different styles for different audiences, so there'll be something for everyone," Mitchell says of his franchise plans. "You want a quick bite, there's the drive-through, just like at the KFC. You want a quick meal here, you go through the service line. In the back we'll have table service. And at the pig bar, you can get together with your buddies, have some beer and some pig, and watch the game."

Perhaps most innovative, however, is Mitchell's system for pit-roasting whole hogs, a system he calls "banking." North Carolina barbecue, in the eastern part of the state where Mitchell is from, is synonymous with the whole hog. While it's a fairly simple matter to create automated equipment for roasting chickens or racks of ribs, nobody before Mitchell has attempted to create a scientifically based system for pit-roasting whole hogs. Thus, whole-hog barbecue remains the most mysterious form of barbecue, requiring 24/7 attention and continuous adjustment to the barbecue pits, and is practiced only by a few idiosyncratic pitmasters at hard-to-reach locations in the rural South.

What Mitchell's system achieves is a degree of standardization that can allow a properly trained employee to pit-roast a pig like the great pitmasters, without the need to stay up all night. Mitchell's specially constructed all-brick aboveground "pits" are wired with temperature probes, they have special valves to control airflow, and they are backed up by redundant state-of-the art exhaust and fire-suppression systems. For each weight of hog, Mitchell's team has computer-generated graphs demonstrating the pit temperature and internal temperatures for the entire length of the roast. So it is possible, using his system, for the cook to prep and leave the pig on the fire at night, reduce the pit's airflow to the proper level for that size animal, and return in the morning to a fully barbecued whole hog. Then, in the morning, the quicker-cooking items like ribs and chicken can be added to the pits, and by lunchtime there's a full barbecue inventory ready to serve.

When I enter the room housing Mitchell's pits—they are indoors at the back of the restaurant, right where any standard restaurant kitchen would be—I'm reminded of my first barbecue road trip through North Carolina, Tennessee, and Texas. As I set out on the trip, I vowed to visit the pits everywhere I could. I figured there would be resistance—pitmasters have a reputation for secretiveness —but I'd persevere and get behind the scenes. At Wilbur's bar-becue in Goldsboro, North Carolina, I summoned up the courage to ask, "May we see the pits?"

"You want to see the pits?" asked a puzzled owner, chewing a cigar and leaning against his white pickup truck. "Sure." We walked around back to a long brick shed lined with smokestacks exhaling gray soot and vaporized grease, and Wilbur opened the door and gestured for us to enter.

It was like walking into an oven in Hell, without any air, surrounded by the sight, aroma, and vapor of dead baby pigs. I lasted just long enough to have the vision recur to me over the years in early morning nightmares. I didn't ask for very many pit tours after that. Wilbur was, I think, amused.

In Mitchell's pits, the thermometer on the wall reads 70 degrees. There is no aroma. The pigs are under metal domes and, in moments of denial, even look kind of cute. You can read a book, take a nap, or have a picnic in Mitchell's pit area and never know there are whole hogs roasting six feet away from you. And by extension, you may be able to have a Mitchell's barbecue franchise next door to your apartment in a large city yet not be inconvenienced. That, at least, is Ed Mitchell's hope.

"Once this place is set up and the franchises are flying solo, I'm going to get in that barbecue truck and drive. We'll go to festivals, we'll make barbecue everywhere. That's my retirement."

A year later, Ed Mitchell is back with his crew at the second annual Big Apple Barbecue Block Party. This time he's expecting an even larger crowd than last year's, and he's preparing ten whole hogs of approximately 150 pounds each. Now an Ed Mitchell groupie, I hang around with his crew for most of the weekend. On the last day, as a particularly fearsome hog comes off the smoker, Mitchell holds up a pair of thick black welder's gloves and signals to me, "You ready to pick a whole hog?"

Even through those gloves, the steaming flesh of the hog sends burning sensations through my hands and up my arms. By the time I pull the meat out of half the hog and place it in a plastic bin, I'm drenched with perspiration. By the time I finish the hog, I'm about to pass out. Not satisfied to have me still conscious, Ed Mitchell holds up two cleavers: "You ready to chop the hog?"

I make it through about five pounds of meat before my forearms go numb and I slink off to sit on a nearby park bench, eating one of Mitchell's chopped barbecue sandwiches while nursing my wounded hands, arms, and pride.

A Critic at Every Table

by Frank Bruni
from *The New York Times*

> When *The New York Times*' chief dining critic
> goes backstage (so to speak) to work as a
> waiter, he discovers a whole new perspective
> on what goes on in the dining room.

It's 7:45 PM, the East Coast Grill is going full tilt and I'm ready to throttle one of the six diners at Table M-8.

He wants me to describe the monkfish special. For the fourth time. I hoarsely oblige, but when I return yet again to my riff on the apricot lager mustard, which comes right before my oratorical ode to the maple pecan mashed sweet potatoes, his attention flags and he starts to talk to a friend.

Does he mistake me for a recorded message, paused and played with the push of a button? Doesn't he know I have other tables to serve?

I need to go over and massage the mood at R-5, where one of the two diners has a suspiciously shallow pool of broth in her bouillabaisse, perhaps because I spilled some of it near M-2.

And I need to redeem myself with the two diners at X-9, who quizzed me about what the restaurant had on tap and received a blank stare in response. I'm supposed to remember the beers? Along with everything about the monkfish, these oddly coded table references, more than ten wines by the glass and the provenance of the house oysters?

I had no idea.

I usually spend my nights on the other side of the table, not only asking the questions and making the demands but also judging and, I concede, taking caustic little mental notes. And it's been twenty years since I walked in a waiter's shoes, something I did for only six months.

But last week I traded places and swapped perspectives, a critic joining the criticized, to get a taste of what servers go through and what we put them through, of how they see and survive us. My ally was Chris Schlesinger, a well-known cook and author who owns the East Coast Grill, in Cambridge, Massachusetts, and has no business interests in New York. So that my presence in the restaurant wouldn't become public knowledge, he introduced me to his staff as a free-lance writer named Gavin doing a behind-the-scenes article to be placed in a major publication.

In some ways this restaurant, which opened in 1985 and special-izes in fresh seafood and barbecue, was an easy assignment. Its service ethic is casual, so I didn't have to sweat many niceties. Its food is terrific, so diners don't complain all that much.

But its pace can be frenetic, and servers have little room to maneuver among 100 or so tightly spaced seats.

From Monday through Saturday, I worked the dinner shift, showing up by 3:30 and usually staying past 11. I took care of just a few diners at first and many more as the week progressed.

And I learned that for servers in a restaurant as busy as the East Coast Grill, waiting tables isn't a job. It's a back-straining, brain-addling, sanity-rattling siege.

MONDAY

Every day at 4 PM, the servers take a pop quiz. This afternoon's ques-tions include ones on how the restaurant acquires its oysters and the color, texture and taste of mahi-mahi.

Before and after the quiz they tackle chores: moving furniture, hauling tubs of ice from the basement, folding napkins. I pitch in by chopping limes into quarters and lemons into eighths. I chop and chop. My fingers go slightly numb.

The servers range in age from their early twenties to their late for-ties. Some go to school or hold other jobs on the side. Many would like to do less physically demanding work. All would like to earn more money.

If they put in a full schedule of four prime shifts a week, they might make $45,000 a year before taxes. Almost all of it is from tips. They wonder if diners realize that.

Bryan, a young server with whom I'm training, brings me up to speed on the crazy things diners do. They let their children run rampant, a peril to the children as well as the servers. They assume that the first table they are shown to is undesirable and insist on a different one, even if it's demonstrably less appealing. They decline to read what's in front of them and want to hear all their options. Servers disparagingly call this a "menu tour."

I acquire a new vocabulary. To "verbalize the funny" is to tell the kitchen about a special request. "Campers" are people who linger forever at tables. "Verbal tippers" are people who offer extravagant praise in lieu of 20 percent.

The doors open at 5:30 and soon two women are seated at L-3. They interrogate Bryan at great length about the monkfish, which, in changing preparations, will be a special all week long. He delivers a monkfish exegesis; they seem rapt.

They order the mahi-mahi and the swordfish.

"It's amazing," Bryan tells me, "how unadventurous people are."

How unpredictable, too. During a later stretch, Bryan has a man and a woman at L-3 and two men at L-4. The tables are adjacent and the diners receive the same degree of attention. The men at L-4 leave $85 for a check of $72—a tip of about 18 percent.

L-3's check is $58, and Bryan sees the man put down a stack of bills. Then, as the man gets up from the table, the woman shakes her head and removes $5. The remaining tip is $4, or about 7 percent.

TUESDAY

I'm shadowing Tina, who has worked at the East Coast Grill for decades and seen it all. She is handling the same section Bryan did. She offers a psychological profile of a woman sitting alone at L-3, who declared the chocolate torte too rich and announced, only after draining her margarita, that it had too much ice.

"Some people are interested in having the experience of being disappointed," Tina says.

Some people are worse. Arthur, a young server who is fairly new to the restaurant, recalls a man who walked in and announced that he had a reservation, a statement Arthur distrusted. The East Coast Grill doesn't take reservations.

Arthur tried to finesse the situation by saying he was unaware of the reservation but hadn't worked over the previous three days.

"You haven't worked in three days?" the man said, according to Arthur's recollection. "You're going to go far in life!"

At about 9:30, a half-hour before the kitchen stops accepting orders, I take my first table, two women and a man. I ask them if they want to know about the half-dozen specials.

"We want to know everything," the man says.

The statement is like a death knell. I mention the monkfish, but forget to say that it comes with a sweet shrimp and mango salsa. I mention the fried scallops, and I'm supposed to say they're from New Bedford, Massachusetts. But that detail eludes me, so I stammer, "Um, they're not heavily breaded or anything." They seem puzzled by my vagueness and poised to hear more. I've got nothing left.

What unnerves me most is trying to gauge their mood. Sometimes they smile when I circle back to check on them. Sometimes they glare.

In addition to dexterity, poise and a good memory, a server apparently needs to be able to read minds.

WEDNESDAY

I'm under Jess's wing. She's young, funny and generous with her encouragement. That final quality turns out to be crucial, because after I greet four diners at M-7, I'm informed that one of them has an affiliation with the Culinary Institute of America.

As I walk toward them with a bowl of house pickles, which is the East Coast Grill's equivalent of a bread basket, my hand shakes and several pickles roll under their table. I can't tell if they notice.

But I can tell they don't trust me. I'm tentative as I recite the specials, and I ask one of them if he wants another Diet Coke. He's drinking beer. They all look at me as if I'm a moron.

Jess tells me that enthusiasm is more important than definitive knowledge, that many diners simply want a server to help them get excited about something.

"You've got to fake it until you make it," she says.

I take her pep talk to heart, perhaps too much so. I handle three men at M-6, one of whom asks, "Between the pulled pork platter and the pork spareribs, which would you do?"

I tell him I'd change course and head toward the pork chop.

"It's that good?" he says.

"It's amazing," I say. I've never had it, but I've seen it. It's big, and so is he.

He later tells me, "Dude, you so steered me right on that pork chop."

I serve four young women at M-9. They order, among other dishes, the "wings of mass destruction." Per the restaurant's script, I warn them away from it, pronouncing it too hot to handle. They press on and survive.

One of them later wonders aloud whether to have the superhot "martini from hell," made with peppered Absolut. I didn't even know it was on the menu before she mentioned it.

"Why worry?" I say. "With those wings, you climbed Everest. The martini's like a bunny slope."

She orders it and drinks it and she and her friends leave a 22 percent tip (which, like all the tips I receive, will be given to the other servers). The three men at M-6 leave 20 percent.

Have I become a service God?

THURSDAY

Divinity must wait.

It's on this night that I spill bouillabaisse, confront my limited beer knowledge and silently curse Mr. Monkfish at M-8. I move up to an evening-long total of eight tables comprising twenty diners; on Wednesday I served five tables and seventeen diners.

I encounter firsthand an annoyance that other servers have told me about: the diner who claims an allergy that doesn't really exist. A woman at X-10, which is a table for two, or a "two top," repeatedly sends me to the kitchen for information on the sugar content of various rubs, relishes, and sauces.

But when I ask her whether her allergy is to refined sugar only or to natural sugars as well, she hems, haws and downgrades her condition to a blood sugar concern, which apparently doesn't extend to the sparkling wine she is drinking.

She orders the sirloin skewers, requesting that their marginally sweet accouterments be put on a separate plate, away from her beef but available to her boyfriend. He rolls his eyes.

Pinging from table to table, I repeatedly forget to ask diners whether they want their tuna rare or medium and whether they want their margaritas up or on the rocks. I occasionally forget to put all the relevant information—prices, special requests, time of submission—on my ordering tickets.

At least everyone at M–8, including Mr. Monkfish, seems content. As I talk to one of the women in the group, another server noisily drops a plate bound for a nearby table. A rib-eye steak special skids to a halt at the woman's feet.

"Is that the cowboy?" she says, using the special's advertised name. "That looks really good!"

About an hour later M–8's spirits aren't so high. They're motioning for me, and it's a scary kind of motioning. The two credit cards I've returned to them aren't the ones they gave me.

One of my last tables is a couple at X–1. They take a bossy tone with me, so when the woman asks if it's possible to get the coconut shrimp in the pu pu platter á la carte, I automatically apologize and say that it's not.

It turns out that I'm right. (I guiltily check a few minutes later.) It also turns out that servers make such independent decisions and proclamations, based on the way diners have treated them, all the time.

FRIDAY

Apparently everything up to now has been child's play. Business will double tonight. People will stand three deep at the bar, closing lanes of traffic between the kitchen and some of the tables.

"Like a shark," Chris Schlesinger tells us, "you've got to keep moving or you die."

My chaperone is Christa, who's as down to earth and supportive as Jess. She's supposed to watch and inevitably rescue me as I try to tackle an entire section of five tables, each of which will have at least two seatings, or "turns."

By 7:30, all of these tables are occupied, and all have different needs at the same time. One man wants to know his tequila choices. I just learned the beers that afternoon.

Another man wants directions to a jazz club. Someone else wants me to instruct the kitchen to take the tuna in one dish and prepare it like the mahi-mahi in another. That's a funny I'll have to verbalize, a few extra seconds I can't spare.

I've developed a cough. It threatens to erupt as I talk to three diners at M-6. Big problem. I obviously can't cough into my hand, which touches their plates, but I can't cough into the air either. I press my lips together as my chest heaves. I feel as if I'm suffocating.

The kitchen accepts orders at least until 10:30 on Fridays and Saturdays. I'm dealing with diners until 11. By then I've been on my feet for more than six hours.

Over the course of the night I have surrendered only two tables and six diners to Christa. I have taken care of eleven tables and thirty-two diners myself. Except I haven't, not really. When my tables needed more water, Christa often got it. When they needed new silverware, she fetched it, because I never noticed.

Truth be told, I wasn't so good about napkin replacement either.

SATURDAY

My last chance. My last test. The restaurant ended up serving 267 diners on Friday night. It will serve 346 tonight.

Between 5:30 and 5:50, I get five tables, each of which needs to be given water, pickles, a recitation of the specials, and whatever coddling I can muster.

The couple at one table want a prolonged menu tour. I'm toast.

Once again I try to tackle an entire section, seven tables in all. Dave is my minder. He tells me to make clear to diners that they need to be patient.

"If you don't control the dynamic, they will," he says.

I don't control the dynamic. Around 6:30 I ask him to take over a table I've started. As some diners leave and new ones take their places, I ask him to take over a few more tables.

I deliver a second vodka on the rocks with a splash of Kahlua to a woman at L-9. Before I can even put it down, she barks, "There's too much Kahlua in that!" Nice to know you, too, ma'am.

I do some things right. I point a couple at L-6 toward the tuna taco, because by now I've tasted it and I know it's fantastic. They love it and tell me they love me, a verbal tip supplemented by 17 percent.

The next couple at L-6 barely talk to me, seek and receive much less care and leave 50 percent. Go figure.

I do many things wrong. I fail to wipe away crumbs. I don't write the time on one ticket. I write M-12 instead of L-12 on another, creating a table that doesn't exist.

Around 8:45, my shirt damp with perspiration, I hide for five minutes in a service corridor, where I dip into the staff's stash of chocolate bars. Then I suck on a wedge of lemon, a little trick I learned from Bryan, to freshen my breath.

By the end of the night I've served a total of fifteen tables comprising thirty-eight people. Some of these people were delightful, and mostly tipped well, keeping my weeklong average—for a comparatively light load of tables—at about 18 percent.

Some weren't so great. They supported an observation that Dave made about restaurants being an unflattering prism for human behavior.

"People are hungry, and then they're drinking," he noted. "Two of the worst states that people can be in."

I recall a young woman at a six-top who bounced in her seat as she said, in a loud singsong voice: "Where's our sangria? Where's our sangria?" Her sangria was on the way, although she didn't seem to need it, and the bouncing wasn't going to make it come any faster.

Around 11:30 all the servers are treated to a shot of tequila. I drink mine instantly. I'm exhausted. I'll still feel worn out two days later, when I chat briefly on the telephone with Jess, Christa, and Dave, who by that point know the full truth about me.

"I think you got a good sense," Dave says.

I think so, too, if he's talking about trying to be fluent in the menu and the food, calm in the face of chaos, patient in the presence of rudeness, available when diners want that, visible when they don't.

It's a lot, and I should remember that. But I still like frequent water refills. And a martini from hell. Straight up.

A Letter from New Orleans

by Lolis Eric Elie

from *Gourmet*

Restaurants have always been a vital part of New Orleans's lifeblood—but as *Gourmet* contributor Lolis Eric Elie recounts it, in the first weeks after the Hurricane Katrina disaster, restaurants literally kept the city alive.

I am writing to you from my usual desk, only now there is plywood to my right, covering the broken window. The ceiling above me is dry, though there is a stain where rainwater dripped through my 170-year-old roof. Behind me is a small patch of moldy Sheetrock. I must preserve it as evidence to show the insurance adjuster, if he ever comes. . . . As you have gathered, I'm lucky. My fence is horizontal, my car is drowned, but in New Orleans as it exists since Hurricane Katrina, I am one of the fortunate ones. I know that you are hungry for news of your favorite people and places. Much of the news is good. The French Quarter, the Garden District, and many of the other places you have visited escaped with relatively little damage. Mardi Gras will still take place, at the end of February, though the planned eight-day celebration will be four days shy of the usual duration. Jazz Fest will take place at the end of April. But with its fairgrounds so badly damaged, no one knows exactly what it will look like. The most devastating images you have seen were primarily from newer residential areas of the city, far from our historic architecture and legendary restaurants. If you confine your movements to these places, life can have that elusive quality we so long for these days: normalcy.

Right after the storm, our chefs were among the first responders. John Besh, the former Marine who commands the four-year-old kitchen at Restaurant August, was cooking red beans and rice for emergency personnel in Slidell, across Lake Pontchartrain from the city. Paul Prudhomme, unable to cook at K-Paul's Louisiana Kitchen, in the French Quarter, set up his kitchen equipment in a tent outside his suburban spice factory. Nearly 30,000 relief workers got their own relief from army-issue meals-ready-to-eat in the form of fresh salads, chicken Creole, and made-from-scratch desserts. "We're not firemen. We're not policemen. The only thing we could do is feed people," Prudhomme said.

Food is identity. We New Orleanians eat our share of typical American fare, but we are not fully ourselves unless we are serving and eating the food that defines us. Louis Armstrong often played "Struttin' with Some Barbecue," but he always signed his letters "Red beans and ricely yours." Emergency measures may have dictated a limited menu, but we were determined that such measures would not endure for long. By early October, very few New Orleanians had returned to the city, but chefs had more options. "We didn't want to just open and serve the easy stuff like hamburgers and chicken fingers. We wanted to bring back the cuisine of New Orleans," said Dickie Brennan, the owner of Bourbon House, Palace Café, and Dickie Brennan's Steakhouse. The opening-day menu at Bourbon House was dressed to impress: Soft Shell Crab Po' Boys, Shrimp Chippewa, Gulf Fish Pecan, and Bread Pudding.

Our food, which has long served as both our sustenance and our emblem, is the bedrock on which we are building our recovery. It has been the local restaurants, not the national chains or even the deep-pocketed fast-food places, that have bounced back first. Even three months after the storm, it was a lot easier to find a po' boy than it was to find a Whopper or a Chicken McNugget.

JoAnn Clevenger, owner of the Upperline, in the Garden District, understands her expanded mission. She is the philosopher queen of our restaurateurs. "I think that just one restaurant opening gives people hope. Optimism can be contagious." Clevenger believes our population will return. And she and other restaurateurs got an unexpected boost from another phenomenon. When people returned, they didn't dare open their reeking refrigerators. They just taped the doors shut and placed the appliances on the curb with the trash. Lacking functioning home kitchens, people went out in search of food and fellowship. "My restaurant is now a gathering place," Clevenger said. "It might sound Pollyannaish, but it is cheerful. I watch the people in here night after night run to another table to see each other. They run!"

I started dining at the Upperline in the 1980s. As I enter this night, I'm immediately struck by the contrasts of old and new. These layers tell their own Katrina story. The warm hug of Clevenger's greeting is timeless, but the carpet smelled of storm decay, she tells me. It was discarded in favor of the terrazzo floor it covered. Her eclectic art collection still crowds the walls, but familiar pieces, moved in advance of the storm, have been rearranged in unfamiliar places.

In the kitchen, chef Ken Smith aims for a balance of home and haute. The arrival of a signature dish—roast duck with ginger peach sauce and sweet-potato french fries—makes me feel at home and at ease. The bacon-blessed richness of the Cane River country shrimp is cut by a crisp grit cake. As I taste it, I am anchored in a moment of prehurricane bliss.

Clevenger gives you the determination to make it all work, and so does Jay Nix. A contractor by trade, he bought the Parkway Bakery in 1996 because it was next to his house and he feared that a liquor store might replace the business that had baked bread and served po' boys since the 1930s. Inspired by that history, Nix renovated the place and taught himself the restaurant business. He had been serving nostalgia on French bread for less than two years when Katrina hit. In December, he was still cleaning up. But he was also plotting his return. "I tell you what. New Orleans is coming back through people's stomachs and their appetites. If you've been following it, it's the restaurants that are getting people excited."

Willie Mae Seaton is determined, too. She had been cooking great soul food in relative obscurity until last year, when she was recognized at the James Beard Foundation Awards as one of America's Classics. The audience, moved by the slow resolve of her eighty-eight-year-old gait and the sincere sparseness of her acceptance speech, cheered and cried. She promised them that whenever they made their way to the Crescent City, she would be there.

She is eighty-nine now. The shotgun double house that is both home and restaurant was flooded. The furniture, the fixtures, all lost. But she had a plan. Her son Charlie serves as sous-chef, purveyor, and handyman. He would get the place ready. It didn't seem to occur to her that, at seventy-one, Charlie might not be the ideal candidate. She still hopes to open, but where will she find the money and man-power to do so? The owners of Gautreau's, Dooky Chase, Gabrielle, and Commander's Palace would also like to return soon, but they, too, face costly repairs.

All true New Orleanians, born or transplanted, have a Creole spirit. Our joie de vivre, we have long joked, marks us as redheaded stepchildren in the vanilla American mainstream. But what was once humor is now a dreadful cloud. We worry that our nation will not help us rebuild our homes and levees. We live and we cook now with an intensity that reminds the world and ourselves of what will be lost if New Orleans is lost. The day Restaurant August reopened, red beans and rice were on the menu. And the Friday lunch menu boasts a down-home seafood and sausage gumbo among John Besh's decidedly nontraditionalist offerings. "I've got something I've got to get off my chest, and here it is," he said. "I don't want to serve a damn thing here unless it has roots that stem from all those crazy bloodlines that built New Orleans."

To understand us now, you must learn the most popular phrase of our new lexicon. We speak of "pre-K." It has nothing to do with early childhood education and everything to do with that long-ago period before the hurricane. This reference point precedes the answers to such questions as "Do they have valet parking?" Post-Katrina, the storm is invariably the main topic of our conversations. But, as in pre-K days, breakfast talk is spiced with anticipatory statements about where one will go for lunch or dinner. No restaurant is more talked about than Donald Link's Herbsaint. Meatloaf remains on his lunch menu as a vestige of those days immediately after his October opening, when he sought to serve comfort food. But it is his chile-glazed pork belly with beluga lentils and fresh mint and his banana brown-butter tart that now dominate discussions of his restaurant.

Fears were raised a year and a half ago when chef Thomas Wolfe bought Peristyle from the popular Anne Kearney. Would the hearty fare from his self-named restaurant across town run roughshod over her meticulous, classic creations? The answer is that, both pre-K and post-K, Wolfe has proved adept at serving dishes as elegant as those Peristyle diners had come to expect.

Two restaurants that were scheduled to open around the time of the hurricane simply altered their debut dates and moved forward. Uptown, Alberta serves elegant bistro food. An hour's drive across Lake Pontchartrain in Abita Springs, Slade Rushing and Alison Vines-Rushing have transplanted the award-winning food they created at Jack's Luxury Oyster Bar in Manhattan to an environment closer to their Mississippi and Louisiana roots. At the Longbranch, their bacon-topped reinvention of Oysters Rockefeller may be the most exciting new dish I've tasted, though the smoked lamb rib served alongside the rack of lamb with wilted romaine and tomato jam has had my taste buds dreaming.

These days, you feel more a part of the restaurant family than before. You know that some of the cooks may well be doubling as dishwashers and that dress codes have been relaxed. Cuvée still requests attire befitting the opulence of its gold-leaf ceiling and its wine list. Chef Bob Iacovone is aiming for lushness, as is evidenced by his opening salvo of foie gras crème brûlée. But post-K fine dining means jeans are acceptable, though not encouraged. Of course, the waiter will still swap the standard white napkin for a black one that won't get light lint on your dark pants.

Once you leave the restaurants, you are often confronted with stark reality. Many neighborhoods are still empty; many streets unlit. This is already a long letter. I didn't intend it to be. But it has taken me this many words to explain to myself what I want you to understand about my hometown. Despite the pronouncements that our beloved city is too dangerous, too hurricane-prone for human habitation, we fully intend to rebuild. Put simply, this place, above all others, is where we wish to live.

Red beans and ricely yours,
Lolis

Reviewing Life

Spy vs. Spy

by Robb Walsh

from *Houston Press*

Once the staff recognizes you, how can you
tell if your excellent meal represented the
restaurant's typical fare? Walsh—author of
The Tex-Mex Cookbook and *Are You Really
Going to Eat That?*—faces this quandary with
his usual down-to-earth, cantankerous wit.

Scott Tycer, the chef and owner of Gravitas, the hip new
bistro on Taft, was standing at the end of the stone counter
in the kitchen looking out over the sleekly modern dining
room. The restaurant's new construction is intriguingly fashioned
from the distressed concrete and vintage bricks of an older
building. The effect is new, yet comfortably worn-looking, like
a pair of stonewashed designer jeans. Not coincidentally, the uni-
form for the waitstaff is an apron over jeans.

Tycer lingered for quite some time at his observation post, and he
seemed to be staring directly at me. Then the manager of the restaurant came by and shooed away a bunch of busboys who had con-
gregated near our table with a low whisper and a slight nod in our
direction. A steady procession of managers and chefs walking down
the aisle seemed to glance furtively at me as they went by.

"I think you're busted," one of my dining companions said.
It certainly looked that way, although I had no idea how the
staff at Gravitas had recognized me.

The extra attention didn't make our appetizers taste any better.
One of my compatriots had ordered the prix-fixe dinner, which
included an appetizer of duck confit salad, an entrée of slow-cooked

pork and a peach cobbler for dessert. I tend to like more salt than most people, so when he kept complaining that his salad was over-salted, I ignored him. Then I tasted it. It was so salty, it had an almost mineral aftertaste. It was awful.

I got some suckling pig ribs, which sounded like a good idea. They looked delicious too, but there was scarcely any meat on the bones. The gazpacho was a huge bowl of bland tomato soup with some avocado cream on top. The corn chowder was the only starter that we all liked, and that was owing mainly to the abundance of applewood-smoked bacon.

Our entrées were uniformly excellent, although a gaffe in the service resulted in only three dinners being delivered to our table of four. Three of us sat there awkwardly watching our food get cold for nearly ten minutes while the fourth urged us to go ahead and eat and the waiter repeatedly came by to reassure us that the fourth dish was on the way.

"Maybe you're not busted," my friend remarked. "Surely they wouldn't do this to a restaurant critic."

The dish that kept us waiting was roast chicken breast with fried corn bread and caramelized shallots, and it was the best thing we sampled that night. It tasted like Sunday-dinner roast chicken with an awesome cornbread stuffing. My entrée of silky, tender black cod piled on top of a rustic green bean cassoulet was a close second. The pan-fried trout with roasted tomatoes, wilted greens, and fresh creamer peas also was sensational.

Gravitas reverses my usual experience with bistros, wherein I start off with an exciting spicy appetizer and end up with a boring slab of meat for the main dish.

My favorite appetizer at Gravitas isn't the least bit spicy. It's an artisanal spin on macaroni and cheese: housemade German spaetzle baked with Gruyère. But it wasn't until my last visit that I finally got to sample it. The first time I visited Gravitas, one of my dining companions ordered it, and I asked for a bite. She blushingly admitted that she had inhaled the entire bowlful without saving any for me. I was extremely disappointed, both because I wanted to include it in the review, and because it looked luscious.

On that first visit, I tried the braised beef bourguignon with potato puree and asparagus. The meltingly tender meat and buttery potato puree were served in a big shallow bowl with a pool of inky purple wine sauce on the bottom.

I hadn't had beef Burgundy since my mom made it when I was in high school. The version served at Gravitas reminds me of how good the original dish was before Mom's recipe, made with cream of mushroom soup and Gallo Hearty Burgundy, turned it into suburban convenience food. The slow-cooked beef in wine sauce and comfortingly creamy mashed potatoes were so good, I had to remind myself to eat slowly so I could savor each bite with a sip of Pinot Noir.

The light and not-too-sweet lemon tart was both the simplest and the best of the desserts, although the flaky-crusted peach cobbler was excellent back when peaches were in season. The cobbler was the last of the three courses the night my tablemate ordered the prix-fixe dinner, but when the rest of us got our desserts, his didn't show up. The waiter claimed that he was confused because my friend hadn't said anything about the cobbler. Evidently, he thought it was our duty to remind him what was on the prix-fixe menu.

The service problems were relatively minor, but they caused my friend to remark, "Nah, they must not have known it was you."

But as it turns out, they did recognize me. While I was talking to an old friend on the phone a few weeks later, she told me to be careful when I went to Gravitas. A guy I had met a couple of years ago at some of her parties now worked there, she said. Suddenly the pieces fell into place.

On a recent Thursday evening, my dining companion and I sat down at the bar at Gravitas to kill a few minutes before our eight o'clock reservation. We asked the bartender if the restaurant had a cocktail list. He said it didn't. So we asked for Mount Gay rum and pineapple juice. They didn't have pineapple juice. We finally settled for rum and OJ.

The only other person sitting at the bar at that moment was Scott Tycer. He took a good look at me, and I took a good look at him. I wanted to be sure he recognized me.

A few minutes later we were shown to a prime table along the front windows. Just as we were seated, *Houston Press* staff writer Josh

Harkinson and his date showed up for their eight o'clock reservation. I had asked Josh to book a table at the same time in order to perform a little experiment.

The point of dining anonymously is to experience a restaurant the same way the general public does. Restaurant critics who aren't anonymous say there is no significant difference between the food and service they get and what the general public experiences. So I asked Josh to help me put that claim to the test.

On this visit, we received excellent service. Our waiter was well informed, low-key and instantly attentive. And the food was terrific.

I finally sampled the creamy spaetzle baked in milk with nutty, full-flavored Gruyère cheese. My date was indifferent about her arugula salad and the enormous disk of goat cheese that came with it. But she liked my homemade noodles and stinky cheese so much, she said she would like to curl up in a bathtub full of the stuff.

For dinner, I ordered steak frites and got a big, thick, tender New York strip steak cooked perfectly to medium rare with a pile of Belgian-style frites so high, I could barely make a dent in them. She got mussels steamed in Belgian beer. I think wine makes a better broth; the beer gets a little bitter.

With my steak, I asked for an obscure beer that I saw on the drink list called Dogfish Head 90 Minute IPA (India pale ale). When it turned out they didn't have any, our waiter said that he would have the chef suggest something else. He came back with a Saint Arnold's Elissa and asked if that would be all right. I said sure, I love Saint Arnold's hoppy new IPA-style beer. "But I have a refrigerator full of the stuff," I added. "It would have been nice to try something new." Before I was halfway through with my Elissa, the waiter returned with a plain brown bottle.

"Scott wants you to try this," he said, as if Tycer and I were on a first-name basis. It was a bottle of the chef's own home-brewed porter. If Tycer ever wants to get out of the restaurant business, he ought to consider becoming a brewer, because the porter was outstanding—just the beer to drink with a thick steak and a pile of fries. And, of course, only the chosen few will ever get a chance to sample Tycer's homebrew. That beer didn't show up on the bill.

I think I could get used to this celebrity-restaurant-critic thing. Meanwhile, across the restaurant, Josh, our representative of the general public, was not doing nearly as well. His waiter, a gentleman with a goatee, was unenthusiastic, uninformed and prone to mumbling, according to Josh.

When asked about the house martinis, his waiter expressed complete ignorance. But it turned out that there was a list of house martinis on the wine list, which Josh pointed out. The waiter asked Josh if he wanted him to go to the bar and find out about them. Finally, after much ado, Josh and his date ordered two of the signature martinis. Fifteen minutes later, the drinks still hadn't shown up.

When they finally flagged down the waiter again, they faced a dilemma. Their appetizers were coming out, but they still hadn't gotten their aperitifs. After some negotiations, the waiter put a hold on their food and slogged off to the bar in search of the cocktails.

Coincidentally, Josh ordered the same steak frites that I did. But oddly, his chunk of New York strip wasn't juicy and tender like mine was. He said it was gristly and a bit tough. (Do you think they might have sorted through the steaks and picked out a special one for the restaurant critic?) His dining companion's dish of trout and peas was excellent, he said. Josh says he wouldn't go back to the restaurant because the service is lackluster and the prices are too high for casual bistro food.

The general public has spoken. But our pampered restaurant critic doesn't agree.

I think Gravitas is a new restaurant with some high points and some problems that need to be worked out. Its strength is in "slow food" entrées like the roasted chicken and cornbread and the braised beef Burgundy, which have instantly become the best upscale comfort food dishes in the city.

Its weaknesses are the slow service and the bar. Some members of the waitstaff are quite good, but overall the kitchen-to-table flow just isn't happening yet. And the bar, with signature cocktails that neither the waiters nor the bartender has ever heard of, advertised beers that aren't available, and a lack of ordinary mixers, is a mess.

As for the experiment, it's clear I was treated much better than Josh. The point isn't to punish Gravitas for recognizing a restaurant critic. That's not their fault. But their natural reaction—lavishing me with superior service, providing special items not available to the general public at no charge, and making sure to give me a better piece of meat than the average guy on the other side of the restaurant —clearly illustrates the value of anonymity.

When I eat at a restaurant unrecognized, I can provide readers with a good idea of what their own experience might be like. When I'm spotted, I can only describe what it's like to be pampered. And unless you're a celebrity, that kind of restaurant review doesn't do you much good.

Twelve Meals a Day

by Jane & Michael Stern

from *Two for the Road*

For years the Sterns have crisscrossed the USA, writing their guidebook *Road Food* and a monthly *Gourmet* column. This memoir divulges the tools of their trade: a full tank of gas, a quirky sense of humor, and truly awesome appetites.

When we tell people that we research roadfood by eating twelve meals a day, they think it's poetic license. But it is true. As travel became a way of life for us, we learned to start very early so we could eat a lot all day long. We woke up around 4 AM, showered, dressed, threw the luggage into the car, and headed out to find breakfast, either alongside the road or, better still, on a town square or Main Street. The kind of place we fell in love with hits its peak at six in the morning, so we wanted to be ensconced in a good booth by that time, ready to order, to eat, and to learn about where we were in America.

For the first meal of the day, we overordered and overate, especially if the menu listed such local specialties as beignets (Creole doughnuts), migas (Tex-Mex tortilla-laced eggs), huevos rancheros, Down East blueberry muffins, Lancaster County waffles, or Tennessee ham with biscuits and red-eye gravy.

We could eat just about anyone under the table, so the first few breakfasts of the day were no problem at all. We awoke ravenous, and with healthy appetites like ours, it was nothing to polish off multiple plates of sourdough French toast in northern California or monster pancakes in Billings, Montana. In the early days of travel, we never met anyone who ate boring sensible breakfasts of Special K with skim milk. Skim milk probably wasn't available even if you asked for it. Our memory of most cafés is that just about everyone smoked cigarettes while they chatted and chewed and welcomed the break of day.

Coffee was a constant problem. We both like it dark and strong, whereas most of the people with whom we rubbed elbows liked theirs farmer-style, which means weak enough for you to drink four or five cups at breakfast as you sit with your friends and neighbors. (Needless to say, this was long before the era of Starbucks and three-dollar lattes.) Furthermore, at many of these roadfood stops, regular customers had their own personal coffee mugs, kept on pegboard hooks, which they reached for and filled the moment they walked in. We felt odd grabbing for Clem's or Elmer's mug, so we dutifully waited for the waitress to bring us house mugs, usually already brimming with coffee and outfitted with a spoon. Once that first cup had arrived, waitresses patrolled the counter and dining room with fresh pots. Refills were automatic unless you did something dramatic like turn an emptied cup upside down or place your hand over the top as she approached. The latter proved to be a dangerous tactic if the waitress was gabbing with other diners and pouring on autopilot.

So we drank weak coffee and cleaned our plates, then moved on to breakfast number two, then breakfast number three. By mid-morning, when our appetites started to lag and we weren't eating everything we had ordered, we began to face the worried-waitress problem.

"You don't like your food? What's the matter, dears?"

"It's great. We're just not hungry."

"But you ordered so much." Sometimes the waitress was so upset that she went back to the kitchen to notify the cook. Then a white-haired granny would run out, looking dismayed.

Having survived upbringings with our Jewish mothers, we thought we knew guilt. Nothing had prepared us for how bad we felt trying to explain our way out of the situation. At the time, writing *Roadfood* was only an ambition; we had never published anything, and so we had no food articles or books to show as an explanation of what we were doing. The very idea of a restaurant writer would have been ludicrous to most of these people, let alone a restaurant writer concerned about flapjacks.

And so to scores of kind old ladies across America we must have appeared to be liars, fakers, or—worst of all—wastrels who thought it was perfectly all right to waltz into Madge's Café in western Nebraska and leave behind half of a three-egg omelet and all of our buttered toast. We could read their minds: "Sausage links do not grow on trees . . ." So we pushed the food around on our plates and used whatever garnishes there were to hide what we hadn't eaten.

After the third or fourth breakfast, it was generally time to make miles. Depending on how far apart towns were and how many likely roadfood places each one had, we tried to travel a few hundred miles a day. In southern Louisiana, we might not go more than fifty miles, the good-eats possibilities were so dense. In the Dakotas, five hundred miles between meals was common.

Since we spent so much time in the car, what we drove seemed very important. After destroying the vomit-green Suburban in a crash, we went through a seemingly endless series of replacements, every one of which had something wrong with it, either a fatal flaw or a huge annoyance. One car spit ice crystals through the air-conditioning vents. A convertible leaked profusely whenever it rained. One pickup truck would not start if the humidity was over 50 percent; another had an exhaust system that fed fumes into the passenger compartment, making us dizzy and faint after thirty minutes. Then there was the coupe that stank of what must have been the four-pack-a-day habit of its former owner, and a primitive four-by-four so tall and nonaerodynamic that it behaved like a mainsail in the wind. All our cars were cheap and ugly. The only one that was not was a black stick-shift 1959 Mercedes with cherry-red leather seats and a mere few hundred thousand miles on the odometer, which we got for the bargain price of $500. It had a minor problem, though; it would not start if there was any moisture in the air at all, and to get it going we had to remove the distributor cap and spray the copper contacts with roach spray—a trick taught us by the seller.

A large number of our early cars were Volkswagens, then the lowest form of four-wheel transportation. They were inexpensive to operate and easy to drive, and while frighteningly unsafe by modern standards, they did have their advantages in poor driving conditions.

Once in a blizzard on Route 80 in western Pennsylvania, Jane hit the brakes on our Beetle too hard. The car did a full 360-degree spin, missed a passing semi, and wound up in the median between the eastbound and westbound lanes. We simply got out and pushed it back onto the roadbed like a toy, climbed in, and drove away.

Whatever we drove, it usually got us to lunch, which is Jane's favorite meal of the day. Michael was and still is a breakfast guy, but Jane is a lady who lunches. Whenever we found ourselves at a wonderful place like the old Miller's Tea Room of Cleveland, Ohio, eating chicken a la king served in a deep-fried potato nest, Jane's eyes brightened. Confronted by the sight of a dozen shimmering individual Jell-O salads brought to the table on a tray so each diner could select a favorite color and combo, followed by a battered silver tray stocked with little sticky buns, cloverleaf rolls, cornbread sticks, and blueberry gem muffins, she would begin to moan that this was simply the best food in the United States, in the world, maybe in the universe. It was all just too good, too delicious; she wanted one of everything . . . And that is pretty much what we would consume.

Opportunity to eat a lunch like this absolutely eclipsed any feelings of fullness left over from breakfasts. Our stomachs were growling, for we were blessed with the best and only tool absolutely necessary for the job we set out to do: a healthy appetite.

After the first lunch, we would move on and find another, stopping in Cleveland at the Balaton for chicken paprikash and apple strudel, at Renée's for Polish pierogi, at Rick's Café for ribs, or at the Flat Iron Café for perch. By the fourth midday meal, we were beginning to unnerve waitresses again by not cleaning our plates. Sometimes we tried to avoid the whole situation and ask for the food to go, then eat what we could in the car. But Michael is a stickler for seeing the whole meal presented as it should be on a table, so unless we were having barbecue or something that seemed right and proper out of a paper bag, we sat at the table or counter and faced what the menu offered.

Michael, the documentarian, entered the restaurants loaded down like a Mexican donkey with heavyweight Rolleiflexes and Hasselblads with tripods and flash attachments to take beauty shots of the food as soon as it arrived at the table. Needless to say, this caused some commotion. People simply couldn't understand why someone would want to take a picture of a slice of pie or a cup of chowder. The idea that we might be food writers meant absolutely nothing, and the Food Network was a few decades away from being a gleam in a TV producer's eye, so Michael with his camera was usually regarded as some kind of nutcase passing through town. As he did not seem dangerous to himself or others, people generally humored him.

"Do you want to take a picture of my chicken sandwich?" someone would call out, and if the plate of food looked good, Michael would go over and snap away. This caused gales of laughter, and Jane would swivel her head to see people making the universal sign of craziness. She would benignly nod in agreement, which was much easier than trying to explain that we were attempting to write a guidebook to regional food, which would have sounded at least as crazy.

Michael, a compulsive note-taker, also spread his pads of paper and pens and notebooks all over the table as we ate. Jane, a more discreet researcher, carried a manual typewriter in the car and relied on her memory for everything. Then, back in the motel at night, she two-finger-typed her thoughts on everything she had eaten that day.

Before we got to the motel, however, there were dinners to eat. We generally tried to take a midafternoon digestive break as we sailed along after lunch, but this rarely worked out well. While we may not have stopped for too many full lunches after around 2 PM, we constantly found pie slices that needed sampling, cheese curds to investigate, local apples from a farmstand, roasted chile sandwiches sold by the side of the road, maple candy, pepperoni rolls, salmon jerky, boiled peanuts, and countless essential snacks.

If we ever hit a wall appetite-wise, it was at dinner. We always tried to start no later than five o'clock. In most parts of rural America, this is no early-bird special; it is the time people eat. Dinner servings tend to be bigger and take longer than other meals, and since we had already had eight or nine meals that day and traveled a few hundred miles, we just didn't have the stamina for more than two or three dinners. Often nauseated, clinging tightly to our supply of Alka-Seltzer, we drove "home" to our little motel in the pines, on the highway access road, near a cornfield, alongside the railroad tracks, or behind the whorehouse. We bolted the door, turned the TV to one of the three available channels to watch primitive pro wrestling or *The Late Show,* and tried to relax. We should have looked horrible in the bathroom mirror, but we did not. Our clothes had food dribbles on them, and sometimes our eyes looked bloodshot, but it was obvious that we were as well fed as a pair of Kobe steers and as happy as two Ipswich clams.

Stealth and guile became essential tools if we were to survive eating twelve meals a day. Jane scrounged or bought plastic bags to hide in her purse. The ideal size was a big one, the kind you find in a nice hotel room so you can send your clothes to the cleaner. However, since we didn't stay in nice hotels, such bags were only a distant dream. Regular plastic bags from the 7-Eleven worked fine. When we were feeling that we simply couldn't eat another bite, we waited for the waitress to turn her back, then scooped up the remains on our plates and slid them into the plastic bag, held open in Jane's waiting purse on her lap. Usually this worked well, but not with waitresses who paid close attention to what they had served us and wondered how we had managed to swallow clamshells, chicken bones, olive pits, and lobster carapaces. We smiled like a couple of ninnies, paid the bill, and left.

Despite getting out of the restaurant without suffering through an inquisition, we felt awfully guilty about just tossing good food into the trash. But what are you going to do with half a meal heaved into a plastic bag? Or even with half a meal if you ask to have it packed in a doggie bag? Who wants somebody else's sampled waffle?

On some occasions we walked out of restaurants with food without bite marks in it. One time, traveling through easternmost Tennessee, we got a couple of slabs of ribs at an excellent barbecue. We ate one, but then a few more dinners on the road from Tennessee into Virginia came between us and the other one. Late that night we arrived in Roanoke with a rack of ribs and no appetite to eat them.

We decided that before we even found a motel, we would drive along the city streets and give our prize to someone who would appreciate some of Tennessee's best barbecue. The ribs were neatly wrapped in aluminum foil—a tidy bundle that we slid inside a clean brown paper bag. What hungry person wouldn't love this gift?

On a corner near the Roanoke railroad tracks we spotted three down-at-the-heels guys standing in a cluster looking uncomfortable: homeless people whose distress might well be relieved by the delicious pork we bore. We stopped the car and got out, Michael carrying the bag, Jane accompanying him as part of our beneficent procession. As we reached them, holding out the brown paper bag, we suddenly heard sirens. Flashing police lights were all around, and the road was instantly crowded with cruisers. The five of us were set upon and frisked as one of the officers grabbed the bag and emptied it onto the hood of his Crown Vic. The look on his face when he unfurled the foil was pure poison. His drug bust had turned into a rib bust, and it was only after a few hours of explaining in the Roanoke police station that we were snarlingly released to find a room for the night. That was the last time we tried to gift perfect strangers with surplus food from a day of eating on the road.

Reality Bites

by Charles Ferruzza
from *The Pitch*

There's so much more to "eating out" than
just the food on your plate, yet many critics
don't parse the whole experience. Ferruzza
does; his readers become comrades-in-arms
on nightly forays into the Kansas City dining
scene.

I never watched the NBC reality show *The Restaurant,* starring
celebrity chef Rocco DeSpirito, for the same reason I won't
watch any reality TV series: My own personal reality is complicated
enough. If I even turn on the television, I want to see something featuring not real people but idiotic caricatures of them—say, *The
O'Reilly Factor.*

But sometimes life takes a funny turn and becomes more like a
reality TV show than actual reality. Take, for example, my second
dinner at the cozy little bistro called SORedux. I was dining with
my friends Bob and Lou Jane, waiting for the fourth course of our
eight-course *prix fixe* dinner to arrive, when we all happened to look
out the window at the same time. Our jaws dropped in unison. "Am
I really seeing what I think I'm seeing?" asked Lou Jane.

Right there outside the restaurant, chef and co-owner Ray
"Pete" Peterman stood in front of an occupied van, demanding that
the driver stop. Flailing his arms behind Pete was, I think, the dishwasher. Suddenly Peterman's wife, Heather, ran out the front door
of the restaurant, and there was a brief flurry of yelling before the
van drove off—mercifully, not with Peterman under its wheels.

A few minutes later, the incredibly tall co-owner of the restaurant, former pro basketball player Todd Jadlow, sheepishly stooped over our table and whispered, "Sorry about that. We had a table walk out on a $900 bill." Gulp! Bob, Lou Jane and I all worked in restaurants in our past lives, where each of us experienced at least one horrible dine-and-dash. I suffered several, and they were particularly brutal because the restaurants demanded that I cover the unpaid check out of my own pocket. Years later, I'm still fuming about the injustice of it.

"What should I do?" asked Jadlow.

Call the fucking police, I insisted. And he did, because at some point between the salad course and the cheese plate, two broad-shouldered Kansas City Police Department officers walked in. If only there had been a camera crew following them, taping the incident for a segment of the trashy Fox series *Cops*. But I'm getting ahead of my story, and the beginning was almost as colorful as the climax.

Let's rewind the imaginary videotape back to 7:08 PM on a Sat-urday. Bob, Lou Jane and I arrived a few minutes late for our 7 PM reservation—reservations are mandatory here, by the way. We were seated fortuitously next to one of the big picture windows in this storefront building. The building that now houses SORedux was, for decades, a neighborhood pharmacy; in more recent years, it was a sort of catch-all shop that sold, according to former Columbus Park resident Lou Jane, "booze, cigarettes and sundries." This yet ungentrified corner of the historic "North End" seems poised for a renaissance. But will SORedux lead the way?

Bob and I had eaten at SORedux when it first opened last October, back when Peterman was ambitiously—and perhaps foolishly—attempting to offer four different prix fixe menus. "I used to offer a three-course, a five-course, a seven and a ten," Peterman told me later. "Talk about a nightmare in the kitchen."

What I remember about that autumn dinner was that the food was creative and delicious but the kitchen's pacing was glacially slow. I think I nearly fell asleep before the dessert course. But Peterman recently streamlined his prix fixe to an eight-course affair that's priced quite reasonably at $38. The menu changes every day, but typ-ically there are a couple of "supplemental" courses that bump up the price and the dining experience.

"I don't remember the dining room being so noisy," Bob said, unfurling his napkin. Well, there are many hard surfaces in the narrow, forty-five-seat room. But this particular evening's acoustic level was intensified by the ear-piercing screech of a beautiful, expensively dressed blonde at an adjoining table. She was having a wonderful time with her entourage and expressed her glee in much the same manner that a black-capped chickadee sends out a mating call. By the time I finished my first course, a delicate portion of pan-roasted veal sweetbreads with yams, I didn't know whether to scold her or call the Audubon Society.

Sweetbreads are an eccentric delicacy, in this case the thymus glands of baby calves. I would never have actually ordered the dish—not for any politically correct reason but because the only sweet breads I really crave are made with dough, yeast, and sugar. Still, ordering isn't an option here, and I didn't want to insult the chef, so I reluctantly nibbled at the smooth-textured meat, which Peterman roasts with shallots and wine. It was actually better than I expected.

My appetite perked up for the second course, a tiny portion of Holland sole in an amber-colored "vanilla-tainted winter tomato butter." I told Lou Jane that *tainted* isn't a word that one sees on a menu very often, given its sort of unsavory connotation. I thought of other possibilities. Infused? Dappled? Perfumed? Despite the odd description, it was a wonderfully flaky, delicately vanilla-scented piece of fish . . . and it was gone in two bites.

We decided to share the two supplemental dishes offered that night. Both were sensational and well worth the extra dough. A 3-ounce "pee wee" Maine lobster tail was described as "double fat basted" (in bacon fat and butter, I learned later), which was why the portion—slightly smaller than a business card—tasted so fantastic. And for ten bucks, the succulent little slab of roasted foie gras, its exterior just slightly caramelized and perched on a bed of sweet red cabbage and raisins, was an extraordinary deal. We practically arm-wrestled for the last bite.

It was during the next course—officially the third—that I realized we had been eating, modestly and elegantly, for two hours. And there were five more courses still to come! The epiphany that this would probably be a four-hour dinner had me squirming in my seat before the duck course, which was a tender burgundy sliver of Moulard Magret with a dollop of lentils and rutabagas.

Suddenly Lou Jane tapped my hand. I turned my head and watched a lithe, tan little chicklet in a tight white halter top (which barely contained her mammoth mammaries) get up from her seat, walk over to where her date was sitting and climb into his lap.

"She's giving him a lap dance," whispered Bob. I noticed that every other patron in the dining room had also turned to look at the performance. The clean-cut quartet of suburbanites at the next table giggled with embarrassment. The groping twosome were so hot for each other that they didn't seem to mind.

Later, looking back on their demonstration, I found it hard to accurately remember which course I was eating when the floor show started. Was it before or after the five-top split without paying the tab? And had the group with the 8 PM reservation already stomped off angrily because the table with the screeching blonde was lingering too long? So many details, so many courses.

It was definitely before the cops arrived, because I had already polished off the fourth course, a New Zealand lamb rib served with a spoonful of olive-studded polenta. In fact, I was halfway through the next dish, a dainty little salad of bitter greens splashed with fresh orange juice, before the squad car pulled up.

The sixth course was all *fromage:* a china plate with slivers of brie, goat cheese and Jarlsberg accompanied by a glass bowl containing pencil-thin slices of bread. Each serving on this menu is a miniature version of a traditional full-sized portion, but by this point, I was getting full. I took one bite of cheese and pushed the plate away. Bob and Lou Jane ate every morsel.

It was 10:30 PM when the first dessert—course seven—was served. Bob griped that he was missing a favorite TV show, but Lou Jane had settled in for the long run and ordered another glass of wine. I greedily wolfed down a sweet spoonful of an apple *tatin,* the traditional French upside-down tart, which Peterman had baked in a cornmeal crust and sided with thyme-and-vanilla ice cream. It wasn't just wonderful; it gave me a second wind.

By this point, Ms. Halter Top and her companion had left after eating only the first three of their eight courses. "They had to go home and, uh, pay the baby-sitter," our server informed us. Bob and Lou Jane burst into hysterical laughter. "I'm serious," insisted the waiter.

Then a relieved-looking Todd Jadlow came over and said, *sotto voce,* that the host of the runaway table had apparently realized the error of his ways (it was a felony, after all) and had returned to pay the bill.

Shortly before 11 PM, the finale was brought to the table: a 2-inch rectangle of baked chocolate mousse that was the consistency of the most luscious fudge, accompanied by slivers of banana and splashed with a cocoa-bean-Merlot syrup spiked with star anise. By the time I paid the bill, we had been sitting at the table for exactly four hours. That's one hour and 15 minutes longer than *The Lion King,* and without an intermission.

Still, this evening had all the elements of fabulous theater: drama! sex! costumes! And the food was scene-stealing, too. "It was one of the worst nights of my life," Peterman told me a few days later.

Too bad, because it was one of the best of mine.

Back to the Zak

by Matthew Amster-Burton

from *www.rootsandgrubs.com*

Another perennial challenge: What if a restaurant actually pays heed to your review and improves itself? *Seattle Times* reviewer Amster-Burton ponders variations on this scenario in his food-and-more weblog.

Like politicians, some restaurant critics get a palpable thrill from going negative. English writer A. A. Gill, who never goes anywhere without the word "acerbic" attached to his name, once referred to a Jean-Georges Vongerichten dish as "fishy, liver-filled condoms."

Me, I try to avoid writing negative reviews. I don't mean to be holier-than-Gill. I certainly understand the appeal of writing a good zinger. But I think readers are better served by being told about someplace good than someplace bad. However, sometimes I have no choice—maybe the restaurant is highly anticipated, or has changed ownership, or is in a visible location.

And sometimes, I have to admit, I write a negative review because it would be infeasible for me to do otherwise. If I decide a restaurant is unreviewable, the newspaper doesn't reimburse me for what I spent there, and you know, caviar don't come for free. Okay, I'm on the cheap eats beat, so when I say "caviar," I mean fries.

The first negative review I ever wrote was of a place called Best Toast, which served grilled bagel sandwiches. For some reason I will never understand—possibly the owners were not from Earth—the sandwich maker squirted a large quantity of cheese sauce on the top surface of the bagel before lowering the top of the panini grill. You'd think this would result in crusty burnt cheese sauce, and you'd be right.

The primary role of a restaurant critic is as a consumer advocate. Most people are not going to demand their money back after a mediocre meal, so my goal is to try to steer you toward places I like and that I hope you'll enjoy, too. The secondary role of the critic is to raise the bar, to elevate the average level of quality. You can't deliberately make this your beat, though, or you will be ineffective and insufferable. Restaurant reviews that lecture the restaurant are tedious to read, and I try to avoid doing that.

People often ask me what kind of response I get to a negative review. Generally, I get a couple of e-mails from fans of the restaurant telling me how wrong I am. Sometimes I get an e-mail from the restaurant owner, defending his restaurant. Usually my editor gets a copy of those, too. Mostly the owner will blame me for the bad review and indicate that I'm biased, incompetent, and unprofessional. I totally understand this response. If a Roots and Grubs reader told me that I use too many adjectives, my first impulse would be to call the writer a malodorous insufferable boorish jerk rather than to examine my own work.

Thankfully, I've never gotten a reaction like my colleague Bill Daley of the *Chicago Tribune*. Bill once said that he used to cover the mafia, but never received a death threat until he started reviewing restaurants for the *Hartford Courant*. He wasn't joking.

The only response I truly dread (other than an armed response) is one telling me that I got a factual detail wrong. Once I reviewed an Italian gelateria and restaurant, found the gelato good and the food unacceptable, and said so. I also described the restaurant has having wood paneling and tourist posters on the walls. It had neither, and the owner said that my error called the credibility of my whole review into question. He was right. Later the place stopped serving food, and then shut down altogether, but it was hard to feel vindicated after such a dumbass mistake. Since then, whenever I go to a restaurant, on duty or off, I spend a lot more time looking around.

I have received two totally unexpected responses to negative reviews.

Last year, I reviewed a hot new Belltown bar called Black Bottle.

I thought the wine list was terrific and the prices very reasonable, but found problems with a lot of the food, particularly a certain broccoli dish:

> One of the most, well, interesting items on the menu is a crime scene of a dish called Broccoli Blasted. Take a bunch of broccoli florets and place them in a red-hot oven until the flower buds are burned to charcoal and the stem sides are still raw. Then throw on a handful of salt and serve. I envy the person who got "blasted" enough to think this was tasty.

I gave the place 1.5 stars. After the review ran, I got separate phone calls from both of the owners. When I picked up the phone and heard, "I'm one of the owners of Black Bottle," I cringed, expecting a tirade. Instead, both owners thanked me for the review. Admittedly, they did want to gloat that all sorts of people were coming in to try this broccoli for themselves. I'm still a little puzzled by their response, but they seem like savvy businesspeople, so I figure they concluded that my review was unlikely to do them any harm.

They were right, of course. As someone wrote this month on Chowhound, "Unfortunately, I'm now in the Yogi Berra camp: 'Nobody goes there anymore—it's too crowded.'"

But the most unexpected response to a negative review came from Zak's. Zak's is a burger joint in Ballard, next to Cupcake Royale on the same block as the Majestic Bay theater. I reviewed Zak's in December. The service was fantastic. The decor was fun. The milkshakes were good. The burger was not:

> The toasted bun, studded with sesame and poppy seeds, looked great but tasted of some kind of grain that should not be in a hamburger bun. The toppings were piled too high. I asked for my burger cooked medium; it came beyond well done and had almost no meat flavor. And rather than crisp strips of bacon, this burger sported something like a mushy bacon spread, with crumbly chunks of what was once thick-cut bacon.

I hated to give Zak's a negative review, since they were so nice, but what could I do? A couple of months went by, and then I got an e-mail from Larry Johnson, owner of Zak's:

I thought you might be interested to know that I reacted objectively and sought out honest opinions from my friends and family about our menu items (asking them to spare my feelings and just let it out.) I did have a few mention that they too thought our burger was on the dry side, although most liked the rest of our menu items enthusiastically. I have since changed the fat content of our meat specs and worked to get my kitchen line more adept at not letting items sit too long on the grill.

He also said he'd dealt with the bacon problem. I'd never heard anything like this from a restaurant owner before. I promised Larry I'd go back and give them another try.

Last night, I did. If the previous burger was a grainy "before" picture from a plastic surgery ad, this burger was the bodacious "after" shot. The bacon was crispy. The meat was juicy. The toppings were well-proportioned. I still didn't like the bun—I think it's the poppy seeds that bother me—but this is well into opinion territory.

The review column I write for, Dining Deals, only awards two ratings: Recommended or Not Recommended. Here's my standard for deciding between them, if I'm on the fence: if a friend called me up and said, "Hey, we're going to Zak's. Wanna come?" would I tell them I'm busy washing my hair? If not, it's recommended. Zak's burger makeover puts them well into the recommended category.

Great—now you, my twelve readers, know about this. But that negative review is still out there on the *Times* Web site, and it's no longer valid. How could I make this right?

I e-mailed my editors, and they cooked up a new feature called Second Helpings. It will enable the paper to offer a revised opinion when a place has improved or changed but it's not time for a whole new review. Look for the inaugural installment of Second Helpings in an upcoming Friday paper—I'll post when it runs. In the meantime, have a burger.

One Last Meal in the Old New Orleans

by Brett Anderson
from *Times-Picayune*

Numbly taking stock amid the wreck of post-Katrina New Orleans, restaurant critic Brett Anderson sought to make sense of the tragedy the only way he could: by cherishing memories of a meal.

F ive years ago this month, my girlfriend and I flew to New Orleans so I could interview for a job that, like everything, changed irreversibly August 29. As part of the interview process, I was asked to write sample reviews of two New Orleans restaurants. One of them was Clancy's.

I had two meals at the restaurant in three days, the second of them a Saturday evening dinner, after which we took a cab to see Los Hombres Calientes at Tipitina's. It was that night that convinced me I wanted this job, that this was my kind of town, and it was at Tips where I ran into Keith Spera, a future colleague and great friend who, the Saturday before Katrina hit, just eight hours before I fled my house, picked me up in his convertible. His top was down. It was a beautiful night.

We were headed to Clancy's.

For me, getting to the restaurant is part of its draw. I live down-town, in the Faubourg Marigny. Clancy's is an Uptown institution. The distance between the two coordinates is, by my measure, as far as you can travel from my house without crossing the parish line or settling for less. And the drive can't be beat. We traced the edge of the French Quarter and then sped through the Garden District via

St. Charles Avenue, where gnarled oak trees obscured our view of a bright moon. The table we thought we'd have to wait for was ready when we arrived at Clancy's.

I didn't expect many restaurants to be open on the Last Saturday Night in Old New Orleans. The fearful, mobilizing citizenry had rendered westbound traffic insane all day, and the restaurants I was currently reviewing—the ones I called first—were all closed.

That Clancy's was packed in spite of it all—"Can you say that again?" the host asked when I called about a table, struggling to hear over the crowd noise—says volumes about why it was an ideal setting for what we were calling our "last supper"—a glib joke in retrospect, but one that, mixed with a pre-prandial round of cocktails, helped dull the edge of the moment. It felt good to set our elbows on pressed white linens and stare into a room of people in the same predicament, drunk on rye whiskey, wine, and lump crabmeat.

Keith and I were perusing the menu when our friend Cynthia walked through the door to join us. The dishes are printed in a font that matches the cursive "Clancy's" sign hanging outside the converted po-boy shop: Fried Oysters with Brie. Rabbit Sausage en Croute. Shrimp Remoulade. Smoked Soft Shell Crab with Crabmeat. Lamb Chops Webster. When the tuxedoed waiter informed us of the evening's appetizer special, I mentioned it could be a long time before anyone on earth utters the phrase "andouille-crusted duck livers in Creole mustard sauce" again.

"Our crabmeat salad tonight has a horseradish-sour cream-mayonnaise dressing," the waiter continued. "It's topped with Louisiana caviar. And there's a splash of vodka in there, too."

"Sold!" I howled, before also claiming the Panee Veal Annunciation: Two tender, pan-fried cutlets covered in béarnaise and crabmeat, a house specialty.

Cynthia ordered the proscuitto-wrapped shrimp over stone-ground grits and the smoked softshell. Keith had a taste for drum, and the waiter, who Keith, a native of eastern New Orleans, has known for years, recommended it pan-sautéed with meuniere sauce. "It's not on the menu, but I'll get it for you," the waiter assured him. When the massive drum filet arrived under a mound of crabmeat, I blurted an answer to a question that's no doubt crossed a lot of CNN-watchers' minds recently. "This is why we live here," I said.

There are other reasons, of course, and to the list I've added things I saw when I returned to New Orleans after Katrina trashed it. In a week of reporting alongside colleagues infinitely better suited to the task than I, I stepped over dead bodies. I rode through flooded streets on the back of a military truck designed to haul rockets. I scribbled quotes from countless soldiers and cops and survivors. I met a guy who, having just been rescued by boat from his flooded Gentilly home, openly questioned the wisdom of his decision to leave. He had plenty of Sterno, spices, water, smoked turkey. He'd just cooked up a batch of red beans.

Most of all I felt that resting on the precipice of existence was not just a magical city but my home. Returning to a death-stricken New Orleans was heart-breaking, but abandoning it for a more comfortable place, even my birthplace, would have been even harder to bear.

Coming to this realization helped me understand that there are reasons beyond stubbornness, ignorance or lack of means that compel people to ride out storms—and then, even more astonishingly, endure the nightmare that follows. They stay because they love New Orleans, love it with an intensity you would a human being. They'll be damned if they're going to turn their back on it, particularly now.

I'm lucky to live here, even today, but that doesn't mean I wouldn't give anything to turn back the clock. We finished our meal at Clancy's with a slice of lemon-icebox pie. "You have to," our waiter said. Out on the sidewalk we posed for a picture that, when I finally saw it, I longed to crawl inside.

Recipe Index

Acknowledgments

Grateful acknowledgment is made to all those who gave permission for written material to appear in this book. Every effort has been made to trace and contact copyright holders. If an error or omission is brought to our notice, we will be pleased to remedy the situation in further editions of this book. For further information, please contact the publisher.

"A Grass-Fed Meal" from *The Omnivore's Dilemma* by Michael Pollan. Copyright © 2006 by Michael Pollan. Used by permission of The Penguin Press, a division of Penguin Group (USA) Inc. ✤ "A Grand Experiment" by Bill McKibben. Copyright © 2005 by Conde Nast Publications. Used by permission. Originally appeared in *Gourmet*, July 2005. ✤ "Proud Heritage" by Patric Kuh. Copyright © 2005 by Patric Kuh. Used by permission of the author. Originally appeared in *Bon Appetit*, November 2005. ✤ "Fleshy and Full of life" from *The Scavenger's Guide to Haute Cuisine* by Steve Rinella. Copyright © 2005 Steve Rinella. Reprinted by permission of Miramax Books. All rights reserved. ✤ "Stuffed Animals" by Jeffrey Steingarten. Copyright © 2006 Conde Nast Publications. All rights reserved. Reprinted by permission. Originally appeared in *Men's Vogue*, Spring 2006. ✤ "Mackeral Punts and Pilchards" by Megan Wetherall. Copyright © 2006 by Megan Wetherall. Reprinted by permission of the author. Originally appeared in *Saveur*, May 2006. ✤ "Fulton Street Fish Market" by Maria Finn Dominguez. Copyright © 2005 by University of California Press—Journals. From *Gastronomica*, Volume 5, Number 4, Fall 2005. Republished with permission of University of California Press—Journals in the format of Trade Book via Copyright Clearance Center. ✤ "Tales of a Supertaster" by David Leite. Copyright © 2005 by David Leite. Used by permission of the author. Originally appeared in *Ridgefield Magazine*, November/ December 2005. ✤ "Italian Butcher Shop Blues" by Matthew Gavin Frank. Copyright © 2006 by University of California Press—Journals. From *Gastronomica*, Volume 6,

permission of the author. Originally appeared in *The New Yorker*, September 5, 2005. ❖ "Lobster Killer" from *Julie and Julia* by Julie Powell. Copyright © 2005 by Julie Powell. By permission of Little, Brown and Co. Inc. ❖ "La Belle France" from *My Life In France* by Julia Child with Alex Prud'homme. Copyright © 2006 by the Julia Child Foundation of Gastronomy and the Culinary Arts and Alex Prud'homme. Used by permission of Alfred A. Knopf, a division of Random House, Inc. ❖ "Putting Le Bec-Fin to the Test" by Pete Wells. Copyright © 2005 by Pete Wells. Used by permission of the author. First published in *Food & Wine*, July 2005. ❖ "Vive le Restaurant" by James Villas. Copyright © 2006 by James Villas. Reprinted by permission of the author. Originally appeared in *Saveur*, April 2006. ❖ "My Parents Are Driving Me to Drink" by Chip Brown. Copyright © 2005 by Chip Brown. Used by permission of the author. Originally appeared in *Food & Wine*, October 2005. ❖ "The Fish That Surpasses All Understanding" by Jeff Gordinier. Copyright © 2005 by Jeff Gordinier. Used by permission of the author. Originally appeared in *Breathe*, September / October 2005. ❖ "Ho Chi Min City" by Brett Martin. Copyright © 2006 by Brett Martin. Used by permission of the author. Originally appeared in *Bon Appetit*, January 2006. ❖ "Eating Space" by John T. Edge. Copyright © 2005 by John T. Edge. Used by permission of the author. Originally appeared in *The Oxford American*, Fall 2005. ❖ "Mama's House" by Jason Sheehan. Copyright © 2006 by Jason Sheehan. Used by permission of the author. Originally appeared in *Westword*, January 5, 2006. ❖ "Two Cooks" by Adam Gopnik. Copyright © 2006 by Adam Gopnik. Used by permission of the author. Originally appeared in *The New Yorker*, September 5, 2005. ❖ "Southern Exposure" by Todd Kliman. Copyright © 2006 by Todd Kliman. Used by permission of the author. Originally appeared in *Washingtonian Magazine*, May 2006. ❖ "The Reach of a Chef" from *The Reach of a Chef* by Michael Ruhlman. Copyright © 2006 by Michael Ruhlman. Used by permission of The Penguin Press, a division of Penguin Group (USA) Inc. ❖ "Pasta Maker" from *Heat* by Bill Buford. Copyright © 2006 by William Buford. Used by permission of Alfred A. Knopf, a division of Random House, Inc. ❖ "A Mentor Named Misty" by Gabrielle Hamilton. Copyright © 2005 by Gabrielle Hamilton. Used by permission of the

About the Editor

Holly Hughes is a writer, the former executive editor of Fodor's Travel Publications and author of *Frommer's New York City with Kids*.

Submissions for
Best Food Writing 2007

Submissions and nominations for *Best Food Writing 2007* should be forwarded no later than June 1, 2007, to Holly Hughes at *Best Food Writing 2007*, c/o Avalon Publishing Group, 245 W. 17th St., 11th floor, New York, NY 10011, or emailed to bestfoodwriting@avalonpub.com. We regret that, due to volume, we cannot acknowledge receipt of all submissions.

Best Food Writing 2000
Foreword by Alice Waters
1-56924-616-5
$14.95
Contributors include Maya Angelou, Eric Asimov, Anthony Bourdain, Rick Bragg, Fran Gage, Jeffrey Steingarten, Jhumpa Lahiri, Nigella Lawson, and Ruth Reichl.

Best Food Writing 2001
1-56924-577-0
$14.95
Contributors include Jeffery Eugenides, Malcom Gladwell, David Leite, Molly O'Neill, Ruth Reichl, David Sedaris, Jeffrey Steingarten, and Calvin Trillin.

Best Food Writing 2002
1-56924-524-X
$14.95
Contributors include Anthony Bourdain, Greg Atkinson,
Rand Richards Cooper, John T. Edge, Barbara Haber, Paric Kuh,
John Mariani, Mimi Sheraton, and James Villas.

Best Food Writing 2003
1-56924-440-5
$14.95
Contributors include Susan Choi, Fran Gage, Adam Gopnik,
Amanda Hesser, David Leite, Jacques Pépin, Inga Saffron, Nigel
Slater, and John Thorne.

Best Food Writing 2004
1-56924-416-2
$14.95
Contributors include Steve Almond, Greg Atkinson, John
Kessler, David Leite, Dara Moskowitz, Molly O'Neill,
Mimi Sheraton, James Villas, and Robb Walsh.

Best Food Writing 2005
1-56924-345-X
$15.95
Contributors include Ruth Reichl, Rick Bayless, Gabrielle
Hamilton, Colman Andrews, Judith Jones, Robb Walsh, Monique
Truong, Eric Asimov, Frank Bruni, and Diana Abu-Jaber.

Please note that limited quantites are available on some previous
editions in the Best Food Writing series. Your local bookseller
should be able to help you obtain previous editions.